Postmodern Music,
Postmodern Listening

Postmodern Music, Postmodern Listening

By
Jonathan D. Kramer

Edited by
Robert Carl

Bloomsbury Academic
An imprint of Bloomsbury Publishing Inc

B L O O M S B U R Y
NEW YORK · LONDON · OXFORD · NEW DELHI · SYDNEY

Bloomsbury Academic

An imprint of Bloomsbury Publishing Inc

1385 Broadway
New York
NY 10018
USA

50 Bedford Square
London
WC1B 3DP
UK

www.bloomsbury.com

BLOOMSBURY and the Diana logo are trademarks of Bloomsbury Publishing Plc

First published 2016

© Jonathan D. Kramer, 2016

Library of Congress Cataloging-in-Publication Data
Names: Kramer, Jonathan D., 1942-2004, author. | Carl, Robert, 1954- editor.
Title: Postmodern music, postmodern listening / by Jonathan D. Kramer ;
edited by Robert Carl.
Description: 1st edition. | New York : Bloomsbury Academic, 2016. | Includes
bibliographical references and index.
Identifiers: LCCN 2016003590 (print) | LCCN 2016004278 (ebook) | ISBN
9781501306020 (hardcover : alk. paper) | ISBN 9781501306044 (ePub) | ISBN
9781501306037 (ePDF)
Subjects: LCSH: Music–20th century–Philosophy and aesthetics. | Music–21st
century–Philosophy and aesthetics. | Postmodernism.
Classification: LCC ML3845 .K8127 2016 (print) | LCC ML3845 (ebook) | DDC
780.9/05–dc23
LC record available at http://lccn.loc.gov/2016003590

ISBN: HB: 978-1-5013-0602-0
PB: 978-1-5013-0601-3
ePDF: 978-1-5013-0603-7
ePub: 978-1-5013-0604-4

Cover design: Jesse Holborn / Design Holborn
Cover image © Jonathan Kramer

Typeset by Fakenham Prepress Solutions, Fakenham, Norfolk NR21 8NN
Printed and bound in the United States of America

Contents

List of Illustrations

Editor's Introduction

Robert Carl

The book you are holding has been in limbo for over a decade, and at times it seemed it would never see the light of day. The fact that it is now in your hands is a tribute to the efforts and faith of several people devoted to the author and his ideas, and a story of intellectual rescue that I'll detail below.

Jonathan Kramer was a composer and theorist, and one of the most original thinkers about music of his generation. And I would go so far as to say that his being a composer lent his thinking its particular originality. His work in the 1970s is one of the most clearly articulated syntheses between modernist and minimalist practice, a rarity at the time, and one that bespoke an exceptional openness to new experience. But he also was always drawn to the power of the classic repertoire, something that he saw and heard with unusual freshness. [In fact, he was the program annotator for the Cincinnati Symphony for over a decade, resulting in a collection of those pieces entitled *Listen to the Music*.]

As a theorist, his magisterial accomplishment was *The Time of Music*, a book that attempted to understand and categorize the many ways that musical time is conceived and its flow articulated. It was *not* a treatise on rhythm, even though it treated the topic as part of its agenda; rather, it attempted to see the very medium within which music exists in new terms. As such it raised far more questions than it could answer, but it also laid the groundwork for an entirely new field of study.

Jonathan (as all who knew him called him, and as do most of those who contribute ancillary pieces to this edition, including myself; in the text when that personal contact is evident we'll call him so; when the consideration is more abstract, it will be Kramer) came to New York in 1988 as Professor of Music Theory at Columbia, and at the turn of the century was at the height of his powers on all fronts. He had seen his musical vision as both composer and writer develop into one that embraced the multiplicity of postmodern thought and art, and he was hard at work on a comprehensive text that sought to explain the technical and philosophic bases of that aesthetic, *Postmodern Music, Postmodern Listening*. But in 2004, a congenital blood disease made a virulent appearance, and carried him off suddenly and shockingly to all who knew him.

And so his manuscript, without the sort of maintenance and advocacy the author gives towards shepherding it to publication, fell off the radar. Jonathan's widow, Deborah Bradley-Kramer, and his friend and colleague, musicologist Jann Pasler, tried to find publishers, but their efforts were rebuffed, for reasons I'll describe later.

It is at this point I come into the picture. Around 2010 my friend, the composer/

musicologist/critic Kyle Gann, made an offhand remark to me about Kramer's last book, and that he had a copy of the manuscript. I knew Jonathan, having been a former student and remaining a friend over the years, and knew of the project, but was not intimately acquainted with it. I asked Kyle for a copy and he sent it on. As I read it, I was astonished to see that the book was almost complete, not the sort of husk I'd expected. Of its eleven chapters, only the tenth seemed about half-finished, and Jonathan himself had annotated that this was the only aspect of the book he considered insufficient. Other editorial issues seemed quite manageable.

I contacted Deborah Bradley-Kramer, who was the owner of the text, in early 2013, and offered my services to once again start the process of finding a publisher and to edit the book, should the search be successful. She gave her blessing, and over the next two years I formulated a proposal, and on a hunch contacted Continuum books, which eventually became Bloomsbury Academic. In late spring 2014 the book finally found a home for publication, and the contracts were signed.

I near the end of my editorial role as I write this, and it's important to understand what's been done with the manuscript to reach this level of presentation. First, for an excellent and detailed description of the evolution of the text, and of Kramer's ideas, please read Jann Pasler's preface. Second, when examining files from Jonathan's computer with Deborah, we found a Word version of the text that was even more complete than the one I had worked from earlier. Above all, Chapter 10 was now basically complete (or at least twice as long as its earlier truncated form). As a result, I'm happy that my own role does not involve any "completion" of the manuscript; it can now speak fully for itself. My major role has been to create a bibliography, which involves both documents of Kramer's from earlier versions of the book and his classes, as well as using every citation in the text. In a few cases, citations had to be hunted down that were left incomplete, as well as correcting infrequent typos and rendering certain stylistic and scholarly conventions consistent (in some cases these bibliographic issues are detailed in my interjections to the footnotes). Finally, I have located most of the book's musical examples. Those that are still missing are marked—an example is #10 of the Mahler chapter. The most glaring omission is a series of examples in Chapter 7, dealing with issues of listeners' ambiguous perception of common sources. Fortunately, the core example is the Schumann *Soldier's March*, and John Halle in his essay helpfully has included it, so readers should refer to that point when the citation comes up in Kramer's text.

Another (and indeed substantial) aspect of the book that was incomplete was a "Book II" consisting of analyses of works, both from the repertoire and contemporary. It was clear that Kramer hoped these pieces would augment his more general argument in the body of the text, presenting a detailed model of an analytic method tailored to postmodern concepts and practices. When the later version surfaced, his analysis of the Finale from Mahler's Seventh Symphony was discovered. (Kramer had originally thought to put it in the body of the text, but then decided to make it part of this extended appendix.) Also, he repeatedly referenced his article on the Nielsen Sixth Symphony (already published in *The Nielsen Companion* (London: Faber and Faber; Portland, OR: Amadeus Press, 1994), and it has been included as well. Other contemporary composers suggested in the table of contents included Bernard Rands' ... *Body and Shadow* ..., Steve Reich's *Proverb*, and unspecified pieces by Louis Andriessen, Aaron Kernis, and John Adams. Of these, only the Rands is available, published in *Contemporary Music Review* (vol. 20, Part 4, 2001), an issue that I edited. Finally, there is passing mention of a Glossary in the original table of contents. This seems never to have been made, and it's unclear if it was designed as a lexicon of musical terms for non-professionals, or of more arcane critical terminology. I personally think the text communicates its intent without needing such.

The earlier mention of Halle brings up the largest addition and expansion to the book, the inclusion of a series of essays commenting on Kramer's life and work. Originally I thought of these as a way to create a distinctly "multiple" answer to the incompleteness of Chapter 10 (very much in keeping with the book's theme), but with the discovery of the more recent version, the aim changed. It was obvious that Deborah Bradley-Kramer, as the primary interpreter of Jonathan's music, should write on it, presenting him as a composer. Jann Pasler, due to her long intellectual interchange with him about the text, was obviously the person to write the Preface. Beyond that, Deborah and I agreed on a set of contributors who had some connection to Jonathan, either as colleagues or students ... and all, interestingly, composers. But they are composers also noted for the clarity of their thought and writing. This was never intended to be just a "memorial wreath," but rather an ongoing dialogue with the issues raised in the text, seen from the perspective of a decade further down the road. And the group of composers—of different ages, stylistic stances; peers, colleagues, former students of Jonathan's—I think amply fulfills this mandate. In a brief introduction to the section I detail what I feel are the special strengths and insights of each.

But no matter how insightful the contributors, the star of the show is of course the manuscript. And I'd like to make a few observations of my own, in part to prepare the reader to get the most from the encounter.

Like more than one essayist here, I too feel that much of the original buzz about postmodernism has abated in the interim. Much of what seemed radical at the moment, in its reaction to modernism, now seems self-evident. Of course that *is*, to a degree, a sign of the triumph of its agenda. But Kramer from the outset was after far more than a manifesto for a particular aesthetic. He had a deep sense that somehow, as we left the twentieth century, *things were no longer the same*, indeed, a new paradigm had emerged that was unprecedented. And he couches his argument in the fundamental premise that postmodernism is not a movement or style, rather it is an *attitude*. And even more than an attitude on the part of artistic creators, it is one assumed by art's *receivers*. The critical role of the *listener* in the interpretation of music, and not just contemporary, is fundamental to his world view. Older works can be seen as "postmodern" not because they are presages of works to come, but because they embody aspects and values that postmodern listeners share and appreciate. In short, postmodernism is a way of experiencing the world. And as a consequence, we begin to experience all art differently. This aspect of the book, certainly the most original, also I feel remains one of the most resonant and enduring in contemporary culture. As we have moved into an age of mass communication and social media, it seems that every act, statement, and product now is subject to an inexhaustible stream of commentary and criticism from anyone who wishes to offer it. More and more, nothing is considered autonomously, but rather in an infinite web of interrelated opinion and judgment. We all experience *interconnection and multiplicity* continually now, as agents in a stream of infinite experience. Kramer did not live to see this online explosion, but somehow his take on the postmodern seems uncannily adaptable to this development.

As one reads the book, slowly it dawns on one that the amount of reading, research, and critical thinking Kramer devoted to the project was monumental (just look at the bibliography). I don't think anyone has ever attempted to untangle the Gordian knot of issues associated with musical postmodernism with so much comprehensiveness and courage (indeed *chutzpah*). The precision of thought involved in assessing the nature of such concepts as musical surrealism, the avant garde, radical/conservative postmodernism, and the relation to antimodernism—all this examination and taxonomy bespeaks an intellectual passion that is deep and wide-ranging.

And that leads to the nature of the text itself. Early on I referred cryptically to the response of readers for other presses. I was able to read a few of the (anonymous) juried evaluations of the manuscript that led to its initial refusal a decade back. Some were quite complimentary, but the recurring theme was its "unacademic" quality. I feel now that this is something rather to be embraced. Kramer was a true scholar, and yet he had a great aversion to undue formality or pomposity that might be tied to "academicism." I think his own innate perspective and humor made it impossible for him to accept the role of an "authority" doling out judgment. The book, while obviously grounded in unquestionable research, also preserves a marvelously conversational tone. Kramer is not averse to questioning himself, to letting an internal dialogue go on for a while. He may move for a moment into the arcana of his personal life and scholarly disputes, then suddenly leap into an overarching point lurking in the margins, confirmed by what he's just related. And above all, in Chapter 11, he sets out to create a model of postmodern scholarship, one that relates seemingly silly personal stories, even at the risk by being labeled foolish by his peers. But just like an earworm you can't get out of your head, that may be the approach that seals the deal—I now can never forget the Otana Bee.

In short, this is a text we *need*, because no matter how much we may think the time of "musical postmodernism" is past, we still live in it, like fish not knowing they live in water. We *need* the perspective Kramer gives us.

I'll conclude with a couple of personal remarks. The first is my own set of acknowledgments. To Deborah Bradley-Kramer I am indebted for her preservation of so many essential materials, and her valiant efforts to keep this project alive over a decade. To Jann Pasler, the same, in particular for her meticulous preservation of her correspondence with Jonathan and certain materials I would never have found otherwise. To James Stewart, who solved several problems of presentation for musical examples and notation in the text. To Promisek Inc. in Bridgewater, Connecticut, which hosted me for a brief but intense residency where the final wave of this editing was accomplished. For Continuum, to editor David Barker for his initial enthusiasm and support, and above all to Ally Jane Grossan of Bloomsbury Academic, who took over the project with the institutional transfer, and who has been its true "shepherd" to its completion, once it came into her fold. Her support and level-headed judgment have been essential to its success. And to Michelle Chen, who took over the final stages of this job.

Finally a word about Jonathan Kramer and me. In spring 1974 I was a sophomore at Yale, a history major but desperate to write music. Through a series of contacts I met Jonathan and he took me as a student. My own experience of his intelligence, openness, and insight was very similar to that described by Duncan Neilson in his essay. I had no idea at the time of his intensive study of time, but it fit entirely with issues that have preoccupied me for my entire creative life. Jonathan was a marvelous teacher, but his greatest simple gift was to take me seriously (I will never forget when he responded to my worries about being a "real" composer by saying, "The moment you put a note on paper you were a composer. Now worry about being a good one.") By the time I graduated, even though I remained a history major, the Yale Symphony had played a piece of mine and I was on my way to further professional study. We stayed in touch. We shared a program in a Philadelphia loft just months before he died, something I had no inkling of as we sat together on a couch. Jonathan was essential to my life trajectory, and I owe him. Karmically I can only hope someone would take up an incomplete project of mine in a similar manner if such were the case. And of course, even if not, this is more than worth the effort.

Preface

The evolution of a book in music, dialogue, and analysis

Jann Pasler

This book began as a journey of self-exploration by a composer who never entirely identified with the major tenets of American high modernism and who reached out to the realm of ideas for sustenance and inspiration. Jonathan Kramer began his career in the 1960s when, despite "wild experiments that sought to overturn virtually every other musical value," "the desire for total unity and total consistency was so pervasive that it touched even composers with little interest in serialism," including John Cage and Philip Glass. Music theorists too, he observed, tended to seek "unity in (or force unity onto) the music." Frustrated with the convention of structural unity in music, Jonathan began to question the need for it as well as consistency and linear logic, as if these "guarantee coherence" or "make the composition succeed aesthetically." Such preoccupations did not take into account so much of what he loved in music, including the "drama" that can result from "manipulating degrees of surprise." From this concern came an important insight: "Both listening and analyzing create as well as discover unity."[1]

Postmodernism offered Jonathan a way of thinking with which to deconstruct the meta-narrative of unity in music. Approaching music as a postmodern listener, he began to explore other aspects of music often left unexplained or even unperceived: discontinuity, conflict, and contradiction—major themes in *Postmodern Music, Postmodern Listening*. Yet, given its multiple associations and the ongoing debate over whether postmodernism has been a regressive or progressive force, this book does not attempt a "rigorous or consistent definition of postmodernism in music nor does it offer a comprehensive survey of postmodern practices in composition or in music analysis." As much as Jonathan considered postmodern music to be "inclusive," he gives little attention to postmodern popular music. At the same time, he conceived the book as postmodern in its shape and processes, allowing it "to unfold circuitously—to take many routes through the thicket of ideas surrounding the postmodern impulse." Its organization thus was meant to suggest "a field of ideas that in themselves are not wholly consistent or constant." Topics come and go and return again. He hoped that, "from savoring all sides of a contradiction," readers will "become more accepting, less rigid, and more enriched."[2]

---

[1] These citations come from "Cross-Culturalism and Postmodernism in Music (or How visiting Korea did and did not influence my composing)," a lecture at the Seoul Arts Center on 19 November 1993, typescript provided by the author; his introduction to *Postmodern Music, Postmodern Listening* (draft, 1997); and *Postmodern Music, Postmodern Listening*, Sections 5.1, 5.5, and 6.2.

[2] Ibid.

The project, in essence, began with Jonathan's fascination with the perception of musical time.[3] In the 1970s, he studied how Beethoven's Opus 135 seemed to begin with a sense of an ending and he investigated moment forms that eschew a beginning-middle-end. As Stockhausen, one of Jonathan's former teachers, put it, in such music "a given moment is not merely regarded as the consequence of the previous one ... but as something individual, independent, and centered in itself, capable of existing on its own."[4] We met in the early 1980s through our shared fascination with temporal multiplicity, the interplay of linearity and nonlinearity in Stravinsky's music, and music in which the experience of time seems to stand still. Jonathan's work on moment form helped me think about formal mobility in *Jeux* and the subtle links that underlie its discontinuities; he shared his work on discontinuity in Stravinsky's music at my International Stravinsky Symposium.[5] As members of the International Society for the Study of Time, we both learned much from its conferences and publications. While Jonathan theorized what he called moment music, process music, and nonprocess vertical music, I explored similar developments in the context of composers' deconstruction of narrative, which I called anti-narrative, nonnarrative, and music without narrativity.[6] As noted in his *The Time of Music* (1988), finding it more accurate than Stockhausen's notion of the "statistical" or the "stochastic," Jonathan looked to the "cumulative impact, rather than moment to moment logic" I described in much recent music, such as *Canti Lunatici* by my colleague Bernard Rands.[7]

Theorizing time in the twentieth century led both of us to postmodern theory as a new way to think about the past and present and as inspiration to develop new approaches to music and musical analysis. In seminars on postmodernism and hermeneutics at UC San Diego in 1992, my students and I read broadly outside music (Hal Foster, Frederic Jameson, Jean-François Lyotard, Andreas Huyssen, Marjorie Perloff, among others). David Harvey's discussion of London as a labyrinth and Los Angeles as an aleph presented notions of structure as episodic and contingent on perception. We interrogated the limits of high modernism and began to conceptualize a musical

[3] Jonathan Kramer, "Multiple and Nonlinear Time in Beethoven's Opus 135," *Perspectives in New Music* 11, no. 2 (1973): 122–45; "Moment Form in Twentieth-Century Music," *Musical Quarterly* 2, no. 64 (1978): 117–94; and "New Temporalities in Music," *Critical Inquiry* 3, no. 7 (Spring 1981): 539–56.

[4] Karlheinz Stockhausen, "Momentform," in *Texte sur elektronischen und instrumentalen Musik*, vol. 1 (Cologne: DuMont, 1963), in Seppo Heikinheimo, *The Electronic Music of Karlheinz Stockhausen*, trans. Brad Absetz (Helsinki: Suomen Musikkitieteellinen Seura, 1972), pp. 120–1.

[5] Jann Pasler, "Debussy, *Jeux*: Playing with Time and Form," *19th Century Music* (June 1982): 60–72; Jonathan Kramer, "Discontinuity and Proportion in the Music of Stravinsky," in *Confronting Stravinsky: Man, Musician, and Modernist*, ed. Jann Pasler (Berkeley: University of California Press, 1986) and "Discontinuity and the Moment," in his *The Time of Music* (New York: Schirmer, 1988), pp. 201–20.

[6] Jann Pasler, "Narrative and Narrativity in Music," in *Time and Mind: Interdisciplinary Issues. The Study of Time VI*, ed. J. T. Fraser (Madison, CT: International Universities Press, 1989), pp. 232–57, first delivered at the International Society for the Study of Time, Dartington Hall, England, 9 July 1986; reprinted in idem, *Writing through Music: Essays on Music, Culture, and Politics* (Oxford University Press, 2008), Chapter 1; Kramer, *The Time of Music*, pp. 410–11, n. 57.

[7] Pasler, "Narrative," p. 252; Kramer, *The Time of Music*, pp. 408–9, n. 34.

postmodernism. Jonathan commissioned an article out of this and published it in a special issue of *Contemporary Music Review* he edited in 1993, *Time in Contemporary Musical Thought.*[8]

Jonathan's first public discussion of how he understood postmodernism came in a lecture at the Seoul Arts Center on November 19, 1993.[9] Here he referred to postmodern music as that which "freely intermixes styles, techniques, and reference to other music;" he also revealed that he had been composing such music in recent years. After defining "musical postmodernism" as characterized by "discontinuity, eclecticism, quotation, pastiche, disunity, focus on the surface more than on deep structure, lack of concern for personal communication, and juxtaposition of vernacular and high-art styles," he explained how these came to permeate his music, beginning with *Atlanta Licks* (1984), *Musica Pro musica* (1987), and *About Face* (1989, rev. 1991), each of which refer to other music. *Musica Pro musica* was written after returning from his first trip to Korea where he had found "an uncomfortable amalgamation of centuries-old culture and brand-new Western influences." He had begun to think about "incongruity" and "the confrontation of disparate experiences." *Musica Pro musica*, "rich in paradoxes," "is certainly postmodern in its juxtapositions of different kinds of music, its reference to various styles, its discontinuities, its pointed challenge to the aesthetic of organic unity, and its cross-cultural aspects." At the same time, he realized that composers should beware of cultural appropriations as they "are not immune from cultural imperialism." Two years later Jonathan published his analysis of postmodern music, building, as I had, on Foster's binary categorization of postmodernism as one of reaction or resistance to explain differences between, for example, the music of George Rochberg and John Zorn.[10]

Yet, for both of us, the postmodern turn emerged as far more than a desire to critique modernism or tradition, whether using quotation or radically transforming perception of the past. It involved a shift in our understanding of musical meaning. For me, this came from studying the most recent music of John Cage and Pauline Oliveros, which was dependent on the perceiver's ever-changing experiences, not the creator's control. It suggests that musical experience is cooperative, collaborative, and contingent, and that the past is not just something to embrace or reject, but also the repository of memory. Their compositions call on the listener to recall his or her own experiences, and not only those of an aesthetic nature. They include elements that

[8] Jann Pasler, "Postmodernism, Narrativity, and the Art of Memory," *Contemporary Music Review*, vol. 7, part 2 (London: Gordon and Breach, 1993): 3–32; reprinted in idem, *Writing through Music*, Chapter 2.
[9] Kramer, "Cross-Culturalism and Postmodernism in Music."
[10] Hal Foster, "Postmodernism: A Preface," in *The Anti-Aesthetic: Essays on Postmodern Culture*, ed. Hal Foster (Seattle: Bay Press), pp. xi–xvi; Jonathan Kramer, "Beyond Unity: Toward an Understanding of Musical Postmodernism," in *Concert Music, Rock, and Jazz since 1945: Essays and Analytical Studies*, ed. Elizabeth West Marvin and Richard Hermann (Rochester: University of Rochester Press, 1995), pp. 11–33. Mark Barry, in his "Music, Postmodernism, and George Rochberg's Third String Quartet," in *Postmodern Music, Postmodern Thought*, ed. Judy Lochhead and Joseph Auner (New York: Routledge, 2002), points out these similarities in our approaches to these two composers, but finds them limiting. Focusing on Rochberg's adoption of Mahler's music, Barry suggests a new way to interpret the composer's intentions (pp. 235–48).

are not musical *per se*. What I have called a third kind of postmodernism—based on the emancipation of memory, interpenetration, and relationships—goes further than what most postmodernist scholars deem simply "eclectic." They constitute occasions for us to come to understand the disparate part of our lives as fundamentally related. In this sense, both Jonathan and I recognized a capacity for ethical implications in postmodern music.

Whereas in the late 1960s Jonathan "accepted as self-evident that music communicates to listeners, and that listeners' experiences are shaped by music," later he too "began to credit the listener as a *source* (not just a receptor) of musical signification."[11] Indeed, under the influence of semiotics and postmodern thinking, Jonathan came to understand that musical significance lies "not with the composer or the composition, but the listener," or "at least from a complex interaction of composer, score, score editor, performance, recording engineer, playback system and—above all—the listener."[12] This challenged him, especially as a composer, in productive ways. In a diary he kept while composing *Remembrance of a people*, a response to the Holocaust, on May 21, 1996 he wrote, "It always takes some time for me to learn to hear my music as a listener rather than as the composer—to hear what is in the music, not what I wanted to put there. Now, after several listenings, I think I understand the Holocaust piece. It surprises me in its emotional intensity and pathos—qualities not common in my music." The diary is full of insights which, when approached as a listener, Jonathan had into his own works, some written years earlier.[13]

When, ironically, he turned to analysis of music of the past—even as he considered himself an "anti-historian"[14]—Jonathan embarked on a bold and original approach to postmodernism, with no true predecessor. Plumbing his deep understanding of music, he suggested that even music before the 1960s, when philosophers and cultural critics date the "crisis of modernity," could be postmodern.[15] Postmodernism, he posited, is "more an attitude than a historical period," "not simply a repudiation of modernism or its continuation," but a composite of attitudes, characteristics, structures that can be found throughout music history.[16] Returning to his previous work on "temporal multiplicity in twentieth-century culture,"[17] Jonathan began to think that "multiple musical time" was, by its nature, postmodern.

In spring 1994 Jonathan gave a graduate seminar at Columbia University on three early twentieth-century compositions that had been resistant to traditional analytic

[11] Jonathan Kramer, "Coming to Terms with Music as Protest and Remembrance: One Composer's Story," typescript provided by the author (55 pages, including musical examples).
[12] Kramer, "Cross-Culturalism and Postmodernism in Music"; "Postmodern Concepts of Musical Time," *Indiana Theory Review* (Fall 1996): 22; and "Coming to Terms with Music as Protest and Remembrance."
[13] This diary, from 18 January 1996 to 7 January 1997, is part of Kramer's "Coming to Terms with Music as Protest and Remembrance."
[14] Kramer, *Postmodern Music, Postmodern Listening* (c. 1997), Chapter 4.
[15] This idea first arises in "Cross-Culturalism and Postmodernism in Music." Here, in the context of presenting his own music, he suggests that "there are certainly non-postmodern works, old as well as recent," that contain aspects of postmodernism.
[16] Kramer, "Postmodern Concepts of Musical Time," pp. 21–62.
[17] Kramer, *The Time of Music*, pp. 163–8.

methods: the finale of Mahler's Seventh Symphony, Nielsen's Sixth Symphony, *Sinfonia Semplice*, and "Putnam's Camp" from Ives's *Three Places in New England*. Where does analysis succeed and fail in such music, "quirky in their embracing of the unexpected, the unmotivated, the unpredictable. What analytic approaches are possible for music that partially lacks unity?" He asked students to study new scholarly fields that were questioning the assumptions or methods of analysis, including feminism/gender/sexuality, narrative, phenomenology, criticism, semiotics, and psychoanalysis—interestingly, not yet postmodern theory.[18] In 1996, he published a forty-page essay on temporal structures in the first two, plus Beethoven's Opus 135, entitling it "Postmodern Concepts of Musical Time." Analyzing the five temporalities he found in the finale of Mahler's Seventh Symphony, he called the work "proto-postmodern" but later "actually postmodern"[19]—this discussion returns in *Postmodern Music, Postmodern Listening* as Chapter 12. Nielsen's *Sinfonia Semplice*, which, like the Mahler, took years to be accepted, became the focus of an article in 1994, here returning as Chapter 13.[20] With its mixture of contradictory styles and techniques, its reveling in eclecticism, its delight with ambiguity, and its refusal to recognize any boundaries between vernacular and art music, the vulgar and the sublime, Jonathan found *Sinfonia Semplice* "the most profoundly postmodern piece composed prior to the postmodern era." And yet, as he later clarified, "these works and works like them are not the sources of postmodernism." It is "only now," when we understand the postmodern attitude, that it makes sense to listen to such works "in a postmodern manner."[21]

In many ways, Jonathan's concept of postmodernism developed concomitantly with his composition, his analysis of these pieces, his reading, and his interaction with others, all of which evolved over time. We can see this most clearly in the list of characteristics he considered postmodern. The eight in his 1993 lecture in Seoul, mentioned above, became an enumerated list of fourteen "traits" in 1996, revised and expanded to sixteen traits in 2000/02 and in *Postmodern Music, Postmodern Listening* (2016). In 1996 trait 1 notes that postmodernism has "aspects of both" modernism and its continuation—in 2000/02 and 2016, he clarifies, "aspects of both a break and an extension." In 1996 and thereafter, he adds the concept of irony as trait 2—perhaps because trait 1 in itself is an irony. In 1993, he had explicitly excluded it: "postmodern music often avoids irony. It takes from history, but it does not distort, interpret, analyze, or revise."

Much of the book is devoted to wrestling with the problem of trying to define or classify postmodernism as entirely distinct from modernism, a preoccupation we shared. In my 1993 and 1994 articles, Cage emerges as not only a postmodernist in such works as *Musicircus* (1967), wherein he shifted to the listener the burden

---

[18] Jonathan Kramer, "Graduate Seminar in Analysis," Spring Semester 1994, Columbia University.

[19] Introduction, *Postmodern Music, Postmodern Listening* (1997 draft).

[20] Jonathan Kramer, "Unity and Disunity in Carl Nielsen's Sixth Symphony," in *A Nielsen Companion*, ed. Mina Miller (London: Faber and Faber; Portland, OR: Amadeus Press, 1994), pp. 293–334.

[21] Kramer, "Postmodern Concepts of Musical Time," pp. 21–2, and Kramer, "The Nature and Origins of Musical Postmodernism," in *Postmodern Music, Postmodern Thought*, ed. Lochhead and Auner, p. 19.

of making sense of his "play of intelligent anarchy." Using structural devises such as repetition and variation, ideas he learned from Schoenberg to ensure structural coherence, and constructing his reputation on the shoulders of his predecessors, whom he frequently cited earlier in his career, he was also a modernist. Cage's vision too was modernist: "to teach through music and embody a way to a better future."[22] In *Postmodern Music, Postmodern Listening* (2016), Jonathan devotes part of Chapter 3 to John Cage as "Modernist *and* Postmodernist," making him the poster-child for his trait 1. In *Postmodern Music, Postmodern Listening*, he likewise considered "influence anxiety" as "a critical issue for modernists" (2000/02), but added a not entirely convincing psychological spin: postmodernists are "adolescents" who have "passed beyond their oedipal conflicts with their modernists parents, although they may still have an uneasy relationship with them." Maybe the point was that Jonathan identified with postmodernists because they "like to feel that they can be whatever they wish."

Over time, Jonathan's earlier preoccupation with critiquing structural unity became less pronounced. After his 1994 article on unity and disunity in Nielsen's music came the 1995 article, "Beyond Unity," in which he defines "disunity" as the basis for musical postmodernism. One reviewer noted that this strong stance risked "creating a meta-narrative of his own."[23] Whether he agreed with this or not, thereafter "disunity" (from the 1993 paper) disappears from his lists, as does "focus on the surface more than on deep structure." And in 1996 and 2000/02, "disdain for structural unity" comes only fifth among postmodern characteristics, moving to eleventh in 2016. At the same time, in 2016 Jonathan supplements trait 10, on "fragmentations and discontinuities," with the notion of "incongruities" and "indeterminacy," perhaps in recognition of John Cage's importance to many postmodernists.

Jonathan's interest in time and eclecticism underlies trait 3—postmodernism "does not respect boundaries between sonorities and procedures of the past and of the present" (1996, 2000/02)—which, "in fact, sometimes goes so far to question the distinction between the past and the present" (2016). Trait 4, in challenging "barriers between 'high' and 'low' styles," reflects how important popular music has been to postmodern theorists (1996, 2000/02) as does trait 6, it "refuses to accept the distinction between elitist and populist values (1996), and "questions the mutual exclusivity of elitist and populist values" (2000/02, 2016). Suggesting some ambivalence about this characteristic in 2016, he adds to trait 4, "sometimes resulting in music that can be considered of questionable taste." These changes imply an important philosophical shift and the introduction of value judgments normally not associated with an aesthetic based on relativism.

Other concepts posited as postmodern in 1993 also grow in complexity over

---

[22] Pasler, "Postmodernism, Narrativity, and the Art of Memory," p. 80, and Jann Pasler, "Inventing a Tradition: John Cage's *Composition in Retrospect*," in *John Cage: Composed in America*, ed. Marjorie Perloff and Charles Junkerman (Chicago: University of Chicago Press, 1994), pp. 125–43, reprinted in Pasler, *Writing through Music*, Chapter 6.

[23] Jonathan Kramer, "Beyond Unity: Toward an Understanding of Musical Postmodernism," in *Concert Music, Rock, and Jazz since 1945: Essays and Analytical Studies*, ed. Elizabeth West Marvin and Richard Hermann (Rochester: University of Rochester Press, 1995), pp. 11–33; David Brackett, review of this book in *American Music*, 15, no. 1 (Spring 1997): 96.

time. Jonathan couples "pluralism" to "eclecticism"; "quotation" becomes "of many traditions and cultures;" but he drops "pastiche" from the lists and "lack of personal communication," the latter perhaps realizing how important autobiography had become for postmodern performance artists such as Laurie Anderson. In 2016, trait 9 on quotations becomes trait 6 and refers to new concepts and concerns, important in the discourse in recent years, especially intertextuality. Here again we hear the composer's critical opinion, resistant to quotation when it is "sometimes so extreme in its intertextual references that it calls into question the validity of artistic originality."

The 2000/02 and 2016 lists include two new characteristics that reflect Jonathan's increasing sensitivity to cultural aspects of postmodernism: one "considers music not as autonomous but as relevant to cultural, social, and political contexts"—an idea possibly influenced by the work of such scholars as Susan McClary and other feminists—and another "considers technology not only as a way to preserve and transmit music, but also as deeply implicated in the production and essence of music." The central insight from 1996 to 2016 is the last trait: postmodernism "locates meaning and even structure in listeners, more than in scores, performances, or composers." In Chapter 11, Jonathan uses Jean-Jacques Nattiez's concept of the "poietic," the "neutral," and the "esthetic" to explain the distinctions between how music is "conceived by a composer," "represented in a score," and "understood by a listener." All traits return as themes throughout *Postmodern Music, Postmodern Listening*, helping one to navigate its complexity. The book ends with arguably the "postmodern attitude" Jonathan most hopes to leave with the reader: "trait 8: embraces contradiction."

Between 1997 and 2004, *Postmodern Music, Postmodern Listening* also evolved in substantive ways.[24] In Chapter 1, Jonathan clarifies that these 16 attributes came from studying compositions that "open themselves up to a postmodern understanding," as well as from reading and contemplating the lists of David Harvey and Ihab Hassan.[25] Like the 2000/2002 article, it ends with another list: ten explanations of why composers write postmodern music. Beginning his book in this way, Jonathan reminds the reader that he is coming, above all, from the perspective of a composer. Besides reusing and

[24] Chapter 1, "Postmodernism (Not) Defined," from the 1997 version became Chapter 2, placed after the 2000/02 article, now revised as Chapter 1. Other chapters from previous articles and the 1997 book also remain, but in new places: Chapters 4, 5, and 6 earlier appeared as Chapter 3 and the two parts of Chapter 2; Chapters 8, 9, and 10 earlier appeared as Chapter 5 and the two parts of Chapter 4. From the Lochhead/Auner volume, he may have taken note of Anne LeBaron's analysis of surrealism in postmodern music, motivating him to develop this topic, only mentioned in the 1997 version, into Chapter 9 in the 2016 book, albeit taking it in different directions than Anne LeBaron ("Reflections of Surrealism in Postmodern Musics," in *Postmodern Music, Postmodern Thought*, pp. 75–92). While she concentrates on automatism, collage, and free improvisation, Jonathan takes issue with these as postmodern, though also examines Satie's *Parade*. He also takes off from Daniel Albright, *Untwisting the Serpent: Modernism in Music, Literature, and Other Arts* (Chicago: University of Chicago Press, 2000). See below, Chapter 9, n. 354.

[25] Jonathan's list is shorter and more focused than the extremely general terms of Ibab Hassan, on "Modernism" vs. "Postmodernism," but not as culturally evocative as the concepts of David Harvey, addressing "Fordist Modernity" vs. "Flexible Postmodernity." These are reproduced in Timothy Taylor's contribution to *Postmodern Music, Postmodern Thought*, "Music and Musical Practices in Postmodernity," pp. 95–7.

expanding his previous work, Jonathan also wrote new chapters after 1997: Chapter 3 on the avant garde and Chapter 7 on "postmodern listening."

As the purpose of *Postmodern Music, Postmodern Listening* and its intended readership evolved from primarily addressing composers and other musicians to participating in the larger debates about postmodernism, postmodern scholarship had perhaps the greatest influence on how the book evolved in its final version. If it began as the personal and intellectual memoir of a composer, music theorist, teacher, and world-traveler, if it allowed Jonathan to reflect on and theorize "the orderly disorder of a chaotic system," it also evolved into a repository of research on the "traits" he had identified as postmodern. As such, the book embodies David Harvey's concept of postmodern subjectivity, that is, multilayered and performative.

If there is anything I wish he could have addressed in this important book before his untimely death, it would have been the resistance to postmodernism among composers then and today, not only in Europe but also the United States. Perhaps this would help explain why the term and all that it embodied seems now like just another passing intellectual fad, merely a watershed for modernism. Yet, the "postmodern attitude" challenges us to reject all forms of elitism, arrogance, and nationalist egocentrism, to cross the boundaries that have separated disciplines, musics, Western and non-Western ways of thinking, and to renew meaningful communication with the public who are, after all, our listeners.

Postmodern Music,
Postmodern Listening

Jonathan D. Kramer

Foreword

The majority of writings that link music and postmodernism fall into one of two areas. They either study popular music as an exemplar of postmodern social, cultural, political, and possibly (but often not) aesthetic thinking. Or else they use postmodernist ideas to study music of the past in new ways, concentrating on such previously ignored areas as gender implications, relevance to cultural and social values prevalent at their time of creation, political and power undertones, etc.

This book does neither of these things. It considers "postmodern classical music" of the present, and also of the past, and studies its relevance to today's listeners. It suggests ways this music can be heard and understood *now*.

Actually, the phrase "postmodern classical music" in the previous paragraph is a misnomer. Not only is "classical" a poor label for the kind of music studied in this book, but also I argue against thinking of "postmodern music" as a category. There is a postmodern musical attitude, which I try to delineate in Chapter 1. This attitude informs a large variety of music, and also it influences the listening process. Some compositions exhibit some characteristics of the postmodern musical attitude, and other compositions display different postmodern characteristics. There is probably no music that is thoroughly postmodern in every conceivable way, and there is not too much music of today that is totally unaffected by the postmodern attitude.

What does it mean to posit that "postmodern music" is not a category? We hear about postmodern music all the time, and you will indeed encounter this term in this book. When I write "postmodern music," what I really mean is "music exhibiting a substantial number of attributes that readily stimulate a postmodern disposition in composers and/or listeners." It is pointless to label works simply as postmodern or not postmodern. When we try to do this, we quickly get caught up in a jumble of contradictions, because postmodernism is not one thing. When someone asks me if the piece we just heard is postmodern, I do not like to say yes or no. Most recent pieces, and several older pieces, are postmodern in some ways and not in other ways. Still, the habit of talking about postmodern music is too deeply ingrained to avoid it totally. To try to do so would be to force the employment of cumbersome phrases. Such jargon works against clearly setting forth my ideas, so I do allow myself to call pieces postmodern, although I hope you will always remember that there really are no such things as simply or exclusively postmodern pieces.

Since I take postmodernism as an attitude, I prefer not to think of it as a historical period. When I write about postmodern aspects of certain pieces of Beethoven, Mahler, Ives, Nielsen, and others, I truly mean that they are compositions that have certain characteristics that listeners of today can understand from the standpoint of a postmodern attitude. I do not mean that these works of the past are precursors of postmodernism. They are as much postmodern as are many works written considerably more recently.

Although I prefer not to think of postmodernism as a period, I am quite aware that postmodern values are more prevalent today than at any time in the past. Thus I may write loosely about a postmodern era (today). What I really mean by this is that our era is one in which postmodern values are particularly widespread.

Another way that this book differs from other writing on music and postmodernism is that it does not simply look to see how postmodern ideas and values are reflected in music. Although I frequently use sources outside of music, I do not assume that what is postmodern is somehow constituted externally to music and then applied to music by composers, commentators, performers, or listeners. I believe that music, just as much as architecture, literature, and painting, has helped to form and to formulate postmodernism. The postmodernism that music has forged naturally has a lot in common with other arts' postmodernisms, but it is also distinct in some ways. But I do not dwell on the ways that musical postmoderism is different. To do so would be to (continue to) cast it as the other, as defined in part by its difference. Instead, I take music to be central to the postmodern enterprise (how odd that I should even have to say that, except that music is often ignored and/or poorly understood by theorists of postmodernism). Some of the aspects of postmodernism I discuss are peculiar to music. Some emanate from music and spread to other disciplines. And some have been imported into the arena of music by composers, commentators, and listeners who are deeply involved in postmodern thinking in other areas of human thought and action.

Postmodernism is not a monolithic aesthetic with a consistent agenda. Different composers, different critics, and different apologists use and see postmodernism differently. Hence its categories and subcategories are impossible to delineate rigorously. There are always exceptions. If my prose seems sometimes contradictory as a result of the fuzziness of categories, I accept that as the inevitable result of trying to study an aesthetic, one of whose tenets is the embracing of contradiction. From savoring all sides of a contradiction, we can become more accepting, less rigid, and more enriched. Resolving aesthetic conflicts, by contrast, can be stultifying and can discourage further creative thought.

Because postmodernism seeks other kinds of logic than the linear, it is appropriate for this study to unfold circuitously—to take many routes through the thicket of ideas surrounding the postmodern impulse. Thus, discussions of several topics are spread across different chapters. When a topic returns, its new context gives it a different twist. In this manner I try to give a flavor for postmodernism as a field of ideas that in themselves are not wholly consistent or constant.

Acknowledgments

I am indebted above all to Margaret Barela, who carefully read and dutifully criticized several drafts of this book. Her tireless dedication, penetrating insights, and extraordinary editorial skills are without equal. I am also grateful to Candace Brower, John Halle, Mina Miller, Severine Neff, Karen Painter, Jann Pasler, and John Rahn for penetrating readings of earlier drafts of some of these chapters and for several useful suggestions. Warren Burt, Stuart Feder, George Fisher, Allen Gross, Stefan Litwin, Robert Morris, and Allen Otte were also helpful. I appreciate Elizabeth West Marvin's urging me to write an article that became the basis of Chapters 2 and 3, and I am grateful to Mina Miller for encouraging me to write what became Chapter 13. As they evolved, portions of the book were presented in several public forums: as a keynote address to the Florida State University Music Theory Society, January 19, 1991; as an informal talk at the third annual Montana International Composers Conference, Talloires, France, July 11, 1991; as a paper read at the Fourth International Music Analysis Conference, City University of London, 19 September 1991; as the keynote address to the Indiana Theory Symposium, Indiana University, April 4, 1992; as an invited address to a regional conference of the Society for Composers, Bates College, April 25, 1992; as an invited paper at the Music and Psychoanalysis Conference at Bates College on April 8, 1995; as a keynote address to the University of Melbourne Centennial Conference on June 8, 1995; as a paper delivered to the International Society for the Study of Time in Sainte-Àdele, Québec, Canada, on July 6, 1995; as an invited paper at a conference on music and time at the University of Geneva, October 28, 1995; and in lectures at the University of Kentucky on March 20, 1991, Northwestern University on November 19, 1992, City of New York Graduate Center on February 22, 1993, Carleton College on January 29, 1994, Ohio State University on November 1, 1994, the Danish Musicological Society on February 22, 1995, the Faculty of Music of the University of Copenhagen on February 22, 1995, the Hochschüle für Musik in Saarbrücken (Germany) on April 3, 1995, Cornell University on April 14, 1995, the Eastman School of Music on April 15, 1995, the University of Western Australia on May 9, 1995, the University of Wollongong on May 29, 1995, and the University of Pennsylvania on November 30, 1995. I appreciate useful comments and criticisms of several audience members on these occasions.

Portions of this book were written under a grant for nonfiction writing from the New York Foundation for the Arts. Other portions were written at the Rockefeller Study Center and Conference Center in Bellagio, Italy. I deeply appreciate the generous support of both the NYFA and the Rockefeller Foundation.

BOOK I

IDEAS

Part One

Chapters on Postmodern Concepts of Music

1

The Nature and Origins of Musical Postmodernism

1.1. The Postmodern Attitude

Postmodernism is a maddeningly imprecise musical concept. Does the term refer to a period or an aesthetic, a listening attitude or a compositional practice? Is postmodern music still seeking to define itself, or has its time already passed? Does postmodernism react against or continue the project of modernist music? Is it a positive or a negative force? Is postmodern music original, or does it recycle older music? How widespread is it? Why does postmodernism seem to embrace many cultural values previously thought to be inimical to successful art and even to simple good sense? Is postmodern art serious or frivolous?

And, simply, what *is* musical postmodernism? For some critics, postmodernism's defining compositional practice is its deliberate attempt to reach out by using procedures and materials audiences are believed to relish: diatonicism, singable melodies, metric regularity, foot-tapping rhythms, tonality, and/or consonant harmonies. Nostalgia for the good old days of tunes and tonality, however, is actually opposed to certain strains of postmodernism. It is not so much postmodernist as antimodernist.[1] There is a significant difference between these two aesthetics: antimodernist yearning for the golden ages of classicism and romanticism perpetuates the elitism of art music, while postmodernism claims to be anti-elitist.[2] An important first step in understanding musical postmodernism, therefore, is to divorce it from nostalgic artworks. Only in antimodernist music (such as the flute and piano concertos of Lowell Lieberman, George Rochberg's *Ricordanza* and Viola Sonata, and Michael Torke's piano concerto *Bronze*) is the use of traditional sonorities, gestures, structures, and

---

[1] I discuss antimodernism vs. modernism vs. postmodernism further in Chapter 4.

[2] Postmodernist music is generally less elitist than modernist music, much of which appeals to a relatively small audience of initiates—people who know how to appreciate atonality, jagged melodies, irregular rhythms, asymmetrical meters, pungent dissonances, etc. But postmodern music rarely achieves the total overthrow of elitism. By incorporating popular music into symphonic compositions, for example, postmodern composers do not really create pop symphonies so much as they embrace pop while preserving its otherness. On this general point, see Georgina Born, *Rationalizing Culture: IRCAM, Boulez, and the Institutionalization of the Musical Avant-Garde* (Berkeley: University of California Press, 1995), pp. 61–5. The effectiveness of pop references in a symphony often derives in part from the fact that they do not totally belong there.

procedures tantamount to a re-embracing of earlier styles. In contrast to such compositions, postmodernist music is not conservative. Compositions such as Zygmunt Krauze's Second Piano Concerto, John Adams' Violin Concerto, Henryk Gorecki's Third Symphony, Alfred Schnittke's First Symphony, George Rochberg's Third Quartet, Steve Reich's *Tehillim*, John Corigliano's First Symphony, and Luciano Berio's *Sinfonia*[3] do not so much conserve as radically transform the past, as—each in its own way—they simultaneously embrace and repudiate history.

Many reviewers of the popular press do not distinguish antimodernism from postmodernism. They identify as postmodern any composition that was written recently but sounds as if it were not. Composers who use the term are not much more informed than the reviewers. Many composers I know use "postmodernism" in the corrupted sense of the press, in apparent ignorance of the thinking of critical theorists such as Eco or Lyotard. Yet the ideas of such writers *are* relevant to today's postmodern music.

A more subtle and nuanced understanding of postmodernism emerges once we consider it not as a historical period but as an attitude—a current attitude that influences not only today's compositional practices but also how we listen to and use music of other eras. Umberto Eco has written tellingly, "Postmodernism is not a trend to be chronologically defined, but, rather, an ideal category or, better still, a *Kunstwollen*, a way of operating. We could say that every period has its postmodernism."[4] Jean-François Lyotard suggests a still more paradoxical view of the chronology of postmodernism: "A work can become modern only if it is first postmodern. Postmodernism thus understood is not modernism at its end but in the nascent state, and this state is constant."[5] Lyotard seems to believe that before a work

---

[3] Much has been written about this work, particularly its third movement, in which Berio incorporates almost complete the third movement of Mahler's Second Symphony, onto which he grafts myriad quotations. One of the more perceptive descriptions is this one by John Rea: "Not unlike a mosquito drawing a bit of blood and then flying away only to leave behind a potent bit of venom, the New York City première in 1968 (European première in 1969 at Donaueschingen) of Berio's Sinfonia—with its fluvial rendering (in its third movement) of Mahler's scherzo movement (the third) from his Second Symphony, itself a rendering (the third) of Mahler's youthful *Das Knaben Wunderhorn* setting, 'St Anthony Preaches to the Fishes'—prompted an immunological mutation in the circulatory system of American and European musical life, a change of consciousness from which there could be no return. The cascading torrent of musical references and citations in the Berio work, notably with respect to the past but also to the present (music critics disparagingly identified this as collage technique), speaks well for it as the sonic precursor of that visual collage as postmodern critique," Rea, "Postmodernisms," *Einaudi Enciclopedia* (ed. Jean-Jacques Nattiez), vol. 2. English translation www.andante.com/reference/einaudi/EinaudiRea.cfm. [Editor's note: this link is no longer active, though the *Einaudi Enciclopedia* remains in print, with this translation included.]

[4] Umberto Eco, *Postscript to the Name of Rose* (New York and London: Harcourt Brace Jovanovich, 1984), p. 67. Similarly, Kathleen Higgins writes: "The term 'postmodernism' has an oxymoronic sound. How, if the word 'modern' refers to the present, can currently living people be 'postmodern'? This question arises almost as a gut reaction. The word seems a little uncanny. A 'postmodernist' sounds like one of the living dead or perhaps one of the living unborn—or maybe our sense of temporality is simply offended. We can recall Kurt Vonnegut and conceive of postmodernists as 'unstuck in time,'" "Nietzsche and Postmodern Subjectivity," in Clayton Koelb (ed.), *Nietzsche as Postmodernist: Essays Pro and Contra* (Albany: State University of New York Press, 1990), p. 189.

[5] Jean-François Lyotard, *The Postmodern Condition: A Report on Knowledge*, trans. Geoff Bennington and Brian Massumi (Minneapolis: University of Minnesota Press, 1984), p. 79.

can be understood as truly modern, it must challenge a previous modernism. Thus, to take Lyotard's example, Picasso and Braque are postmodern in that their art goes beyond the modernism of Cézanne. Once their art has achieved this postmodern break with the past, it becomes modernist. Similarly, certain music of Mahler, Ives, and Nielsen, for example, becomes postmodern by going beyond the modernist practices of such composers as Berlioz, Liszt, and Wagner.

1.2. Postmodern Views on Unity, Intertextuality, and Eclecticism

Beyond the relevance (or lack thereof) of the critical theories of Eco, Lyotard, and others, one other thing that distinguishes antimodernism from postmodernism is the attitude toward the notion of musical unity, cherished by traditionally minded composers as well as by critics, theorists, and analysts.[6] For both antimodernists and modernists, unity is a prerequisite for musical sense; for some postmodernists, unity is an option. I believe that unity is not simply a characteristic of music itself but more pointedly a means of understanding music, a value projected onto music. As such, it is necessarily demoted from its previous position of universality. It is no longer a master narrative of musical structure. Many postmodern composers have accordingly embraced conflict and contradiction and have at times eschewed consistency and unity. Similarly, postmodern audiences do not necessarily search for or find unity in the listening experience. They are more willing to accept each passage of music for itself, rather than having—in accordance with the strictures of modernist analysis and criticism—to create a single whole of possibly disparate parts.

Freed from the dictates of structural unity, some of today's postmodern music offers its listeners extraordinary discontinuities that go beyond contrast, variety, consistency, and unity. Such pieces as John Zorn's *Forbidden Fruit* and William Bolcom's Third Symphony, for example, continually challenge their boundaries by redefining their contexts. References to musical styles of any era or of any culture can intrude, possibly unexpectedly. Of course, some modernist (and earlier) music also includes unexpected quotations. One need only recall the sudden appearances of *Tristan und Isolde* in Debussy's *Golliwog's Cakewalk* and in Berg's *Lyric Suite* to understand that quotation and surprise are not the exclusive province of postmodernist composers. Such examples demonstrate one way among several that postmodernism does not necessarily contradict but rather extends ideas of modernism. Intertextuality has become more pervasive as postmodernism has become more widespread: the references in the Zorn and Bolcom works are far more extensive than the isolated Wagner quotations in the Debussy and Berg pieces. In some postmodern works, essentially all of the music is quotation. There is no other music, no "normal" music of the piece

---

[6] The postmodern challenge to the concept of unity is the topic of Chapter 4.

itself, which the quotations interrupt, as in the Debussy and Berg examples. In works like *Quasi una sinfonietta* by Pawel Szymański or *Jackie O* by Michael Daugherty, you take away the whole piece.[7] According to Björn Heile, in Mauricio Kagel's *Ludwig van*, "all the musical material was composed by someone else."[8]

Long before postmodernism was widely recognized, and long before recording technology brought distant musics into the present, there were pieces that juxtaposed styles. How does the eclecticism of such music as Ives' *Three Places in New England*,[9] Mahler's Seventh Symphony,[10] or Nielsen's *Sinfonia Semplice*,[11] for example, differ from that of the 1980s and 1990s and 2000s? It is tempting to understand such earlier works as precursors of (but not necessarily formative influences on) today's postmodernism—somewhat as early repetitive works, such as Ravel's *Boléro* or the first movement of Shostakovich's *Leningrad Symphony*, can be understood in retrospect as precursors of minimalism.[12] But there is a more intriguing way to view pieces like those of Ives, Mahler, and Nielsen: they are not so much proto-postmodern as they are actually postmodern—by which I mean not only that they exhibit postmodern compositional practices but also that they are conducive to being understood in accordance with today's postmodernist musical values and listening strategies.

[7] David Brackett makes a similar point in "'Where It's At?': Postmodern Theory and the Contemporary Musical Field," in Judy Lochhead and Joseph Auner (eds.), *Postmodern Music/Postmodern Thought* (New York and London: Routledge, 2002), p. 211. Brackett calls the music surrounding quotations in music by, for example, Ives and Mahler "real." In discussing the Daugherty work, he suggests that "there is no longer the sense of what might constitute the real."
Furthermore, there is a difference in perspective between modernist and postmodernist quotation. Modernist composers often want to take over, to own, to demonstrate their mastery of that which they are quoting, either by placing it in modernist contexts or by distorting it. Postmodernists are more content to let the music they refer to or quote simply be what it is, offered with neither distortion nor musical commentary. Hence postmodern music readily accepts the diversity of music in the world. It cites—in fact, appropriates—many other musics, including that of modernism. In a sense it challenges the notion of the past, since it may include references to music of virtually any era or culture. Wide-ranging quotations are readily included in postmodern works and are easily understood by postmodern listeners because—thanks to recording technology—music of all times and places can be a living force for composers and listeners alike.
[8] Bjorn Heile, "Collage vs. Compositional Control: The Interdependency of Modernist and Postmodernist Approaches in the Work of Mauricio Kagel," in Judy Lochhead and Joseph Auner (eds.), *Postmodern Music/Postmodern Thought* (New York and London: Routledge, 2002), p. 291.
[9] For a discussion of the postmodern aspects of *Putnam's Camp*, the middle movement of *Three Places*, see Jonathan D. Kramer, "Postmodern Concepts of Musical Time," *Indiana Theory Review* 17/2 (1997): 48–60.
[10] Chapter 12 discusses postmodern aspects of the finale of Mahler's Seventh Symphony.
[11] See Chapter 13 for an analysis of postmodern aspects of Nielsen's *Sinfonia Semplice*.
[12] It is impossible to prove lack of influence decisively. However, none of the writings by or interviews with early minimalists with which I am familiar cites either of these works as influences, and I suspect—for aesthetic and stylistic reasons—that the music of Glass and Reich would be unchanged had Ravel and Shostakovich never composed these particular pieces. But I cannot prove this contention. Similarly, I feel (but cannot prove) that postmodernism of today would be essentially unchanged if the cited compositions of Ives, Mahler, and Nielsen did not exist.

1.3. Characteristics of Postmodern Music

Naming music that is nearly a hundred years old postmodern is not willfully perverse but rather is a consequence of viewing postmodernism more as an attitude than as a historical period. This anti-historical stance results in a blurring of rigid distinctions among modernism, postmodernism, and antimodernism, resulting in the term "postmodernism" resisting rigorous definition. Attitudes toward structural unity, intertextuality, and eclecticism, as explained in the previous section, further problematize (to use a favorite term of writers on postmodernism) attempts to demarcate the word's meaning. Despite such complications, however, it is useful to enumerate characteristics of postmodern music—by which I mean music that is understood in a postmodern manner, or that calls forth postmodern listening strategies, or that provides postmodern listening experiences, or that exhibits postmodern compositional practices.

Musical postmodernism

1. is not simply a repudiation of modernism or its continuation, but has aspects of both a break and an extension;
2. is, on some level and in some way, ironic;
3. does not respect boundaries between sonorities and procedures of the past and of the present, and, in fact, sometimes goes so far as to question the distinction between the past and the present;
4. challenges barriers between "high" and "low" styles, sometimes resulting in music that can be considered of questionable taste;
5. questions the mutual exclusivity of elitist and populist values;
6. includes quotations of or references to music of many traditions and cultures, and, in fact, is sometimes so extreme in its intertextual references that it calls into question the validity of artistic originality;
7. encompasses pluralism and eclecticism;
8. embraces contradictions;
9. distrusts binary oppositions;
10. includes fragmentations, incongruities, discontinuities, and indeterminacy;
11. shows disdain for the often unquestioned value of structural unity;
12. avoids totalizing forms (e.g. does not want entire pieces to be tonal or serial or cast in a prescribed formal mold);
13. presents multiple meanings and multiple temporalities;
14. considers technology not only as a way to preserve and transmit music but also as deeply implicated in the production and essence of music;
15. considers music not as autonomous but as a commodity responsive to cultural, social, economic, and political contexts;
16. locates meaning and even structure in listeners more than in scores, performances, or composers.

It may seem bizarre to offer a seemingly orderly list of characteristics of postmodernism, which by its nature defies orderliness, categories, and taxonomies. Indeed, this list has been criticized a number of times for being contrary to the postmodern spirit. I would encourage my readers to consider the nature of these traits, the way they overlap and refuse to form neat categories, rather than to be put off by the unpostmodern appearance of a list.

Not many pieces exhibit all these traits, and thus it is futile to label a work as exclusively postmodern. Also, I would find it difficult to locate a work that exhibits none of these traits. I caution, therefore, against using these 16 traits as a checklist to help identify a given composition as postmodern or not: postmodern music is not a neat category with rigid boundaries. These traits try to circumscribe the postmodern attitude, which is manifest in a variety of ways and to a variety of degrees, in a large amount of music produced today (and yesterday); but the traits cannot really define specific pieces as postmodern or not, or even as postmodern to a particular degree.

I must emphasize how wrongheaded it would be to use these traits as a checklist for determining whether or not a work is postmodern. This is simply not a very interesting question, nor is it one that can be answered in any meaningful way. Postmodernism resides in cultural values and in people—listeners—but *not in pieces of music*. Although I do refer informally throughout this book to "postmodern music" and "postmodern compositions," I do not strictly believe that such things exist in the world out there. Where they exist is in listeners' minds, since it is listeners—operating under the influence of various traits (in my list) that they can discover in the music they are hearing—who constitute the postmodern musical experience.

I am particularly insistent on these 16 characteristics not being used as a checklist because, despite disclaimers such as this current one, people have tended to take this set of traits as just that. This has happened in discussions after numerous lectures I have given, and at least once in print. Björn Heile writes of "the 'checklist approach' in which the perceived characteristics of a certain music are compared to a list of standard features of postmodernism[,] and the music is segregated along the modernist/postmodernist divide (… the checklist approach is particularly evident in J. Kramer 1995 …)."[13]

Tellingly, Heile goes on to provide a brief list (!) of his own binaries: "Modernism emphasizes unity, postmodernism highlights heterogeneity; likewise modernism features closure and hermetic systems prominently, while postmodernism stresses openness. This list of divergences between the postmodern and the modern could be extended almost indefinitely into issues of hierarchy, order, pluralism, or intentionality." Heile softens the stark contrasts implied in his list: "I consider modernism/ postmodernism as a dialogic relation …, that is, as fundamentally intertwined and interacting, rather than opposing and mutually exclusive principles. There is no definite antagonism between modernism and postmodernism." This is precisely my position, which Heile has missed, apparently because the appearance of a list in my article caused a knee-jerk reaction. He was unable to see beyond the binariness— more apparent than real—of my chart to the spirit in which, and purpose for which, it was offered. I deeply hope that readers of this book will be able to avoid this pitfall.

[13] Heile, "Collage vs. Compositional Control," pp. 287–8.

To a certain extent, my list forms the underlying theme of this book.[14] These attributes are addressed in the course of several chapters, although some more directly and some more extensively than others. For now, as we begin our journey toward an understanding of postmodernism in music and in music listening, we should restrict ourselves to trait 1, considered in the light of trait 9.

1.4. Postmodernism vs. Modernism

In many discussions postmodernism is set against modernism. Numerous distinctions between these two aesthetic attitudes are routinely drawn. Indeed, understanding postmodernism as modernism's "other" is useful up to a point. As I began to explore just what postmodernism is, and how it feels in the context of music, I found binary distinctions such as the following quite useful. But it is necessary finally to move beyond the modernist habit of seeing modernism and postmodernism as opposites.

The list of 16 characteristics of the postmodern attitude in music came from studying compositions that seem, in some intuitive sense, to open themselves up to a postmodern understanding. The list also comes from reading several books and articles on postmodernism in fields other than music, and thinking about which aspects of postmodernism elucidated in these writings are relevant to music. One of the most useful books is David Harvey's *The Condition of Postmodernity*. Harvey (and those he quotes) believes that postmodernism is related to modernism but also distinguished from it—by an acceptance of discontinuity over continuity, difference over similarity, and indeterminacy over rational logic. Some of Harvey's contrasts between modernism and postmodernism are nicely summarized in a chart by Ihab Hassan, who offers his analysis in full knowledge of the dangers of depicting "complex relations as simple polarizations."[15] The idea of listing oppositions between postmodernism and modernism is in itself distinctly unpostmodern, since postmodernism and modernism exist in a symbiotic relationship that is not well served by stark dichotomies, and also because postmodernism dismisses either/or oppositions in favor of fuzzy boundaries (or even no boundaries at all). Nonetheless, Hassan's chart offers a useful preliminary way to get at postmodernism, by contrasting its principles with the possibly more familiar tenets of modernism. Of the many contrasts Hassan draws, I include only those that are directly relevant to music:[16]

In discussing Hassan's oppositions, Harvey focuses on the totalizing aspects of modernism vs. the pluralism and eclecticism of postmodernism (all the terms in quotation marks appear in Hassan's original table):

[14] I refer to these 16 traits by number repeatedly throughout this book. It may be useful for you to bookmark this page for easy reference to this list later on.
[15] David Harvey, *The Condition of Postmodernity* (Oxford: Blackwell, 1990), p. 42.
[16] Ihab Hassan, "The Culture of Postmodernism," *Theory, Culture, and Society* 2 (1985): 123–4.

Table 1.1

Modernism	Postmodernism
form (conjunctive or closed)	antiform (disjunctive or open)
purpose	play
design	chance
hierarchy	anarchy
totalization/synthesis	deconstruction/antithesis
narrative/grande histoire	anti-narrative/petite histoire
determinacy	indeterminacy

"Modernist" town planners, for example, do tend to look for "mastery" of the metropolis as a "totality" by deliberately designing a "closed form," whereas postmodernists tend to view the urban process as uncontrollable and "chaotic," one in which "anarchy" and "change" can "play" in entirely "open" situations. "Modernist" literary critics do tend to look at works as examples of a "genre" and to judge them by the "master code" that prevails within the "boundary" of the genre, whereas the "postmodern" style is simply to view a work as a "text" with its own particular "rhetoric" and "idiolect," but which can in principle be compared with any other text of no matter what sort.[17]

Modernist composers, we might add, often "design" "hierarchic" "forms" with "purpose." With their precompositional plans and with their tendency not to be public performers, they maintain a "distance" from music as performed. Their music concerns itself more with internal syntax than with external reference. Postmodernist composers, by contrast, often take a loose, almost "playful" approach to form, which can seem in its extreme eclecticism "anarchic." They often "participate" directly in the performance of their works. Their music is sometimes more concerned with references to other bodies of music than with the syntax of form.[18]

Similar in spirit to Hassan's binary distinctions, yet more directly aimed at music, is a chart offered by Larry Solomon in his article "What is Postmodernism?"[19]

Solomon acknowledges that "any such chart is bound to be an oversimplified generalization. Nevertheless, distinctions are necessary and useful. ... The contrasts between the two [modernism and postmodernism] are rarely clear-cut, and postmodern thought normally embraces modernism within it."

---

[17] Harvey, p. 44. Hassan's chart is also discussed in Margaret A. Rose, *The Post-Modern and the Post-Industrial* (Cambridge: Cambridge University Press, 1991), pp. 42–53.

[18] Harvey also mentions (p. 44) postmodernism's "total acceptance of ephemerality, fragmentation, discontinuity, and the chaotic. ... Postmodernism swims, even wallows, in the fragmentary and the chaotic currents of change as if that is all there is. Foucault ... instructs us, for example, to 'develop action, thought, and desires by proliferation, juxtaposition, and disjunction,' and 'to prefer what is positive and multiple, difference over uniformity, flows over unities, mobile arrangements over systems.'"

[19] I have removed some of Solomon's binaries that seem irrelevant to this book, some with which I disagree, and some which duplicate Hassan's binaries. I have altered some of Solomon's other entries. His original chart can be found at http://solomonsmusic.net/postmod.htm (accessed April 24, 2016).

Table 1.2

Modern	Postmodern
monism	pluralism
utopian, elitist	populist
patriarchal	non-patriarchal, feminist
totalized	non-totalized, fragmented
centered	dispersed
European, Western	global, multicultural
uniformity	diversity
determinant	indeterminant
staid, serious, purposeful	playful, ironic
formal	non-formal
intentional, constructive	non-intentional, deconstructive
theoretical	practical, pragmatic
reductive, analytic	nonreductive, synthetic
simplicity, elegance, spartan	elaboration
logical	spiritual
cause-effect	synchronicity
control-design	chance
linear	multi-pathed [or, multi-directional]
harmonious, integrated	eclectic, non-integrated
permanence	transience
abstraction	representation
material	semiotic
mechanical	electronic

Oppositions between modernism and postmodernism, such as those of Hassan and Solomon,[20] are certainly useful for someone possessing an understanding of modernism and seeking to comprehend postmodernism. But such charts do not do justice to the ways in which postmodernism continues, as well as repudiates, the project of modernism. In its attempt to offer a new world view and to challenge people through art (and other means) to rethink their values, postmodernism is indeed modernist. In its more extreme incarnations, postmodernism is deliberately disturbing, troublesome, and unsettling.[21] The negativity with which many audiences and critics—even those who have championed modernist music—have reacted to

---

[20] For other lists, see Marjorie Perloff, "Postmodernism / Fin de siècle: The Prospects for Openness in a Decade of Closure," *Criticism* 35/2 (March 1993): 161–92; Martin Irvine, "The Postmodern, Postmodernism, Postmodernity: Approaches to Po-Mo," http://www.georgetown.edu/irvinemj/technoculture/pomo.html; and Dougie Bicket (K.I.S.S.—Keep It Simple Stupid—of the Panopticon), "Modernism and Postmodernism: Some Symptoms and Useful Distinctions," http://carmen.artsci.washington.edu/panop/modpomo.htm.

[21] The music of postmodernism, like the music of modernism, can be disturbing, whereas the music of antimodernism (as seen, for example, in several of Ellen Zwilich's concertos) rarely seeks to unsettle listeners in comparable ways. Among the types of modernist music that can be challenging are the music of neoclassicism and surrealism (discussed in Chapter 9) and of the avant garde (see Chapter 3).

music replete with postmodern characteristics is telling. As modernistic musical traits have become more understood, accepted, and institutionalized (in critical writings, newspaper reviews, educational institutions, and what are ironically still considered adventurous concerts), the tendency to see postmodernism as the opposite of modernism has been rampant.

1.5. Postmodernism and History

If postmodernism were simply a period, we could readily understand it as the chronological successor to modernism. Then it would be reasonable to search for postmodernism's origins in earlier times and to understand it as a reaction to and/or a refinement of aesthetic ideas of previous periods. But postmodernism taken as an attitude suggests ways listeners of today can understand music of various eras. It is in the minds of today's listeners, more than in history, that we find clues to the sources of postmodernism. It comes from the present—from ourselves—more than from the past. Music has become postmodern as we, its late twentieth- and early twenty-first-century listeners, have become postmodern.

To look for historical precedents leading toward postmodernism would be to accept the idea of historical progress, which postmodernists challenge. The literature on postmodernism is full of statements about the death of history, but it is not necessary to go to the extreme of seeing our age as anti-historical (or, better stated, post-historical[22]) in order to understand the uneasy relationship between postmodernism and progress. Postmodernism questions the idea that, if one artwork was created after another, the earlier one may have—or even could have—caused or uniquely influenced the creation of the later one. Every artwork reflects many influences, some from its past, some from its present cultural context, some from its creator's personality, and even some from its future (as subsequent generations come to discover or invent new ways to understand it).

Although they reject the linearity of historical progress, postmodern artworks regularly quote from history (trait 3). How can we understand such a paradox? How can postmodernism both repudiate and use history? Since the quotations and references in postmodern music are often presented without distortion, without commentary, and without distancing, composers treat them just as they might use citations of the present. If a musical style of two hundred years ago is employed in the same way—with the same degree of authenticity (i.e. composed as it was when it was current) and belief (in its viability as a vehicle for musical expression)—as is a newly developed style, then history is indeed challenged. As the past becomes the present, the concept of historical progress becomes problematic.

The avant-gardists of early modernism (such as Luigi Russolo, Satie, Cowell, and Varèse) sought to escape history, but were hopelessly trapped in the continuity of

---

[22] I prefer the term "post-historical," which is more accepting of (the now dead) history than is "anti-historical."

historical development.[23] To see themselves on the cutting edge, such avant-gardists (and also early modernists like Schoenberg, Webern, and Stravinsky) had no choice but to accept history as linear progress, even as they rejected historical concepts of what music is. But recent postmodern composers have moved away from the dialectic between past and present that constrained these early avant-gardists and modernists and that continued to plague their mid-century descendants, such as Boulez, Stockhausen, Nono, Cage, Carter, and Babbitt. Because they recognize history as a cultural construct, postmodernists (such as Aaron Kernis, John Tavener, Paul Schoenfield, and Thomas Adès) can enter into a peaceful coexistence with the past, instead of confronting it as latter-day modernists do. For postmodernists, "history is recast as a process of rediscovering what we already are, rather than a linear progression into what we have never been."[24]

The situation for modernists was and is Oedipal: they are in conflict with their antecedents, whom they reinterpret in order to possess, shape, and control their legacy. Modernists sought to displace the major figures in their past, because they were in competition with them despite their owing their very (artistic) existence to them. Influence was a critical issue for modernists.[25] Postmodernists, however, are more like adolescents than like children: they have passed beyond their Oedipal conflicts with their modernist parents, although they may still have an uneasy relationship with them (thus, postmodernists may accept historical succession even while rejecting the idea of progress). Postmodernists like to feel that they can be whatever they wish. Their music can happily acknowledge the past, without having to demonstrate superiority to it. Postmodern composers understand that their music is different from that of modernism, but they can nonetheless include modernist (and earlier) styles without having to make them something other than what they were or to relegate them to the inferior status of historical artifacts. But, like adolescents, they can maintain ambivalent feelings toward the modernists whom they view as parents.[26] If these attitudes of postmodernists seem naïvely utopian, that quality is certainly consonant with their adolescent nature.

Can we really dismiss history to the extent that we do not look for the origins of the very attitudes that try to turn us away from the concept of the past? We may be willing to accept postmodernism because it exists, but we are also aware that there were times when it did not exist.[27] What happened? What changed? To the limited extent

---

[23] I discuss avant-gardism in Section 3.2.

[24] I owe this perceptive formulation to an anonymous reviewer of the article on which this chapter is based, "The Nature and Origins of Musical Postmodernism," in Judy Lochhead and Joseph Auner (eds.), *Postmodern Music/Postmodern Thought* (New York and London: Routledge, 2002), pp. 13–26.

[25] Joseph Straus offers a theory of influence in modernist music, based on the ideas of Harold Bloom, in *Remaking the Past: Musical Modernism and the Influence of the Tonal Tradition* (Cambridge, MA: Harvard University Press, 1990), pp. 1–20.

[26] Modernists have also acted like rebellious teenagers in overthrowing accepted musical norms, such as tonality and metric regularity.

[27] While I have suggested that postmodernism is an attitude more than a period, and that instances of postmodern musical practice can be found in compositions of the distant past, I want to make clear that I do not believe that postmodernism is ubiquitous throughout history.

that postmodernism had causes,[28] we should look to recently developed (or at least recently accepted) ideas, perhaps more pervasive in the United States than elsewhere, in order to understand its musical origins. I say this in full realization that I have posited postmodernism in music as far back as that of Ives and Mahler, and believe that there are embryonic postmodernist ideas that can be found in (or projected onto) certain music by Berlioz, Beethoven, Schumann, and Haydn. However, since I regard postmodernism as an attitude more than as a historical period, and since I believe that an important aspect of that attitude is the location of meaning in the listener (trait 16), it is reasonable to suggest that postmodernism did begin rather recently and subsequently spread to the past as listeners of today began to find postmodern meanings in music from earlier periods.

The best place to search for the origins of musical postmodernism is not, therefore, in the history of music. It is wrongheaded to look to those pre-contemporary works I have called postmodernist for influences on today's postmodern attitudes or for sources of the kind of postmodernist thinking that has recently become widespread. Postmodernism *is* a recent phenomenon. It is only now, given the spread and acceptance of postmodern attitudes, that it makes sense to listen to music like Ives' *Putnam's Camp*, Mahler's Seventh Symphony, or Nielsen's *Sinfonia Semplice* in a postmodern manner. But those works and works like them are *not* the sources of postmodernism.

1.6. The Origins of Postmodernism in Contemporary Culture

One source of today's postmodernism, not surprisingly, is the psychological and sociological tenor of our technology-saturated world. Technology and its uses (trait 14) have created a context of fragmentation (trait 10), short attention spans leading to constant discontinuities (trait 10), and multiplicity (trait 13)—all characteristics not only of contemporary society but also of postmodern thinking. In his book *The Saturated Self*, social psychologist Kenneth J. Gergen offers insights into the psychological dimensions of postmodernism. Gergen traces the changing concepts of the self from the romantic age (when each person was thought to possess depth of passion, soul, and creativity[29]) through the modernist age (which particularly valued logic, rationality, and conscious intentions) to the current era of postmodernism, which is characterized by "social saturation."

By "social saturation" Gergen means the condition in which we continually receive messages of all sorts, coming (often electronically) from many corners of the globe, all competing for our attention and involvement. There is no time to reflect, no time to savor, no time for contemplation, no time for considered choice, no time for

---

[28] It is somewhat naïve to look only for cultural factors that "caused" postmodernism to develop. Postmodernism shaped as well as was shaped by certain Western cultural ideas.

[29] Kenneth J. Gergen, *The Saturated Self: Dilemmas of Identity in Contemporary Life* (New York: Basic Books, 1991), p. 6.

depth. Conflicting claims on our attention, as well as constant bombardment with information, lead to the fragmented sensibility associated with postmodern attitudes. Gergen writes:

> The postmodern condition ... is marked by a plurality of voices vying for the right to reality—to be accepted as legitimate expressions of the true and the good. As the voices expand in power and presence, all that seemed proper, right-minded, and well understood is subverted. In the postmodern world we become increasingly aware that the objects about which we speak are not so much "in the world" as they are products of perspective. Thus, processes such as emotion and reason cease to be real and significant essences of persons; rather, in the light of pluralism we perceive them to be imposters, the outcome of our ways of conceptualizing them. Under postmodern conditions, persons exist in a state of continuous construction and reconstruction; it is a world where anything goes that can be negotiated. Each reality of self gives way to reflexive questioning, irony, and ultimately the playful probing of yet another reality.[30]

Gergen's concept of the saturated self resonates with my own experiences. In a given afternoon, I may find myself sitting in my office, communicating via e-mail or fax with professional colleagues in London and Perth, advising former students in Warsaw and Taipei, and carrying on personal correspondence with friends in Evanston and San Diego. I may then turn my attention to some journal articles and books, which are rarely read through in their entirety and several of which I find myself studying more or less simultaneously. I may receive phone calls (or messages on my voice mail) from faraway colleagues, old friends, prospective students, performers who are rehearsing my music in distant cities, someone who wants me to do a guest lecture. Each phone call picks up a continuity broken off hours, days, weeks, or even years ago, or else initiates a relationship to be continued in the future. These activities, which continually intrude upon one another, may in turn be interrupted by a knock on my door. A student in need of help? A textbook publisher's representative wanting to convince me to use a certain book in my harmony class? A workman wanting to fix my air conditioner? All of this, and some days still more, within the space of two or three hours! Fragmentation. Discontinuity. Lack of connection. Lack of linear logic. Postmodernism.[31]

Since technology allows me to stay in contact with people I know in many different contexts and those I knew in many periods in my past, the past in a certain sense is no longer as remote as it would have been had I lived before telephones, e-mail, faxes, airplanes, cars, or trains. Two hundred years ago people moved around a lot

---

[30] Ibid., p. 7.
[31] Gergen writes (pp. 15–16): "We are now bombarded with ever-increasing intensity by the images and actions of others; our range of social participation is expanding exponentially. As we absorb the views, values, and visions of others, and live out the multiple plots in which we are enmeshed, we enter a postmodern consciousness. It is a world in which we no longer experience a secure sense of self, and in which doubt is increasingly placed on the very assumption of a bounded identity with palpable attributes."

less and maintained far fewer contacts than they do today. When someone moved from one community to another, acquaintances were lost, relegated to memory and imagination. Not necessarily so today. I am in touch with my first friend (from kindergarten), my high school buddies, my college roommate, my grad school colleagues, many of my former teachers and students, and people I have met lecturing in several countries. My past lives not only in memory but also through contacts in my present.[32] My friends may get older and change, but they are still the same friends. Their identity keeps our shared past alive (although their aging makes me more acutely aware of what is loosely called time's passage than I might have been had I continually traded my friends for newer ones).

The blurring of the distinction between past and present (trait 3) is one postmodern cultural value that is reflected in postmodern music. There are others. Gergen cites as results of social saturation an increasing sense of pastiche and otherness (similar to the way postmodern music refers to or quotes other music—traits 6 and 7). Intertextuality is not solely a condition of postmodern literature or music, but also of the postmodern self. People come into contact with so many other people, with divergent personalities and values, that the self is constantly in flux, always bending under the influence of others.

> As social saturation proceeds we become pastiches, imitative assemblages of each other. In memory we carry others' patterns of being with us. Each of us becomes the other, a representative, or a replacement. To put it more broadly, as the [twentieth] century has progressed selves have become increasingly populated with the characters of others.[33]

Robin Hartwell acknowledges this condition and relates it directly to postmodernism in music.

> We are an inconsistent, incoherent mixture of external forces, absorbed to varying degrees. Postmodernist music is mimetic in that it attempts to present a picture of this incoherence and the play of these forces.[34]

Other aspects that social saturation shares with postmodern art are multiplicity (trait 13) and disunity (trait 11). Gergen again:

> Increasingly we emerge as the possessors of many voices. Each self contains a multiplicity of others. ... Nor do these many voices necessarily harmonize. ... Central to the modernist view was a robust commitment to an objective and knowable world. ... [Yet] as we begin to incorporate the dispositions of the varied others to whom we are exposed, we become capable of taking their positions, adopting their attitudes, talking their language, playing their roles. In effect, one's

---

[32] Gergen discusses the "perseverance of the past" on pp. 62–3.

[33] Ibid., p. 71.

[34] Robin Hartwell, "Postmodernism and Art Music," in Simon Miller (ed.), *The Last Post: Music after Modernism* (Manchester and New York: Manchester University Press, 1993), p. 50. I recommend this article as a context in which to encounter an account of postmodernism in music that is quite different from, and at times at odds with, the one offered in this book.

self becomes populated with others. The result is a steadily accumulating sense of doubt in the objectivity of any position one holds.[35]

Robert Morgan has written perceptively on how social forces can shape postmodern music.

> The plurality of styles, techniques, and levels of expression appears both plausible and meaningful in a world increasingly shedding its common beliefs and shared customs, where there is no longer a single given "reality" but only shifting, multiple realities, provisionally constructed out of the unconnected bits and pieces set loose by a world stripped of all attachments. If traditional tonality … adequately reflected a culture characterized by a community of purpose and well-developed system of social order and interpersonal regulation, its loss, and the musical atomization that has ensued, reflects a fragmented and defamiliarized world of isolated events and abrupt confrontations.[36]

1.7. Why Today's Composers Write Postmodern Music

I would not argue that social saturation, however potent a force in contemporary Western societies, inevitably leads to the creation of postmodern art. There is always the possibility of protest. For example, some (indeed, many!) may find social saturation to be alienating, and seek antidotes or alternatives or escapes. The persistence of modernism in the arts—and the antimodern resurgence of traditionalism—can be understood in part as a resistance to social saturation. But the forces that are transforming the self from a modernist to a postmodernist entity are undeniable. That some artists should create works expressive of a saturated personality, whether by intention or not, is hardly surprising. Composers, like others who live in a saturated society, have personalities shaped in part by their social contexts. The same is true of listeners who, immersed in postmodern social values, find meaningful resonances in musical compositions that reflect postmodern attitudes and practices.

Uncritically adopting or thoroughly repudiating postmodern values are not the only possible responses of late twentieth-century composers to a socially saturated culture. Some composers—probably more Europeans, steeped as they tend to be in dialectical thinking, than laid-back, naïvely utopian Americans—enter into a struggle with postmodern cultural forces. It is beyond the scope of this chapter, however, to probe the manner in which the music of certain composers (such as Bernd Alois Zimmermann, Gyorgy Ligeti, and Louis Andriessen) dialectically grapples and contends with postmodernist ideas, rather than simply accepting or rejecting them.

---

[35] Ibid., pp. 83–5.
[36] Robert P. Morgan, "Rethinking Musical Culture: Canonic Reformulations in a Post-Tonal Age," in Katherine Bergeron and Philip V. Bohlman (eds.), *Disciplining Music: Musicology and Its Canons* (Chicago: University of Chicago, 1992), p. 58.

Various composers respond differently to their postmodern culture. Whether they accept, deny, or do battle with postmodernism, it is an undeniable force. Even those who embrace it outright may do so for a variety of reasons. It is appropriate, therefore, to conclude this chapter by enumerating some of the reasons today's composers are drawn to postmodern values.

1. Some composers react against modernist styles and values, which have become oppressive to them.
2. Some composers react against the institutionalism of modernism—against, in other words, its position of power within the musical establishment, particularly in the United States, Germany, France, England, and Italy.
3. Some composers respond to what they see as the cultural irrelevance of modernism.
4. Some composers (antimodernists as well as postmodernists) are motivated by a desire to close the composer-audience gap, created—they believe—by the elitism of modernism.
5. Some young composers are uncomfortable with pressures from their teachers to like and respect one kind of music (tonal) yet write another (atonal).[37] Like adolescents in the world of postmodernism, they rebel against the values they learn in school. They want to create the music they love, not that which they are told to love.
6. Some composers today know and enjoy popular music. While there were always "classical" composers who liked pop music, nowadays some composers who appreciate it (such as Steve Martland [*ed. note: d. 2013*] and Michael Daugherty) see no reason to exclude it from their own stylistic range—a further instance of composing what they love, regardless of how respectable it is.
7. Some composers are acutely aware that music is a commodity, that it is consumable, and that composers are inevitably part of a materialist social system. Such composers understand postmodernism as an aesthetic whose attitudes and styles reflect the commodification of art (trait 15). They see postmodern music as concerned with, rather than ignoring (as they see modernism doing), its place in the economy.
8. Some composers, like their predecessors in earlier eras, want to create music that is new and different. Yet they have become disillusioned with the avant-garde's search for novel sounds, compositional strategies, and formal procedures, and with its adversarial stance with regard to tradition. Rather, they seek originality in the postmodernist acceptance of the past as part of the present (trait 3), in disunifying fragmentation (trait 10), in pluralism (trait 7), and in multiplicity (trait 13).
9. All composers live in a multicultural world. While some choose to keep the ubiquitous musics from all parts of the globe out of their own compositions,

[37] Several students of one well-known modernist composer-teacher have told me how they simultaneously work on two different pieces, one that they truly believe in and one that they think their professor will approve of.

others are so enthralled by coming in contact with music from very different traditions that they accept it into their own personal idioms. Although such appropriations are sometimes criticized as instances of cultural imperialism, they do abound in postmodern music.

10. Most contemporary composers are aware of the postmodern values in their culture. These values inform not only the music they produce but also the ways it is heard and used. However varied its musical manifestations may be, and however diverse the reasons for its appeal to composers and listeners, musical postmodernism is—as I have tried to suggest—the all but inevitable expression of a socially saturated civilization.

The reasons behind the creation of postmodern music today are varied. The characteristics of postmodern compositions and postmodern listening are numerous. The origins of the postmodern attitude in music are diverse, as are the responses to it and social uses of it. Hailed by some and reviled by others, postmodern music and postmodern listening are exciting—yet sobering—statements of who and what we are.

Postmodernism (Not) Defined

2.1. Postmodernism

Since this book is about music and postmodernism, it may appear unavoidable to define these two words. But we run into problems immediately. Aestheticians have debated for centuries how to define music, and, while I have my own favorite attempt,[1] to enter this debate here would take us too far afield. I should say something about what kind of music is studied in this book, however. It is curious that this kind of music has no adequate label. Some call it "classical" music, but that suggests music of the classical period. Others call it "serious" music, but surely there is serious jazz and serious popular song. "Concert" music also does not work, because many other kinds of music are heard in concerts. "Art" music is inadequate, because who could reasonably deny that music of, say, the Beatles or of Duke Ellington is art? That Cecil Taylor's *Unit Structures* or the Grateful Dead's *Dark Star* are art? By now you probably know the kind of music I intend to discuss, even if there is no good label for it. I do not wish to ignore popular music or jazz or certain ethnic musics, which have brought forth exciting instances of postmodernism and which some critics take as the locus of postmodern musical thinking, relegating classical/serious/concert/art music to a dusty museum status. But postmodernism in classical/serious/concert/art music, less studied and less understood, is of considerable importance today, particularly as this music seems to be under attack as culturally irrelevant.

Defining postmodernism is an even greater challenge than defining music. This slippery term—coined as early as the 1870s[2]—has been used in a large variety of ways by critics. One example of the variability of the word's meaning: while the representation of reality is pervasive in visual arts labeled postmodern, so-called postmodern drama (e.g. that of Beckett) turns away from reality.[3]

It is in the very nature of postmodernism to resist definition. That is why I continually caution against reading my list of 16 attributes of postmodernism (Section 1.3)

---

[1] See Jonathan D. Kramer, *The Time of Music* (New York: Schirmer, 1988), p. 385. I take my ideas from those of Morse Peckham. See footnote 32 in Chapter 6 of the present book.

[2] Charles Jencks, "The Post-Modern Agenda," in Jencks (ed.), *The Post-Modern Reader* (New York: Saint Martin's Press, 1992), p. 17. For a brief history of the changing uses of the term "postmodernism" from the 1870s through the 1980s, see Steven Best and Douglas Kellner, *Postmodern Theory: Critical Interrogations* (New York: Guilford Press, 1991), pp. 5–16.

[3] I am indebted on this point to Claudia Clausius.

as a definition. Still, it is important to offer at least some flavor of the concept. To show the range of meanings the term has, and to give a sense of what this aesthetic attitude is all about, I offer a lengthy series of quotations. Taken together, they should add up to an understanding of the nature of postmodernism. But I do not believe that there is a viable definition among these quotations, because to define postmodernism is to misread it. I want to deconstruct the concept of postmodernism, not to construct its meaning(s).

2.2. Quotations in Search of a Definition

These quotations should help to explain what I think the postmodernism that is relevant to music is all about. My reasons for using extensive quotations are twofold: (1) theorists of the postmodern have come up with many illuminating formulations, on which I cannot hope to improve; and (2) the act of quotation is quintessentially postmodern, and I hope that this book not only discusses but also in certain ways exemplifies postmodernism.

The ideas of Kenneth Gergen quoted and discussed in Section 1.6 include the notion that postmodernists often assume the voices of others. Hence I am comfortable letting the authors I quote here speak for me. Since I have removed these quotations from their original contexts, these authors actually are unknowingly assuming my voice, just as I assume theirs. Since I have chosen the quotations, suppressed the original contexts, and selected the order of presentation here, I actually *am* offering my own ideas, but—in a quintessentially postmodern manner—in *their* words.

Many writers have agonized over the term "postmodernism." They ask questions such as those listed at the beginning of Section 1.1. The lingering binary oppositions in some of these questions, as well as in the charts of Hassan and Solomon quoted in Section 1.4, indicate the difficulties in trying to use linear logic, ordinary language, and concepts of causality to investigate an idea that challenges the validity of such discourse. Yet, we should at least try to elucidate postmodernism by means of traditional explanatory prose; to use postmodern prose would be more to exemplify than to illuminate (which is what I try to do in Chapter 11). Here are some of the ways David Harvey, Ihab Hassan, Linda Hutcheon, Charles Jencks, and others have dealt with these issues:

> **Hutcheon:** "Of all the terms bandied about in both current cultural theory and contemporary writing on the arts, postmodernism must be the most over- and under-defined. It is usually accompanied by a grand flourish of negativized rhetoric: we hear of discontinuity, disruption, dislocation, decentering, indeterminacy, and anti-totalization. What all of these words literally do (precisely by their disavowing prefixes—*dis, de, in, anti*) is incorporate that which they aim to contest—as does, I suppose, the term postmodernism itself."[4]

[4] Linda Hutcheon, *A Poetics of Postmodernism: History, Theory, Fiction* (New York and London: Routledge, 1988), p. 3.

Harvey: "Postmodernist philosophers tell us not only to accept but even to
    revel in the fragmentations and the cacophony of voices through which the
    dilemmas of the modern world are understood."[5]

Hutcheon: "Postmodernism cannot simply be used as a synonym for the
    contemporary. … And it does not really describe an international cultural
    phenomenon, for it is primarily European and American."[6]

Hassan: "Postmodernism appears to be a mysterious, if ubiquitous, ingredient—
    like raspberry vinegar, which instantly turns any recipe into *nouvelle cuisine.*"[7]

Jencks: "Mixing of categories and genres became common. In this era of
    eclecticism the past was consulted (and plundered), lovingly revived (and
    ridiculed). Often it was hard to tell whether the artist or architect was making
    a serious attempt at critically contrasting traditions, or was simply confused."[8]

Harvey: "The most startling fact about postmodernism: its total acceptance of
    ephemerality, fragmentation, discontinuity, and the chaotic."[9]

Monelle: "Perhaps the main difficulty with postmodernism is the fact that its
    unifying factor is, specifically, a rejection of unification, of manifestos, of
    centralizing and totalizing forces. It is both a return to pluralism after the
    modernist experiment and—its true novelty—an embracing of pluralism as a
    fundamental tenet."[10]

Jencks: "The attempt to go beyond the materialist paradigm which characterises
    modernism; an intense concern for pluralism and a desire to cut across the
    different taste cultures that now fracture society; an obligation to bring back
    selected traditional values, but in a new key that fully recognises the ruptures
    caused by modernity; an acknowledgement of difference and otherness, the
    keynote of the feminist movement; indeed the re-emergence of the feminine
    into all discourse; the re-enchantment of nature, which stems from new
    developments in science and AN Whitehead's philosophy of organicism;
    and the commitment to an ecological and ecumenical world view that now
    characterises post-modern theology."[11]

Hutcheon: "Postmodernism questions centralized, totalized, hierarchized, closed
    systems: questions, but does not destroy. … It acknowledges the human urge
    to make order, while pointing out that the orders we create are just that:
    human constructs, not natural or given entities."[12]

Ward: "Because we have the single word 'postmodernism,' we assume that there
    is also a single thing in existence to which the word corresponds. The *name*

[5] Harvey, *The Condition of Postmodernity*, p. 116.
[6] Ibid., p. 4.
[7] Hassan, *The Postmodern Turn: Essays in Postmodern Theory and Culture* (Columbus: Ohio State
    University Press, 1987). Reprinted in Jencks, *The Post-Modern Reader*, p. 199.
[8] Jencks, "The Post-Modern Agenda," p. 23.
[9] Harvey, *The Condition of Postmodernity*, p. 44.
[10] Raymond Monelle, "The Postmodern Project in Music Theory," in Eero Tarasti (ed.), *Music
    Semiotics in Growth* (Bloomington, IN and Imatra: Indiana University Press, 1996), p. 37.
[11] Jencks, "Post-Modernism—The Third Force," in *The Post-Modern Reader*, p. 7.
[12] Hutcheon, *A Poetics of Postmodernism*, pp. 41–2.

'postmodernism' has thus in effect given rise to the *thing* so that we can now find ourselves asking 'what is postmodernism?' rather than the more appropriate question 'what does the word postmodernism do?'"[13]

Kramer: "Postmodernism: finding the mundane in the profound and the profound in the mundane."[14]

2.3. Postmodernism and Modernism

The first trait of postmodern music listed in Section 1.3 can be the most challenging to accept: postmodernism has a decidedly ambiguous relationship to modernism.[15] There is certainly tension between the two, as Hassan's and Solomon's dichotomies (sampled in Section 1.3) demonstrate. But, as I have been trying to emphasize, postmodernism is not a wholesale rejection of modernism. Since the word "postmodernism" includes the word "modernism," it proclaims that the two aesthetics are inseparably bound up with one another.

What does "post" mean in this context? What can it mean to be "after" the modern, after that which is supposedly up to date? Although the apparently self-contradictory term "postmodernism" bothers a number of writers, I rather like it, since the very name of the movement it labels challenges a linear view of history and thus seems to embrace a literal impossibility. The "post" in "postmodernism" must be taken to indicate something other than, or at least something in addition to, "after." It suggests a rethinking, a rereading, a reinterpretation of modernism.

The paradoxes entailed in this quirky prefix have led various authors to construct the whole term in slightly, but significantly, different ways:

postmodernism
post-modernism
Postmodernism
Post-modernism
post-Modernism
Post-Modernism
(post)modernism

Do these words mean the same thing? Some versions place emphasis on the problematic "post," others on the hardly less innocent "modernism." Some separate the "post" and the "modernism" into an opposition, while others (including the version I use in this book) push the two together into an uneasy alliance.

Here are some of the things critical theorists have written about postmodernism in relation to modernism. Notice the different versions of the term they employ.

---

[13] Glenn Ward, *Teach Yourself Postmodernism* (New York: McGraw-Hill, 2003), p. 98.

[14] Jonathan D. Kramer, *Postmodern Music, Postmodern Listening*, Chapter 2, footnote 51.

[15] I am aware that it is necessary to discuss not only what postmodernism is but also what modernism is. I touch on the question in Section 3.1 and discuss it more fully in various parts of Chapter 4.

Zavarzadeh and Morton: "For many, the (post)modern is a direct contestation
of the modern and, above all, its regime of rationality, its elitism, and its
notion of 'progress' that locks human history into linear movement towards
a pre-set goal. But the opposition to the modern does not mean that the
(post)modern is a total negation or rejection of modernity: the '(post)' in
(post)modern ('post' in parentheses) marks the problematic relation between
the two. It certainly does not mean 'after,' since such an understanding of
it will take us back to history as 'progress' again. ... If one takes '(post)' in
the sense of an 'after,' one has posited a traditional notion of history based
upon 'period'—a unique, homogeneous segment of time which in its totality
represents the 'spirit of an age.' Only traditional modernists read (post)
modernism in this way. ... Those who oppose such a progressive, linear
notion of history and believe that history is in itself a problematic issue
(since it is only a representation ...), regard '(post)' to be a sign of 'reading,'
interpretation, and 'textuality.' For these, (post)modernism would mean the
re-reading or textualization of modernity."[16]

Another way to read the "post" in "postmodernism" is suggested by Gary
Tomlinson,[17] taking a cue from Terry Eagleton. Postmodernism, Tomlinson
suggests, is a product of modernism. It not only comes after but also
descends from modernism.

Barth: "The proper program for postmodernism is neither a mere extension of
the modernist program ... nor a mere intensification of certain aspects of
modernism, nor on the contrary a wholesale subversion or repudiation of
either modernism or what I'm calling premodernism—'traditional' bourgeois
realism."[18]

Compagnon: "There is a flagrant paradox in the postmodern that claims to have
done with the modern but, in breaking away from it, reduplicates the modern
process par excellence: the rupture."[19]

Hutcheon: "Modernism literally and physically haunts postmodernism, and
their interrelations should not be ignored. Indeed there appear to be two
dominant schools of thought about the nature of the interaction of the two
enterprises: the first sees postmodernism as a total break from modernism
and the language of this school is the radical rhetoric of rupture; the
second sees the postmodern as an extension and intensification of certain
characteristics of modernism."[20]

Barth: "I deplore the artistic and critical cast of mind that repudiates the
whole modernist enterprise as an aberration and sets to work as if it hadn't

[16] Mas'ud Zavarzadeh and Donald Morton, *Theory, (Post)Modernity, Opposition: An "Other" Introduction to Literary and Cultural Theory* (Washington, DC: Maisonneuve, 1991), p. 108.
[17] *Current Musicology* 53 (1993): 36.
[18] John Barth, "The Literature of Replenishment: Postmodernist Fiction," *The Atlantic Monthly* 254/1 (January 1980). Reprinted in Jencks, *The Post-Modern Reader*, p. 176.
[19] Antoine Compagnon, *The 5 Paradoxes of Modernity*, trans. Philip Franklin (New York: Columbia University Press, 1994), p. 115.
[20] Hutcheon, *A Poetics of Postmodernism*, pp. 49–50.

happened; that rushes back into the arms of nineteenth-century middle-class realism as if the first half of the twentieth century hadn't happened. It *did* happen ... and there's no going back to Tolstoy and Dickens & Co except on nostalgia trips."[21]

Wolff: "The rejection of modernism can be the rejection (from the right) of its original radical project, or the attempt (on the left) to revive that project in terms appropriate to the late twentieth century."[22]

Jencks: "Post-Modernism as a cultural movement, or agenda, does not seek to turn the clock back, is not a Luddite reaction, but rather a restructuring of modernist assumptions with something larger, fuller, more true."[23]

Huyssen: "Postmodernism is far from making modernism obsolete. On the contrary, it casts a new light on it and appropriates many of its aesthetic strategies and techniques, inserting them and making them work in new constellations. What has become obsolete, however, are those codifications of modernism in critical discourse which, however subliminally, are based on a teleological view of progress and modernization."[24]

Hutcheon: "The modern is ineluctably embedded in the postmodern ..., but the relationship is a complex one of consequence, difference, and dependence."[25]

Mann: "Postmodernism is the death of modernism or its latest avatar or a perpetual disruptive tendency within it; it is the current period of one already past or the end of all periodizing; it is postavantgarde or postmovement or postart or postpolitical or posthumous or postpost; it is posthistorical or a new way to articulate the presence of the past, for instance through past-iche, which is or is not subversive, is or is not conservative ...; it is bourgeois reality deconstructed or simulated or imploded or reasserted ...; it is the end of the age of the signified and the beginning of the age of the signifier (Barthes); it is the final mutual assimilation of high art and mass culture prepared for by the avantgarde, and this marks either the tragic destruction of standards of quality ([Hilton] Kramer et al.) or a new 'opportunity' (Huyssen); ... it is Culture giving way to cultures (Hutcheon) ...; it is media hypnosis or the latest mannerism or *realkulturpolitik*."[26]

Marzorati: "Surrealism without the dark edge of night, surrealism for the fun of it."[27]

Barth: "My ideal postmodernist author neither merely repudiates nor merely imitates either his twentieth-century modernist parents or his

[21] Barth, "The Literature of Replenishment," p. 177.
[22] Janet Wolff, *Feminine Sentences: Essays on Women and Culture* (Berkeley and Los Angeles: University of California Press, 1990), p. 93.
[23] Jencks, "The Post-Modern Agenda," p. 11.
[24] Andreas Huyssen, *After the Great Divide: Modernism, Mass Culture, Postmodernism* (Bloomington: Indiana University Press, 1986), pp. 217–18.
[25] Hutcheon, *A Poetics of Postmodernism*, p. 38.
[26] Paul Mann, *The Theory-Death of the Avant Garde* (Bloomington: Indiana University Press, 1991), pp. 121–2.
[27] Gerald Marzorati, "Kenny Scharf's Fun-House Big Bang," *Art News* (September 1985): 81.

nineteenth-century pre-modernist grandparents. He has the first half of our century under his belt, but not on his back."[28]

Harvey: "In a modernist classic like *Citizen Kane* a reporter seeks to unravel the mystery of Kane's life and character by collecting multiple reminiscences and perspectives from those who had known him. In the more postmodernist format of the contemporary cinema we find, in a film like *Blue Velvet*, the central character revolving between two quite incongruous worlds—that of a conventional 1950s small-town America with its high school, drugstore culture, and a bizarre, violent, sex-crazed underworld of drugs, dementia, and sexual perversion. It seems impossible that these two worlds should exist in the same space."[29]

Rea: "Modernists see the future in the present. Postmodernists see the future in the past, an attitude about life and things in general that has probably existed for much longer than most people are prepared to admit."[30]

Deak: "The shock of recognition instead of the shock of the new."[31]

2.4. Irony and Parody

Another important characteristic of postmodern art is irony (trait 2), which may take many forms and, furthermore, appears in non-postmodern art as well. The irony of postmodernism is the opposite of the nostalgia of what I call antimodernism. It is also different from making fun of the past. A work like Hindemith's string quartet *Overture to the "Flying Dutchman" as Played at Sight by a Second-Rate Concert Orchestra at the Village at 7 O'clock in the Morning*, for example, may exhibit several of the characteristics of postmodernism listed in Section 1.3, but it is an irreverent mockery, not an ironic reworking. This work is an exaggeration—but not by much!—of exactly what its title says it is. It mingles sounds of the past and present, is a lowbrow travesty of some very highbrow music, is not unified in any normal manner, is a populist spoof of some elitist music, is formally more loose than totalized, refers to music outside itself, includes discontinuities, is pluralistic, and can be appreciated on multiple levels.[32] But it is not postmodern in that it ridicules without irony or parody.

It is because a work such as Hindemith's parodistic quartet can satisfy most of the conditions of postmoderism listed in Section 1.3 and still not feel postmodern that I insist that these sixteen traits do not constitute a definition. They are neither necessary nor sufficient to determine the postmodernism of a piece of music,

---

[28] Barth, "The Literature of Replenishment," p. 70.
[29] Harvey, *The Condition of Postmodernity*, p. 48.
[30] John Rea, "Postmodernisms."
[31] Edit Deak, "The Critic Sees through the Cabbage Patch," *Artforum* (April 1984): 56.
[32] The same might be said of a frankly humorous work like P. D. Q. Bach's *Unbegun Symphony*, which is a collage of such recognizable music as "Beautiful Dreamer," Brahms's Second Symphony, "Ta Ra Ra Boom De Ray," "Camptown Races," the "Ode to Joy," "Joy to the World," Schubert's Ninth Symphony, the *Jupiter Symphony*, "Onward Christian Soldiers," the *Pathétique Symphony*, "You Are My Sunshine," *Marche Slav*, Jack Benny's violin warm-up exercise, and many others.

because *postmodernism is not a category.* Finding several of these characteristics in a composition does not determine that the work is postmodern. Rather, our listening experience tells us in what ways the music is, and is not, postmodern. Thus, as this book argues, postmodernism resides in the listener but is not independent of the work. Hindemith's parody is not postmodern—simply because it does not invoke a postmodern listening attitude.

Several critical theorists have considered the roles of irony and parody in postmodernism.

> **Gaggi:** "A degree of wit, whimsy, and irony may be involved, as a past work is recycled, but the new work is never a lampoon of the old; the old work is viewed as a source for creative reworking, but it is not held sacred and the new work is never simply neo-classical, neo-romantic, or 'revivalist' in nature."[33]
>
> **Hutcheon:** "It is always a critical reworking, never a nostalgic 'return.' Herein lies the governing role of irony in postmodernism."[34]
>
> **Hutcheon:** "The postmodernist ironic rethinking of history is definitely not nostalgic. It critically confronts the past with the present, and vice versa. In a direct reaction against the tendency of our times to value only the new and novel, it returns us to a re-thought past to see what, if anything, is of value in that past experience. But the critique of its irony is double-edged: the past and the present are judged in each other's light."[35]
>
> **Hutcheon:** "Postmodernism is a fundamentally contradictory enterprise: its art forms (and its theory) at once use and abuse, install and then destabilise convention in parodic ways, self-consciously pointing both to their own inherent paradoxes and provisionality and, of course, to their critical or ironic rereading of the art of the past."[36]
>
> **Hutcheon:** "Parodic echoing of the past, even with this kind of irony, can still be deferential. It is in this way that postmodern parody marks its paradoxical doubleness of both continuity and change, both authority and transgression. Postmodernist parody, be it in architecture, literature, painting, film, or music, uses its historical memory, its aesthetic introversions, to signal that this kind of self-reflexive discourse is always inextricably bound to social discourse."[37]

According to Charles Jencks, Umberto Eco presents an "amusing illustration of why postmodernism must use irony when dealing with the past."[38] Eco: "The moment comes when the avant-garde (the modern) can go no further, because it has produced a metalanguage that speaks of its impossible texts (conceptual art [Eco cites, among

---

[33] Silvio Gaggi, *Modern/Postmodern: A Study in Twentieth-Century Arts and Ideas* (Philadelphia: University of Pennsylvania Press, 1989), p. 21.
[34] Hutcheon, *A Poetics of Postmodernism*, p. 4.
[35] Ibid., p. 39.
[36] Ibid., p. 23.
[37] Ibid., p. 35.
[38] Jencks, "The Post-Modern Agenda," p. 22.

other works, John Cage's silent music]). The postmodern reply to the modern consists of recognising that the past, since it cannot really be destroyed, because its destruction leads to silence, must be revisited: but with irony, not innocently. I think of the postmodern attitude as that of a man who loves a very cultivated woman and knows that he cannot say to her, 'I love you madly,' because he knows that she knows (and that she knows that he knows) that these words have already been written by Barbara Cartland. Still, there is a solution. He can say, 'As Barbara Cartland would put it, I love you madly.' At this point, having avoided false innocence, having said clearly that it is no longer possible to speak innocently, he will nevertheless have said what he wanted to say to the woman: that he loves her, but he loves her in an age of lost innocence. If the woman goes along with this she will have received a declaration of love all the same. Neither of the two speakers will feel innocent, both will have accepted the challenge of the past, of the already said, which cannot be eliminated; both will consciously and with pleasure play the game of irony. ... But both will have succeeded, once again, in speaking of love."[39]

2.5. Past and Present

Postmodernism's relationship with the past is complex, as we might well expect from an aesthetic that calls into question the very notion of history. For some postmodernists, the past has not passed but still lives on in the present. For others, the past represents an otherness which postmodernism should embrace precisely because of its difference, not because of its alleged indistinguishability from the present. Is it useful to reconcile these views? A true postmodernist would probably say so, since postmodernism embraces contradiction (trait 8). But is this truly a contradiction? Does the past as "other" preclude the past existing in the present? How can something which cannot be distinguished be nonetheless recognized for its otherness? These unresolvable complexities indicate postmodernism's ambivalent stance with regard to the past. Several theorists have considered these problems.

> **Hassan:** "A new relation between historical elements, without any suppression of the past in favour of the present."[40]
> **Hassan:** "A different concept of tradition, one in which continuity and discontinuity, high and low culture, mingle not to imitate but to expand the past in the present. In that plural present all styles are dialectically available in an interplay between the Now and the Not Now, the Same and the Other."[41]
> **Jencks:** "Postmodernism's "root meaning, to be beyond or after the modern, remains common to diverse usages, but, as we will see, some authors use the phrase perversely to mean a cultural movement that *precedes* the modern;

---

[39] Eco, *Postscript to the Name of Rose*, pp. 67–8.
[40] Hassan, *The Postmodern Turn*, p. 197.
[41] Ibid.

and others, such as Umberto Eco, see it as a metahistorical category that cuts across periods of cultural history."[42]

Hutcheon: "The naïveté of modernism's ideologically and aesthetically motivated rejection of the past (in the name of the future) is not countered … by an equally naïve antiquarianism. … On the contrary, what does start to look naïve … is this reductive notion that any recall of the past must, by definition, be sentimental nostalgia."[43]

Hutcheon: Postmodernists "'try hard to misread [in Harold Bloom's sense of the term] their classicism in a way which is still functional, appropriate and understandable' [Hutcheon here quotes Jencks]. It is this concern for 'being understood' that replaces the modernist concern for purism of form. The search is now for a public discourse that will articulate the present in terms of the 'presentness' of the past and of the social placement of art in cultural discourse—then and now. Parody of the classical tradition offers a set of references that not only remain meaningful to the public but also continue to be compositionally useful."[44]

2.6. High and Low

One aspect of postmodern music that seems to upset purists is its free mixture of classical and vernacular traditions (traits 4, 5, and 6). Postmodernism attempts to break down what some see as artificial barriers—stronger in music than in any other art—between high and low culture. It is probably more for social than artistic reasons that musical comedies attract different audiences and critics (and composers and performers) than operas do, or that a ballad by Bob Dylan is understood to be fundamentally different in kind from a ballad by Franz Schubert. Several commentators hail the interpenetration of high and low art, while others disparage it. As we shall see, completely removing the barrier between high and low art can be problematic, although there certainly exists a postmodern impulse to do just that.

> **Jencks:** "The agenda of post-modern architects—and by extension post-modern writers, urbanists, and artists—is to challenge monolithic elitism, to bridge the gaps that divide high and low culture, elite and mass, specialist and non-professional, or most generally put—one discourse and interpretive community from another. There is no overcoming these gaps it is true: to believe so would be to return to the idea of an integrated culture, whether traditional or modern, that is another form of universalising control. Rather, the different ways of life can be confronted, enjoyed, juxtaposed, represented

[42] Jencks, "The Post-Modern Agenda," p. 10.
[43] Hutcheon, *A Poetics of Postmodernism*, p. 30.
[44] Ibid., p. 34.

and dramatised, so that different cultures acknowledge each other's legitimacy."[45]

Huyssen: "Postmodernism ... operates in a field of tension between tradition and innovation, conservation and renewal, mass culture and high art, in which the second terms are no longer automatically privileged over the first; a field of tension which can no longer be grasped in categories such as progress vs. reaction, left vs. right, present vs. past, modernism vs. realism, abstraction vs. representation, avantgarde vs. Kitsch."[46]

Jencks: "By the 1960s, 'postmodern' had only been used with any consistency concerning fiction and it was considered a regression from High Modernism, a compromise with mass culture and midcult. Irving Howe and Harold Levine formulated this negative assessment and, since mass culture was increasing in strength, it led to a certain paranoia; intellectuals and the avant-garde saw their positions under threat. The top-down view of cultural politics, the elitism which modernists took over from traditionalists, was hardly ever stated, but it was the usual premise behind debate. Of course not all intellectuals, modernists, and avant-gardists held this elitist position. But enough of them did to create a loose consensus that the citadel of high culture must be defended from the onslaughts of mass culture. The metaphor of the gap between the 'two cultures' (the literary and the scientific) was extended in all directions—highbrow, lowbrow, midcult, mass cult—until the cultural site resembled a battlefield criss-crossed with trenches. Thus the scene was set for a new strategy, and it created the first positive phase of post-modernism."[47]

Hutcheon: "Postmodernism ... does indeed 'close the gap' ... between high and low art forms, and it does so through the ironizing [i.e. rendering ironic] of both. ... Postmodernism is both academic and popular, elitist and accessible."[48]

Hayles: "To live postmodernism is to live as schizophrenics are said to do, in a world of disconnected present moments that jostle one another but never form a continuous (much less logical) progression. ... The people in this country who know the most about how postmodernism *feels* (as distinct from how to envision or analyze it) are all under the age of sixteen."[49]

---

[45] Jencks, "The Post-Modern Agenda," pp. 12–13.
[46] Huyssen, *After the Great Divide*, pp. 216–17.
[47] Jencks, "The Post-Modern Agenda," p. 18.
[48] Hutcheon, *A Poetics of Postmodernism*, p. 44.
[49] N. Katherine Hayles, *Chaos Bound: Orderly Disorder in Contemporary Literature and Science* (Ithaca, NY: Cornell University Press, 1990), p. 282.

2.7. What *Is* Musical Postmodernism?

I would prefer not to have to use the postmodernist label for almost all music of today that does not sound modernist. But popular usage is too widespread to combat in one book. So I modify the term "postmodernism." Although suspicious of binary oppositions such as those listed in the charts in Section 1.4, I invoke (but not extensively) conservative vs. radical postmodernism. These terms, like progressive vs. radical modernism, label not binary oppositions and not categories but extremes of a continuum. I believe that the postmodern music close to the radical extreme is deeply related to the ideas on postmodernism referred to in this chapter's quotations. We can think of various kinds and degrees of musical postmodernism as offering alternatives to high modernism; as turning away from modernism as if it had never happened (antimodernism); as opposing the elitism and purity of modernism; as continuing and possibly intensifying modernism's exploratory spirit but in an atmosphere of populism; as playing with history's chronology.

For those who see musical postmodernism as a nostalgic return, an important characteristic is the re-emergence of diatonic melodies and/or triadic sonorities. This idea is problematic. Re-emergence from what? Were diatonicism and tertian harmonies ever really absent from twentieth-century Western concert music? Those of us trained in academia may think so, or may at least see mid-century traditionalism as peripheral. Some modernist critics and professors have encouraged a belief in a mainstream linear historical continuum in atonality from Schoenberg and Webern through the Darmstadt and Princeton composers of the 1960s to composers of today such as Ferneyhough and Dench. This view marginalizes composers who did not abandon the diatonic and tonal centers, such as Copland, Hanson, Piston, Britten, Shostakovich, et al.[50] I doubt that the critics who equate postmodernism with diatonicism would call these composers postmodernists. Why not? We might say that these composers' music has little to do historically with ideas on postmodernism such as those quoted in this chapter. But, as I often argue in this book, chronology is not a defining aspect of postmodernism. Hence these composers may, in fact, be listened to from a postmodernist perspective. Or they may not.

The dubious activity of deciding whether traditionalist music composed today is or is not truly postmodern is only one problem in trying to categorize recent compositions. Many—indeed, most—pieces refuse to ally themselves totally with any one aesthetic position. For example, because of its overriding unity and its avant-garde attempt to create a new kind of musical theater, Philip Glass's opera *Einstein on the Beach* can be thought of as modernist. But it is also postmodernist in its embracing of simplicity and diatonicism, in its attempt to speak to audiences directly, and in its

---

[50] Critics and academics usually admit the quality of such composers' music, even as they marginalize it with respect to the modernist canon. "The difficulty," according to Rose Rosengard Subotnik, "is that this music is felt to have sidestepped the central historical problem of contemporary music as laid out by Schoenberg." That problem is artistic progress, as promulgated by modernists following the ideas of Schoenberg, *Developing Variations: Style and Ideology in Western Music* (Minneapolis: University of Minnesota Press, 1991), p. 274.

use of tonal materials in non-directional, non-functional (in the sense of the triadic functionality of tonal harmony) ways. Certain music of John Cage, to take another example, is modernist because of its purity, experimental nature, and elitism, but it is also postmodernist because of its indeterminacy, dismissal of formal structure, and encouragement of the individual creativity of listeners (Section 3.4 discusses Cage as modernist *and* postmodernist). Thus to ultimately classify a work as essentially either modernist or postmodernist is unproductive. While there certainly are predominantly modernist works (e.g. Schoenberg's Five Pieces for Orchestra) and quintessentially postmodernist works (e.g. William Bolcom's Third Symphony), there are very many pieces that exhibit characteristics of both modernism and postmodernism.

The question of classification as postmodernist vs. modernist recalls the problematic labeling of earlier works as classic or romantic. Do these terms name styles or historical periods? The answer, of course, is both. Is romanticism a negation or a continuation of classicism? Again, both. The parallels to the ensuing discussion of modernism vs. postmodernism are striking. Classicism and modernism are neat and pure, romanticism and postmodernism are messy. There are proto-romantic works that were composed during the classical period (Mozart's G Minor Symphony, or the *Stürm und Drang* works of Haydn), just as there were proto-postmodernist works composed during the modernist period (several compositions by Ives). And there was lingering classicism (certain aspects of Mendelssohn's *Italian Symphony*, for example, or many works of Brahms) during the romantic age, just as a lot of modernist music continues to appear today (e.g. the string quartets of Carter and Babbitt), during what some call a postmodernist era.

Postmodernism exists today. It is important to understand it in relationship to modernism, even though separating individual works into one of two piles is pointless. Therefore, in what follows there will be discussions of postmodernism vs. modernism, of radical postmodernism vs. conservative antimodernism, and of the traits, styles, and underlying meanings of all these pseudo-categories. Outright attempts at taxonomic categorization of pieces, however, will be largely (but not totally) avoided.

3

Modernism, Postmodernism, the Avant Garde, and Their Audiences

3.1. Musical Modernism and Postmodernism

To understand postmodernism entails understanding modernism, a formidable challenge. One place to begin is the fascinating book *Disappearing Through the Skylight*, in which author O. B. Hardison, Jr., draws a distinction between what he calls "modern" and "modernist" art.[1] While I do not particularly care for Hardison's uses of these terms (and will shortly offer replacements), I find his distinction quite useful. For him the *modernists* are those who, no matter how forward-looking their art, have extended tradition or sought to integrate their work with tradition. They understand themselves to be in history: earlier art leads to later art. They know where their roots lie, and even their most extreme experiments have eventually sought a continuity with the past. Hardison's creators of *modern* art, on the other hand, are avant-gardists who create radical breaks with the past.

While this distinction is helpful to my purposes, Hardison's terms are too similar. I would prefer terminology that is clearly different, allowing the words "modern" and "modernist" to remain close in meaning. Hardison's terms are confusing for another reason beyond their similarity: he idiosyncratically uses "modern" in a way that no other critic I know of does. For most critics (including Hardison), "modernist" refers to new artistic and cultural movements born in the mid-nineteenth century (although later in music). For most critics (but *not* including Hardison), "modern" characterizes modernity, the period beginning with the renaissance (the dawn of the "modern world," around 1450) and culminating in the eighteenth-century enlightenment—the period extending from the end of the Middle Ages to the advent of our present era of postmodernity. Hence postmodernity (a term rarely used in this book) is not the same as postmodernism, not only because of the distinction between the *modern* (this term is here not used in Hardison's sense) period of history and the *modernist* movement in art and culture but also because postmodernism is not simply a historical era. After all, how could an aesthetic that seeks to destroy history (trait 3) become a period within history? How could a movement that tries to overthrow meta-narratives (trait

---

[1] O. B. Hardison, Jr., *Disappearing Through the Skylight: Culture and Technology in the Twentieth Century* (New York: Viking, 1989), pp. 129–34.

12) nonetheless fall under the power of the grandest of all narratives, that of historical progress and periodization?

To avoid these confusions I use the terms "radical" and "progressive" in place of Hardison's "modern" and "modernist," respectively. When I use "modernist," and particularly when I write "progressive modernist," my intended meaning is close to his. However, where Hardison uses "modern" I prefer "radical modernist" or simply "avant garde" (not quite the same thing, but close to it). For me "modern" is not opposed to "modernist" but is almost its synonym.

Although Hardison does not write specifically about music in regard to the distinction between radical and progressive modernism, it is not difficult to name progressive composers of the first half of the last century: Schoenberg, Berg, Stravinsky, Debussy, and Bartók come immediately to mind. These men's compositions exhibit complex relationships to various musical traditions of their pasts. The more radical artists, by contrast, tried to redefine their art by freeing it from a heritage that had come to seem oppressive and limiting. While the distinction between progressive and radical art is not ironclad, we can nonetheless identify certain radical composers of the twentieth century: Italian futurists (e.g. Russolo and Pratella), Varèse, Partch, Babbitt, and Cage are good examples. Significantly, there have been fewer radicals than progressives among composers. Perhaps most fascinating are those figures whose work displays aspects of both radical and progressive sensibilities: Ives, Webern, Reich, and Carter, for example.

Despite its roots in the progressive harmonic structures of Liszt and Wagner, musical modernism is usually identified with the progressive and often atonal music composed after approximately 1909. Early modernist composers sought new languages in uncompromising and challenging works of great purity, complexity, severity, autonomy, originality, and perfection. These composers were (and their descendants today are) often unconcerned with mass culture or with popular acceptance; sometimes they were/are contemptuous of the average listener,[2] for whom they rarely compromise(d). They remain(ed) true to their own private expression, creating art for art's sake. Thus isolation, or alienation, was/is a common characteristic of modernism.

How did early modernists like Schoenberg and Webern, and also Stravinsky and Bartók, come to be promoted as central to the canon of twentieth-century art music? After all, atonality was never universal, even after it became broadly practiced by composers and carefully studied by theorists. I am referring not to the performance canon, since these composers (particularly Schoenberg and Webern) have never been widely played, but to the canons of analysis and theory. In the United States the canonization of such early modernists was a result of composers entering the academy *en masse*. They sought to legitimate their art by (1) situating themselves as direct

---

[2] Nicholas Cook believes that "one of the main forces underlying the apparently puzzling evolution of modern music is in fact a profound distrust of the popular," *Music, Imagination, and Culture* (Oxford: Clarendon, 1990), p. 178. Cook (p. 183) traces the source of this modernist distrust of popularity to Adorno's quintessentially modernist belief "that for the artist to give his audiences what they want is simply a betrayal of his artistic integrity."

descendants of the European modernists,[3] and (2) promoting this lineage and its sources as somehow more important, longer lasting (a self-fulfilling prophecy), and frankly better than others.

But why Schoenberg in particular? Why did this one composer come to be deified above all others in many American academies of higher learning? He had come to America, as had Stravinsky and Bartók, where he (in contrast to the other two) had many students. The force of his intellect and music mesmerized even composers who did not study with him directly. And, though he did not teach it to his American students, his twelve-tone method of composing seemed to offer—to those who understood it only superficially—easy answers to difficult questions of aesthetics and craft. Furthermore, Schoenberg provided a way for American composers to see themselves not as outsiders but as part of a venerated European (specifically German) heritage. The tendency of American composers to look for their spiritual and intellectual forbears in Europe rather than in their native country is as old as art music in the Western hemisphere, and it is one of many ways in which American classical music differs from jazz and pop, which do not trace their lineage to Europe.

Schoenberg represented an ideal for those would-be modernists who sought refuge and nurturing in American colleges, universities, and conservatories.[4] He was seen as both an avant-gardist and a traditionalist; originally viewed as a radical modernist, by the time he arrived in America he was known as a progressive. He had struck out in truly new directions, but he had also maintained contact with his heritage. For mid-century American composers, tradition was not oppressive in the way it was for many of their European contemporaries, but rather it was something to be envied and adopted. It was easy to see Schoenberg not only as a fierce individualist but also as carrying on from Brahms, Wagner, and Mahler. By following Schoenberg, the Americans sought to place themselves as direct descendants of those late-romantic giants. The Americans used Schoenberg's techniques to suit their own purposes, in often pale imitation of how Schoenberg had "misread" (in the sense of Harold Bloom and Joseph Straus; see Section 4.4) the music of Brahms (see Section 5.4). As the aesthetics of party-line modernism hardened, the American descendants of Schoenberg forced themselves to reject competing ideologies and to indoctrinate (the term is not too strong) their students.

Perpetuating an American modernism traceable to Schoenberg is a political as well as aesthetic act. Not only do some in the older generation seek to indoctrinate their students within those great bastions of conservatism, American universities, but also their establishment mentality brought many of them to positions of considerable power. More often than not, it is the latter-day modernists who are in positions

---

[3] For the most part, these American modernists did not "misread" (in Harold Bloom's sense of the term, discussed in Section 5.4) the art of their forbears, in the way (discussed in Section 4.3) that Schoenberg recast music of Brahms to make him into his antecedent. In Schoenberg's mind, Brahms was cast as a proto-Schoenberg. The Americans were less ambivalent, however. They situated themselves in the line of the great modern masters, rather than recasting them as precursors.

[4] What they sought was legitimacy, membership in an elite circle of self-proclaimed important artists, *and* a paycheck!

to hand out—to their colleagues and students—prizes, commissions, awards, and grants.[5] They use their positions of power to promote an aesthetic in which they deeply believe but which ever greater numbers of composers and performers find outmoded.

After the Second World War, European composers seemed to associate themselves with Webern (who had not left for America) in much the same way that Americans connected with Schoenberg. The war had produced a cultural rupture in Europe, and these composers were able to re-establish contact with contemporary music by relating to a composer who, more than Schoenberg, had made a radical break with the past. Needing to split off from what they felt to be an oppressive tradition, the Darmstadt avant garde could not abide Schoenberg's lingering traditionalism—his sonata forms, his row transpositions by perfect fifth, his Brahmsian rhythms—any more than they could accept Stravinsky's triads, diatonic tunes, or octatonic pitch collections. No neoclassicism for them! Webern did have an allegiance to tradition, notably in his use of double canons which he derived from the renaissance music he had studied as a musicology student. But Webern, unlike Schoenberg, did largely repudiate—in his music, though not in his tastes—his immediate past. Although it is possible in his early works to trace his development from chromatically tonal late romanticism to atonal modernism, it is hard to hear much of the late nineteenth century echoing in his twelve-tone works, the way one can in Schoenberg's dodeca-phonic pieces.

Why did Berg never become central to latter-day modernists? His music was always too romantic, too close to tonality, too impure stylistically. Also, he was one of the first to lay claim to his lineage. He was proud of his studies with Schoenberg, whom he revered to such an extraordinary degree that he willingly took on menial tasks and waited eagerly for any small praise that might fall from the master's lips or pen. Late modernists, I suspect, are uncomfortable with Berg's almost obeisant vener-ation of his mentor, perhaps because they feel on some level awkward about coveting (or at least accepting) comparable loyalty from their own students.

And why was Ives not a father figure? American modernists, needing to place themselves in the European tradition, were not about to venerate one of their own, particularly one whose music is highly unsystematic. For a long time, Europeans seemed to value Ives's music more than Americans did, although in Europe it was seen as an exotic curiosity—on an equal footing with, for example, music of the Russian nationalists and the Javanese gamelan—more than as part of any respectable mainstream.

And what about the other early progressive modernists, Stravinsky and Bartók? In some ways, their modernism was of a different sort from that of the Second Viennese School. Lingering diatonicism, folk elements, and temporal disjunctions mark their music far more than such traits are found in the compositions of Schoenberg, Berg, and Webern. These aspects place the music of Stravinsky and Bartók closer to postmodernism, although its unity, austerity, complexity, and novelty situate it squarely in the modernist camp.

---

[5]   Jann Pasler, "Musique et Institution aux Etats-Unis," *Inharmoniques* (May 1987): 104–34.

The atonal canon has been promoted in American academia not only by composers but also by theorists, who have found in the music of Schoenberg, Webern, Berg, Stravinsky, and Bartók fertile ground for their analytic studies. Music which lends itself to systematic analysis tends to be analyzed in universities more readily than that which does not, and the music which is often analyzed is the music that students naturally are expected to think of as the most significant and relevant. This is the music they often imitate (hence their reverence for self-conscious and contrived unity, which I mention at the outset of Section 4.1). Their modernist teachers reinforce these imitations with praise and encouragement. And why have theorists concentrated on this small body of music? Part of the reason is expediency: it is easier to analyze consistent music than pluralistic music, in which no one system of thought will explicate an entire piece. Another part of the reason is political. When theories of atonal analysis began to spread through academia, this music was already well entrenched, thanks to several influential progressive modernist composers who held major teaching posts. Theorists were thus able to assure their own importance by providing keys that unlocked the secrets of this highly valued but little understood repertory.

Audiences have come around to some modernist music (such as the early ballets of Stravinsky, the quartets of Bartók, and the sonatas of Ives), but the compositions of the Second Viennese School still fail to attract a large public. The reason often given is the unrelieved dissonance in the music of Schoenberg, Berg, and Webern, but I doubt that this is the whole story. There is also a lot of dissonance in those Stravinsky and Bartók works which have found audiences, as there is in some downright popular Ives compositions, like his massively dissonant Fourth Symphony. Is the reason, then, atonality? I think not. *The Rite of Spring*, for example, may use some tonal materials, but it is not tonal. Stravinsky's neoclassic works, which come closer to tonality, are less widely appreciated than the *Rite*. Schoenberg's tonal works, such as *Pelleas und Melisande* and the Suite in G, are no more accepted by the public than are his atonal compositions. It seems that Schoenberg's musical values and personality, more than his use of atonality or tonality, put listeners off. Is the reason for the gap between modernist music and the general public, then, the alleged lack of emotional content (whatever that vague term might mean)? Again, I think not, because some of Schoenberg's most hermetic scores are also his most emotional (or so they seem to me). I think the main reason why some of the modernist works most prized by academics have little audience appeal is their elitism: you need to be a sophisticated listener to understand Stravinsky's Symphony in C, or Schoenberg's Fourth Quartet, or Webern's Orchestral Variations. You need to learn how to listen to these works. They are an acquired taste.

Whatever the reasons for the failure of audiences to enjoy much modernist music— and the failure of most modernist composers to write music capable of appealing to a large audience—modernism's hermeticism has become almost a badge of honor. Late modernists, adopting a defensive posture, often act proud of the inaccessibility of their works to a general public. No pandering to the masses for them! No compositions with easily discernible structures! No postmodernism!

3.2. The Avant Garde

In delineating radical and progressive modernism in the previous section, I came close to equating the former with the avant garde. When considering the most radical of postmodern music, I will need to address the question of whether or not an avant garde of postmodernism exists, or is even possible. Before that issue can be taken up meaningfully, however, we should consider just what the musical avant garde entails.

A wide variety of music has been labeled "avant garde." What does this term really mean when applied to music? Some writers seem to take the avant garde as synonymous with modernism; for others it apparently equates with innovation. Some identify it with originality, and others with novelty—not quite the same thing.

I cannot survey all or even most meanings of avant-gardism, nor do I expect to resolve disagreements. What I do plan to discuss is characteristics shared by many musical works reasonably thought of as avant garde—whether those traits are inherent in the music, relate to how the music is received and used, or emanate from the social and cultural contexts that first greeted it.

Some uses of the term "avant garde" ought to be dismissed outright. Avant-gardism is not the same as utter originality, for example. To my ears, two of the most original works of the twentieth century were composed by men not regularly thought of as vanguardists: Sibelius's *Tapiola* and Janáček's Sinfonietta (discussed briefly in section 4.7). I am awe-struck at the visionary quality of this music. In admiration I wonder how these composers managed to find such striking and stunning ideas. These pieces are not unprecedented, however. It is possible to hear their special sound-worlds presaged in earlier pieces by the same composers. Yet these works are unquestionably original—in part for the techniques employed in their making but more substantially because of their amazingly fresh ways of thinking of musical impulse, gesture, form, continuity, and expression.

Why are these not avant-garde works? Is the reason simply that they were created toward the ends of their respective composers' careers, whereas avant-gardism is a youthful phenomenon? While there surely is more to the avant garde than the age of an artist, I do not completely discount this factor. Most avant garde music is the product of brash young artists out to show the world something revolutionary, to state starkly what is wrong with mainstream music, to redefine what music can or ought to be, and to challenge listeners by shaking the foundations of their understanding of the musical art. The Sibelius and Janáček works are not pathbreaking in any of these ways, but they are special for more subtle, interior, and personal reasons. Instead of breaking with tradition, as youthful vanguard art relishes doing, they build on lifetimes of music-making within a known tradition. They represent an ultimate refinement of their composers' art and heritage, not a breaking away from the past.

These qualities contrast considerably with those of music normally considered avant garde. Such music focuses on its surface and on its technical means of production, while works like those by Sibelius and Janáček are deep, with their technical means operating in the service of expressive ideas, and with their intriguing surfaces serving as gateways to their inner depth. These qualities differ markedly from those of such avant-gardisms as indeterminacy (as in works of Cage from the 1960s onward), minimalism (such as in the early works of Philip Glass and Steve Reich), and integral serialism (as practiced briefly by Boulez, Stockhausen, Krenek, and Nono), where the procedures by which these composers made their sounds or constructed their forms actually *become*, rather than just serve, the music.

Novel sounds help to focus the listener's attention on musical surfaces. Avant-garde works may be rich in ideas, since they can call for rethinking what music is: they brashly suggest—to stick with my few examples—that music can be so variable from one performance to the next that a listener may not recognize that the same piece is being performed, or that music can be the result of rigidly applied arithmetic algorithms rather than emotional impulses, or that music can consist of large stretches of almost unchanged repetition. However rich in combative intellectual ideas such avant-garde music may be, it tends to lack emotional depth and structural subtlety.

If focusing on procedures and surfaces defines (at least in part) the avant garde, then should such figures as Schoenberg, Webern, and Stravinsky disappear from the avant-garde canon?[6] It was undoubtedly the radical newness of the surface sounds of these composers' early works that first caused them to be hailed or condemned as revolutionary. Listeners were challenged—indeed shaken—by massive unresolved dissonances, lack of tonal resolution, wildly irregular rhythms and meters, intimate and fragile wisps of sound, lack of repetition *and* excessive repetition, new sonorities, and extreme discontinuities. Over time, however, audiences came to understand the profundities behind these once new sounds and procedures.

The parallel cases of Schoenberg and Stravinsky show how what once seemed a historical break came to be part of tradition's continuum. Pathbreaking works like *Pierrot Lunaire* and *The Rite of Spring*, for example, were taken as avant-garde statements by their first audiences. This music surely sounded unusual if not bizarre to listeners still having trouble with Strauss and Debussy. The composers were thought to be deliberately debunking their heritage. They were accused of assaulting both their audiences and the institution of music. By the ends of their long careers, however, Schoenberg and Stravinsky—both of whom had continued to grow in depth and singularity—were generally understood to be well within the cultural mainstream. Late visionary works like the String Trio and the Orchestral Variations are unique, but they are not avant garde. They, like *Tapiola* and Sinfonietta, do not flout but rather belong to a tradition.

What changed? Surely Schoenberg and Stravinsky changed as they matured, and their music did as well. But so did our understanding of their early rebellious works. Today we can understand *Pierrot* in relation to nineteenth-century German *Lieder* and *The Rite* in relation to folk-inspired Russian nationalism and to Debussyan orchestration—they are simultaneously a repudiation and a continuation, a disdaining and a refinement, of their antecedents. These pathbreaking works not only challenged but

---

[6]   See Jochen Schulte-Sasse, "Foreword: Theory of Modernism versus Theory of the Avant-Garde," in Peter Bürger, *Theory of the Avant-Garde*, trans. Michael Shaw (Minneapolis: University of Minnesota Press, 1984), p. xxix.

also continued tradition as they pushed it in unexpected directions. Looking back, we see *Pierrot* and *The Rite* not solely as breaks in history's continuum but also as stages in the development of musical style.

In contrast to such pillars of early twentieth-century music, thoroughly avant-garde works may not reveal much inner profundity once they have lost their initial impression of audacity—once the dust they have stirred up has settled. Regardless of their original impact, Luigi Russolo's compositions for orchestras of noisemakers, Erik Satie's unpretentious and guileless piano solos, and Henry Cowell's works that call for strumming directly on piano strings do not shake our souls—or at least *my* soul—to their/its emotional core.[7] As composer-critic David Schiff has written, "By definition, avant-garde works have a short shelf life. Whatever is merely new soon becomes merely old."[8] The impudence of the avant garde is found essentially in the music's exterior, where it has its most immediate impact. If the interior is impoverished, that lack seems beside the point. Impressed mainly by the impertinence of the avant garde, contemporary audiences may not even notice its superficiality. Whereas profound works open up gradually as they become understood over time, the impact (although not necessarily the comprehension) of the avant garde is instantaneous.

Music that is *more than* avant garde may eventually enter the cultural mainstream, but music that is *only* avant garde may not. Thus Russolo's futurist works seem forever to be avant garde—in part because they continue to be dismissed as marginal curiosities. Also, Harry Partch remains an avant-gardist for us, because of his rejection of several generations of music history. The tradition he connected with was not of his immediate past but of centuries earlier.[9] Even with the advantage of time's objectivity, we do not see Partch primarily in relationship with his recent musical past. Similarly, much of the music of Cage continued to be avant garde, perhaps because of the extent of his rejection of tradition (although he, like Partch, did not spring from nowhere—his relationship with the music of Satie, for example, is frequently acknowledged). Furthermore, Cage continued to experiment[10]—often in different veins—well into old

---

[7] It may seem strange to invoke the romantic ideal of emotional profundity as an artistic criterion in a book on postmodernism. What I actually mean is that these works do not offer—at least to me but perhaps to other listeners as well—a context for deeply emotional experiences. I do not mean to imply that emotions are, or even could be, in music, nor that music directly and single-handedly evokes emotional responses. See my discussion of musical communication in Chapter 7.

[8] David Schiff, "Ah, for the Days When New Music Stirred the Blood," *New York Times*, October 4, 1998, p. 34.

[9] Partch's music is not *totally* divorced from his recent past. There is a relationship to the early works of Cage, for example. But Partch, more than most composers, sought specifically to deny the course that mainstream music had taken for centuries. Curiously, another composer who tried to connect with a distant past while ignoring a more immediate past was Orff, whom we tend not to think of as an avant-gardist.

[10] It may be an oversimplification to equate the avant garde with the experimental in music. In his book *Experimental Music: Cage and Beyond* (New York: Schirmer Books, 1974), Michael Nyman carefully distinguishes the two. For Nyman, experimental music (e.g. that of Cage and Feldman) is concerned with new processes of and new attitudes toward composing, performing, and listening, while avant-garde music (e.g. that of Boulez and Stockhausen) is concerned with new musical objects—unprecedented kinds of notation, instruments, sounds, etc. See pp. 1–26. It is beyond the scope of this chapter to explore Nyman's dichotomy.

age. His mesostics, for example, are as unprecedented as his silent piece *4'33"*, or as his indeterminate music. Much of Cage's output questions—often in different ways—not only what music is but also what a composer does, what a listener does, and what is usable as musical sound.

What is the difference, we might ask, between Schoenberg and Stravinsky, who were initially understood as avant-gardists but who continued to develop their ideas so that the label came to fit them less and less, and Cage, who changed a lot during his lifetime yet remained an avant-gardist?[11] Cage's ideas developed as much as Schoenberg's and Stravinsky's did, but with the Europeans the changes were more in the spirit of developing and refining, and with Cage they were more in the sense of remaining ever fresh and ever open to new kinds of experiments. The Europeans tried to work through the implications of their initial avant-gardisms, and in so doing they made clear the historical continuity underlying the apparent ruptures in their early music. Cage instead moved from one avant-garde statement to another, in a spirit of eternal youth.

The additive and phase-shifting early works of Steve Reich stand out as quintessential examples of avant-garde music in which the compositional processes produce music of the surface. Pieces like *Pendulum Music* (in which a microphone swings back and forth over a loudspeaker, producing intermittent feedback until the motion finally ceases), or the two tape-loop compositions *Come Out* and *It's Gonna Rain*, or the early phase pieces *Violin Phase* and *Clapping Music*, are avant-garde statements. Their surfaces offered their first listeners a strikingly new kind of music. Their processes of composition in a sense *are* their formal structures. They neither seek nor find depth of feeling.

Some people still doubt whether such pieces are actually music, rather than simply experiments in sound or exercises in perception. Whether or not they are music depends on how one defines the word, a debate I do not want to enter here. But there is no denying that such works are presented to audiences *as* music. They are usually (not always) realized by performers, they are presented in concert halls or on recordings or on the radio: their context is that of music. Audiences are being invited, or dared, to hear them as music. Yet, they are so different from normal music that an uninitiated audience member may feel confused, or used, or even mocked. But this is exactly what the avant garde tries to do: to shake listeners out of their complacent attitudes about what music is, and thereby to challenge them to rethink the whole process of listening to, understanding, and enjoying the musical art.

The relationship of such works to tradition is adversarial. They defy more than seduce the listener, and they extend by potentially unsettling means the very idea of what music is. Reich's later pieces, by contrast—works like *Different Trains* and *The Cave*—also embody innovative statements. In fact, they are *more* original than his early pieces. They are original in the same way that *Tapiola* and Sinfonietta are: they situate themselves at the intersection of certain traditions, including that of their composer's own earlier works. They do not negate traditions, but rather use them in

---

[11] I am indebted to Chadwick Jenkins for raising this important question.

the service of unique musical ideas, expressions, and contexts. Hence they do achieve expressive profundity.

So we have Reich, Schoenberg, and Stravinsky as one-time avant-gardists who continued to grow and whose late music is thoroughly original but in no way avant garde. And we have composers like Cage and Partch, who remained avant-gardists their entire creative lives. In addition, we have composers who were self-consciously avant garde in their youth, but who finished up as reactionaries. Composers such as Richard Strauss, Henry Cowell, and George Antheil began as active avant-gardists, seeming to enjoy the way their music shocked its first listeners; but then they turned back from the brink. Their later works—regardless of their inherent quality,[12] which in at least the case of Strauss was considerable—do not move along in the tradition initiated by their early avant-garde creations, nor do they seek to reconcile the vangardism of their youth with the heritage they were initially seen to be mocking. These composers backed away, choosing another course.

An important question to consider is whether avant-garde music becomes so because of its composer's intentions and procedures, because of characteristics in its sound palette, or because of the way people react to it.[13] I believe that avant-gardism resides in all three areas: the composer's intentions, the essence of the music, and its reception. Thus, it is an oversimplification to label a work simply as avant garde or not: there are several ways a composition can exhibit avant-gardism, each to varying degrees. Not only the sounds in the music but also what its composer intends matters,[14] as does how the music goes out into the world.

An avant-gardist is self-conscious, knowing well what he or she is doing. There is a political dimension to avant-garde music: it is art that intends to provoke audiences out of their complacency. Thus it is necessarily extremist. Innovation and novelty may be necessary components of an avant-garde work, but they are not sufficient: as I have tried to indicate, there is innovative or novel music that is not avant garde because it does not challenge listeners to reconsider what music is.

---

[12] The idea that quality can be inherent in an artwork is contentious and is certainly challenged from within postmodernism. Whereas I cannot here embark on an extended discussion of value judgments from a postmodern perspective, I should state that I am expressing a personal opinion that is partially informed by the actual music out there, in the world. I find that the late works of Strauss are full of sumptuous harmonies and gorgeous orchestration that evoke for me a wonder-fully bittersweet autumnal quality. I do not find comparable beauty in the late music of Cowell and Antheil. Their late works strike me as rather pedestrian, not as exciting or even as well crafted as their earlier pieces. Are these qualities literally in the music? Not totally. They are in my perception and understanding of the music, which does have, I trust, something to do with the actual music. If someone were to argue that she or he finds extraordinary beauty or meaning or originality in late Cowell or Antheil, I would not denigrate this person's values. If someone can find these works as satisfying as I find the late works of Strauss, that does not at all bother me. But I cannot. For further discussion, see Section 11.7, "Good and Bad Music."

[13] These three possibilities correspond loosely to Jean-Jacques Nattiez's tripartite division of the locus of musical meaning into the poietic (the composer's meaning), neutral (what is inherent in the score), and esthesic (the listeners' meanings) levels. See *Music and Discourse: Toward a Semiology of Music*, trans. Carolyn Abbate (Princeton: Princeton University Press, 1990), pp. 10–32, 139–49. See also Bürger, *Theory of the Avant-Garde*, pp. 47–54.

[14] Chapter 7 considers whether or not a composer communicates with his or her listeners.

There is also innovative or novel music that is not avant garde because it is not aggressive. Such music may seek aesthetic beauty but not the shock value central to the avant-garde act. Challenging accepted artistic values is necessarily contentious. The avant garde does not seek to convince through careful reasoning or through seductive sonorities: it confronts its audiences with aggressively new statements and sound objects. Artistic manifestos—whether essays or compositions (such as *4'33"*)— antagonistically challenge audiences. This is surely true of Varèse's massive sonorities, Iannis Xenakis's dense textures, Cage's indeterminacy, and the repetitiveness of Reich's and Philip Glass's early minimalism. The aggressiveness of such music openly courts rejection. It is rarely met with outright acceptance, and its composers tend to prefer hostility to indifference.

But what of inventive but less contentious music, such as that of Debussy? Or of postmodernist music like that of John Adams, Arvo Pärt, or Alfred Schnittke? This music is innovative and challenging, but it aspires more to aesthetic beauty than to confrontation, and hence is not fully avant garde. And what about Webern? His fragile textures do not reflect the harshness of the avant garde. They can be understood as reactions against the gigantism of Mahler's symphonies, Wagner's music dramas, and perhaps (in Webern's later works) Stravinsky's ballets. Webern's miniatures can seem avant garde in reverse, as challenging by their refusal to be aggressive.[15] Similar things can be said about the intimate sounds of Morton Feldman.

Whether or not Webern and Feldman were avant-gardists, they were certainly radical modernists. What, indeed, *is* the relationship between avant-gardism and radical modernism? Both types of music share several traits: novelty, extremism, and breaking with the past. But modernist music is complex and elitist, appealing to a small group of initiates, while avant-garde music does not aim to appeal so much as to upset, and it tries to upset not a small elite but as many people as possible. Modernist music is created in the spirit of "art for art's sake"; it is pure and autonomous,[16] divorced from political, social, or cultural contexts (there are exceptions, of course).[17] But the act of creating avant-garde music is necessarily political, social, and cultural, since avant-gardism challenges social and artistic values. Avant-gardism and modernism become confused, however, when we find some of the same composers placed in both camps. Schoenberg, Webern, and Stravinsky are quintessential modernists of the early twentieth century, and—as mentioned above—their early works were understood as

[15] The research of Felix Meyer and Anne C. Shreffler has uncovered the significant fact that the original textures of some of Webern's early transparent miniatures were considerably thicker than their final versions, revised for publication some fifteen years after they were first completed. This fact further problematizes the classification of Webern as an avant-gardist, because his so-called innovations were not so new or unprecedented when he actually incorporated them into his scores. See "Webern's Revisions: Some Analytical Implications," *Music Analysis* 12/3 (October 1993): 355–79.

[16] The concept of the autonomy of art is complex and fraught with potential contradictions. See Bürger, *Theory of the Avant-Garde*, pp. 35–41.

[17] The independence of art from politics is a modernist ideal which, postmodernists seem to feel, is finally impossible. The very act of trying to divorce art from politics is political. To set art above or beyond politics is to take account of—if only by denial—the fact that art is unavoidably of the world: of the political and social world.

radical and provocative, whether or not the composers intended them to provoke. Hence they have been labeled as both modernists and avant-gardists (although, as indicated, I question whether the avant-gardist label is really appropriate). Latter-day modernists, such as Elliott Carter, Milton Babbitt, György Ligeti, Witold Lutosławski, and Luciano Berio, may have been provocative at early stages of their careers, but their modernism was not conceived for the purpose of goading an audience. Rather, these composers set themselves above the general (as opposed to the specialist) audience. They responded to charges of incomprehensibility with disdain or indifference, whereas hardcore avant-gardists like Cage, Karlheinz Stockhausen, LaMonte Young, and Dick Higgins have at times seemed to relish their status as *provocateurs*. While it is difficult to maintain such broad generalizations in the face of certain exceptions that could be cited, I do wish to acknowledge a distinction between the radical modernist spirit and the avant-garde act.

If avant-gardism and radical modernism are distinct but overlapping categories, what about avant-gardism and postmodernism? In other words, is an avant garde of postmodernism possible? Possibly it is, but I think that a postmodern avant garde has, or would have, considerably less impact than did the modernist avant garde. The concept of the avant garde depends on a linear view of history. To be out front, ahead of everyone else, doing daringly new things, implies that there is only one line of history and that you are at its forefront. Only if we believe that music history is a linear move toward greater complexity, or greater abstraction, or greater dissonance, or greater *anything,* can we identify which composers are out front. But postmodernism denies the linearity of history (trait 3). Postmodernism sees history not as a line but as a direction-less field. It is certainly possible for an avant-gardist to step beyond such a field by creating something utterly new, utterly unprecedented, and quite challenging. The collage movement of Berio's *Sinfonia* is a good example, I think, of a work that has a lot of postmodernist traits and is also avant garde. However, when there was a perceived linearity to history, it was much easier to identify the next frontier and, with avant-garde brashness, to cross it. Without a solitary line of historical progress, it is much harder to find something that is beyond the purview of current musical practice. But not, I would insist, impossible. Since I do occasionally encounter music that strikes me as both postmodern and avant garde, I would not suggest that the two are mutually exclusive.

It is because composers of a postmodernist persuasion view history as a direction-less field that they accept sounds and procedures of the past alongside those of the present (or of a more recent past) (trait 3). Postmodernists are not trying to exclude types of music that they feel are worn out, because they do not believe that any music can become unusable. Theirs is an inclusive and pluralistic art, trying to bring as much as possible into the here and now.

Not all composers of today identify themselves with postmodernism, however. Modernism is still very much alive (as is antimodernism, which some view as synonymous with or at least part of postmodernism while others—including this author—view as a separate phenomenon).

The following chart should clarify how I see modernism and postmodernism with respect to their subcategories. Under each broad category (modernism and

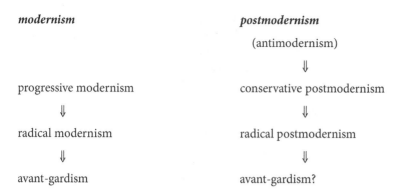

Figure 3.1

postmodernism), subcategories are listed in increasing degrees of radicalism (top to bottom, as indicated by arrows). Antimodernism is listed as the extreme of conservative postmodernism, but it is in parentheses because I, in contrast to many critics, do not see antimodernism as having substantive connections to postmodernism.

The question before us is whether or not it makes sense to posit a postmodern avant garde that is still more challenging and novel than what I have been calling radical postmodernism: hence the question mark in the chart. I have said that a postmodern avant garde is possible, but not very widespread and not having nearly the impact that the avant garde of modernism had.

Actually, we can also question whether an avant garde of modernism is possible *today*. The modernism of the 1990s and 2000s is very different from that of the 1910s. For one thing, much music of current modernism is not disturbing in the ways that the music of early modernism was. In other words, today's modernists may be progressive but are generally not radical (at least since the death of Cage). Hence I am tempted to suggest that avant-gardism is dormant if not dead, in both the modernist and postmodernist arenas and in a cultural climate where everything goes and where nothing shocks. But it is risky to predict the future of the avant garde. The very complacency implied in the suggestion that avant-gardism is all but defunct could be taken as a sign that we are ripe for a new wave of vangardism—whether it would be of postmodernism or of a reborn modernism—which may shake us out of a self-satisfied anything-goes attitude.

I do not find much music of today that I would consider avant garde. Berio's *Sinfonia* is a rather isolated instance. French spectral music (by composers such as Tristan Murail and Gérard Grisey), for example, is strikingly new, but it is not avant garde. It arose in reaction to the way serialism had moved ever farther from the realities of the human perceptual mechanism and hence from audiences. An attempt to reach rather than confront audiences—even an attempt to do so in an utterly uncompromising and novel manner—precludes an avant-garde confrontation. Similarly, I find a lot of vitality in today's computer music (such as that of Paul Lansky and Brad Garton), in microtonal music (such as that of Johnny Reinhard), in polystylistic music (such as that of Alfred Schnittke or John Zorn), in crossover music (such as that of Steve Martland or Michael Gordon), and in the "new complexity" (of composers like Brian Ferneyhough and James Dillon). Yet none of this music strikes me as avant garde. Although at first blush it seems radical, it is actually progressive, as it seems more to extend the traditions of, respectively, analog tape music, experimental scales, Ivesian eclecticism, mixtures of jazz into "classical" music, and Darmstadt serialism. These types of new music are not utterly unprecedented, nor do they aggressively defy musical tradition, however controversial they may be.

It is symptomatic of the avant garde's dormancy that the term has become trivialized and institutionalized. The label "avant garde," for example, is routinely applied to music involving extended instrumental techniques and/or non-traditional notation. How ironic it is that a term that once signified aggressive challenges to the *status quo* should now become essentialized and frozen! And how far it is from the original spirit of the avant-gardists to have some of the most superficial aspects of their compositional techniques taken as defining traits of compositions that do not in any way confront the institution of music!

3.3. The Avant Garde in the 1960s: Modernist or Postmodernist, American or European?

Some theorists of the postmodern would not completely accept my suggestion, in the preceding section, that an avant garde of postmodernism is a rarity. For example, cultural critic Andreas Huyssen, who considers postmodernism to be primarily an American phenomenon,[18] places its roots in the 1960s' attempt to recreate a vital avant garde. He labels this 1960s avant garde the "Duchamp-Cage-Warhol axis." Huyssen explains[19] that the artistic revolts of the 1960s were not directed against modernism *per se*. After all, the works of the Duchamp-Cage-Warhol axis certainly have a lot in common with modernism. What such artists were rejecting, rather, was the image high modernism had attained, its acceptance into society as chic, its use in advertising and media, its cultural acceptability. Modernist music may not have had as widespread acceptance as abstract painting, but the atonality and jagged lines of many Hollywood film scores and television soundtracks attest to the mainstreaming of the sounds of modernist music.

The postmodernist revolt against what modernism had come to mean was carried out in the spirit of what modernism had originally been—radical. The avant-garde music of Cage (discussed in greater detail in the next section) and similar composers and artists was at least as revolutionary as the music of Schoenberg, Webern,

---

[18] Antoine Compagnon also locates postmodernism first in the United States, with 1960s' critics (such as Irving Howe) who decried it as anti-intellectual, antimodernist, and consumerist, and in the 1970s with polemical defenses (such as that by Ihab Hassan) of it as a new aesthetic paradigm. See Compagnon, *The 5 Paradoxes of Modernity*, pp. 113–15.

[19] Huyssen, *After the Great Divide*, pp. 189–90.

Stravinsky, and Ives had been a half-century earlier. Yet the avant-garde music of the 1960s was as postmodernist in its aesthetic ideas as it was modernist in spirit. Part of the reason 1960s music was modernist was that it still accepted—indeed, strove for—unity, although of a new kind: consistency more than organicism, synchronic over diachronic unity (these types of unity are explored in Chapter 5). Yet, in its attempt to transfer structure and even meaning from the artist to the perceiver (trait 16), as well as in its embracing of indeterminacy (trait 9), the music of the Cage-Warhol-Duchamp axis was decidedly postmodernist.

Huyssen believes that the 1960s' experimentation in Europe, particularly Germany, was an attempt to recapture the modernist impulse, but for a reason quite different from what motivated American avant-gardism: the Second World War had cut European artists off from modernism, because Hitler and Stalin suppressed it—its creation, its dissemination, and its preservation. This explains why Darmstadt music, for example, and also sound-mass music in Poland, represented a resurgence of modernism more than a birth of postmodernism. America had not been torn apart by the war; it had, furthermore, accepted as refugees from Europe many modernist artists (including Schoenberg, Stravinsky, Hindemith, and Bartók), whom American artists revered but against whom postmodernists eventually rebelled. By the 1960s the time was ripe for an artistic revolution in this country.

That revolution took place at the aesthetic intersection of modernism and postmodernism. But the 1960s were long ago. The principals of the Duchamp-Cage-Warhol axis are no longer with us. Modernism and postmodernism *are* both still here, of course, but they no longer interact in a way that can be fairly characterized as avant garde. I may find an isolated work of today that seems to instantiate avant-garde attitudes, but I find no sustained avant-garde movement.

Huyssen's hypothesis that postmodernism flourished more strongly in America than elsewhere is more difficult to defend for music than for other disciplines. Consider the striking postmodernism called forth in compositions of Pärt, Gorecki, Andriessen, Berio, Adés, Martland, Szymański, Krauze, Eloy, Kancheli, Schnittke, et al.—postmodernisms that do not seem to derive much of their nature from American cultural values. The ideas underlying musical postmodernism (e.g. my 16 traits) may have an American flavor, but the music which is animated by these ideas is as often as not European.

Given the vitality of this and other European music of a postmodern persuasion, we may wonder why postmodernism received slow and grudging acceptance in Europe, particularly in France and Germany, where a great many musicians still dismiss it outright. Perhaps one reason is that many Europeans tend to think of history as linear, as progress to ever greater heights. It may seem strange that a culture that has seen the dénouement of progress in the ravages of Hitler, Stalin, and Mussolini continues to believe in progress, but the linear view of history—strongly promoted by Adorno and perpetuated by those whose modernism derives from his—does not die easily. People who think in this manner are unlikely to be attracted to an aesthetic that, despite—or maybe because of—its free appropriation of historical artifacts, has little respect for the concept of history. Composers who espouse the linear view of history face a difficult problem. They see the evolutionary increase of musical complexity as having reached a culmination in music of the "new complexity," such as that of Michael Finnissy and Richard Barrett. They see unity as having peaked in total serialism. They see extended instrumental techniques pushed to an extreme in music of Lachenmann. Linear history seems to demand that such composers go beyond these extremes to new heights of complexity and unity (and, hence, of modernism).[20] But some European (particularly German) composers (possibly subconsciously) fear that there are no greater heights to be scaled. What are they to do? Since they see postmodernism as not just conservative but reactionary, they refuse to adopt its tenets, for that would appear to be a move backward along history's linear continuum. And they are uncomfortable about standing still, although that is what many of them seem to be doing: at several European new music festivals I have attended in the 1980s, 1990s, and 2000s, I have found young composers offering new compositions depressingly similar to but lacking the vitality of those of the Darmstadt school a generation earlier. But there *are* European composers, such as those listed above, who see ways out of this dilemma—ways that point toward some sort of postmodernism.

3.4. The Music of Cage: Modernist *and* Postmodernist

Many discussions of postmodernism in music eventually confront the music and the impact of John Cage. Cage's indeterminate music, long reviled in some circles and hailed in others, is still not well understood. It is not, despite what several commentators believe, a music where "anything goes." A music as austere and cerebral as his hardly fits that description. He may have randomly chosen the ways he would determine the sounds of a given work, but he remained faithful to those initially arbitrary decisions. In some of his music, the arbitrary becomes the fixed.

Was the grand avant-gardist also a postmodernist? His populism would seem to suggest so. Yet his music shares with high modernism a degree of its elitism. Despite his personal populism, his music *is* elitist: I have yet to meet a listener who appreciates Cage's indeterminate music without first being tutored in what it means and how to listen to it. It is, like its modernist antecedents, abstract, pure, austere, and uncompromising.

Yet, as I have said, in its attempt to transfer structure and even meaning from the artist to the perceiver (trait 16) Cage's music is also postmodernist. Can Cage's works be both modernist *and* postmodernist? They nicely demonstrate a point echoed

---

[20] Boulez has written of "the utopia which directed integral serialism: besides the desire to unify the system, to do justice to previously neglected constituent parts, to rehabilitate them, there existed no less strongly, a belief in the infallibility of *order*, something approaching a superstition concerning its magic virtues which, if they did not form a complete substitute for the personality of the composer, sustained him unfailingly in his battle against uncertainty, at the price of an agreed element of anonymity," "Le système et l'idée," in *InHarmoniques* 1 (1986): 97. This text is expanded in an edition of Boulez's course at the Collège de France: *Jalons pour une décennie* (Paris: Christian Bourgeois, 1989), pp. 316–90.

frequently in this book: postmodernism is not simply a repudiation of modernism but also its continuation (trait 1). As I suggest in Section 1.5, postmodernism is like a rebellious teenager, busy more with not being his or her parents than with exploring who she or he actually is. Postmodernism tries to displace the modernism from which it was born and some of whose tenets it continues to perpetuate, but also, as Linda Kouvaras writes, it "seeks to embrace much of the radical and redemptive qualities which were—and to many, still are—an integral part of the modernist project."[21]

Cage's status as both modernist and postmodernist is particularly evident when we consider his music from the standpoints of order and unity (trait 11). Cage created and promoted a music that was disordered in one sense, since in it no event responds to any other event, but ordered in another sense: it is a music of overwhelming consistency, at least as usually performed. In all performances I have heard of *Atlas Eclipticalis*, for example, every event is so much like every other event that, even though they are not interrelated in any functional or implicative manner, they belong together and to the piece. This music *is* unified: while one thing may not lead to another, there is certainly an utmost relatedness between all the parts.[22]

Cage wanted to liberate the audience by refusing to structure his music, thereby encouraging the listener to provide mental structuring in order to make sense of the music. I do not think his music succeeds very often in making listeners into mental composers, however. Most listeners do not have, or do not know how to use, the mental ability to create musical structures from unstructured sounds. Music must give its listeners some material with which to work. Music with ambiguous or contradictory structures (rather than no structures), or music that presents familiar materials in disorienting juxtapositions—the music of postmodernism—succeeds, more than the typical Cage composition does, in implicating the spectator in the work's production. Cage's abstract sonorities, with little reference outside themselves,[23] give most listeners too little to work with in their attempts to create meaningful musical experiences. The *tabula rasa* Cage sought may ideally allow listeners to imagine their own music unfettered by any impositions of a composer's personality, but in practice most people are more creative listeners when confronted with material not devoid of association but rich in (possibly contradictory) references. Using John Zorn as an archetypcal postmodernist in contrast to Cage the late modernist, Kevin McNeilly writes percep- tively on the different stances of these two aesthetics *vis-à-vis* the listener:

> Cage's is a politics of exclusion and abandonment, his music demanding a willful participation which the comfortable, impatient, media-saturated listener is often unwilling to give. Zorn, on the other hand, offers the semblance of that comfort,

---

[21] Linda Kouvaras, "Postmodern Temporalities," in Broadstock et al. (eds.), *Aflame with Music: 100 Years of Music at the University of Melbourne* (Melbourne: Centre for Studies in Australian Music, 1996), p. 401.

[22] I am invoking Webern's definition of unity, discussed in Section 5.2.

[23] Some of Cage's open works allow the inclusion of environmental sounds, which are likely to be saturated with connotations for many listeners. Hearing works like *Variations II* or *Fontana Mix*, for example, can be a far different experience from listening to abstract works like *The Four Seasons* and *Cartridge Music*.

simulates the attributes of popular culture, in order to confront and to engage that same listener, whose thirty-second attention span, so programmed by television advertising, can be accessed directly by thirty-second blocks of sound. Cage stands aloof from his audience, at a somewhat elitist distance, while Zorn unashamedly baits a hook with snatches of the familiar and the vulgar.[24]

Several theorists characterize Cage as a postmodernist.[25] Indeed, his 1960s music displays several aspects of what theorists outside of music often consider postmodern: open form, chance, anarchy, listener participation, and indeterminacy. Nonetheless, because of its experimentation and its continued engagement with unity (of performance if not of score), it can also be understood as radically modernist—and undeniably as avant-gardist.

There was another avant garde back in the 1960s, in addition to the Duchamp-Cage-Warhol axis. It was, according to Huyssen, the avant garde of "happenings, pop vernacular, psychedelic art, acid rock, alternative and street theater."[26] This avant garde, more than that of the Duchamp-Cage-Warhol axis, not only rebelled against institutionalized high modernism but also looked forward to 1970s and 1980s postmodernism in its eclecticism (trait 7), its collages and pastiches (trait 6), its disregard of the canons of structural unity (trait 11), and its double coding (trait 4). When these traits burst forth in great profusion in 1970s and 1980s and later music, they were actualized in music that was too populist (trait 5), too familiar (trait 6), and too socially engaged (trait 15) to offer the kinds of challenges normally associated with an avant-garde movement. Just as earlier avant-garde movements in the arts brought forth innovations that sometimes, sooner or later, were assimilated by mainstream artists, so Huyssens's avant garde of happenings, etc., led to an upsurge in postmodern characteristics of music that was no longer in any substantial sense avant garde. The institutionalization of Huyssen's 1970s avant garde happened very quickly—which is hardly surprising, given the increased speed of dissemination of new ideas in the arts.

3.5. Modernism, Education, and Lineage

One latter-day modernist teaching in a prestigious American university greets his new graduate students each year with a speech welcoming them into an exclusive club: they, and only they, will save music from philistine postmodernism, they are told (but not in those terms). One of my own modernist composition teachers believed that

---

[24] Kevin McNeilly, "Ugly Beauty: John Zorn and the Politics of Postmodern Music," *Postmodern Culture* 5 (1995): accessible from http://pmc.iath.virginia.edu/text-only/issue.195/mcneilly.195, para. 11.

[25] Gregory L. Ulmer, for example, discusses the manner in which Cage "postmodernizes" verbal texts. See "The Object of Post-Criticism" in Foster, *The Anti-Aesthetic, Essays on Postmodern Culture* (Port Townsend, WA: Bay Press, 1983), pp. 102–7. For a discussion of how various current trends in composition do and do not relate to postmodernism, see Benjamin Thorn, "Why Postmodern Music Is Impossible," *Sounds Australian* 33 (Autumn 1992): 39–42. The bulk of this issue is devoted to articles on postmodernism. The editor is Warren Burt.

[26] Huyssen, *After the Great Divide*, p. 193.

there were only two composers of the twentieth century whose music he could (and hence we should) accept unequivocally: Schoenberg and Sessions. Schoenberg was this composer's idol, and Sessions had been his teacher. Contemporary composers readily seek to prove themselves by means of academic pedigrees. Their professional biographies proudly list their famous teachers, as if to say that their own music is validated by the music (or, actually, by scholarly opinion of the music) of their teachers. Some composers even trumpet their lineage back to their "grandteachers." When I was a young student, before I had worked with such prestigious instructors as Stockhausen and Sessions, I used to brag that my grandteachers included Schoenberg (through Leon Kirchner), Webern (through Arnold Elston), Hindemith (through Billy Jim Layton), and Strauss (through Arnold Franchetti). Nowadays, I even see the process of validation in reverse: older composers applying for faculty positions brag about not only their famous teachers but also their famous students! What a telling instantiation of the linear view of history!

Studying with prominent teachers is nothing new, of course. Beethoven studied with Haydn, after all. But what was Beethoven's attitude? In marked contrast to composers of today, Beethoven steadfastly refused to acknowledge himself as a pupil of an old master, and he was quite critical of Haydn's teaching.[27] Beethoven's having studied with Haydn influenced his music and helped his career less than, for example, Charles Wuorinen's having studied with Babbitt or Earl Kim's having studied with Schoenberg.

3.6. Alienation from the Audience

The modernist avant garde of the early twentieth century thrived on being different, on going against the grain. The arrogance of Schoenberg's Society for the Private Performance of New Music, which held private concerts that excluded the general public,[28] may have been partly a defensive reaction to public hostility, but it was also a celebration of difference. This music undeniably was different from anything the world had previously heard. Its difference may in part account for its vitality: going against the grain can be a heady experience. The aggressiveness of pieces like Stravinsky's *Rite of Spring*, Schoenberg's *Erwartung*, Berg's *Three Pieces for Orchestra*, Webern's *Six Pieces for Orchestra*, Prokofiev's *Scythian Suite*, or Bartók's *Miraculous Mandarin* alienated some audiences, but this music was nonetheless known. It was controversial. It was discussed and debated. Opinions of it were polarized.

Today's modernists, particularly in the United States, suffer a more profound alienation: not difference (since their music often reworks ideas of high modernism) but indifference. They are not so much controversial as they are peripheral. Early modernists such as Schoenberg and Webern thrived despite, or partly because of,

---

[27] For an excellent discussion on the relationship between Beethoven and Haydn, see Maynard Solomon, *Beethoven* (New York: Schirmer, 1977), pp. 67–77.
[28] See Charles Rosen, *Arnold Schoenberg* (New York: Viking, 1975) pp. 63–9.

the lack of public acceptance of their work (at the same time that they deplored it): they knew, whether consciously or not, that the music they were producing was unprecedented, radically new, and profoundly challenging. Thus they could console themselves by saying that the public was not yet ready for the new music. But today's audiences have made little progress toward accepting and enjoying the works of high modernism, so it is hardly surprising that latter-day modernism has few adherents. (There remains a nucleus of enthusiasts in the general public, to be sure, but their number is small.) Today's modernists cannot comfort themselves with the idea that they are breaking new ground, because they are not. Thus modernists in the 1990s and 2000s can hardly look to the future the way modernists in the 1910s may have. Since listeners still have trouble with the music of Schoenberg and Webern, how likely is it that a large public will rally around the music of, say, Babbitt and Boulez? This dilemma, it seems to me, is producing a widespread despondency among our modernists, particularly as they see segments of the public excited by the postmodern music they deplore.

Composers are not the only ones upset by the often lamented gap between modernist composers and audiences. Critics, music enthusiasts, performers, and musicologists bemoan this situation. For example, Rose Subotnik, an astute observer of the position of music in society, paints this depressing picture:

> Composers have forfeited the prospect of any direct relationship between their music and the public at large; and conversely, we in society have forfeited our rights as individuals to make our own judgements about contemporary [i.e. modernist] music. If we don't like what we hear, we are branded as uneducated or vulgar, even if there is no reasonable way of understanding what we hear, indeed, even if it is central to the composer's aesthetic and moral integrity that we not like what we hear.[29]

Although her tone is not particularly ironic, I think Subotnik's statement is exaggerated. Composers may adopt a defensive posture by claiming the moral integrity of alienation from the public, but all reasonable modernist composers I know do want audiences to hear, understand, and appreciate their music. Still, exaggeration or not, Subotnik's description is disheartening.

I regret this state of affairs, which I blame as much on the poor education of American audiences (caused by the marginalization of music in public education, which led all too readily to the removal of funding from music programs a generation or two ago) as I do on the arrogance of modernist composers. It bothers me that only a few people I meet, other than some composers and some performers, appreciate the beauties and profundities I hear in such works as Roger Sessions's Third Symphony, Leon Kirchner's Music for Twelve, Elliott Carter's *Night Fantasies*, Donald Martino's Triple Concerto, Charles Wuorinen's *The Golden Dance*, or Mario Davidovsky's *Quartetto*. I respect the tenaciousness of these and other latter-day modernists, who continue to compose the music in which they deeply believe, despite dwindling

---

[29] Subotnik, *Developing Variations*, p. 251.

financial support, shrinking audience sizes, disdainful reviews, and death of some brilliant ensembles that specialized in performing modernist music.

It is fashionable for modernists and their defenders to fault audiences for not understanding, but the composers must also take responsibility. They are not innocent. They have seen how time has not brought large audiences to the music of Schoenberg or Webern. When they write the kind of music they prefer, late modernists should know what to expect. I respect them enormously for continuing to create the kind of music they feel they must write, regardless of its reception. And I wish their music were more appreciated. But it is not. And no amount of defensive posturing or retreating to academia or giving each other awards seems to affect public opinion.

In the United States, the contemporary composer is more estranged from society than are other artists. Among non-professionals, I hear intelligent debates about the theater of Edward Albee or the art of Julian Schnabel far more than I witness discussions about the music of Elliott Carter or Milton Babbitt (though a crossover figure like Philip Glass does attract some attention). The alienation of the "classical" composer is also evident in our larger newspapers, which usually have two different staffs of reviewers, one for "classical music" and one for jazz/rock/pop. But the same newspapers are happy to allow one critic to cover plays of Neil Simon and the Ridiculous Theatrical Company, another to write up retrospectives of Norman Rockwell and Jasper Johns, and a third to review novels by Harold Robbins and Kathy Acker. This double standard shows up even in arts and entertainment listings, where all theater appears in one place, all movies in another, all art galleries in a third, but music is divided into two separate groups: pop and classical. The modernist composer is thus doubly alienated: she or he works in a genre ("classical" music) marginalized in society, and even within the rather small world of classical music she or he is further ghettoized and ignored as a modernist. It is hardly surprising, then, that postmodern composers seek to break down barriers between genres and styles (traits 4 and 6), and between elitist and populist values (trait 5)! Or that modernists resent their success.

The situation in Europe may be somewhat better. The intellectual level of newspaper criticism, and of audiences, is noticeably higher than in the United States (the difference is directly traceable to education, I believe). Serious debate about current music appears regularly in newspapers, whereas in America it is rare (although not unheard of). Furthermore, European musicologists publish not only in academic journals but also in popular magazines, and they study the music of today far more than do their American counterparts. The long-lived magazine *Musical America* was certainly not an in-depth music journal, but its demise nonetheless removed virtually the only big-circulation magazine that spoke to the consumer about "classical" music. Perhaps the turn to opera of some American postmodernist composers (John Adams, David Lang, Steve Reich, Philip Glass, Michael Torke, and John Corigliano, for example) is partially an attempt to use the still vital arena of the theater to reach audiences and to be noticed in the press.

Postmodernists, particularly of the more conservative persuasion, often do seem more concerned with reaching an audience than do modernists. Furthermore, antimodernists often court audiences more openly than do postmodernists. Postmodernists and antimodernists seek not a faceless audience expected to make whatever effort is needed to comprehend, as with modernism, but an audience of real people willing to meet the composer halfway.

But the postmodern composer is under a sentence of death: the birth of the listener's creativity is at the cost of "the death of the composer," to paraphrase Barthes (see Section 7.2). How does a composer approach an audience that is rejuvenated by his or her own "death," and onto whom is thrust creativity (the listener creates the work, and perhaps—as suggested in Section 7.3—even creates the composer)? For conservative postmodernists, the answer is nostalgia: nostalgia for the good old days when audiences cared about new music, waited for it eagerly, discussed it, were engaged by it. Thus we hear a lot of conservative postmodernists citing as motivation for their no-longer-modernist styles the desire to reach audiences. They do not want to compose the music of modernist alienation, but they also stop short of wanting to give the audience the antimodernism they think it wants and/or believe it can enjoy and/or imagine it can understand. But for radical postmodernists, "pandering to the public" (as latter-day modernists are wont to characterize the postmodernists, particularly the conservative postmodernists) is not the answer.

How *does* a radical postmodernist approach an audience? By using references to and/or quotations of other music (trait 6), some of which is well known to some listeners, they invite listeners to bring to the piece personal associations with the music referred to or quoted. Every listener will have different associations, and there will be many degrees of familiarity with the quoted materials. Thus, quotation and reference are not superficial aspects of postmodernist music, but are a vital means by which creativity is handed to listeners, who constitute pieces from what composers and performers present to them. The pieces are uniquely their own, and they do not require (though they surely admit) any special abilities to construct musical forms mentally.[30]

---

[30] These issues are discussed more fully in Chapter 7.

Part Two

Chapters on Concepts of Postmodern Music

Postmodernism and Related Isms in Today's Music

4.1. Meta-Narratives

Jean-François Lyotard, one of the leading theorists of postmodernism, defines the postmodern simply as "incredulity towards meta-narratives."[1] The term "meta-narratives" refers to all-encompassing ideas or thought systems, the absolute truth, utility, and universality of which are taken to be self-evident (trait 12). For example, meta-narratives govern the gestures, rituals, and social customs that contribute to cultural identity. They are often invisible and automatic—until we step into another context, with different meta-narratives. Then they become quite visible.

I had an experience that strikingly demonstrated the clash of cultural meta-narratives. I was visiting Korea for a performance of a solo piano composition of mine. The pianist invited me to her apartment to rehearse. As soon as I arrived, she offered me tea. In accordance with my meta-narrative about how busy Americans interact with new professional colleagues, I declined: I did not want to inconvenience her, and I did not want to waste her or my valuable time with anything other than rehearsing. So I politely suggested that we should get right to work. She led me uneasily to her studio and sat down at the piano, placing my music before her and her hands on the keyboard. But she could not bring herself to play. After an awkward silence, she turned to me and explained that she could not work with me until we had gotten to know each other a bit. She asked me to reconsider the tea. I realized how important to her cultural ritual it was to sit over tea with a new acquaintance before beginning to work with him. This was part of her cultural meta-narrative.

Meta-narratives are so ingrained in the ways we think that they are often unexamined and may even go unnoticed. *They are the contexts within which we think and act.* We do not consider them to be optional or arbitrary, even though they may be. They are assumptions, and possibly sets of expectations, the truth of which is taken as self-evident to the extent that people often do not question them. Once we step outside and start questioning, they may be dethroned *as meta-narratives.* They may become less than universal, although they may remain in place: my having confronted in Korea the relativity of my American rehearsal behavior did not mean that I gave

---

[1] Quoted in Harvey, *The Condition of Modernity*, p. 45.

it up, although I now understand better that the ways in which American musicians enact their rehearsal rituals are not the only ways.

But questioning meta-narratives *can* make them begin to crumble. The way early twentieth-century composers interrogated the meta-narrative of functional tonality, for example, led to its demotion (but not, as is sometimes claimed, its demolition). Composers came to understand that there are other viable ways to organize their musical sounds. Tonality did not disappear, but it became no longer a context, no longer an assumption. It became an option, to be used or not. Once composers began to explore atonality, modality, exotic scales, polytonality, sound masses, timbre, composition, etc., traditional tonality could no longer function *automatically* as the context of a piece of music. Composers had to decide: should their pieces be tonal, atonal, modal, polytonal, or some mixture? A composer like Schubert, for example, would not think to ask himself such a question upon commencing a new work; a composer like Stravinsky could hardly avoid asking it, in some form or other.

For tonal composers, and for theorists and analysts, a tonal piece was expected to contain only pitches that could be heard as belonging to (or as being connected by step to) triad-derived sonorities; it was expected to establish a tonic, contradict it, and eventually reaffirm it; it was expected to utilize a prescribed hierarchy in which chords are related in various functional ways to the central tonic; and its dissonances and their resolutions were expected to operate according to certain constraints. These characteristics define the meta-narrative of traditional tonality.

A few paragraphs back I characterized meta-narratives as "often unexamined." This idea needs to be explored. Let us remain with the example of the meta-narrative of traditional triadic tonality. In one sense tonality was not an unexamined assumption during the eighteenth and nineteenth centuries. Many theorists tried to formulate the principles by which tonality operated. Many composers sought, whether consciously or not, to extend the harmonic and modulatory possibilities within tonality. No, tonality was not unexamined, but the examinations all took place *within* the context of a basic assumption, namely that music (in the West, in the so-called "common practice" period) was necessarily and obviously tonal. It did not seriously occur to composers or theorists to ask what might lie beyond tonality (the rare excursion outside tonality would most likely not be taken seriously, as the ending of Mozart's *Musical Joke* demonstrates), or how sounds might be coherently organized in ways that did not depend on tonal principles. Once that kind of examination began to take place—in some of Liszt's late piano pieces, in some of Busoni's writings, in Debussy's excursions into modality and artificial scales, in Strauss's flirtations with bitonality— then a new kind of examination of tonality was underway, whether or not composers and theorists fully realized the consequences of their new questioning attitude. They had begun to examine the meta-narrative of tonality not only from within but also from without. They glimpsed a potential world of music outside the bounds of tonality.

More than any other turn-of-the-century composer, Schoenberg questioned the meta-narrative of functional tonality. But did he succeed in replacing tonality with another meta-narrative? Was his twelve-tone system a meta-narrative? It was certainly not unexamined—quite the contrary. Its detailed examination may have led, paradoxically, to its failure to become established as a meta-narrative. Many theorists and composers probed the depths of the serial principle, but in so doing they—sometimes inadvertently—exposed some of its limitations, so that many subsequent composers resisted it, in part if not entirely. Today many composers are affected by serial thinking, but only a few are true serialists. Schoenberg may have felt that twelve-tone principles assured the hegemony of (at least) German music for the upcoming century, and Boulez may have felt that the serial system was an inevitable evolutionary development, but in fact serialism never became ubiquitous. Only a few composers internalized their twelve-tone rows and serial operations to the extent that they no longer thought much about them consciously, so that they became part of their intuitive musicality; for most twelve-tone composers, however, writing music remained a conscious, indeed a self-conscious, procedure. Hence, although some composers (including Schoenberg and Boulez) may have had personal meta-narratives *about* serialism, and although it allowed some composers to create some truly wonderful music, in itself it never really achieved the status of a meta-narrative of musical culture.

Schoenberg may have contributed more than anyone else to the overthrow of one meta-narrative (tonality), and he may have striven to create another (serialism), but he was still bound by—was still operating within the strictures of—yet another meta-narrative, namely structural unity. He no doubt did not have the term or even the concept of a meta-narrative, and hence he did not see that the status of unity was like that of tonality: a context waiting to be challenged. He defied tonality while he continued to embrace unity. It remained for postmodern composers to take the fateful next step, to examine *from without* and hence to reject the ubiquity of musical unity. Radically postmodern music demotes unity from the status of a totalizing meta-narrative to one of many smaller narratives (trait 11). Musical unity becomes not the context in which music unfolds but rather a strategy available to be used (or ignored) in generating or analyzing or listening to a piece, or even just a part of a piece.

Whether unity is a meta-narrative or an option is one factor that distinguishes modernist from postmodernist music. In general, postmodernism's rejection of meta-narratives sets it apart from modernism (trait 12). Although he is not writing about music, urban theorist David Harvey's ideas are relevant here. He sees

> postmodernism as a legitimate reaction to the "monotony" of universal modernism's vision of the world. "Generally perceived as positivistic, technocentric, and rationalistic, universal modernism has been identified with the belief in linear progress, absolute truths, the rational planning of social orders, and the standardization of knowledge and production." Postmodernism, by way of contrast, privileges "heterogeneity and difference as liberative forces in the redefinition of cultural discourse." Fragmentation, indeterminacy, and intense distrust of all universal or "totalizing" discourses (to use a favored phrase) are the hallmark of postmodernist thought.[2]

---

[2] Harvey, pp. 8–9. His quotations are from the architectural journal *PRECIS* 6 (1987): 7–24.

After listing examples of postmodernist ideas in philosophy, science, history, mathematics (including chaos theory), ethics, politics, and anthropology, Harvey goes on to explain:

> What all these examples have in common is a rejection of "meta-narratives" (large-scale theoretical interpretations purportedly of universal application), which leads [Terry] Eagleton to complete his description of postmodernism thus: "Postmodernism signals the death of such 'meta-narratives' whose secretly terroristic function was to ground and legitimate the illusion of a 'universal' human history. We are now in the process of [a]wakening from the nightmare of modernity, with its manipulative reason and fetish of the totality, into the laid-back pluralism of the postmodern, that heterogeneous range of life-style and language games which has renounced the nostalgic urge to totalize and legitimate itself."[3]

The adjective "totalizing" occurs frequently in writing about postmodernism, often in conjunction with the noun "meta-narratives." It should already be evident that I have chosen to adopt this terminology, despite its near redundancy. Can there be, after all, a meta-narrative that is not totalizing? "Totalizing"—which means ubiquitous and omnipotent—conveys the flavor of subversion, oppression, or (as Eagleton says) terrorism. What I call the "totalizing meta-narrative of musical unity" is not simply an idea that used to be taken as a universal truth (i.e. all good pieces are unified). It is an unspoken assumption that theorists and analysts have accepted, often uncritically. It prejudices music analysis, and it can prevent critics (and listeners who read and believe their criticism) from finding other values in music. It can subvert some of the meanings of a piece, meanings that become more directly accessible once analysts and listeners move away from the narrowness of this meta-narrative (the meta-narrative of musical unity is discussed more fully in Chapter 5). Subversion, oppression, and terrorism are rather strong terms to apply to the aesthetic of unity, but by calling attention to the totalizing aspect of this particular meta-narrative I hope to underline the notion that musical unity is not an objective fact nor a universal good, but rather an idea of considerable, if not always beneficent, power—a power that postmodernism has been vigorously challenging.

Like musical unity, history itself is a meta-narrative. We used to think of ourselves as in history. History was our context. But now postmodernism encourages us to think of history as a construct, or a text, made by people (not just historians) according to their needs and desires (trait 3). Postmodernism rejects the meta-narrative of historical progress, although it does not seek to overthrow smaller historical narratives—the stories by which we understand our origins, our values, and ourselves. Hence postmodern artworks can be thought of as "post-historical" despite their appropriation of artifacts from history.

It is not difficult to identify meta-narratives that are no more or that never were:

---

[3]   Harvey, *The Condition of Postmodernity*, p. 9. He quotes from Terry Eagleton, "Awakening from Modernity," *Times Literary Supplement*, February 20, 1987.

history, unity, tonality are meta-narratives that were overthrown; serialism is an idea that never made it to meta-narrative status. What is more difficult is to understand new meta-narratives, or meta-narratives that are still so deeply ingrained in our way of thinking that they are unrecognized as such. Is postmodernism itself such a meta-narrative, or are some of the sixteen traits I have enumerated meta-narratives of postmodernism? Are disunity, distrust of binary oppositions, or distrust of history meta-narratives? Is distrust of meta-narratives itself a meta-narrative?

The demise of one totalizing meta-narrative, and possibly the rise of another, is similar to the paradigm shifts posited by Thomas Kuhn in his influential book *The Structure of Scientific Revolutions.*[4] Kuhn shows that the truths of science are not immutable but are subject to widely held assumptions: even science has its meta-narratives. Euclidean geometry was accepted as universal until mathematicians began to think about non-Euclidean geometry. In other words, they examined traditional geometry *from within* for centuries, and then finally began to look *outside*. Similarly, Newtonian mechanics was believed to rule the world until Einstein's theories of relativity showed a world beyond Newton. Physicists used to study mechanics from within the Newtonian paradigm; starting with Einstein, they examined mechanics from the outside.

Perhaps we should think of the transition from predominantly modernist to predominantly postmodernist aesthetic ideas a paradigm shift, comparable to such shifts in the sciences. Central to the shift from modernism to postmodernism is the changing of meta-narratives.

4.2. Styles of Postmodernism

In its rejection of the meta-narrative of historical progress, postmodernism is opposed to the historical consciousness of progressive modernism. Yet the art of postmodernism utilizes gestures, materials, or procedures from the past (trait 3), which would appear to place it in opposition also to radical modernism's quest for the new. Thus postmodernism would seem to react to (as well as to perpetuate) some of the tenets of both radical and progressive modernism. It is therefore not surprising to find that there are two strains of postmodernism (radical and conservative) that are roughly parallel to radical vs. progressive modernism.

My differentiation of postmodernism into radical and conservative derives from art critic Hal Foster. He calls the two types the "postmodernism of reaction" and the "postmodernism of resistance"; he also calls the former "neoconservative postmodernism" and the latter "poststructuralist postmodernism."[5] The neoconservative postmodernism of reaction, which Foster feels is better known, is

---

[4] Second edition, enlarged, vol. 2, no. 2 of *International Encyclopedia of Unified Science* (Chicago: University of Chicago Press, 1970).

[5] The terms "postmodernism of reaction" and "postmodernism of resistance" appear in a brief discussion in Foster's "Postmodernism: A Preface," in Hal Foster (ed.), *The Anti-Aesthetic: Essays on Postmodern Culture* (Port Townsend, WA: Bay Press, 1983), p. xii. A later essay

conceived in therapeutic, not to say cosmetic, terms: as a return to the verities of tradition. ... Modernism is reduced to a style ... and condemned, or excised entirely as a cultural mistake; pre- and postmodern elements are then elided, and the humanist tradition is preserved. But what is this return if not a resurrection of lost traditions set against modernism, a master plan imposed on a heterogeneous present?[6]

Eager to avoid a proliferation of jargon, I will stick with the terms "conservative" and "radical" rather than adopting Foster's "resistant," "reactive," "neoconservative," or "poststructuralist." But I must add that conservative postmodernism at its most extreme blends into what I have been calling antimodernism (see the chart in Section 3.2).

As I stressed when exposing my list of 16 traits of the postmodern musical attitude (Section 1.3), it is an exercise in futility to label a composer or a composition as postmodern, whichever style of postmodernism is invoked. Postmodernism is an attitude that a sympathetic listener may find reflected in some ways in a variety of works or parts of works. It is not an absolute quality that does or does not inhere in a certain body of music or in a certain group of composers. I find, for example, much of George Rochberg's latest music to have aspects of postmodernism. But the composer may well disagree, even though he has written an article that condemns modernism as a mistake,[7] and even though his compositions do indeed align themselves with conservative postmodernism as they elide pre- and postmodernist elements.

When a composer or a piece is labeled postmodern, particularly in music reviews, the postmodernism referred to is usually conservative. Rochberg often composes music of a conservatively postmodern bent. In my opinion, however, a work like his Third String Quartet has aspects of radical postmodernism in the way that unmistakable stylistic references to music of Beethoven, Mahler, and Bartók (that stop short of literal quotation) are played off against each other. I feel the Third Quartet to be radically postmodern in some respects; Rochberg would probably disagree. I

expands considerably on these concepts. Foster substitutes the terms "neoconservative postmodernism" and "poststructuralist postmodernism" in "(Post)modern Polemics," in *Recordings: Art, Spectacle, Cultural Politics* (Seattle: Bay Press, 1985), pp. 120–35. George Edwards offers a similar distinction between "postmodernism as utopia" and "postmodernism as protest." See "Music and Postmodernism," *Partisan Review* 58 (1991): 701–4. Also relevant are Peter Bürger's categories of antimodern postmodernism, pluralistic postmodernism, and postmodernism that continues the project of modernism. See *The Decline of Modernism*, trans. Nicholas Walker (University Park, PA: Pennsylvania State University Press, 1992), pp. 42–6.

6   Foster, "Postmodernism: A Preface," p. xii. See also E. Ann Kaplan's discussion of Foster's ideas in *Postmodernism and its Discontents* (London: Verso, 1988), pp. 2–3. Jann Pasler offers an interesting and useful discussion of Foster's categories with respect to music; she also sketches a third species of postmodernism. See her "Postmodernism, Narrativity, and the Art of Memory," in Jonathan D. Kramer (ed.), *Time in Contemporary Musical Thought*, which is *Contemporary Music Review* 7/1 (1993): 19–20.

7   Rochberg, "Can the Arts Survive Modernism?" *Critical Inquiry* 11 (1984): 317–40. Although I still have trouble with several of Rochberg's ideas, particularly those in his response to me in "Kramer vs. Kramer" (*Critical Inquiry* 11/3 (1984): 509–17), I would revise some of the formulations in my response to his original article. See Jonathan D. Kramer, "Can Modernism Survive George Rochberg?" *Critical Inquiry* 11/2 (1984): 341–54.

feel much of his other recent music to be conservatively postmodern, some of it to be antimodern, and a lot of his earlier music to be modernist. So what? These labels do not tell us too much about the pieces, but they do suggest (but not determine) ways to understand them.

Several works of John Zorn seem to exemplify a radically postmodernism aesthetic. Pieces like *Carny* or *Forbidden Fruit*, for example, offer a considerable dose of postmodern chaos, despite their nostalgia for other musics. Zorn writes about his stylistic eclecticism:

> I grew up in New York City as a media freak, watching movies and TV and buying hundreds of records. There's a lot of jazz in me, but there's also a lot of rock, a lot of classical, a lot of ethnic music, a lot of blues, a lot of movie soundtracks. I'm a mixture of all those things. ... We should take advantage of all the great music and musicians in this world without fear of musical barriers, which sometimes are even stronger than racial or religious ones.[8]

Listening to *Forbidden Fruit* or *Carny* can be as dizzying as it is electrifying. We never seem to know what is coming next, nor when.[9] The stylistic juxtapositions are amazingly bold: the disunity of musical styles can be disorienting.[10] To unify the apparent disorder perceptually requires a listener to invest considerable mental effort and creativity.[11] If there were any discernible thread of continuity, the music would surely be more tame, more predictable, more ordinary. But there is not. Yet, despite the chaotic (my description, not his) nature of his music, Zorn espouses a surprisingly conservative aesthetic *vis-à-vis* unity (notice the added italics in this quotation):

> A composition needs some kind of stamp, a sense of cohesion. That's what I was taught in school by uptight professors in thin ties and thick glasses who made me

---

[8] John Zorn, notes to recording of *Forbidden Fruit*, Elektra/Asylum/Nonesuch, 1987.

[9] In a private communication, composer John Halle (who interviewed Zorn) has explained that *Forbidden Fruit* was conceived in relationship to a Japanese film of the same title. The music apparently mimics quite closely the narrative sequence of the movie, which is not particularly unpredictable. Thus *Forbidden Fruit* exemplifies a process hardly unknown in previous music: a musical structure that seems imaginative (or even whimsical) when experienced in a concert or recorded performance owes its origin to a decidedly less whimsical extra-musical source. Another example of this procedure is Jacques Ibert's *Divertissement* (discussed in Section 9.2), a suite that is full of wonderful surprises. Once we recontextualize the piece in accordance with our knowledge that it was originally incidental music for a farce—a fact not usually mentioned in program notes— we may be less in awe of the composer's imagination, but the piece remains a delightful study in unpredictability. Nonetheless, changing the work's context does change some of its meaning.

[10] Zorn's chamber work *Cobra* is equally eclectic. According to Kevin McNeilly, it "not only uses conventional orchestral instrumentation including harp, brass, woodwinds, and percussion, but also incorporates electric guitar and bass, turntables, cheesy organ, and sampled sounds ranging from horse whinnies and duck calls to train whistles, telephone bells, and industrial clanging. Zorn, while affirming his own position as a 'classically-trained' composer, fuses the materials of the 'classical' world with pop music, hardcore punk, heavy metal, jazz (free and traditional), television soundtracks, and sound effects. ... His work is consistently eclectic, hybridized, and polysemous," "Ugly Beauty," para. 3.

[11] Simply listening to the piece—letting its chaos wash over you—is not such a formidable task. But it is a creative challenge to extract and create structures that make listening to the piece into a unified and coherent experience in time.

study pitch sets. I mean, give me a break from that sterile bullshit! But what all that schooling did impress upon me was the realization that *every note needs to have a function, and that there always has to be a sense of going somewhere*, the feeling that a personal vision is being realized. ... My works often move from one block to another such that the average person can hear no development whatsoever. But *I always have a unifying concept that ties all the sections together.*[12]

It is fascinating to find a composer like Zorn composing more radical music than his prose writings suggest he realizes. In Section 4.3 I discuss similar phenomena with regard to Rochberg's Third Quartet and an article of York Höller; earlier I considered Schoenberg, who continually wrote of his music as if it carried on in the tradition of nineteenth-century romanticism (which to a large degree it did), at the same as time as it was pushing forward the frontiers of nontonal pitch organization. These examples are symptomatic of the needs of some composers (but certainly not all—I know composers who claim to be more radical than their music would suggest) to see themselves as part of a tradition, no matter how original their works are. Harold Bloom's anxiety of influence (see Section 4.3) operates even in Zorn's "misreadings" of the music of his "heroes"—Ives, Partch, Varèse, and Stravinsky—whose compositions he sees as precursors of his own discontinuous style.[13]

4.3. Postmodernism, Latter-Day Modernism, and Antimodernism

Individual artworks are rarely so cooperative as to be subsumed readily by a single category (e.g. modernist or postmodernist). While it is pointless rigidly to label a given composition as progressive modernist, radical modernist, conservative postmodernist, or radical postmodernist, these four terms do name specific aesthetic positions—not to create a taxonomy but to identify ideas that have informed twentieth-century composition in varying ways and in varying degrees.

It can also be difficult to distinguish conservative postmodernism from antimodernism, in which artists try to return nostalgically to what is perceived as a golden age before the advent of modernism.[14] "New Romantic" works like Rochberg's

---

[12] McNeilly, "Ugly Beauty," para. 3.

[13] Jean-Jacques Nattiez discusses several other examples of contemporary composers' studying past works in order to find antecedents and justifications for their own compositional procedures: Boulez analyzing *The Rite of Spring* and a Debussy etude, Berg studying Schumann's *Träumerei*, and Pousseur writing on Schumann's *Dichterliebe*. See *Music and Discourse: Toward a Semiology of Music*, trans. Carolyn Abbate (Princeton: Princeton University Press, 1990), pp. 183–5.

[14] Andreas Huyssen writes about "postmodern nostalgia ... [as a] sentimental return to a time when art was still art. But what distinguishes this nostalgia from the 'real thing,' and what ultimately makes it anti-modernist, is its loss of irony, reflexiveness and self-doubt, its cheerful abandonment of a critical consciousness, its ostentatious self-consciousness," *After the Great Divide*, p. 180.

In his discussion of what he feels are the contradictions in the antimodernist aesthetic, Peter Bürger paints a picture of antimodernism that makes it look something like right-wing fundamentalist political extremism: "Since the anti-modern version of the post-modern theorem can preserve

Ricordanza, Easley Blackwood's Cello Sonata, and Michael Torke's piano concerto *Bronze*—all of which are almost indistinguishable from nineteenth-century music—are extreme examples; several pieces of David del Tredici, Ellen Zwilich, Joel Feigin, Paul Alan Levi, and Stefania de Kenessey also qualify, as do some recent compositions of Krzysztof Penderecki (such as his Second Violin Concerto).

One intriguing aspect of antimodernism is the way its composers seem to return, to some extent, to styles they were expected to master as students and then expected to abandon as young professionals. Although traditional pedagogy in harmony and counterpoint is usually presented to students as necessary steps in the building of their craft, it is surely true that several composers maintain a nostalgia for composing the tonal music they spent years mastering. John Rea has written perceptively on this issue:

> The composer who in his professional life flirts openly with counterfeits and simulacra—openly, since postmodern artists are above all honest if not naïve—does so because it may be economically advantageous, and because he is capable of regressing to an earlier stage of psychotechnical development, to the apprenticeship studies that had obliged him to *faire semblant* (working with models and outmoded paradigms) before passing on to the stage of perfection courses, those dealing with autonomous creativity and authenticity. Not surprising then that, especially at the end of the twentieth century, postmodern artists seem to be suffering a form of arrested development. In giving spectators and audiences unusual new copies of their old school book studies, they also are either dissimulating voluntarily or exposing involuntarily their genuine selves. So an artist takes to symbolically wearing masks or carrying iconic images.[15]

Both postmodern and antimodern aesthetics reject some of the sounds and procedures of modernism and embrace some of the sounds of music from the past, but there are decided differences in aesthetic attitudes and in the ways those sounds are put together. To complicate the matter further, aspects of postmodernism, modernism, and antimodernism sometimes occur in the works of one composer (Berio and Penderecki, for example). Thus the terminology offered here is useful only as an overview, not as a taxonomic means to place individual works or composers into convenient "isms." Classifications and oppositions, fuzzy as their boundaries may be, do relate to real cultural divisions, however. These categories have exerted a discernible influence on composers and listeners, and to some extent recent music has participated in shaping the categories. Thus the relevance to music of these dichotomies is undeniable.[16]

---

nothing of modernism, it comes to contradict its conservative self-understanding. That unmasks it as a badly secured polemical position which has nothing to contribute to the comprehension of the possibility of art today." See *The Decline of Modernism*, trans. Nicholas Walker (University Park: Pennsylvania State University Press, 1992), pp. 42–3.

[15] Rea, "Postmodernisms."

[16] For a useful discussion of the difficulties yet necessity of categorization, especially as exemplified by a discussion of one particular composer's work, see Keith Potter, "James Dillon: Currents of Development," *Musical Times* 131 (1990): 253–60. Dillon's compositions—such as the piano piece

The coexistence of latter-day musical modernism, antimodernism, and postmodernism is not particularly cordial. Cultural critic Andreas Huyssen describes these categories in terms of dominant trends in thinking in three recent decades in America:

> In the American debate, three positions can be schematically outlined. Postmodernism is dismissed outright as a fraud and modernism held up as the universal truth, a view which reflects the thinking of the 1950s. Or modernism is condemned as elitist and postmodernism praised as populist, a view which reflects the thinking of the 1960s. Or there is the truly 1970s proposition that "anything goes," which ... recognizes that the older dichotomies have lost much of their meaning.[17]

Several of today's modernists—whether they are composers who continue to create in a modernist style, performers who play mostly modernist music, or reviewers who praise only modernist music—scornfully dismiss postmodernism, in which they see a rejection not only of modernism's purity and austerity but also of the cultural relevance (which should not be confused with popular acceptance) that modernism once had. Hal Foster writes of "a modernism long ago purged of its subversive elements and set up as official culture in the museums, the music halls, the magazines";[18] and, we might add, in musical academia and in the awarding of composition grants and prizes. Since in my experience latter-day modernists generally do not recognize a difference between radical and conservative postmodernism, they reject all postmodern music as conservative, superficial, simplistic, pandering to popular taste, and—ironically, from my point of view—disunified.[19]

Spleen—belong to the so-called "new complexity" school and yet exhibit decidedly postmodern characteristics, including some wonderfully imaginative non-sequiturs and occasional unexpected references to vernacular music. See also Arnold Whittall, "Complexity, Capitulationism, and the Language of Criticism," *Contact* 33 (1988): 20–3.

[17] Huyssen, *After the Great Divide*, p. 202. See also Madan Sarup, *An Introductory Guide to Poststructuralism and Postmodernism* (Athens, GA: University of Georgia Press, 1989), p. 131. Foster, in contrast to Huyssen, questions the identification of postmodernism with populism: "to a great degree ... postmodernism seems a front for a rapprochement with the market and the public—an embrace that, far from populist (as is so commonly claimed), is alternately elitist in its allusions and manipulative in its clichés," *Recodings*, p. 122. Many postmodernist composers claim to be striving for a new rapprochement with their audiences, but significantly the public they seek is not that of the working class (as was sought both by the 1930s' American populism of Copland and others and by Soviet composers working under the dictates of Socialist Realism) but that of the symphony-going, grant-giving social elite. Edwards discusses this "opportunism" briefly in "Music and Postmodernism," *Partisan Review* 58 (1991): 704–5. Also relevant is the question of how readily listeners can assimilate the nontonal structures of modernist music vs. those of tonal (or, by extension, neotonal) music. See Fred Lerdahl, "Cognitive Constraints on Compositional Procedures," in John Sloboda (ed.), *Generative Processes in Music: The Psychology of Performance, Improvisation, and Composition* (New York: Clarendon, 1988), pp. 231–59.

[18] *Recodings*, p. 125.

[19] Huyssen (p. 199) discusses the way modernist critics confuse radical postmodernism with conservatism: critics "took them to be compatible with each other or even identical, arguing that [radical] postmodernism was the kind of affirmative art that could happily coexist with political and cultural neoclassicism. Until very recently, the question of the postmodern was simply not taken seriously on the left, not to speak of those traditionalists in the academy or museum for whom there is still nothing new and worthwhile under the sun since the advent of modernism."

The continued viability of modernism is evident in both late twentieth-century music and polemics by its composers. In the latter category is a 1984 article by German composer York Höller. Höller's music, at least from the time of this article, adheres to a modernist aesthetic. Yet his vehement defense of the meta-narrative of organicism is certainly conservative:

> The work of art seems to me to be above all an *organism*, like an organico-energizing system, comparable to a living organism in nature. In such a system, all elements are linked by functional relations; they do not result from arbitrary formulation, but from the evolution of a process.[20]

Höller takes as desirable the "congruence" between top-down and bottom-up generative processes of composition, and he assumes that this congruence is "a guarantee of the quality of a musical work."[21] As he goes on, he reveals an attitude toward musical organicism that is markedly close to Schoenberg's views (discussed in Sections 5.2 and 5.4). Höller typifies a group of middle-aged modernists who are working to preserve the organicist aesthetic of the preceding generation. In the topsy-turvy world of postmodernism, we find a composer like Höller—whose music uses many of the techniques and devices of high modernism—espousing a conservative aesthetic, while the beliefs of radical postmodernists are often actualized in music of almost (but never quite) comfortable consonance and pseudo-tonality.

Consonance and tonality do not in themselves guarantee a postmodern aesthetic, however. Some pathbreaking early minimalist works strike me as just as much—or even more—modernist than postmodernist. The purity, the strong statement, and the radical newness of such pieces as Steve Reich's *Violin Phase* or Philip Glass's *Music in Fifths* are thoroughly modern, even if their use of triadic sonorities, diatonic lines, and regular rhythms suggests antimodernism. These composers' attempts to define a new kind of music are similar in spirit to early twentieth-century experiments, even though the actual music is dissimilar to early atonality. Significantly, early minimalist music is thoroughly unified, and sometimes even pervasively organic: consider the way Reich's *Four Organs* grows inexorably from its initial material.

Perhaps the grandest achievement of early minimalism is Glass's first opera, *Einstein on the Beach*, written in collaboration with Robert Wilson and already discussed briefly in Section 2.7. Its attempt to redefine opera and to create a new kind of musical theater are modernist aspects of *Einstein*, as are the austerity and purity of both the music and the staging. But there are also underlying postmodern sensibilities: the diatonicism, the repetitions, the gestures toward popular music, the anti-elitism. Yet *Einstein* is as structurally unified as any modernist work. There are large-scale musical recapitulations, each scene is motivically consistent, and there are recurrent visual (such as the ubiquitous oblong and the finger dancing) as well as musical motives.

---

[20] York Höller, "Composition of the Gestalt, or the Making of the Organism," *Contemporary Music Review* 1 (1984): 35. Street ("Superior Myths, Dogmatic Allegories: The Resistance to Musical Unity," *Music Analysis* 8 (1989): 78) discusses this article briefly.

[21] Höller, pp. 35–6.

If minimalist diatonicism and repetition can produce works rich in both modernist and postmodernist aspects, then it is hardly surprising that it can be misguided to try to untangle modern and postmodern aesthetic attitudes. A further source of confusion between these two stances is the use of collage and pastiche in both modernist and postmodernist compositions. There is a difference, however. While postmodern music's appropriation of the historically (trait 3) and culturally (trait 6) remote is fundamentally ironic (trait 2), the irony often does not work primarily through distortion.[22] Whereas modernist composers felt they had to alter what they quoted or referred to in order to demonstrate (1) their power over it, (2) their control of the past, and (3) perhaps subconsciously even their music's superiority to that of the past, postmodernists often do not feel in competition with the past. The past is indistinguishable from the present for them (trait 3). Ives' wrong notes are therefore more modernist than postmodernist: he asserted his power over the classical and folk sources he used. Stravinsky's distortion (in *Pulcinella)* of music he thought to be by Pergolesi was similarly modernist in spirit, as was his denigration of the earlier composer. Another example of a piece in which the composer appropriated and distorted an earlier composer's works is Hindemith's *Symphonic Metamorphosis of Themes of Carl Maria von Weber.* Hindemith freely admitted that he had chosen Weber's weakest music, thereby possibly exonerating himself of guilt over having harmed any of Weber's important compositions. Even Tchaikovsky was more modernist than postmodernist when he chose Mozart's weakest music to adapt as his Fourth Orchestral Suite.[23] Despite his statements of admiration for his predecessor,

---

[22] In an article that is essentially an earlier version of Chapters 4–6, I state that postmodern music is not ironic. I now feel that idea to be quite wrong. For my earlier formulation see "Beyond Unity: Postmodernism in Music and Music Theory," Elizabeth West Marvin and Richard Hermann (eds.), *Concert Music, Rock, and Jazz Since 1945: Essays and Analytical Studies* (Rochester: University of Rochester Press, 1995), p. 26.

[23] Tchaikovsky chose a tiny homage to another composer that Mozart had tossed off in an hour, an incomplete minuet, a distorted Mozart transcription by Liszt, and an improvised set of variations on a theme of yet another composer. Could Tchaikovsky really have been motivated, as he claimed to be, only by a sense of wanting to preserve these obscure pieces (Mozart's *Ave Verum Corpus*, which Liszt transcribed, is hardly an obscure Mozart piece, though it was in Tchaikovsky's time, but he tellingly chose to use the Liszt lavish and rather questionable transcription rather than the Mozart original; Tchaikovsky even included Liszt's added introduction and coda, plus numerous small changes in details)? Or did he perhaps want to show that *he* was the one who had saved some minor Mozart works from oblivion? Or that he had rendered them less problematic by orchestrating them in *his* own manner? Perhaps this was Tchaikovsky's way of seeing himself as Mozart's equal, or even of making Mozart seem to owe something to him. It is furthermore significant that Tchaikovsky brought forth this collection as his own Suite Number 4, rather than as four pieces of Mozart that he had arranged. Tchaikovsky's three earlier orchestral suites had been his own music, but now he added another suite of which he was the orchestrator but not the composer. This fact, as much as anything else about this strangely conceived work, shows Tchaikovsky's ambivalent feelings toward a composer who had created some extraordinary music a hundred years earlier.

Tchaikovsky may have recognized in Mozart's music something that was beyond his own grasp: the perfection of form, the ability suggesting profundity within a restrained, understated, elegantly classical style. Perhaps, in making a suite of four Mozart piano pieces orchestrated in his own style, Tchaikovsky subconsciously tried to see himself as an artistic descendant of the Salzburg master. If Tchaikovsky's real purpose had simply been, as he claimed, to make Mozart's piano pieces better known, he might have encouraged pianists to play them more often, rather than painstakingly orchestrating them. But by transferring them to the orchestral medium, where they were not

he needed to demonstrate his superiority over even Mozart, much in the way that Joseph Straus feels Schoenberg acted with regard to Brahms (see Section 5.4). The later composers, as mentioned in Section 1.5, had to overthrow their predecessors, they had (in an Oedipal manner) to kill and replace their spiritual fathers, and they needed to claim victory for the present over the past.

Despite their deep involvement with music of the past, Tchaikovsky, Hindemith, and Stravinsky were acting more as modernists than as postmodernists. A postmodernist would not feel threatened by the past, and would not be in competition with the past. Thus distortion of quoted material tends to be less extreme in some postmodern music, as compared to modernist or some romantic music. All John Zorn's *Forbidden Fruit* does to Mozart's B-Flat Piano Sonata, for example, is to orchestrate it *in Mozart's style* for string quartet. Similarly, William Bolcom's music usually enters into the worlds he quotes. There is often no distancing in postmodern music. Gone is the objectivity of neoclassicism, the so-called homages that do not quite pay homage. Thus a composer like Easley Blackwood really can try (in his Cello Sonata), with utmost seriousness and artistic integrity, to enter the world of late Schubert—not a 1990s' view of the 1840s,[24] but the thing itself.

Blackwood's case represents an extreme but not unreasonable use of the past *as* present, not distinguishing between the two in terms of subject/object or natural/ unnatural. The past is more than quoted. Blackwood's antimodernist music enters into the language of a past style and remains there. The style quotation lasts longer than the brief shock of recognition, longer than the joke of hearing the familiar in an unexpected context. It lasts long enough for the listener to begin to believe in the quoted style, to accept it not as object but as context. Like antimodern music, postmodern music often lets its references be. It does not distort them, or possess them, or comment on them (except by association in context), or pay homage to them, or satirize them. The ultimate irony of postmodernism is that it tries (not always successfully, as we shall see) not to recognize as hierarchic the distinction between past and present (trait 3), between the familiar and exotic (trait 6), between highbrow and lowbrow (trait 4). No style has to be subordinate, nor to be in control, nor to make fun of other idioms. The past exists in the present, is the present—not just a reinterpretation of the past in the present but—again—the thing itself

Once a postmodern composition enters a remote musical world, it may stay there, enjoying itself. A postmodern composer may not feel the need to transform the march (as Mahler and Schoenberg did) or *Ländler* or gigue. Rather, she or he uses these types without apologizing and without distancing through distortion. Not, for example, the modernist stylizations of jazz we find in Ravel, Stravinsky, Milhaud, or Copland, but real jazz (as, for example, in certain pieces of Zorn); not a stylization of

---

destined to gain too many more performances than individual pianists could have given them, he made them his own. They became not simply Mozart's piano music, but Tchaikovsky's interpretation—indeed, appropriation—of Mozart's compositions. The suite's orchestral style does not, after all, imitate Mozart's scoring practices but is distinctly Tchaikovskian in its orchestration.

[24] Blackwood tried to imagine the musical style Schubert would have employed had he lived on until 1845.

rock but (in, for example, compositions of Michael Daugherty, Steve Martland, Daniel Roumain, and Derek Bermel) rock itself. Postmodernism's ironic relationship to the past comes not so much through manipulation or ownership but through acceptance. Postmodernism takes from history, but it often does not interpret, analyze, or revise. It may well remove some of the original connotations of the music quoted, but it then leaves what remains as skeletons, rather than trying to inject new (modern) life into them. As opposed to the artist trying to own the past, postmodernism transfers ownership to the perceiver (trait 16). It follows that the quotations in postmodern music are not defended as acts of homage nearly as readily as modernist quotations were (and are). Postmodern quotations, whether of specific pieces or specific composer's styles,[25] are often simply readings, not "misreadings" (in Bloom's sense of the term—see Section 5.4). Appropriately, literary critic Fredric Jameson refers to the "random cannibalization of all the styles of the past" and the "omnipresence of pastiche."[26]

Modernist quotation takes as a challenge making stylistically foreign elements fit the logic of the music. The power of dissociation, though presumably as palpable to high modernist composers as it is to postmodern listeners today, was rarely considered as paramount. Making the quotation organic was the prime value. Thus Berg was not content simply quoting a Bach chorale in the Violin Concerto[27] or quoting *Tristan* in the *Lyric Suite*.[28] He had to make the quotations serially coherent: he sought unity behind the surface disparity.

These conflicts became vivid when I first lectured at the Summer Courses for Young Composers in Kazimierz Dolny, Poland, under the auspices of the International Society for Contemporary Music (September 1990). I was expected to share several of my compositions. I presented works chronologically, demonstrating my gradual transformation from a 1960s modernist to a 1980s postmodernist. Most of the students had been educated in and were working within the central European tradition of modernism. They found themselves intrigued with my pseudo-serial piano piece from 1968, somewhat interested in my quasi-minimalist works from 1974 (clarinet and electronics) and 1980 (piano), but utterly mystified by a stylistically eclectic orchestral piece from 1987. One student, an Austrian, expressed what he intended as a criticism: all the diverse styles in this piece were presented without irony, without commentary.

---

[25] Pasler discusses recent composers' predilection for quoting the style, if not the music, of Beethoven in particular. See "Postmodernism, Narrativity, and the Art of Memory," pp. 17–18.

[26] Fredric Jameson, *Postmodernism or, the Cultural Logic of Late Capitalism* (Durham, NC: Duke University Press, 1991), p. 18. See also Foster, *Recodings*, pp. 127–8. Linda Hutcheon objects to Jameson's characterization of the cannibalization as random. "There is absolutely nothing random or 'without principle' in the parodic recall and re-examination of the past by architects like Charles Moore or Ricardo Bofill [or, I might add, a composer like Alfred Schnittke]. To incur irony and play is never necessarily to exclude seriousness and purpose in postmodernist art. To misunderstand this is to misunderstand the nature of much contemporary aesthetic production—even if it does make for neater theorizing," *A Poetics of Postmodernism*, p. 27.

[27] See Arnold Whittall's excellent discussion in "The Theorist's Sense of History: Concepts of Contemporaneity in Composition and Analysis," *Journal of the Royal Musical Association* 112/1 (1986–87): 1–20.

[28] See Straus, *Remaking the Past*, pp. 144–8.

They did not fit one of his meta-narratives, namely that musical quotations had to be distorted in some way. I had followed my own meta-narrative, just letting the citations be what they are (I feel that leaving them alone does indeed invoke irony, but he did not see it that way). His attitude was decidedly modernist: the only viable way to incorporate the past into the present is with distortion. This attitude shows one reason why radical postmodernism, at least in music, has met with considerable resistance in Western Europe. Many (certainly not all) contemporary European composers seem unwilling simply to savor unmediated historicist juxtapositions. They feel they must impose order and purpose and hierarchy, even if that happens through ironic commentary and distortion of sources.

Modernist pastiche acknowledges history: the past is reinterpreted in the present. But postmodern pastiche is anti-historical: the past coexists with, and indeed is indistinguishable from, the present (trait 3).[29] Jameson refers to postmodernism's cultural productions as "heaps of fragments" resulting from the "randomly heterogeneous."[30] Madan Sarup discusses Jameson's ideas on pastiche:

> The great modernisms were predicated on the invention of a personal, private style. The modernist aesthetic was originally linked to the conception of an authentic self and a private identity which can be expected to generate its own unique vision of the world and to forge its own unmistakable style. The poststructuralists argue against this; in their view the concept of the unique individual and the theoretical basis of individualism are ideological. ... In a world in which stylistic innovation is no longer possible all that is left, Jameson suggests, is pastiche.[31]

If stylistic innovation is truly no longer possible, if pastiche is all that remains, then all new music must in some sense be quotation. While I am not comfortable with this blanket generalization—I think there is still innovative vitality in several areas of new music: computer, spectral, microtonal, and multicultural composition[32]—it is true that many composers have forsaken the avant-garde quest for novel sounds. They have not,

---

[29] According to critic Madan Sarup (*An Introductory Guide to Poststructuralism and Postmodernism*, p. 145), "There seems to be a refusal to engage with the present or to think historically, a refusal that Jameson regards as characteristic of the 'schizophrenia' of consumer society. He believes that there has been a disappearance of a sense of history. Our entire contemporary social system has little by little begun to lose its capacity to retain its own past; it has begun to live in a perpetual present." Foster discusses the complex relationship between postmodernism and history in *Recodings*, pp. 121–8.

[30] Sarup, *An Introductory Guide to Poststructuralism and Postmodernism*, p. 25.

[31] Ibid., p. 133.

[32] Warren Burt has quite rightly pointed out (in a private communication) that there is also considerable vitality in the creation of new social contexts for new music. He feels furthermore that, despite the widespread influence of Cage, composers are only beginning to explore music that is not dominated by their own egos or by the will to express. I accept Burt's point. The reasons for making music and the social uses of music continue to evolve, as well they should. Burt writes, "These things—ego-problem and context—are *not* extramusical or extra-artistic issues. They are intrinsically *musical* or *artistic* (they absolutely affect the music or art that will be written!) and their avoidance by music, art, literature, architecture, etc., is one of the reasons that the feeling of 'it's all been done' has evolved. These issues were too big and too uncomfortable for the arts, and so the arts ... retreated to the safety of postmodernism's endlessly pluralistic boogie of reiteration and recycling." [Editor's note: this comes from private communication with author.]

however, given up on originality. Originality—of vision, of voice, of expression—is always available to profound artists. It never dries up. It is not dependent on aesthetic position. Original statements can be made in antimodernist styles as well as in avant-gardist styles. Even those composers who do not feel the need of new languages or vocabularies of expression still hope to say something unique. For postmodernists, this uniqueness often comes packaged in references to and/or citations of existing music. Since its materials (although not their combination) are rarely new, postmodern music is therefore often a web of quotations,[33] even when the composer does not consciously intend to refer directly to other musics. In this sense postmodern music, like other recent arts, is profoundly intertextual. While high modernists may have sought to create unique and autonomous compositions, postmodernists understand that all music is inevitably heard in a context shaped by listeners' prior experiences with a vast variety of music.

4.4. Postmodernism and Vernacular Music

Discontinuity and pastiche have been important aspects of some modernist art from early in the twentieth century. Why, then, am I positing fragmentation (trait 10) and pluralism (trait 7) as particularly postmodernist musical phenomena? One reason is that high modernists usually sought to unify their quotations within the new contexts into which they were placing them. Another reason is degree: the discontinuities of modernism can be extreme, but those of the late twentieth-century culture were more so. They were readily accepted to the extent that we have become all but immune to their power. Hardison invokes MTV to exemplify the recent increase of discontinuity:

> When Jean Cocteau used abrupt discontinuities in his surrealist film *Orpheus* the art world was enchanted. How advanced, how outrageous! The discontinuities of *Orpheus* are trivial compared to the discontinuities accepted as the normal mode of television by TV aficionados of the developed world. The psychoanalytic surrealism of *The Cabinet of Dr. Caligari* or of Ingmar Bergman's *Wild Strawberries* is timid compared to the surrealism that teenagers ingest as a daily diet from musical videos, to say nothing of the spectacular happenings that have become standard fare at concerts by popular entertainers like Michael Jackson or Kiss or Madonna.[34]

Like Hardison, Katherine Hayles sees the discontinuities of music videos as quintessentially postmodern. Her ideas can with few changes be adapted to postmodern concert music.

> Turn it on. What do you see? Perhaps demon-like creatures dancing; then a cut to cows grazing in a meadow, in the midst of which a singer with blue hair suddenly

---

[33] Robert P. Morgan discusses the ubiquity of quotation in music of the 1970s and 1980s: "Rethinking Musical Culture," pp. 54–7.
[34] Hardison, *Disappearing Through the Skylight*, pp. 178–9.

appears; then another cut to cars engulfed in flames. In such videos, the images and medium collaborate to create a technological demonstration that any text can be embedded in any context. What are these videos telling us, if not that the disappearance of a stable, universal context *is the context* for postmodern culture?[35]

It is interesting that these two theorists, neither of whom as far as I know has worked as a musician or music scholar, turn to popular music as a prime exemplar of postmodernism. Most writings that address musical postmodernism focus on popular music. Postmodernism has indeed come to pop music with less resistance and less controversy than has surrounded its appearance in that other kind of music which I have been discussing, that type of music that lacks a good name (see Section 2.1) and that lacks a mass audience but that many people nonetheless find quite significant. A study of postmodernism in music—such as this one—that marginalizes pop music is admittedly covering the field in a selective if not idiosyncratic manner. One reason is that the impact of postmodern thinking on classical/concert/serious/art music needs to be studied at least to the extent that postmodernism in pop music has. Another reason is that I am writing about what I know, and I am not a student of popular music or its culture. I do acknowledge the importance of pop music as a cultural force and a cultural barometer, and I readily admit that some pop music is quite sophisticated. I just do not know enough about it to offer in-depth analyses.

I do know, however, that many of the traits of postmodern music listed in Section 1.3 characterize vernacular music. For example, it freely incorporates references to or (thanks to sampling technology—trait 14) quotations of music from distant cultures or periods (trait 6). As George Lipsitz perceptively remarks, "Commercial popular music demonstrates and dramatizes contrasts between places by calling attention to how people from different places create culture in different ways."[36] Furthermore, postmodern pop music is often not overly concerned with unity (trait 11), it can avoid totalizing forms (trait 12), include fragmentations and discontinuities (trait 10), encompass pluralism and eclecticism (trait 7), present multiple meanings and multiple temporalities (trait 13), and locate meaning to some extent in listeners (trait 16). It also, to a significantly greater extent than "classical" music, is a commodity (trait 15). It is a powerful economic force, just as it is subject to economic pressures (see Chapter 10).

Many postmodern composers, trained as either classical or popular musicians or both, seek to weaken the barriers between pop and art music (traits 4 and 5). While the split between these two may have existed for some time,[37] it intensified

---

[35] Hayles, *Chaos Bound*, p. 272.

[36] George Lipsitz, *Dangerous Crossroads: Popular Music, Postmodernism, and the Poetics of Place* (London and New York: Verso, 1994), pp. 3–4

[37] For a brief yet interesting discussion of the split between popular and art music through the ages and the attempts of postmodernists to close the gap, see Kyle Gann, "Boundary Busters: How to Tell New Music from Music that Happens To Be New," *Village Voice* (September 3, 1991): 85–7. Gann's ideas are controversial: other scholars place the popular/art split far more recently than he does. Lawrence W. Levine, for example, demonstrates that in America the split is a product of late nineteenth- and early twentieth-century social conditions. See *Highbrow/Lowbrow: The Emergence of Cultural Hierarchy in America* (Cambridge, MA: Harvard University Press, 1988), pp. 84–168.

in the late nineteenth century (with, for example, the waltzes of Johann Strauss). By the middle of the twentieth century, the alienation of modernism brought the music of the concert hall to its farthest remove from pop music. Their purposes were different, their intended audiences were different, their economics were different, and their musical materials and procedures were different. Postmodernism respects no boundaries, however. Wishing to create a music for individual people rather than for all of humankind (trait 5),[38] some postmodern "classical" composers seek to overthrow the isolation of high culture and to cross-fertilize with mass culture (trait 4). They are happy to cross the line that separates vernacular from art music. In so doing they may create discontinuities as chaotic as those of MTV and more extreme than those in, for example, Stravinsky's *Rite of Spring* or *Symphonies of Wind Instruments*. Crossover music, like Zorn's *Forbidden Fruit* or Rhys Chatham's *The Heart Cries with 1000 Whispers* or many other so-called "downtown" compositions, creates powerful discontinuities that are possible only with the suspension of underlying unity—not only of materials and style but also of musical genre (e.g. pop vs. classical).

In Chatham's seventy-minute work the outer sections consist of quasi-minimalist, quasi-rock music for several amplified guitars. The two inner sections contrast totally in both instrumentation and style. In a thoroughly postmodernist manner, Chatham seems unconcerned about integrating these divergent musics. He seems equally unconcerned with bringing them into confrontation. He simply lets them exist. The listener can relish or ponder or ignore or mentally play with their incompatibility. If a composer of modernist sensibilities were to create a comparably eclectic work, he or she would probably seek ways to unite the diverse styles, or else he or she might bring them into confrontation in order to drive toward their eventual reconciliation, or else he or she might comment on them, thereby distancing the listener from the quotation-like references. But not in Chatham's work, which is postmodern not only in its combination of distinctly different musical traditions but also in its refreshing freedom from the need to unify them.

Consider another quintessentially postmodern composer, William Bolcom. That his career spans the worlds of art, popular, and theater music has surely influenced his eclecticism (trait 7). Works like his Third Symphony are sometimes dismissed by latter-day modernists as sprawling, seemingly random series of unrelated styles. True, the symphony does include modernist passages, vernacular passages, and many styles between those extremes, all within the second movement. That movement is not a hodgepodge but rather a dynamic opposition of seemingly incompatible idioms: one reference/quotation either leads to another quasi-organically, or is starkly juxtaposed to it. This pastiche is no collage! In particular, the opposition of high modernism and American pop music gives the symphony its vitality. While he has not produced a whirlwind like Zorn's *Forbidden Fruit*, Bolcom's subtle mastery of timing and surprise makes the symphony a thorough delight. Its seemingly illogical progressions do, in fact, offer listeners deep meaning, whether the *non sequiturs* are humorous or

---

[38] Harvey, *The Condition of Postmodernity*, p. 40.

poignant. Bolcom juxtaposes different kinds of music without distortion, without commentary.[39]

But the work still is called a symphony, and it is played by a symphony orchestra usually dressed in tails, playing in a traditional concert hall. Despite Bolcom's attempts to make the pop and classical elements of his music coequal, the music is offered to the public as art music with a pop flavor, not as pop music with an art flavor. The references to the vernacular retain a sense of otherness. They are the enticing gestures toward lowbrow music. They are the foreigners, invited into a culture that used to disdain them. How different this symphony would seem if it were orchestrated, performed, and marketed as a pop piece with intertextual references to the classical tradition!

The combination of popular and modernist styles in a single work recalls what architectural critic Charles Jencks calls "double coding," which refers to the dichotomies of new vs. old (trait 3) and of elite vs. popular (trait 5).[40] He favors double coding above any possible attempts to reconcile the vernacular and the modernist. Such a postmodern attitude is in direct contradiction to both modernist and antimodernist dictates of unity in artworks. Another architectural critic, Howard Caygill, relates Jencks' double coding to Adorno's "unresolved contradictions" between the two "spheres" of popular and art music. Adorno felt that these two spheres of music are ultimately incompatible.[41] It remained for postmodernists, in both music and architecture, to, as Caygill puts it, erase the "differences between the profession and the public."[42] After all, postmodern composers seem to be saying, we do listen to popular music and to traditional classical music and to modernist music. Why should their art seek to perpetuate the artificial boundaries between different kinds of music that many people regularly enjoy?

Robert Venturi, yet another architectural critic (and also an important architect), believes in eclectic combinations of vernacular and high art. One of his books is an extended appreciation of the architecture of Las Vegas.[43] In another book he states his own meta-narrative: "I like elements which are hybrid rather than 'pure,' compromising rather than 'clean,' distorted rather than 'straightforward,' ambiguous ... rather than direct and clear. I am for messy variety over obvious unity."[44]

The double coding in music of composers like Bolcom, Chatham, and Zorn may cause certain critics to dismiss these works as lacking order. There is something

---

[39] By his Fifth Symphony, composed ten years later, Bolcom permits these different styles to flow one into the next, allowing the listener to accept the work's diversity rather than confront its oppositions.

[40] Jencks, *What Is Postmodernism?* (London: Academy Editions, 1989), p. 14.

[41] Adorno, "On the Fetish Character in Music and the Regression of Listening," in Arato and Gebhardt (eds.), *The Essential Frankfurt School Reader* (Oxford: Basil Blackwell, 1978), p. 275.

[42] Howard Caygill, "Architectural Postmodernism: The Retreat of an Avant Garde?" in Roy Boyne and Ali Rattansi (eds.), *Postmodernism and Society* (New York: St. Martin's, 1990), p. 285. See also Jameson, *Postmodernism or, the Cultural Logic of Late Capitalism*, pp. 62–3.

[43] Robert Venturi, Denise Scott Brown, and Steven Izenour, *Learning from Las Vegas* (Cambridge, MA: MIT Press, 1972).

[44] Venturi, *Complexity and Contradiction in Architecture* (London: Architectural Press, 1966), as quoted and discussed in Hardison, p. 112.

challenging and possibly disturbing in radical postmodern music's double coding. The eclecticism of such works should not be conflated with poor compositional technique (see Section 11.8), or with pandering to audiences' conservatism, or with an attempt to reinstate compositional values from decades past. As Huyssen writes,

> It is tempting to dismiss this historical eclecticism ... as the cultural equivalent of the neoconservative nostalgia for the good old days and as a manifest sign of the declining rate of creativity in late capitalism. But is this nostalgia for the past ... compatible with the status quo? Or does it perhaps also express some genuine and legitimate dissatisfaction with modernity and the unquestioned belief in the perpetual modernization of art.[45]

Questioning, or even attacking, the previously all but unassailable barrier between pop and art music has energized postmodern music. Whereas there have certainly been modernist composers who enjoy vernacular music, only under the influence of postmodernism have art-music composers invited pop music into ostensibly art-music compositions. In the case of conservative postmodernists, the motivation may have been to reach out to an audience increasingly alienated from the world of serious concert music; in the case of radical postmodernists, the reason may have been to create unsettling and challenging contexts in which different styles confront each other. Despite the rhetoric of some composers and critics, most such crossover music does not cross completely freely from one musical world to another. Postmodernism thrives on otherness, on the recognition that something foreign is being embraced.[46]

---

[45] Huyssen, *After the Great Divide*, p. 185.

[46] John Rea offers a wonderfully varied list of postmodernist crossover music. Notice how, in most instances, the composer or performer's stylistic or aesthetic affinity is on clearly one side of the divide, with foreign elements welcomed in precisely for their otherness, their exoticism: "Yehudi Menuhin playing ragas with Ravi Shankar or improvising hot jazz with Stéphane Grappelli; the Swingle Singers interpreting Bach by scat singing; the Beatles using a sitär in the *Sergeant Pepper* album; the settings of *Folk Songs* by Berio; *Switched-on Bach* for synthesizers, where the arranger/ transcriber would change sex by the time he/she had completed the recording project; any one of the innumerable happenings organized by John Cage; the second movement of György Ligeti's Three Pieces for Two Pianos entitled *Selbstportrait mit Reich und Riley (und Chopin ist auch dabei)*; almost any ensemble in the Early Music movement that, in performing to extremely fast tempi, always leaves the impression that it might as well have played music to accompany a cartoon; jazz pianist Keith Jarrett performing Shostakovich or playing the harpsichord; the Kronos String Quartet, dressed in costume and exploiting rock-'n'-roll theatrical lighting, performing *Purple Haze* by Jimi Hendrix; the Koto Ensemble of Tokyo playing Vivaldi; Pavarotti singing with Dalla and Sting; the symphonies of Philip Glass; the *Liverpool Oratorio* by Paul McCartney; Itzahk Perlman playing klezmer music; Gidon Kremer playing tangos; the Shanghai Film Orchestra playing *In C* by Terry Riley on traditional Chinese instruments; the symphonies of Krzysztof Penderecki; Bobby McFerrin conducting and Chick Corea playing a Mozart piano concerto where the cadenzas are jazz-like improvisations; Belgian singer Helmut Lotti singing classical songs and arias but sounding like Mario Lanza's operatic persona-manqué; American pop singer Neil Diamond singing the Hallelujah Chorus from Handel's *Messiah*; jazz saxophonist Jan Garbarek playing in a church while the Hilliard Ensemble sings Lasso and Palestrina; the English pop music group Oasis, feebly copying the Beatles, including their haircuts; the celebratory *Symphony 1997—Heaven, Earth, Mankind* by Tan Dun, written to mark the transfer of power in Hong Kong from Great Britain to China; the very long symphonic poem, *Standing Stone*, by Sir Paul McCartney, which sounds as if it had been written by Rachmaninoff after having taken LSD; and, finally, cellist Yo-Yo Ma playing tangos," John Rea, "Postmodernisms."

When the pop-art barrier is truly broken down, as it is in some works (e.g. Michael Torke's *Vanada*), some of the tension of postmodernism is lost—lost in favor of a celebration of a new, truly all-inclusive aesthetic of music.

In music which truly mixes high and low, as in music which thoroughly combines styles previously understood as quite different if not inimical, the meta-narrative of musical unity is directly challenged. Even if the music still coheres through motivic or some other kind of consistency, or even if there are careful transitions between styles that bind them together, the kind of unity in a deeply polystylistic piece is different from the kinds of unity our composition students used to, and still do, learn about in the classroom.

Consider Schnittke's *(K)ein Sommernachtstraum.* On one level, we might say that this piece is unified, since there is a musical theme that runs through almost the entire work. Yet there are many different musical styles traversed in the course of the piece's ten minutes. The styles seem, at least to this listener, incompatible, and hence I do not have an experience of overriding unity when I hear this music. Its arrangement into a rondo-like structure—defined by style returns more than by theme returns—can perhaps be understood as the music's desperate, or at least conventional, way to achieve formal unity. It does not matter! Despite the rondo principle, I still have trouble experiencing this stylistically diverse piece as unified. Or, perhaps better stated, the unity I experience is of a different sort from the kinds of musical unity we usually study. An analysis can easily point to this work's unifying devices, but I still hear disunity (along with some unity).

Schnittke is hardly the first composer to employ a variety of idioms within a single piece. Stylistic variety can be found in several of Beethoven's late string quartets, for example, as well as in Mahler symphonies and various works of Ives. It is surely possible to hear some amazing stylistic variety in certain movements of Mozart's piano concertos. But there is a difference. For such earlier composers (Ives may be an exception), styles were contexts within which musical expression unfolds. The diverse styles of a Mahler symphony or a Beethoven quartet or a Mozart concerto are in the service of those work's themes and contrasts. But for a late twentieth-century composer like Schnittke, style becomes something different. In part because so many different musical styles—from all historical periods and all musical cultures—are well known today, style is more like an object than like a context. A composer such as Schnittke plays with style in a way similar to how earlier composers play with themes. In *(Not) A Midsummer Night's Dream* styles are developed, transformed, and contrasted, thereby creating the work's narrative and its structure.

In Schnittke's work, the contrasts are enormous: not so much of melodic material (the opening tune is present throughout much of the work) as of type of music. It is with a sense of sardonic wit that we return again and again to the sunny innocence of the Mozartian opening, realizing more and more each time that its simplicity is not to be believed, because it has always led to a wild array of unexpected sounds.

The Schnittke example underlines how unity is a major issue for postmodernism. Hence we should now turn to a study of just what musical unity is and has been, and to the various ways that postmodernism has been challenging it.

Unity, Organicism, and Challenges to Their Ubiquity

5.1. Unity and the Composer

As a composition teacher, I have often experienced the following: a student appears for his or her weekly lesson with some newly composed material. I notice some problems[1] with it, which I try to explain. The student then defends the questionable passage by pointing to its rigorous derivation from materials composed in previous weeks, as if such derivation guarantees coherence, renders any suspect passage immune to structural problems, and magically makes the composition succeed aesthetically.

Or, in an only slightly different scenario, the student comes into my office and, before I am even allowed to look at the music, proudly explains the motivic derivation or set construction or row generation, as if all his or her hard work in making the composition tight and economical magically also makes it work aesthetically. I find these attitudes extremely hard to combat in most students. Their almost religious belief in the power, utility, and necessity of musical unity starts young and dies hard.

The value many of today's student composers place on unity—and on the related but not identical concept of organicism—should not be surprising. These qualities have been important to composers and to the theorists teaching them at least from the beginning of the nineteenth century and perhaps from the start of the tonal era. Unity has been a meta-narrative of music composition and analysis: it has been accepted as self-evident that good pieces are coherent, consistent, tightly constructed, logical, and parsimonious in their choice of material.[2] These are some of the qualities of musical unity, at least as I have been using the word. All parts of a unified piece are understood to be essential, yet the whole is believed to transcend the sum of its parts. Commentary has routinely praised unity in what was understood to be the greatest music.

Until recently, no one seems to have asked why unity is universally valued in Western music. Yet today we are finding in postmodern music serious challenges

---

[1] I discuss the problematic nature of compositional "problems" in Section 11.8.

[2] Or, as Leonard B. Meyer has written, "A composition is considered to be more coherent and intelligible, more significant and aesthetically valuable, if every pitch and every pattern can be traced to a single germinal cell, and if all relationships can be understood as instantiations of a single, underlying principle or scheme." See "A Pride of Prejudices; or, Delight in Diversity," *Music Theory Spectrum* 13 (1991): 241.

to the necessity of unity (trait 11), and we are beginning to hear calls for analytic methods that are no longer biased toward the elucidation of unity.[3] Before turning to these challenging new concepts, I want to survey—briefly and incompletely—the history of the powerful notion that is under attack by postmodernists.

5.2. The Ubiquity of Unity

Most theorists and composers of the past (at least of the recent past) unquestioningly declared their faith in unity. Webern, for example, felt: "to develop everything else from *one* principal idea! That's the strongest unity."[4] He wrote a seemingly straight-forward definition of musical unity:

> Unity is surely the indispensable thing if meaning is to exist. *Unity, to be general, is the establishment of the utmost relatedness between all component parts.* So in music, as in all other human utterance, the aim is to make as clear as possible the relationships between the parts of the unity; in short, to show how one thing leads to another [emphasis added].[5]

Even this direct definition is not devoid of nagging questions, however. Just what *is* "relatedness," for example? Who determines whether "parts" are interrelated—the composer, the analyst, the performer, or the listener? Is relatedness an observable fact, is it a subjective impression, or is it an experience? These are the kinds of questions that postmodern music analysts and theorists are beginning to ask.

Webern's definition is typical of twentieth-century modernist thought. The nineteenth century accepted a weaker concept of unity: a work was thought to be unified if all its parts were understandable in relation to the whole.[6] The twentieth-century idea that the parts had to be related not only to the whole but also to each other is a stronger condition. Since we will be concerned largely with modernist ideas on unity, we will initially accept Webern's stronger formulation. A piece of music is said to be thoroughly unified if all its parts are related to each other and to the whole,

---

[3]   Among the recent challenges to the ubiquity of unity in music analysis are Fred Everett Maus, "Concepts of Musical Unity," in Nicholas Cook and Mark Everist (eds.), *Rethinking Music* (Oxford, UK and New York: Oxford University Press, 1999), pp. 171–92; and Joseph Dubiel, "Hearing, Remembering, Cold Storage, Purism, Evidence, and Attitude Adjustment," *Current Musicology* 60/61 (1996): 26–50.

[4]   Anton Webern, *The Path to the New Music*, trans. Leo Black (Bryn Mawr, PA: Theodore Presser, 1963), p. 35.

[5]   Ibid., p. 42. This passage is discussed in Alan Street, "Superior Myths, Dogmatic Allegories: The Resistance to Musical Unity," *Music Analysis* 8 (1989): 77–8.

[6]   I am indebted on this point to Karen Painter. She quotes Riemann on the parts of a unified work cohering into the whole: "No art can do without form, which is nothing other than the joining together of the parts of an artwork into a uniform whole," Hugo Riemann, *Lexikon* (Mainz: Schott, 1967), p. 420. Nicholas Cook offers a more hierarchic version of the nineteenth-century conception of musical unity: "Most musical analyses can be viewed as attempts to demonstrate specific ways in which the overall structure of a composition lends significance to its smaller-scale events," *Music, Imagination, and Culture*, p. 41.

if all unexpected events are retrospectively integrated into the logic of the piece, if there are structural principles that apply to the entire work, and if the music seems to be ordered, consistent, and coherent. By accepting such a definition, we add to rather than answer or bypass the nagging questions. How does a part relate to the whole? Is it imaginable for a part not to relate to the whole? How can unexpected events be subsequently integrated? Where and how would such integration take place? How can we tell if a piece is consistent? Or coherent? Coherent to whom, under what conditions? If a work is judged incoherent, why does that mean that it is disunified rather than that the critic simply does not understand it? I am starting with Webern's definition, despite all the unanswered questions it calls forth, not because I find it unproblematic but because it represents a typical formulation, one that many of those who have unquestioningly accepted the idea would no doubt approve.

A typical statement on the value of musical unity is found in philosopher Roman Ingarden's "The Question of the Unity of a Musical Work," a chapter from his book *The Work of Music and the Problem of its Identity*, first published in 1966. Ingarden posits "an organized totality in which specific parts belong to each other. In the case of the *best possible composition*, they *postulate* each other or they fulfill the postulates of other parts constituting their fulfillment or completion" [emphasis added].[7] Ingarden does not concern himself with *how* one part of a piece "postulates" another, nor does he consider whether a so-called "best possible composition" is so because of its high degree of unity, or whether a work determined in some other way to be a "best possible composition" will necessarily be highly unified.

For Ingarden any piece lacking in unity is bad. Significantly, he does not cite any examples of disunified music. Instead he constructs hypothetical examples, such as a symphony comprised of the first movement of Beethoven's Fifth followed by a symphonic poem by Debussy, a toccata by J. S. Bach, and an orchestral transcription of an aria from *Madame Butterfly*. He comments, "The total absence of any connection between the putative movements of this kind of 'symphony,' the glaring incompatibility of styles, of atmosphere, of texture and so on, are so profound that surely no one would acknowledge the artistic unity of this amalgam of differing products."[8] While it is true that we may not acknowledge the unity of such a composition, we may nonetheless enjoy its juxtapositions of "incompatible" styles or moods.

Ingarden also scornfully hypothesizes a work made up of the first bars of all the Chopin preludes, played in succession.[9] Ironically, both of his constructed examples, the worthlessness of which he takes to be self-evident, could be serious compositions today. Indeed, software companies are selling digitally recorded excerpts to self-styled composer-arrangers, who are encouraged to string them together in any way they wish to produce their "own" works.[10]

---

[7] Roman Ingarden, *The Work of Music and the Problem of Its Identity*, trans. Adam Czerniawski (Berkeley and Los Angeles: University of California Press, 1986), p. 132.
[8] Ibid., p. 136.
[9] Ibid., p. 129.
[10] See, for example, Edwin Wilson, "Authors' Rights in the Superhighway Era," *Wall Street Journal* 25 January 1995, p. A14.

5.3. Synchronic and Diachronic Unity

The concept of music unity is often conflated with that of organicism. But there are distinctions. A piece is said to be not only unified but also organic if it grows in a teleological, connected, motivated progression from beginning to end. Perhaps the most articulate twentieth-century advocate of organicism in music was Schoenberg:

> A real composer does not compose merely one or more themes, but a whole piece. In an apple tree's blossoms, even in the bud, the whole future apple is present in all its details—they have only to mature, to grow, to become the apple, the apple tree, and its power of reproduction. Similarly, a real composer's musical conception, like the physical, is one single act, comprising the totality of the product. The form in its outline, characteristics of tempo, dynamics, moods of the main and subordinate ideas, their relation, derivation, their contrasts and deviations—all these are there at once, though in embryonic state. The ultimate formulation of the melodies, themes, rhythms, and many details will subsequently develop through the generating power of the germs.[11]

The distinction between unity and organicism is parallel to that between synchrony and diachrony.[12] An analysis that elucidates synchronic unity looks for consistencies that pervade a work, with little regard for their temporal sequence or for the manner in which they might develop during the course of the music. To notice the pervasiveness of the opening motives throughout Beethoven's Fifth Symphony or Violin Concerto,

---

[11] Arnold Schoenberg, *Style and Idea*, ed. Leonard Stein (Berkeley and Los Angeles: University of California Press, 1984), p. 165. This passage is discussed in Meyer, *Style and Music*, pp. 334–5, and in David Epstein, *Beyond Orpheus* (Cambridge, MA: MIT Press, 1979), p. 19. Schoenberg did not believe that a composition simply grows from a source motive, however. He criticized as "sentimental poeticizing" the notion that "a composition might arise from the motive as kernel of the whole, as a plant from a seed. This is a childish notion, quite apart from the fact that it neither questions nor answers the problem that next arises: where does the seed come from, and what is it?" This quotation appears in Arnold Schoenberg, *The Musical Idea and the Logic, Technique, and Art of Its Presentation*, edited, translated, and with a commentary by Patricia Carpenter and Severine Neff (New York: Columbia University Press, 1995).

[12] These terms originated with the early twentieth-century French linguist Ferdinand Saussure. Diachronic relationships are temporally ordered. For example, the words of this sentence are meaningful in relation to one another, and the sentence builds its meaning as it adds on more words, in a specific order. Synchronic relationships are atemporal, and they encompass the whole. Whether or not they appear in a sentence, words derive their meanings from their relationships to other words. For a fuller explanation, see Terence Hawkes, *Structuralism and Semiotics* (London: Methuen, 1977), pp. 20–7. For a brief discussion of diachronic and synchronic conceptions of music, see V. Kofi Agawu, *Playing with Signs: A Semiotic Interpretation of Classic Music* (Princeton: Princeton University Press, 1991), p. 15. These two terms recall what I have labeled, respectively, linear and nonlinear relationships. See Jonathan D. Kramer, *The Time of Music*, pp. 20–2. Also relevant is John Rahn's distinction between in-time vs. time-out explanations of music: "At the in-time extreme is an obsessive concern for the way in which, *at every musical time*, events immediately following that time grow out of events preceding that time. ... At the other extreme (time-out) lie explanations exposing only 'syntactical' or systematic relations, without at all accounting for the disposition of these relations in time, let alone their role in a temporally evolving process." See Rahn, "Aspects of Musical Explanation," *Perspectives of New Music* 17/2 (1979): 213. Other theorists invoke the similar dichotomies syntagmatic/paradigmatic, spatial/temporal, and metaphor/metonymy.

for example, is to elucidate the music's synchronic unity. Such an analysis assumes that the music is unified and then shows that this is so because the motive is found on virtually every page of the score (I will have more to say later about analysis of scores as opposed to performances).

According to Leonard Meyer,

> In [synchronic] thematic transformation, the various versions of a motive, though necessarily successive in practice, are really regarded as members of a temporally unordered class or set. Of course in actual musical composition, the versions of a motive *are* ordered, and this ordering shapes aesthetic experience. ... Most theorists and composers who have discussed motivic unity have adopted the synchronic position; that is, they have explained how the variants of a motive or theme are related to one another—or to some abstracted, imaginary pattern from which the variants are derived—by arguing for their classlike conformance. The diachronic interpretation [by contrast] considers that motivic unity involves a process of gradual growth, development, and variation.[13]

In Webern's definition of musical unity, quoted above, the "utmost relatedness between all component parts" invokes synchronic unity, while "how one thing leads to another" refers to diachronic unity. An analysis of diachronic unity would not so much focus on consistencies as show how a work grows from temporally prior fundamental materials. Thus diachronic unity is essentially equivalent to organicism. To the extent that a synchronic analysis considers growth in any sense, the priority of the source(s) is conceptual, not temporal.[14] In its extreme form, diachronic unity need not entail similarity of materials but rather their constant transformation.[15]

Particularly instructive examples of diachronic unity can be found in several compositions of Fred Lerdahl, such as *Cross-Currents, Fantasy Etudes,* and the two

---

[13] *Style and Music* (Chicago and London: University of Chicago Press, 1997), p. 332. See also p. 41, and "A Pride of Prejudices," p. 244. The concept of derivation of some event from some earlier event is problematic. Who does the deriving? The composer, the listener, the performer (by "bringing out" the similarity), or—metaphorically—the music itself? Interestingly, the verb "to derive" is used mostly in the passive voice when referring to music. Few people—except for the students mentioned at the outset of this chapter, who know very well who does the deriving—seem concerned about the agent of musical derivation.

[14] Nadine Hubbs offers a classification of the attributes of organicism similar to the synchronic/diachronic dichotomy. Among factors contributing to the "unity of parts and whole" (which parallels synchronic unity) she lists necessary form, essential permeation (by which she means that each part reveals the whole), and the whole being greater than the sum of its parts; among factors contributing to "growth" (which corresponds to diachronic unity) she lists metamorphosis and teleology. Hubbs's "Schoenberg's Organicism" presents a thorough historical review of the concept of organicism. It appears in *Theory and Practice* 16 (1991): 143–62. William A. Pastille offers a similar opposition between holism and unity on the one hand, and growth and development on the other. Pastille's formulation is found in "Heinrich Schenker, Anti-Organicist," *Nineteenth-Century Music* 8 (1984): 32. See also Severine Neff, "Schoenberg and Goethe: Organicism and Analysis," in *Music Theory and Its Exploration of the Past,* ed. David Bernstein and Christopher Hatch (Chicago: University of Chicago Press, 1992), pp. 501–22.

[15] According to Meyer, "Coherence by similarity of kind or class is perhaps the least organic sort of unity. ... But an organism ... is an integrated whole precisely because its component parts ... perform different, complementary functions," "A Pride of Prejudices," p. 244.

string quartets. In these works Lerdahl uses a procedure he calls "expanding variations," whereby a small, basic figure is progressively lengthened, eventually achieving
an elaborated shape that may be quite different in its surface manifestations from the
original kernel.

5.4. Unity and Organicism in Schoenberg

Diachronic unity—organicism—was highly valued throughout the nineteenth
century.[16] The concept of organicism also pervaded the ideas of many early twentieth-
century composers and theorists. The above quotation from Schoenberg's *Style and
Idea* is particularly eloquent: Schoenberg was obsessed with organic growth. As Joseph
Straus points out in his book *Remaking the Past*, Schoenberg's analysis of tonal music,
particularly that of Brahms, in terms of motivic organicism

> derives its coherence primarily from the density and richness of its motivic
> structure. ... By analyzing Brahms in this way, by motivicizing him, Schoenberg
> accomplishes two related aims. First, he establishes a link between his music and
> Brahms's. He thus justifies his own music by showing that its structural principles
> are not revolutionary but are hallowed by tradition. Second, he attempts to
> neutralize Brahms as a threat to his compositional autonomy. ... Instead of seeing
> himself as the weak descendent of Brahms, Schoenberg tries to depict Brahms as
> a prototypical Schoenberg. When Schoenberg analyzes Brahms, he is not dispas-
> sionately and neutrally revealing musical structure; he is passionately struggling
> ... to see himself not as the latest and least of a dwindling line, but as the culmi-
> nation of all that has come before.[17]

Straus's ideas derive from literary critic Harold Bloom's concept of "misreading,"[18]
which Straus applies to Schoenberg's understanding of the works of Brahms.

---

[16] See Ruth A. Solie's influential article "The Living Work: Organicism and Musical Analysis,"
Nineteenth-Century Music 4 (1980): 147–56. Also, Brian Hyer discusses the confusion in some
nineteenth-century thinkers between a work being like an organism and a work actually being
organic. See Chapter 3 of *Figuring Music* (Cambridge, UK: Cambridge University Press, 2002).

[17] Joseph N. Straus, *Remaking the Past*, pp. 29–31. Straus claims that Schoenberg's obsession with
the motive took precedence over his concern with harmony and voice leading. Severine Neff has
pointed out (in a personal communication) that there are many Schoenberg analyses that do justice
to voice leading (conceived in his own peculiar manner) and harmony. Furthermore, Neff suggests
that Schoenberg's attitude towards Brahms, whose life overlapped his own, was different from his
feelings towards Bach, Beethoven, and Mozart, with whom he probably felt not competition but
unlimited respect. Schoenberg probably did not see himself as the culmination of *all* that preceded
him; he probably saw Bach as the pinnacle of German music. But he did apparently consider
Brahms a father figure, whom he felt he had to supplant.

[18] Bloom's ideas are set forth in several books, including *The Anxiety of Influence* (New York: Oxford
University Press, 1973). See also Kevin Korsyn, "Towards a New Poetics of Musical Influence," *Music
Analysis* 10 (1991): 3–72, and Michael Cherlin, "Musical Imagination and Other Fictions: Literary
Trope as Musical Process," paper read to the joint conference of the American Musicological
Society, Society for Music Theory, and Society for Ethnomusicology, Oakland, CA, November 1990.

Bloom considers misreading a particularly powerful form of interpretation in which later poets assert artistic freedom from a precursor's domination by using the precursor's work for their own artistic ends. To read is to be dominated; to misread is to assert one's own priority, as the later poet does by making the earlier poet say what the later poet wants or needs to hear. Misreadings are *not* failed or inadequate interpretations. In fact, misreadings are usually the most interesting interpretations. A misreading is distinguished from a simple reading precisely by its power to revise.[19]

Although a composer whose music has been "misread" might vehemently disagree with the analyst or composer who has taken over his or her work, a "misreading" is not a mistaken reading. It is a prejudiced interpretation—not an objective understanding—by a creative mind. A "misreading" may be incompatible with the composer's cultural or artistic values, but it would reflect the intellectual ideals of the analyst and of his or her times. Some of Peter Sellars's opera productions, and some of Glenn Gould's keyboard interpretations, are good examples of "misreadings": they are powerful, original, and creative, even if they are not overly concerned with fidelity to the composers' apparent intentions.

The mechanism by which Schoenberg misread Brahms's subtle and sophisticated motivic transformations was the *Grundgestalt*. Although he wrote little directly about this concept, it was of fundamental importance to his thinking. Despite some vagueness about the nature of the *Grundgestalt*, or basic shape,[20] he took it to be the technical means of realizing what he called the piece's *Gedanke* or fundamental idea.[21] The relationship between Schoenberg's prejudiced "misreading" of tonal organicism and his own compositional procedures can be readily appreciated if we view the row as something like a *Grundgestalt*: an abstract principle from which come not only all the work's melodies and harmonies but its very essence. Not only the whole but also every last detail is row-derived; nothing is merely ornamental.[22] The row pervades the musical space of the work, horizontally and vertically. Through the row the work becomes unified, although it is certainly not the case that the row guarantees unity.

---

[19] Straus, *Remaking the Past*, p. 14.

[20] For useful discussions of the *Grundgestalt* concept, see Patricia Carpenter, "*Grundgestalt* as Tonal Function," *Music Theory Spectrum* 5 (1983): 15–38; David Epstein, *Beyond Orpheus* (Cambridge, MA: MIT Press, 1979), pp. 17–21, 207–11; Walter Frisch, *Brahms and the Principle of Developing Variation* (Berkeley and Los Angeles: University of California Press, 1984), pp. 1–34; and Carl Dahlhaus, *Schoenberg and the New Music*, trans. Derrick Puffett and Alfred Clayton (Cambridge: Cambridge University Press, 1987), pp. 128–33.

[21] I am indebted to Severine Neff for several useful discussions of the *Grundgestalt*.

[22] This alleged lack of ornamentation may suggest a limitation of the twelve-tone method, but it is not as extreme in realization as it is in conception. Filler, ornamentation, quasi-passing and neighbor tones, etc., are still possible, but the composer must work hard to make them function within the twelve-tone universe, because the working premise of the system (its meta-narrative) is that every note belongs to the row and hence is equal in conceptual importance. The key to successful twelve-tone composition lies in respecting its anti-hierarchical basis, while creating on the surface a meaningful hierarchy of degrees of functional importance among tones. The tension inherent in this apparent contradiction has something to do with the intensity of a lot of twelve-tone music (e.g. that of Schoenberg, Berg, Martino, Wuorinen, and many others).

The row is the means by which a twelve-tone composer exercises craft in the service of unity.

5.5. Unity and Organicism after Schoenberg

Schoenberg's analytic work emphasizes motivic unity and diachronic organicism in the music of Brahms in order to cast that music as antecedent to Schoenberg's own. Later twentieth-century theorists have acted similarly: they have taken prejudiced views of the music they studied because of their own obsession with unity. They have searched for consistency of motives or sets or proportions or whatever until they have found it. Joseph Straus's analytic agenda, for example, is as prejudiced as Schoenberg's. Straus accepts analyses of late romantic music from the viewpoint of motivic saturation, yet he relegates the motive to a secondary status in comparison with voice leading, and he embraces Allen Forte's set-theoretic apparatus—all because doing so suits his analytic purposes. But this is as much and as creative a "misreading" as Schoenberg's studies of Brahms's motivic transformations. Straus's goals are theoretical rather than compositional, but his views are thereby no less a distortion (or, in Straus's own terms, a revision) of a body of music for specific purposes. He, as well as others, was drawn to analyzing late romantic and early atonal music from the viewpoint of "motivici-zation" because casting this music in such a light validates the assumptions underlying some theorists' most cherished analytic methods: motivic, *Grundgestalt*, developing variation, set-theoretic. Set theory may be the most nearly objective of analytic strategies, but even it is based on (often unstated) assumptions the adoption of which is anything but objective. Most set theorists use quasi-scientific analytic methodologies because they believe that the atonal music they study is unified and because they believe that the unity comes, at least in part, from an elegant interweaving of abstract pitch-class sets.[23] The near-total separation of unity from audibility in such pitch-class-set analyses marks an extreme of modernist theoretical thought (although, as I argue in Section 7.2, footnote 17, it has elements of the postmodern as well). It represents a deification of structure.

Set theorists are not the only analysts who engage in "misreading." Indeed, "misreading" is not exclusively an activity of modernists. When I, for example, hear in compositions of Ives, Nielsen, Mahler, or Beethoven something that strikes me as postmodern, I am being selective in what and how I choose to observe. Just as Schoenberg made Brahms into a precursor of Schoenberg, I am making these composers into precursors of contemporary postmodernism. Of course my analyses are prejudiced; of course they distort the music they study; of course they are influenced by my own cultural and personal values. It is impossible to divorce the analyst from the analysis.

---

[23] Even analyses that uncover a large number of set types in a given work are usually oriented toward unity, as analysts strive to show the interrelatedness or similarity among the most pervasive set types.

"Misreading" in order to discover postmodernism in certain works from the past helps to validate new ideas by showing how they are, in fact, not new. It hardly matters that Ives, Nielsen, Mahler, et al., probably did not think like postmodernists. For whatever reasons, they produced some music that, listened to today, can be understood in terms of ideas that many late twentieth-century and early twenty-first-century composers are now embracing.

The situation in music is not unlike that in the visual arts, where, as Silvio Gaggi has shown, numerous critics and artists[24] have found validation of their postmodernist ideas in their creative "misreadings" of Diego Velazquez's 1656 painting *Las Meninas*.[25] Similarly, Gaggi discusses how Borges, Foucault, and others have found something akin to postmodernism in Cervantes's novel *Don Quixote*.[26] In Chapters 12 and 13, I offer detailed accounts of pieces by Mahler and Nielsen, which—through my own misreading—I show to be early instances of musical postmodernism.

Theorists and composers have engaged in creative "misreadings" for generations. Some modernist composers (mostly in America), for example, saw in the music of Schoenberg, just as other modernists (mostly in Europe) saw in the music of Webern, prototypes for extension of the serial principle. The approach to the control[27] of time, dynamics, timbre, etc., was very different in the music of Babbitt and Wuorinen on the one hand and of Boulez, Krenek, Nono, and Stockhausen on the other, but all these generalizations can be understood as outgrowths of "misreadings" of classical serialism.

What these later composers needed to find was validation of their music as an extension of that of Schoenberg or Webern. Indeed, their music *is* unified, at least on paper, in an even more thorough way than that of Schoenberg and Webern. The unity may be less obvious in the perception than in the precompositional plans and postcompositional analyses by the composers and/or their students, but it was demonstrably *there*, in the score.[28]

Thus validated by a discovered or constructed historical linearity, the idea of total unity became quite seductive. But late modernists embracing "total" serialism seem to have been little concerned that unity had in their works become synchronic, that it had moved far from Schoenberg's organicism. Most "totally" serialized music does not grow in any organic sense: one event does not lead to, come from, or imply another event. Rather, each gesture, each sound, results from a global and to some extent predictable scheme, which has an atemporal existence prior to and apart from the music.[29]

---

[24] Gaggi refers, among others, to Michel Foucault, John R. Searle, George Kubler, and Pablo Picasso.

[25] Silvio Gaggi, *Modern/Postmodern: A Study in Twentieth-Century Arts and Ideas*, pp. 1–9.

[26] Ibid., pp. 9–12.

[27] The notion of the composer as controller is decidedly modernist. Under the influence of postmodernist thinking, several composers have been moving away from the idea of music as either controlled or controlling.

[28] Schoenberg discusses the difference between unity in music's conception, which he calls its coherence, and in its perception, which he refers to as its comprehensibility. See *Zusammenhang, Kontrapunkt, Instrumentation, Formenlehre*, ed. and with an introduction (that discusses this issue) by Severine Neff, trans. Neff and Charlotte M. Cross (Lincoln: University of Nebraska Press, 1994).

[29] But this can surely be appropriate in certain works embracing synchronic unity, given the rise of

Mid-twentieth-century unity was not only synchronic but also essentialized. Works were thought to possess unity. Unity was a thing that was found in music in varying degrees, from piece to piece. Many composers and commentators seemed to believe that a piece can have unity, and that the more unity a piece has the better it is. Today such notions seem quaint, and indeed they were rarely stated in such a bald fashion. But they were quietly believed. Thus highly serialized pieces were praised for their complex networks of unities. Each pitch, each duration, was justified in numerous ways, and this meant that the pieces had a high degree of unity. Today we tend to think of unity more as an experience than as a quality of the music. If unity is located anywhere, it is in the listener (and in the composer and in the performer), not in the piece. A composer may put more unifying devices into a piece than another composer does, but that in no way guarantees that the first piece has any greater unity than the second. Composers who adopt this point of view are understandably skeptical about the ubiquity or necessity of complex schemes of integration of elements across a piece.

By the 1960s the desire for total unity and total consistency was so pervasive that it touched even composers with little interest in serialism, composers who did not trace their lineage to Schoenberg or Webern. For example, the open works of John Cage (a student, but not a disciple, of Schoenberg) are usually realized with a pervasive synchronic consistency. Although they may not be organic, performances of these pieces are certainly unified by their consistency.[30] Similarly, the early minimalist music of Philip Glass and Steve Reich is thoroughly unified, with no large-scale surprises.

The obsession with synchronic unity thus reaches its logical extreme in multi-parameter serialism, early minimalism, and indeterminate and aleatoric procedures, all of which can produce pieces or sections of unchanging sameness. That a reaction, which I am identifying with the rise of postmodern thinking in music, should appear is hardly surprising. What *is* surprising is the durability of the essentially conservative concept of unity, despite wild experiments[31] that sought to overturn virtually every other musical value. Even those few modernist composers who had created disunified music seem not to have realized the radical nature of overthrowing unity. Ives, the most extreme early exponent of chaos in music, sought to rationalize the inconsistencies in his compositions by appeal to a higher unity in all things.[32] Similarly, Adorno explained away the seeming disarray of modernist music: "Even the … extreme inconsistency and dissonance in non-conformist modern art cannot hide the

---

the aesthetic of stasis in postwar music. See Kramer, *The Time of Music*, pp. 54–7, for a discussion of stasis in contemporary music.

[30] In certain periods Cage openly espoused unity. See David W. Patterson, "Appraising the Catchwords, c. 1942–1959: John Cage's Asian-Derived Rhetoric and the Historical Reference of Black Mountain College," dissertation, Columbia University, 1996, Chapter 4.

[31] Such as conceptual music, musique concrète, stochastic music, randomly generated music, indeterminacy, etc.

[32] Ives's aphorism, "the fabric of existence weaves itself whole," is frequently quoted. See, for example, Eric Salzman, "Charles Ives, American," *Commentary* (August, 1968): 39. It is telling that many latter-day modernists still have trouble accepting the more chaotic works of Ives.

fact that these moments belong to a unity. Without oneness they should simply not be dissonant."[33]

Given the pervasiveness of music created in the spirit of unity, analytic methods aimed at discovering the means by which pieces are unified, and pronouncements on unity even from composers whose music would seem to belie their polemics, where could a composer turn who was disillusioned with obsessive unity? Not to the past, because the quest for unity has pervaded music for generations. Rather the place to turn was to chaos (see Section 6.3).

5.6. Unity and Organicism in Schenker and Others

But I am getting ahead of myself. Before exploring chaos in music, let me return to the idea of unity in early twentieth-century musical thought. Schoenberg had many followers, most of whom lacked his analytic sophistication. Lesser minds failed to appreciate the distinction between organicism and unity. It is ironic that some of the major twentieth-century proponents of synchronic unity claimed allegiance to Schoenberg, whose organicist ideas cast unity as essentially diachronic. Rudolph Réti, for example, analyzed by going on a hunting expedition for motives. He brought back similar shapes no matter where he found them. In the most blatant cases, the principle for choosing one motivic shape over another seems to have been the desire to make as much music as possible fit together according to his preconceptions.[34] Joseph Kerman appropriately characterizes Réti's analyses as "a sort of poor man's organicism."[35]

Analysts such as Réti (Hans Keller and Alan Walker are others) offered little in the way of systematic methodology for selecting certain pitches over others as members of significant motivic shapes. Other theorists, however, did try to formalize the motive, to seek ways of integrating motivic consistency into a larger theory of tonal unity. I am thinking primarily of Schenker, who even in his early writings emphasized the organic nature of music.[36] At first, as Robert Snarrenberg informs us,[37] he referred to the

---

[33] Theodor Adorno, *Aesthetic Theory*, trans. C. Lenhardt (London: Routledge, 1984), p. 225.

[34] Solie ("The Living Work: Organicism and Musical Analysis," p. 152), however, sees Réti's work as more diachronic than synchronic, because of his use of organicist language in justifying his essentially synchronic notions. A typical Réti invocation of organicism is the following: "Music is created from sound *as life is created from matter.* In the organic sphere one cell engenders the other in its own image, yet each of the innumerable cells is different from all the others. ... In an astoundingly analogous way one musical motif, one theme releases another as an expression of its own innermost idea, yet the latter is a being entirely different from the first." [Emphasis in original.] Rudolph Réti, *The Thematic Process in Music* (London: Macmillan, 1961), p. 359. Despite these organicist sentiments, however, Réti's analyses remain essentially synchronic.

[35] Joseph Kerman, "How We Got into Analysis, and How to Get Out," *Critical Inquiry* 7 (1980): 317.

[36] At the very beginning of his career, however, Schenker was opposed to the concept of musical organicism. According to William A. Pastille ("Heinrich Schenker, Anti-Organicist," p. 32), he originally believed that "music lacks both organic growth and organic unity."

[37] Robert Snarrenberg, "Myth and Theory: Stories for Ourselves," paper delivered to the Society for Music Theory, Oakland, CA, November 1990.

intuitive compositional process as organic. But his later theories posit an organicism that operates in a different dimension from that of simple temporal succession. For the later Schenker, organic growth is not simply from beginning to end but mainly from top to bottom of the tonal hierarchy. Conceptually—not perceptually—the music is generated from the *Ursatz* through its various middleground stages to the foreground.[38]

Schenker's concept of organicism is sophisticated. Music is heard two-dimensionally, so to speak. It grows from beginning to end and from *Ursatz* to foreground. While a number of commentators[39] consider Schenkerian theory to be essentially synchronic, I believe that it is fundamentally diachronic. Since the *Ursatz* is itself a motion, it is fair and proper to consider the unity it engenders diachronic.[40] Furthermore, as Richard Cohn points out,[41] "masterful" music is unified for Schenker because all pitches have a specific place within a hierarchy; each pitch is the result of a series of transformations from the *Ursatz*, the ultimate source of unity (Cohn also admits motivic repetition as a generator of unity in Schenker's world, although he believes that Schenker viewed motivic similarities as diachronic transformations).

> Whatever the manner in which the foreground unfolds, the fundamental structure of the background and the transformation levels of the middleground guarantee its organic life. The fundamental structure represents the totality. It is the mark of unity and, since it is the only vantage point from which to view that unity, prevents all false and distorted conceptions. In it resides the comprehensive perception, the resolution of all diversity into ultimate wholeness.[42]

A view divergent from that of Cohn is offered by Nicholas Cook:

> The assumption that Schenkerian analysis is about unity does a disservice to Schenker. Rather, I would maintain that it is predicated on the concept of unity ... but *about* tension, conflict, disunity. ... [For example,] any motivic parallel across different structural levels must, by definition, involve the apparent similarity of formations that have different generative sources; hence motivic parallels don't impose unity, as has been generally assumed, but rather highlight the discrepancy between surface and structure. ... What is being demonstrated [by such analyses] is not some abstract quality of musical unity, but rather the conflict and contradiction that animates the musical experience—"the tension of musical coherence," as Schenker himself expressed it.[43]

In an article that is in part a response to Cook, Cohn argues that Cook's characterization

[38] See *Das Meisterwerk in der Musik* 3 (1930): 20.
[39] Leo Treitler, for example. See *Music and the Historical Imagination* (Cambridge, MA: Harvard University Press, 1989), p. 52.
[40] See Schenker, *Das Meisterwerk in der Musik* 1 (1925): 12.
[41] Richard Cohn, "The Autonomy of Motives in Schenkerian Accounts of Tonal Music," *Music Theory Spectrum* 14 (1992): 150–70.
[42] Schenker, *Free Composition*, trans. Oswald Jonas (New York: Longman, 1979), p. 5.
[43] Nicholas Cook, "The Future of Theory," *Indiana Theory Review* 10 (1989): 71–2.

applies more to latter-day Schenkerian theory than to Schenker's own ideas. Thus the decidedly postmodernist flavor of Cook's idea, which Cohn calls the "Constructive Conflict Paradigm," is fully appropriate to contemporary intellectual values.[44]

And so, if we accept Cook's intriguing "misreading," Schenkerian theory has developed to a point where it is rife with conflict and amenable to disunity. Furthermore, Schoenbergian analysis of musical organicism has, in many hands, degenerated into searches for motivic (or other kinds of) similarity. Equating similarity with unity is problematic because, as we shall see, similarity is not a simple concept, and recognizing it is a more subjective activity than is usually allowed. Moreover, even if we admit that similarity is demonstrable, it is something of a leap from observing that two figures are similar to experiencing them as unified when they are heard.

The powerful traditions of diachronic unity, whether of the Schoenbergian or the Schenkerian variety, have devolved to a position of vulnerability. Musical postmodernists—whether analysts, critics, theorists, or composers—have gone the next logical step by recognizing in the demise of these concepts of unity new possibilities for constructing, listening to, and analyzing music that are not overly beholden to the totalizing meta-narrative of structural unity. We should now look, therefore, at some postmodern challenges to musical unity.

---

[44] See Richard Cohn, "Schenker's Theory, Schenkerian Theory: Pure Unity or Constructive Conflict?" *Indiana Theory Review* 13/1 (1992): 1–19.

6

Beyond Unity

6.1. Music that Defies the Unity Mystique

In traditional analytic methodologies—whether Schenkerian, Schoenbergian, motivic, or set-theoretic—and in other less institutionalized but commonly encountered (in the classroom more than in journals) *ad hoc* modes of analysis, when a passage of striking discontinuity or potential disunity is considered (if it is considered at all), the normal way of approaching it is to remark on, or even marvel at, the power of the surprise, but then to demonstrate (if possible) that the unexpected does, in fact, belong to the piece.[1] Traditional analysis strives to show similarities, whether obvious or hidden, between disparate events. Disunity may be noticed, but it is the underlying unity that is explained. This discrepancy between the observed and the explained indicates both our analytic prejudices and the fact that we have well-developed theories of unity but we rarely turn them around to demonstrate disunity. Traditional analysis studies similarity, not difference (difference is central to postmodern thinking in other disciplines, but not yet in music analysis). This is hardly surprising, since unity has long been universally valued[2] and disunity has always been a bit suspect. We have been conditioned to think of disunity as a negative value: it is the absence of something we are told is an indispensable feature of all good music.[3] Thus we tend to believe in our demonstrations of how a piece is unified, but the notion of showing that or how a piece might be disunified probably strikes us as more than a little bizarre.

As Joseph Kerman has pointed out,[4] the concept of organicism (and, we might expand, the idea of unity) works better for German instrumental music than for other bodies of music. We need not go too far afield to appreciate the truth of his contention; we do not need to invoke the music of happenings to find compositions that are less than comfortably served by the idea of organicism, music for which at least some of our analytic strategies do not work so well. Consider certain Eastern European concert

---

[1] Leo Treitler relates how music historians, unable to account for the apparent disunity in some of Ockeghem's compositions, transformed it into an aesthetic virtue by labeling it a "far-reaching renunciation of rational organization" and a "musical mysticism." See *Music and the Historical Imagination*, pp. 54–5.

[2] Raymond Monelle, *Linguistics and Semiotics in Music* (Chur, Switzerland: Harwood, 1992), pp. 320–1.

[3] Street, "Superior Myths, Dogmatic Allegories," p. 80.

[4] Kerman, "How We Got into Analysis, and How to Get Out," p. 320.

music. Nineteenth-century Russian music, for example, is still sometimes denigrated for its "episodic forms" and "lack of development."[5] The fact that the introductory themes of Tchaikovsky's Violin and First Piano Concertos are never referred to later in those pieces continues to trouble some commentators,[6] who seem to believe in some universal law that requires themes to return.[7] The lack of linear, teleological development in Mussorgsky is still sometimes disparaged (although no one questions the consistency of his music or that of other Russians).

Eastern European music lacking in pervasive unity is not exclusively Russian. What can an analyst who believes in the inevitability of structural unity make of, for example, a nondevelopmental and varied work like Janáček's Sinfonietta? In fact, the one blatant gesture toward formal unity in that piece—the recapitulation of the entire first movement as coda of the fifth movement—strikes at least this listener as a gratuitous gesture toward traditional (i.e. Western European) closure. This superficial bowing to the dictates of Germanic organicism surely does some harm to the work; any resulting unification certainly does not adequately compensate.

I am complaining not that the Sinfonietta's one unifying passage is incongruous with respect to the rest of the piece, but that the composer apparently felt the need to wrap things up by grafting onto his wonderfully disparate piece a traditional and rather automatic recapitulation. But if the coda is structurally unmotivated, then one might argue that it is actually a gesture of disunity. Thus there is a contradiction between its literal relationship to the opening and its unexpectedness in context. This contradiction might be intriguing were the coda not so long: it is a *complete* rehash of the first movement. Indeed, there are other returns in the Sinfonietta that do not seek to destroy the prevailing disunity. While some passages are unrelated to one another, other passages do interrelate: no work is thoroughly disunified. When the first movement returns at the end in an apparent attempt to round out the Sinfonietta, however, the artificiality and superficiality of this closure compromise the work's quirkiness.

Another example of non-Germanic music not overburdened by unity (despite sophisticated motivic interrelationships) is Nielsen's Sixth Symphony, discussed in Chapter 13: of all his symphonies the least interested in the dictates of organicism, this work has also given commentators the greatest difficulty. But, if we stop expecting it to be unified, we can understand it as an astounding and overpowering statement, a vision of chaos, a precursor of late-century postmodernism.

Lack of continuity or development is not the only way a piece can seem disunified. In some music there may be disunity between simultaneous rather than successive structures. Theorist Brian Hyer,[8] for example, cites two examples of music he feels is

---

[5]   I am indebted on this point to Gregory Karl.

[6]   I confess to being among the guilty. See my book of program notes, *Listen to the Music* (New York: Schirmer, 1988), pp. 762–3, 765.

[7]   Introductory material in the works of other composers also fails to return (e.g. in several Haydn symphonies), but the Tchaikovsky melodies are such sweeping melodic statements that we expect more of a future for them. They seem (gesturally if not tonally) expository more than introductory.

[8]   In a preliminary version (read at Columbia University, April 1989) of the unpublished paper "Them

not unified, although nonetheless coherent: French chorale harmonizations from the Schola Cantorum, in which a diatonic melody is incongruously set over a chromatic bass and dissonant inner voices,[9] and Stravinsky's Piano Concerto, which Schenker (in what Hyer considers a rare, perhaps unique, attempt by a theorist to demonstrate that a piece is not a unified whole) analyzed derisively to show the lack of coordination between melody and harmony.[10]

In fact, we might question the unity in any music in which the harmonic implications of a melody are contradicted rather than realized. Arnold Whittall describes certain passages in Berg's Violin Concerto as disunified. He is excited by Berg's anti-organicism but disappointed in analysts' failure to deal adequately with it. This anti-organicism does not mean "that the various elements used in a composition may have absolutely nothing to connect them, but that some kind of contradiction of language occurs which makes analytical demonstrations of interruption or suspension take priority over demonstrations of connection."[11]

Berg's concerto is not the only modernist work in which a "contradiction of language" results from superimposing new music on old models. Other examples include Schoenberg's Concerto for String Quartet and Orchestra (based on Handel), Stravinsky's *Fairy's Kiss* (based on Tchaikovsky), Bartók's Third Piano Concerto (the middle movement is based on the slow movement of Beethoven's String Quartet in A Minor, Opus 132), and Schoenberg's Third (related to Schubert's A Minor String Quartet) and Fourth (related to Mozart's Quartet in D Minor, K. 421)[12] Quartets. Such music demands what Joseph Straus calls

a useful antidote to what has become a virtual dogma in music theory: organic coherence. ... [Critic Harold Bloom] makes possible a shift of critical focus from the demonstration of organic unity to the evaluation of elements of conflict and struggle within a work. ... In most of the works discussed in [Straus's] book, there is a clear delineation of new and old elements. The older elements are recognizable but placed in a new context that confers upon them a new meaning. Works containing this clash of elements may be coherent, although not in an organic sense. Rather, their coherence depends upon the ability of the new musical context to hold the older elements in its grasp. Old and new are not reconciled or synthesized but locked together in conflict. The coherence of these works is won through a struggle.[13]

Bones, Them Bones, Them Dry Bones: Discontinuities in the First Movement of the Mozart G Minor Symphony."
[9] Chromatic harmonizations of simple diatonic tunes can also be found in Reger's sets of variations on other composers' melodies, e.g. the *Variations on a Theme of Hiller*.
[10] Schenker, *Das Meisterwerk in der Musik* 2 (1926): 37–91.
[11] Whittall, "The Theorist's Sense of History," p. 1–20.
[12] Martha Hyde mentions the dialectic interrelationship between these two quartets in her paper "Neoclassic and Anachronistic Impulses in Twentieth-Century Music," presented to the joint conference of the Music Theory Society of New York State and the Arnold Schoenberg Institute, Barnard College, October 6, 1991.
[13] Straus, *Remaking the Past*, p. 16.

Whittall and Straus regret the failure of traditional analytic methods to explain such music. Certainly harmonic analysis can make some sense of diatonic melodies harmonized chromatically, set theory can uncover consistencies in a piece like the Stravinsky Piano Concerto, and twelve-tone analysis can point to the identity of the last tetrachord of Berg's row and the opening of the chorale melody. But these observations do not make us have a unified listening experience. My interest in this music lies precisely in the areas which such analyses ignore: the tension between different kinds of pitch structures operating within the same work, "locked together in conflict," as Straus says.

The finale of Mahler's Seventh Symphony, discussed in Chapter 12, offers yet another species of musical disunity. It contains events that normally connote and/or create structural articulation: perfect authentic cadences, returns to the tonic key after modulatory excursions, and returns of the main theme. These structures *never* act completely in phase with one another. Every articulation in some domain is contradicted in another domain. Thus the movement is temporally disunified, despite a surface of considerable motivic consistency and transformation.

6.2. The Need for Analyses of Disunity

If we study stylistically diverse music, or discontinuous or nondevelopmental music, in the normal ways, our analyses will most likely find unity in (or force unity onto) the music. Yet the analytic project is "problematized" if methodologies are designed to search for unity even in pieces that strike us as less than pervasively unified.[14] When an analysis fails to unify all aspects of a piece that is deemed worthy of study, we tend to blame the analytic method as imperfect or the analyst as lacking sufficient skill or insight. We rarely think to blame the piece: perhaps it is difficult to demonstrate pervasive unity in a given composition simply because it is not totally unified![15]

What should our response be to a piece of music that strikes us as disunified? We might reject it outright, or (more likely) we might try to constitute it in our minds as unified in some manner. Studies in psychology support the notion that perception is an ordering process: to enter a series of stimuli into our minds, we must encode them—group them—in some way. If the series has clear cues to its group boundaries, we use them; if not, we construct them and impose them. Thus all music that is perceived (i.e. that is not ignored or rejected) is unified to some degree, in some way.

---

[14] Hyer, *Figuring Music*, Chapter 3, argues "that to smooth over ... discontinuities in the name of a seamless organic perfection is to impoverish our experience of the music. ... Our uncritical adherence to organicist dogma often causes us to ignore the snags and glitches that occur in our experience of listening to the music. As a result, the music is rendered hermetic, sealed off from the world, no longer the product of a warm-blooded human imagination, immune to lapses in concentration and our all-to-human inclination to misconstrue. In [some] music, at least, the musical continuation—the moment-to-moment grammatical coherence of the music—is sometimes broken asunder."

[15] Street, "Superior Myths, Dogmatic Allegories," p. 95.

So it is hardly surprising that analysis seeks to elucidate unity. There is always a handy analytic method available to demonstrate how (if not that) the music coheres. All we need do is try hard enough, bend the piece or the method sufficiently, or ignore disunifying factors, in order for the music—as well as our perception of it—to come out comfortably unified. Thus the analytic mind mimics the listening mind, as analysts have been telling us for a long time. Both listening and analyzing create as well as discover unity. But is that unity solely in the music? Or is it also—even primarily—in the listener's mind and the analyst's charts and prose?

These challenging questions (at least as just formulated) suggest that we should differentiate between the alleged unity of a composition (whether studied in score or in performance) and that of music as heard, understood, and remembered. I call the former *textual unity*, and the latter *experiential unity*. Textual unity does not exist physically: we cannot point to the unity in a score or a performance but only to the elements that are allegedly unified or, in Webern's terminology, interrelated. Although I informally refer to textual unity "in" music, textual unity actually exists in relationships between events or qualities of music. The simplest kind of textual unity is similarity: two events or figures can be shown to have some degree of similarity. The figures have an objective existence in the piece, but the similarity relationship is something discovered by analysts or listeners: the similarity is in the perceiver.[16] Because the objects which are experienced as similar do exist in the music, textual unity can be demonstrated without reference to what is actually heard.

Experiential unity also does not exist physically but resides in relationships—but not among aspects of the music-out-there but among aspects of music-in-here: music as perceived, as encoded in short- and then long-term memory, and as recalled. To the extent that unity involves similarity, textual unity resides in the perceived similarity between events, while experiential unity is the *experience* of relatedness one may have when noticing similar (or even dissimilar) events. Not all unity is the product of similarity relationships, however. While most textual unity involves—in practice (of traditional music analysis) if not in theory—similarity between events that can be shown to have properties in common, experiential unity—being more an experience than an observation—can go beyond simple similarity.[17] This bears remembering: *the demonstrable textual unity of a score may have something to do with the experiential unity of a performance (although it may not!), but the two are not identical.*

---

[16] Umberto Eco argues essentially the point that similarity, or resemblance, is conventional rather than inherent in objects. See *A Theory of Semiotics* (Bloomington: Indiana University Press, 1976), pp. 191–217.

[17] Nicholas Cook discusses textual vs. experiential unity at some length. "There is a rather glaring disparity between the way in which the arbiters of musical taste approach musical structure and the way in which listeners generally respond to it. For the theorist ... musical forms are to be understood in terms of unitary, integrated structure. ... But it appears that such integrated structure passes over the heads of most listeners most of the time," *Music, Imagination, and Culture*, p. 68. Cook even suggests (pp. 58–9), quoting Kathryn Bailey ("Webern's Opus 21: Creativity in Tradition," *Journal of Musicology* 2, 1983: 195), that there can be "two quite different pieces—a visual, intellectual piece and an aural, immediate piece, one for the analyst and another for the listener."

In an article that is an early version of Chapters 4, 5, and 6, I used the terms "textual" and "perceptual" unity.[18] But I now prefer "textual" and "experiential" unity. Both exist in the mind of the perceiver, but textual unity is projected onto the stimulus, where it is studied using quasi-objective analytic means, such as Nattiez's neutral level or atonal set theory. Experiential unity is more immediate, more visceral—an experience located in and understood to be in the listener's perception and not necessarily related to the structures reputed to "cause" textual unity to be perceived. With much traditional analysis, experiential unity comes from an auditory perception—or, better, from the interaction between an auditory experience and the collection of values, prior experiences, cognitive abilities, predilections, etc., that make up an individual's personality—while textual analysis often comes from (or, is of) a visual perception (of a score). But this is not a necessary distinction. A performance may be the object, the text, of textual analysis, in which case the textual unity is of an auditory perception, a perception of an auditory stimulus believed to be "out there," to have an objective existence. The same musical performance "out there" can be implicated in experiential unity, but the unity of experience (of that performance) is not the same as, nor even necessarily related to, the unity an analyst discovers in, or projects onto, the performance-as-text.

It is indeed all too easy to project the experiential unity of listening or of analyzing back onto the stimulus. If we have a unified listening experience, we may unthinkingly assume that the music is textually unified.[19] The postmodern aesthetic, however, encourages us to separate the two, by conceiving of the text—the music—as autonomous. There is some degree of textual unity "in" most pieces; there is also a measure of textual disunity "in" a lot of music. There is a considerable amount of experiential unity in the mind of the listener or analyst; and, indeed, there is a degree of experiential disunity, or irrationality, in the listener's mind. But the listener's experiential unity/disunity is not identical to the music's textual unity/ disunity.[20]

---

[18] "Beyond Unity: Toward an Understanding of Postmodernism in Music and Music Theory," in Elizabeth West Marvin and Richard Hermann (eds.), *Concert Music, Rock, and Jazz Since 1945: Essays and Analytical Studies* (Rochester: University of Rochester Press, 1995), pp. 11–33.

[19] Or, as Fred Maus says, "Confronted with a demonstration, on the basis of a score, that some kind of musical pattern exists, one may be tempted to conclude that the pattern explains features of one's experiences, even though one does not recognize the pattern as such in listening. The temptation is familiar in analytical reflections on successful twelve-tone music. On the one hand, a twelve-tone piece may seem [i.e. sound] convincing, unified, and beautiful; on the other hand, the twelve-tone patterning seems [i.e. looks] undeniable. So, one feels bound to admit, somehow the patterning must explain the experiences, including the feeling of unity. One should resist such hypothetical analytical explanations—not primarily because they are false (though I think they are not known to be true), but because they change the subject of analysis, leading away from the articulation of experienced qualities of music," "Concepts of Musical Unity," in Nicholas Cook and Mark Everist (eds.), *Rethinking Music*, p. 175–6.

[20] Thomas Clifton wrote that the word "ordered" is "a description of an experience which may be independent of, and other than, the kinds of orderings injected into the work by the composer. Once again, then, the experience of order says nothing about whether order is there in fact. Order is constituted by the experiencing person, who is just as likely to experience it in a collection of natural sounds as in improvised music or a finely wrought fugue by J.S. Bach," *Music as Heard* (New Haven: Yale University Press, 1983), p. 4.

Since perceiving is a process that creates order, experiential unity is certainly not very remarkable. Any music that makes even a modicum of sense to a listener is understood to possess experiential unity. Thus, the probable reason for Roman Ingarden's inability (quoted in Section 4.2) to cite any existing disunified pieces is that, in terms of perception, there actually are none![21] It is impossible to get completely beyond unity in perceived music.

This important point needs to be emphasized: *the textual unity of music, the textual unity of analysis, the textual unity of performance (which results from the performer's experiential unity), and the experiential unity of listening are not the same.* If we have a perceptually unified experience and if we can demonstrate quasi-objective patterns of textual consistency in a score, it is difficult to resist the temptation to relate the two. Yet experiential musical unity and the factors that purportedly create it *are* distinguishable.[22] As Alan Street has stated, "There is simply no reason, still less a necessity, to infer unity of form from that of structure."[23] For, as Leonard Meyer puts it,

> unity is neither an objective trait like frequency or intensity, nor a specifiable relationship like an authentic cadence or a *crescendo*. Rather, it is a psychological effect—an impression of propriety, integrity, and completeness—that depends not only on the stimuli perceived, but on cultural beliefs and attitudes ingrained in listeners as standards of cognitive/conceptual satisfaction.[24]

Once we realize that a unified experience is psychological and cultural, that it is not guaranteed by—nor even necessarily related to—motivic or any other kind of consistency, then we should be in a position to appreciate a work's surprises, *non sequiturs,* detours, etc., *for themselves,* without having to find their fundamental principles of textual unification. We have these experiences of surprise all the time, and analysis *can* help us understand them, if only because it tells us where our thwarted expectations might have led[25] or because it explicates the background of continuity against which a discontinuity stands out. What I am objecting to is the obsession of analysts to find how the surprising events also fit the unified plan of the work. I do not say that such information is not interesting, but only that it can be less important than the impact of the discontinuity.

Schenkerian theory and set theory, arguably the two most common analytic methodologies currently practiced, at least in English-speaking countries, are both intense statements on the necessity of, more or less respectively, textual organicism and textual unity. They are popular because they try to answer a question that has bothered music theorists for generations. But this question—how are works of

---

[21] Surely there are some pieces that make no sense to some listeners, but I would suggest that virtually every piece makes some sense to someone—if only the composer!

[22] Stephen Davies, "Attributing Significance to Unobvious Musical Relationships," *Journal of Music Theory* 27 (1983): 207. Fred Maus makes similar points ("Concepts of Musical Unity").

[23] Street, "Superior Myths, Dogmatic Allegories," p. 100.

[24] Meyer, *Style and Music,* p. 326.

[25] An intriguing analysis of this sort can be found in Joseph Dubiel, "Senses of Sensemaking," *Perspectives of New Music* 30/1 (1992): 210–21. Dubiel analyzes what he calls a "gratuitous" move to F minor in the first movement of Haydn's Quartet in D Minor, Opus 76, Number 2.

music unified?—is not the only one to ask, nor is it the most basic. Today we are witnessing not only a widespread acceptance of these two theories but also a growing dissatisfaction with them, somewhat parallel to the uneasy coexistence of latter-day modernism and postmodernism in composition (which I discuss in Chapter 3). The more thoughtful of the disaffected do not reject Schenkerian or set theory outright; these methodologies do what they do exceedingly well. But we are coming to realize, now that we have amassed a substantial body of very good analyses, that they do not really explain all that much about the *impact* of music. Only now that the mania for unity is being addressed in sophisticated and/or rigorous analyses have we begun to realize how hollow it is. We have begun to understand, as Joseph Kerman has told us in an often quoted passage: "From the standpoint of the ruling ideology, analysis exists for the purpose of demonstrating organicism, and organicism exists for the purpose of validating a certain body of works of art."[26] And dismissing others![27]

One theorist who is willing to confront discontinuities without having to smooth them over into textual unities is Brian Hyer.[28] He has studied one particular passage in Mozart's G Minor Symphony,[29] although he is careful to point out that the discontinuity in this excerpt is typical rather than unique. "The point is that if discontinuities can be found in this most unified of all compositions, then discontinuities can be found anywhere." He feels that "there is something almost cancerous" about mm. 247–51 from the first movement's recapitulation, "something that threatens the well-being of the musical organism, a threat some listeners [and analysts], I believe, are unable to face." Hyer concedes "that the melodic organization of these measures is perfectly continuous. ... It would be a mistake, however, to regard the melodic process as the sole determinant of musical coherence: that the melodic organization is continuous does not prevent the music from being discontinuous in other respects." These measures are harmonically necessary, because of the need to return from a far-flung motion away from the tonic, although they are not tonally or even hypermetrically necessary to the structure of the piece. They furthermore have neither motivic precedent nor consequent, they do not appear in the corresponding place in the exposition, and—most significantly—they are motivated not by any global tonal plan but only by the harmonic logic of the preceding few measures, which move the music into a strange and distant area from which return is locally imperative. This passage is exciting because of its textual disunity rather than any sense of belonging organically. The textual unity it contains is, by comparison, rather ordinary: the realization of implied tonal return. A traditional analysis, Hyer shows, would point to the voice-leading connections between this passage and the

---

[26] Kerman, "How We Got into Analysis, and How to Get Out," p. 315.
[27] I gratefully acknowledge Margaret Barela for this perspicacious addition to Kerman's quip.
[28] Hyer, *Figuring Music*, Chapter 3.
[29] Rose Rosengard Subotnik also offers a discussion of the G Minor Symphony, focusing on the apparent arbitrariness of some gestures, the abrupt discontinuities, and the abrogation of "logical harmonic movement." *Developing Variations*, pp. 106–07. Subotnik also writes about the progression to C♯ (in mm. 175–93 of the finale) as stretching "the unifying functional power of the tonic to the point of raising doubts as to the logical necessity (and inevitable potency) of a resolution into I," p. 109.

previous and subsequent music, thereby positing both unity and continuity. But such an analysis privileges continuity over discontinuity, textual unity over disunity. This excerpt in some ways fits in and in other ways does not; it is the prejudices of analysis that make us more able, and more willing, to understand and accept the former over the latter.[30]

6.3. Chaos and Chaos Theory

In his 1967 book *Man's Rage for Chaos*, literary critic Morse Peckham quotes a critic who praises artistic unity in a typical manner: "What the poem discovers—and this is its chief function—is order amid chaos, meaning in the middle of confusion, and affirmation in the heart of despair."[31] Peckham then comments,

> What heartening words those are! What a cozy glow they offer! It is a pity that they are quite false. At least they are false if what is meant is what all such statements mean: order is a defining character of art.[32]

Peckham does not deny that people like, crave, and need order. He devotes a number of pages to what he calls the "rage for order," which relates to the psychological concept—mentioned in section 4.8—of perception as a unifying process.[33] But he does deny that the purpose of art is to provide order in a chaotic world; the world, he feels, is overly ordered.[34] If order is everywhere, it can hardly be the purpose of art to bring order out of chaos. "Every man experiences order every second of his life. If he did not, he could not cross the room, let alone the street … . That order is a defining character of art is so utterly untrue that it is downright absurd."[35] Peckham believes that the purpose of art is to present disorienting experiences,[36] that we in turn are forced to

---

[30] Hyer goes on to identify the source of analytic discomfort with these measures in an automatic over-reliance on scale degree functionality: "I … sense dread and panic at this moment in the music, stemming from the realization that the music-theoretical logic that has gotten us this far—the logic of scale degrees—won't get us through these five measures," *Figuring Music*, Chapter 3.

[31] The citation Peckham uses is from Elizabeth Jennings, *Poetry Today*, quoted by a reviewer of her volume *Recoveries* in the *London Times Literary Supplement*, June 11, 1964: 512.

[32] Morse Peckham, *Man's Rage for Chaos* (New York: Schocken, 1967), p. 31.

[33] Peckham has written on experiential unity (p. 30): "Unity of any kind is something the human being always tries to perceive if he possibly can. Indeed there is no set of perceptual data so disparate that human perception cannot create order and unity out of it."
Also (p. 41): "Since we value—and often madly overvalue—whatever is ordered, we tend to impute order to whatever we value, even to the point of distorting perceptual data so that we see something as ordered which in fact is not; … perception is not mere passive response to a stimulus but a creative, dynamic act, an act of interpretation."

[34] Contemporary chaos theory, discussed below, takes a more moderate view: the world is both ordered and chaotic.

[35] Peckham, *Man's Rage for Chaos*, p. 33.

[36] J. T. Fraser echoes Peckham's idea in "From Chaos to Conflict," in Fraser, Marlene P. Soulsby, and Alexander J. Argyros. (eds.), *Time, Order and Chaos: The Study of Time IX* (Madison, CT: International Universities Press, 1998), pp. 3–20. He writes of artists perpetuating conflict, rather than bringing order out of chaos. Fraser believes that oppositions between order and chaos are endemic to great art.

order in our minds if we are to make sense of them. By this process of perceptual ordering, we grow as individuals and as a culture. There is both order and chaos in any profound work of art. In order to understand such a work, we must both discover and create its order (although, at least for postmodern music, the imposed order may be more meaningful than the discovered order).

When it was new, *Man's Rage for Chaos* was popular with the artistic avant garde, not only for its attack on textual unity but also for its behavioral definition of art.[37] More recently, however, the book seems to be routinely ignored, perhaps because it poses a deep threat to the beliefs of modernists and traditionalists alike. But it is, in fact, one of the first statements of the postmodern aesthetic of textual disunity. In a limited way, furthermore, Peckham's ideas anticipate recent applications of mathematical chaos theory[38] to the arts.

Despite similarities, however, Peckham's chaos is not the same thing as the chaos of contemporary science. For Peckham, chaos is profoundly disorienting, while chaos theory characterizes it as "an orderly disorder."[39] It is unfortunate that these two distinct but related concepts share the same name; it is difficult today to speak of chaos as total lack of order, owing to the popularity of chaos theory's idiosyncratic construal of the term. According to the theory, an unpredictable, seemingly insignificant event can have enormous consequences. This causal event is characterized as disordered because of its randomness, but the large-scale result remains within predictable and hence ordered limits. In her book *Chaos Bound*, N. Katherine Hayles, a scholar with advanced degrees in both chemistry and English, gives an instructive example: "An inattentive helmsman on the bridge of an oil tanker … can have immediate and large-scale effects on an entire coastal area."[40] The confluence of circumstances which give his inattention the power to destroy a huge area is random, but the *possibility* (though not the actuality) of this result is foreseeable.

A frequently used example of chaos theory concerns weather prediction.[41] It is not simply difficult but virtually impossible to make accurate long-range predictions, because tiny changes in air currents, undetectable in themselves, can lead to ever larger changes, ultimately having considerable impact on the weather. Yet weather is not totally random; some degree of prediction is indeed possible. Weather behavior lies someplace between the orderly and the disorderly. This combination of chaos and order lies at the heart of the science of chaos. "Chaotic systems," writes Hayles, "are both deterministic and unpredictable."[42]

---

[37] Peckham places the burden of creation with the perceiver: "*A work of art is any perceptual field which an individual uses as an occasion for performing the role of art perceiver.* (This assumes, naturally, that any individual who does this has already learned the role of art perceiver from his culture.)" [emphasis in original] Peckham, *Man's Rage for Chaos*, p. 68.

[38] For highly readable accounts of this theory, see James Gleick, *Chaos: Making a New Science* (New York: Viking, 1987); Ian Stewart, *Does God Play Dice?* (Cambridge, MA: Basil Blackwell, 1989); and N. Katherine Hayles, *Chaos Bound*.

[39] Gleick, *Chaos*, p. 15.

[40] Hayles, *Chaos Bound*, p. 5.

[41] Gleick, *Chaos*, pp. 11–23; Hayles, *Chaos Bound*, p. 12.

[42] Hayles, *Chaos Bound*, p. 14.

Similarly in music: an unexpected, unjustified, unexplained event can have a huge impact on the subsequent music (or even on our retrospective understanding of what we have already heard), even if—*particularly* if—it is not eventually integrated, either motivically or harmonically. I hear the subsequent music differently, even when it involves literal recapitulation, because the context has changed radically. Especially when the music refuses in any substantive way to integrate the unexpected into the fabric or logic of the piece, I as listener take on the burden of making sense of it. I mean that quite literally. I create sense, in order to render the passage experientially coherent. This is my rage for order at work.

Consider, for example, the A-major tune in the finale of Bartók's Fifth Quartet, mm. 699ff. This passage provides an example of how wrong-headed a good analysis can be. I remember first coming to know this piece while I was an undergraduate. I was struck, intrigued, overpowered by the seeming irrationality of this simple tune intruding on the last movement. More than one of my professors was quick to point out that what was truly admirable about this seeming *non sequitur* was how it fundamentally *did* fit in, *did* partake of and even further the tight logical consistency of the piece. I am not sure whether or not these learned professors went on to demonstrate the alleged underlying textual unity; and I am not particularly interested in justifying the A major passage in terms of tonal, motivic, melodic, harmonic, rhythmic, or set relationships.[43] Nor was I impressed when, after I explained this point in a lecture, a theorist gleefully responded that a contour analysis reveals that the tune is "actually" a transformation of a prominent earlier melody. (I wonder if Bartók—indeed anyone—*could* have composed something at this juncture that would be impossible to analyze as related to earlier portions of the piece.) The power of that passage lies in its unexpectedness and also in just when in the piece we experience the simple/familiar/tonal interrupting the complex/abstract/nontonal. An analysis—such as my friend's contour study—that shows how the tune is, in fact, textually integrated into the movement may not be false; probably it is demonstrably and objectively true. But it misses the point, if we take the point of analysis to be the explanation of how a piece is heard, how it works, and what it means. Of course if our analytic purpose is something else—e.g. to find consistencies whether audible or not, whether structural or not, whether significant or not—then explaining the unity behind the unexpectedness of the tune can be tempting. This kind of analysis does interest me, I confess, much as solving mathematical games intrigues me. Furthermore, I am not ready to reject textual analysis as irrelevant. To do so would be an overreaction. After all, who is to say *a priori* that a certain analysis is unrelated to perception, to a listener's understanding? What I am calling for is a relaxation of the rigid hierarchy of analysis, where what is easily explained (underlying consistency, in this case) is valued over what may be more striking, more meaningful, more memorable, but less tidily analyzed.[44]

---

[43] After calling the tune "a grotesque contrast," Elliott Antokoletz offers several such justifications for its harmonic and melodic derivation. See *The Music of Béla Bartók: A Study of Tonality and Progression in Twentieth-Century Music* (Berkeley: University of California Press, 1984), p. 179.

[44] Another passage that could be discussed in relation to chaos theory occurs in the first movement of Beethoven's String Quartet in A Minor, Opus 132, where a striking discontinuity (mm. 93ff.) is

From the perspective of chaos theory, the organicist model of music theory is wishful thinking. A *Grundgestalt* or basic motive or *Ursatz* or set complex may explain some of the ways a piece is structured, but it cannot determine—and, in fact, was never intended to determine—every last detail. Artistic inevitability is a fiction. Traditional analysis tries to understand as outgrowths of source materials as many events and aspects of a piece as possible, but there are always anomalies which cannot be predicted, which do not truly fit in,[45] but which should not be ignored (although they routinely are) analytically. Hyer's example from Mozart and Dubiel's (see footnote 25) from Haydn are not that unusual. Chaos theory tells us that the unpredictable is commonplace in complex systems, and music is a complex system.

In her explanation of chaos theory, Kathryn Hayles invokes information theory, which has had an undeniable but less than pervasive influence on music scholarship. Although the mathematics of information theory has proven too cumbersome to become a widespread analytic methodology, I maintain that the underlying concept of information as meaning does have explanatory power.[46] The more expected an event is, the less information it contains, in the technical sense of information. The more an event is a surprise, the more information it contains and hence, according to Leonard Meyer, the more meaning it has.[47] This is an unusual but productive use of the term "meaning." Hayles points out[48] that it is easier to predict the next number in the sequence 2, 4, 6, 8, 10, 12, ... than in the sequence 4, 6, 4, 5, 12, 7, ... The former is generated by the orderly formula $f(n+1) = f(n) + 2$, while the latter is the output of a random number generator. The former is totally predictable, once we catch on to the formula; the latter is unpredictable. In information theoretic terms the latter has more information and, according to Meyer, more meaning. But, Hayles asks, what kind of meaning inheres in a sequence of random numbers? This very specialized concept of meaning may be of little use to the perceiver of the number series. Thus, Hayles notes the demise of the one-to-one correlation between meaning and information. This, she claims, renders chaos a positive force rather than simply the absence of order.

"When information could be conceived of as *allied* with disorder, a passage was opened into the new paradigm of chaos theory."[49] Hayles feels that "maximum infor-

---

unprepared and has no motivic consequence, yet has a tremendous impact on how the movement is understood. See *The Time of Music*, pp. 29–32.

[45] This assertion does not contradict my earlier claim that in twelve-tone music nothing is merely ornamental because everything is row derived. Serially integrated gestures can still be experienced as unexpected, as disunified, as surprising. Consider, for example, Webern's Variations for Orchestra, Opus 30. The trombone move from G to F-sharp in mm. 46–7 is unprecedented: it is the first (but not quite the only) overt contiguous stepwise motion in the piece. This gesture is particularly striking because it has not been prepared in any way: the row is full of interval class 1, but every preceding linear statement has been as a major seventh or minor ninth.

[46] For a good exposition of information theory as applied to music, see Leonard B. Meyer, *Music, the Arts, and Ideas* (Chicago and London: University of Chicago Press, 1967), pp. 5–21.

[47] Ibid.

[48] Hayles, *Chaos Bound*, p. 6.

[49] Ibid., p. 58. For a useful discussion of information theory and chaos applied to music, see Horacio Vaggione, "Determinism and the False Collective: About Models of Time in Early Computer-Aided Composition," in Jonathan D. Kramer (ed.), *Time in Contemporary Musical Thought*, which is volume 7/1 (1993) of *Contemporary Music Review*. Vaggione (pp. 91–104) offers pertinent criticisms

mation is conveyed when there is a mixture of order and surprise, when the message is partly anticipated and partly surprising"[50]—a view with which Meyer would no doubt agree. Thus, for example, music that we tend to feel has a maximum of meaning (e.g. that of Beethoven) lies midway between the extremes of totally random and totally predictable music.[51]

There are two aspects of chaos theory of potential relevance to music. In a chaotic system (1) unexpected events happen, which (2) may or may not have far-reaching consequences. A small air current may be unpredictable in itself, yet it may (or may not) be so situated in space and time that it contributes to a chain of events that culminates in a hurricane. In traditional music, unexpected events do happen. They need not be as unpredictable as Bartók's A-major passage, as the analyses by Dubiel and Hyer show. An unexpected event may or may not have large-scale consequences for how the music is subsequently understood and/or for how it subsequently unfolds. Chaos theory suggests that the unexpected need not be explained in reference to what has preceded it.

In this sense, postmodern music well exemplifies the orderly disorder of a chaotic system. But a music which suggests that anything may happen—where so many unexpected events occur that a listener begins to forsake expectation—is a music that may not be sufficiently integrated for an unanticipated perturbance to have major structural ramifications.[52] In this sense, postmodern music would seem to be a less likely candidate than traditional music for an analysis derived from chaos theory. But we should remember that structures that seem to be located within a piece (whether placed there by the composer, the performer, or the analyst) are not the same as structures a listener constructs mentally. The "piece" constituted in the listener's mind will necessarily have a complicated structure, because of both the intricacy of the music and the complexity of the human mind. Thus the listener's mental representation may possibly be understood from the viewpoint of chaos theory—since small, unpredictable perceptions may (or more often may not) have a considerable impact on cognitions of the piece developed later in the listening process. The partially chaotic representation of music in a listener's mind would, I suspect, be unaffected by whether or not the music that gave rise to that representation is susceptible to a chaos-theory textual analysis. This idea is quite speculative, since to my knowledge there have been no sustained attempts to study either music scores or mental representations of music from the perspective of chaos theory. But chaos theory does offer one attitude relevant to postmodern music: they both upset normal hierarchies, allowing a seemingly insignificant event to take on considerable importance and allowing a particularly portentous event to have few consequences.[53]

---

of simply equating information with randomness and redundancy with determinism, without taking account of the concepts of chaos theory.

[50] Hayles, *Chaos Bound*, p. 53. See also p. 55.

[51] I am, as I trust is clear, referring to internal, syntactic meaning, not to social, political, cultural, or referential meanings: random music (by Cage, Joel Chadabe, and Lejaren Hiller, among others) and predictable music (such as certain early minimalist pieces of Reich, Glass, and Frederic Rzewski) have made powerful statements by their very existence, quite apart from their internal meaning.

[52] I am indebted on this point to John Rahn.

[53] I am indebted for this observation to Robert Morris. A similar attitude may be sought in a postmodern analysis of any music: what is traditionally important may be marginalized, and the

Even if unexpected events are so common in a particular piece that the syntactical impact of any single discontinuity cannot be great, the influence of that unexpected musical event on the listener's understanding can be considerable and can alter his or her experience of an entire work. While one particular quotation of the many in John Zorn's *Forbidden Fruit*, for example, may not be powerful enough to generate the musical equivalent of a hurricane, having heard it may nonetheless irrevocably alter a listener's experience. A piece may seem to ignore (textually) the possible implications of an unprecedented event (just as not every unexpected air current leads to a storm), but this event may still suggest to some listeners a profoundly altered context in which to understand the remainder of the piece.

Chaos theory, then, may some day provide useful hypotheses for an analysis of *traditional* music, particularly if it does not rely on textual unity as a universal principle. Some *postmodern* music, on the other hand, may paradoxically be less efficiently studied from the viewpoint of chaos theory, although the listener to such music may well have an experience that is properly described by the chaos model. Yet psychology, like music theory, has not to my knowledge used chaos theory to explain musical cognition, and least of all the cognition of postmodern music.

Critical theorists like Hayles, on the other hand, *have* applied chaos theory to the study of postmodern artworks. She writes, "[Traditional] literary theorists like chaos because they see it as opposed to order. Chaos theorists, by contrast, value chaos as the engine that drives a system toward a more complex kind of order. They like chaos because it makes order possible."[54] The order that chaos theory enables is of a new, more complex kind. It is an order beyond that which can be elucidated by traditional analysis. Perhaps it is this kind of order that John Zorn seeks (see Section 4.2). And perhaps this new order means that disunity itself becomes a principle of postmodern musical structure. If the sections of a radically postmodern piece are truly not unified, then the difference between them is extreme. Such music may constitute an extreme of moment form.[55] The polystylistic nature of *Forbidden Fruit*, for example, makes its discontinuities more pronounced than any in Stockhausen's moment forms, in which there is at least stylistic similarity between sections. Such an extreme of difference as we find in Zorn forces the listener outward, through quotations and references, into the arena of cultural differences between the kinds of music invoked. Thus difference—among parts of a composition, between the composition and other music to which it refers, and among the many other styles it refers to—paradoxically

analysis may find meaning in normally marginalized details. Raymond Monelle makes a similar point: "If a critic is to look for traces of the hinterland beyond the frame—disunifying and destabilizing features, details that fail to confirm the hierarchies and principles on which the best analysis may depend—then his attention will be drawn to the apparently unimportant." *Linguistics and Semiotics in Music*, p. 310.

[54] Hayles, *Chaos Bound*, pp. 22–3.

[55] Zorn's compositional aesthetic would seem to confirm this notion. He has written: "It's made of separate moments that I compose completely regardless of the next, and then I pull them, cull them together. It's put together in a style that causes questions to be asked rather than answered. It's not the kind of music you can just put on and have a party. It demands your attention. You sit down and listen to it or you don't even put it on." From Edward Strickland, *American Composers: Dialogues on Contemporary Music* (Bloomington: Indiana University Press, 1991), p. 128.

becomes an ordering principle. The order created is not that of similarity relationships between musical materials, not that of organic growth, not that of stylistic consistency, but that of difference—intra- as well as inter-opus. If this possibly odd idea—that pervasive disunity can become a sort of order—has any validity, it just may suggest that the apparent paradigm shift of postmodernism away from unity is finally just the means to define new types of order appropriate to postmodern art and ideas. If the demotion of unity leads finally to new order, then the process would nicely exemplify what Peckham says about the chaotic nature of significant art. Radical postmodernism would at first be disorienting for most perceivers (this much is surely true), but they would eventually come to understand (or discover or invent) new orders from the disorder they initially experienced. And so postmodernism's attack on unity may eventually come to seem less a rupture, less an overthrowing of traditional values, less negative than it appears to many today.

Against the backdrop of radical postmodernism, the attempts of some composers in the 1960s and 1970s to create music of extreme (synchronic) unity seem like last desperate attempts to save music from the onslaught of difference. It should be no surprise that music that steadfastly avoids unpredictability—randomly generated, pure minimalist, and totally serialized pieces, for example—is no longer very widely composed. These types represent extremes of textual unity and consistency (but not of organicism), about which increasing numbers of composers have become skeptical. If radical postmodern music does indeed produce a new kind of order, then such obsessively unified music may seem in retrospect to have been a dead end. Thus, while only a few theorists have yet confronted the musical implications of chaos theory or the decentralization of organicism and unity, substantial numbers of postmodern composers *are* responding to these challenges. Disillusioned with the faith in unity other composers—often their teachers—espouse, they have given up trying to make all or even most aspects of their pieces relate to each other, to a germinating cell, or to an overriding generative idea, or to a meta-narrative. These composers are working at a time when chaos theory has shown how natural the unpredictable is, even within an orderly system. I do not necessarily suggest direct influence (although I do know composers who are fascinated by chaos theory), but rather that chaos in the arts comes at least as much from cultural concerns as from analogies to science.[56]

Why has late twentieth-century culture begun to turn away from order toward chaos? Those who see chaos as a negative[57] will necessarily take a cynical view, but there are those for whom the concept of order has become oppressive and who embrace chaos as a source of freedom. Hayles states: "As chaos came to be seen as a liberating force, order became correspondingly inimical."[58] And, according to Helga

---

[56] Hayles, *Chaos Bound*, pp. 4–5, 17.

[57] George Rochberg is one. In his strongly worded response to an article of mine (which is, in turn, a response to his "Can the Arts Survive Modernism?"), he sees only the negative side of disunity, equating it with "divorce, wife abuse, drug abuse, street crime, and intensifying neurosis." See "Kramer vs. Kramer," *Critical Inquiry* 11 (1984): 509–17.

[58] Hayles, *Chaos Bound*, p. 22.

Nowotny,[59] disorder has become acceptable to a world that looks for an alternative to the order of modernity. The acceptability of disorder and disunity has allowed for the development of the artistic stance known as postmodernism. Thus, as we continue to explore the diminishing importance of textual unity in music, we should turn directly to postmodern music.

6.4. A Taxonomy of Musical Unity

But first let us review and summarize ideas on unity. This chapter has discussed and categorized musical unity in a number of ways. Musical unity can be textual or experiential. Experiential unity is the all but unavoidable sensation that any music that makes sense is, in some way and to some degree, unified, if only because making sense of auditory stimuli is a unifying process. Not only experiential but also textual unity is located in the mind of the perceiver (listener or analyst), but textual unity is metaphorically said to reside in the music. This is because textual unity often relies on similarity relations (as Webern's definition implies). In traditional music analysis, motives, contours, sets, etc., are scrutinized for similarities. When similarities are found, as they usually are, then they are believed (unjustifiably, maybe even falsely) to be the cause of experiential unity.

But textual unity does not have to depend on similarities. Consistency of textures or of timbre can contribute to textual unity. So can organic growth, whereby some musical material is transformed step by step into some other, quite dissimilar material. This kind of organicism is an essentially diachronic unity. It has to do with processes unfolding in time, whereby one thing grows into another. A carefully worked out transition, for example, can bring the listener through time from one point to another, in a unified manner. Diachronic unity, or organicism, may be either experiential or textual. Listeners certainly are capable of experiencing diachronic growth (e.g. transitions) and of feeling unity because of their experience. Diachronic unity can also be textual: an analyst can certainly trace gradual transformations of material in a way that suggests unity.

But analysis that seeks to elucidate the means of textual unity more often studies similarity relations than trace processes of growth, transformation, or transition. Similarity relations tend to be more synchronic than diachronic. They tend to trace classlike resemblances throughout a work more than they trace the temporal unfolding of relationships. Thus, textual unity is likely to be synchronic, though it can be diachronic. But can experiential unity be synchronic? Can listeners experience similarities without concern for temporal order or rate of unfolding? In *The Time of Music* I posited a perceptual mechanism that would indeed allow for synchronic

[59] Nowotny, "The Times of Complexity: Does Temporality Evolve?" in J. T. Fraser, Marlene P. Soulsby, and Alexander Argyros (eds.), *Time, Order and Chaos: The Study of Time IX* (Madison, CT: International Universities Press, 1998), pp. 91–146.

experiential unity. I called this listening mode "cumulative listening,"[60] but I stressed that cumulative listening might be more metaphorical than real. Now, having read more extensively in the psychology of perception, I have come to doubt that cumulative listening is anything more than a metaphor, although it is a useful one. I doubt that listeners can experience synchronic unity in any real sense. Listeners can certainly notice similarities across time, but they can hardly be unaffected by the order of similar events or by their placement within the duration of a piece.

In summary:

Synchronic experiential unity is unlikely actually to be felt, although it can certainly be extrapolated as a metaphor for heard consistency.

Diachronic experiential unity is the type of unity listeners feel, or construct mentally, as they hear a performance unfold in time.

Synchronic textual unity is what analysts most often study, as it deals mainly but not exclusively with similarity relations.

Diachronic textual unity is what more sophisticated analytic methods (e.g. Schenkerian analysis) seek to elucidate in studying how music grows organically.

---

[60] See *The Time of Music*, pp. 52–4 and 367–9.

Postmodern Listening

7.1. The Listener and the Musical Text

The less an artwork is textually unified, the more the perceiver must assume the burden of rendering her or his perception of it experientially coherent. To make sense of a chaotic piece like Zorn's *Forbidden Fruit*, for example, a listener must invest some effort. And, since the ordering is largely the listener's own, a piece might well mean or even *be* very different things to different perceivers. It matters what references or quotations present themselves to the listener, just as it matters in what order and for what durations they are heard: these aspects of the structure will presumably be common to most listeners' understanding of the music. But, since the text apparently lacks structures that can readily be seen or heard as textually unifying, each perceiver constitutes the work's experiential unity mentally in his or her own way. The resulting multiplicity of responses suggests that there are as many pieces as there are listeners (or even *listenings!*), an idea thoroughly appropriate to postmodern thinking.

Robert O. Gjerdingen offers a concrete example of how different listeners can have different musical experiences in the presence of the same piece.[1] In a discussion of the first movement of Mozart's Piano Sonata in E-Flat Major, K. 282, Gjerdingen identifies several conventional gestures that Mozart incorporates and overlays in various ways. He remarks on how these gestures are largely unrecognized by present-day analysts[2] and listeners. Listeners who know and understand the repertory of conventional gestures in the music of Mozart and his contemporaries may well perceive and react to such patterns with greater involvement, and gain from them greater meaning, than they get from attending to and processing the melodic, harmonic, and rhythmic information offered by many brands of musical analysis and tacitly assumed to be an (or even "the"!) appropriate way to hear this music.

There may be different modes of listening to Mozart. I have tried to suggest how a mode of listening that emphasizes the matching of specific learned patterns to the musical presentations at hand may approach the type of listening that rewards experience, attention, and active engagement. For courtiers accustomed

---

[1] Robert O. Gjerdingen, "Courtly Behaviors," *Music Perception* 13 (1996): 365–82.
[2] Ibid., p. 369.

to following the clear presentation of the standard musical behaviors, Mozart's mature style presented a challenge. Ironically, for the listeners of later eras accustomed to a more passive mode of listening to broad harmonic progressions, the very same compositions became synonymous with ease and grace. Both types of listeners hear "Mozart," but I would argue that those who are challenged by his musical behavior ultimately have the richer experience. That experience is grounded not in mere appearances or in some imagined essences but in the real-time evaluation of musical patterns by those listeners with the relevant repertory of learned schemata. The great moments of Mozart's music, then, depend less on how chords progress or how dissonances resolve and more on how an experienced listener evaluates the import of nuances detected in the presentation of complex musical behaviors.[3]

If, as Gjerdingen demonstrates, Mozart's sonata movement (along with many other pieces from the classical period) is full of conventionally defined musical gestures that carried specific meanings in Mozart's time, then it is reasonable to assume that Mozart may have intended his listeners to hear these gestures as constituting the work's narrative. Mozart may well have been trying to communicate specific musical (or even extra-musical) ideas by means of the sequence of these gestures. If so, however, his communication no longer succeeds, since the skill needed to identify such gestures is all but lost today. Yet listeners still have meaningful and unified musical experiences when listening to this sonata, even if these experiences are not closely related to what Mozart intended to communicate. Nowadays, theorists tell us, our experiential unity of Mozart's music has to do not so much with conventional gestures as it does with harmony, voice-leading, rhythm, meter, melody, motives, etc. The sonata is unified for us today, just as it was for Mozart's contemporaries, but in strikingly different ways. This idea may seem odd, unless we understand that it means that different listeners may have different feelings of experiential unity in the presence of the same musical text.

The demise of the notion that the textual unity of music is intimately related to the experiential unity of listening suggests that we should be skeptical as well of the relationship between the composer and the music. The act of composing may (to some degree) be unified behavior, the musical text may (to some degree) be unified, a performance may (to some degree) be unified, an analysis may (to some degree) be unified, and the listening experience may (to some degree) be unified, but these five possible unities are only weakly interrelated. The focus of the creative act is moving away from the composer toward the text and, ultimately, the listener.[4] It is easy to adopt Terrence Hawkes's view of Shakespeare's dramas to music:

---

[3] Ibid., p. 381.
[4] This tripartite division of the analytic subject parallels Jean-Jacques Nattiez's three parts of musical semiology (see Chapter 3, footnote 100). When I delivered part of this chapter as a paper at an analysis conference in London in 1991, the late Derrick Puffett interestingly suggested that the quasi-independence of Nattiez's three levels rescues the composer from Barthes's sentence of death (discussed later in this section).

The point of Shakespeare and his plays lies in their capacity to serve as instruments by which we make cultural meaning for ourselves. . . . They don't, in themselves, "mean." It is *we* who mean, *by* them.[5]

Traditionally, music analysis has been concerned either (1) with the score as perceived by an ideal listener or by the analyst himself or herself (as in analyses of the old Princeton school, influenced by Edward Cone and Roger Sessions—analyses that try to answer the question "how is it heard?"[6]), or (2) with the composer's methods (as in Darmstadt analyses, such as those reported in the journal *Die Reihe*—which ask the question "how was it made?").[7] Now we are finding a shift in interest among several theorists, who study not primarily the score and not the composer's methods but the music as constituted in listeners' minds (trait 16).[8] I am referring to analyses influenced by phenomenology (for example, in David Lewin's influential article "Music Theory, Phenomenology, and Modes of Perception"[9]), to studies of the metaphors by which we describe music (as found in, for example, Marion A. Guck's "Two Types of Metaphoric Transference"[10]), and to perceptual studies (including not only work found in journals such as *Music Perception* and *Psychology of Music* but also such cognitively based music theories as those of Lerdahl and Jackendoff, of Narmour,[11] and of Lerdahl[12]).

7.2. The Listener as Creator

Turning scholarly focus away from the composer toward the listener (trait 16) is related to Roland Barthes's often cited idea of "the death of the author." Barthes

---

[5] Terrence Hawkes, "Bardbiz," *London Review of Books*, 22 February 1990, pp. 11–13.
[6] These analyses are related in spirit, if not in methodology, to those of Schenker. In a quintessentially modernist (and elitist) manner, Schenker wrote not about how music is actually perceived but about how it *ought* to be heard. Nicholas Cook makes this point in *Music, Imagination, and Culture*, p. 21.
[7] Theorist David Neumeyer has called for "analysis papers [that] could be built around 'See how this piece is animated?' rather than the usual 'See how wonderfully it's put together?'" "Reply to Larson," *In Theory Only* 10/4 (1987): 34.
[8] Stephen McAdams, a leading researcher in music cognition, understands the significance of considering the listener's perception. "The will and focus of the listener play an extraordinarily important role in determining the final perceptual results," "The Auditory Image: A Metaphor for Musical and Psychological Research on Auditory Organization," in W. R. Crozier and A. J. Chapman (eds.), *Cognitive Processes in the Perception of Art* (Amsterdam and New York: Elsevier Science Publishers, 1984), p. 319. McAdams goes on to articulate what could be taken as a manifesto of postmodern music composition: "What this proposes to the artist is the creation of forms that contain many possibilities of 'realization' by a perceiver, to actually compose a multipotential structure that allows the perceiver to compose a new work within that form at each encounter. This proposes a relation to art that demands of perception that it be creative in essence."
[9] *Music Perception* 3 (1986): 327–92.
[10] This article appears in Jamie C. Kassler and Margaret Kartomi (eds.), *Metaphor: A Musical Dimension* (Paddington, Australia: Currency Press, 1991).
[11] Lerdahl and Jackendoff, op. cit.; Eugene Narmour, *The Analysis and Cognition of Basic Musical Structures: The Implication-Realization Model* (Chicago: University of Chicago Press, 1990).
[12] Fred Lerdahl, *Tonal Pitch Space* (New York: Oxford University Press, 2002).

writes of the inescapability of postmodern quotation and of the attendant shift of the process of unifying from the creator to the perceiver:

> We know now that a text is not a line of words releasing a single "theological" meaning (the "message" of the Author-God) but a multidimensional space in which a variety of writings, none of them original, blend and clash. The text is a tissue of quotations drawn from … many cultures and entering into mutual relations of dialogue, parody, contestation, but there is one place where this multiplicity is focused and that place is the reader, not, as was hitherto said, the author. The reader is the space on which all the quotations that make up a writing are inscribed without any of them being lost; a text's unity lies not in its origin but in its destination.[13]

Before exploring Barthes's idea in the context of music, let us consider it in general. Needless to say, Barthes was not invoking a literal death. Rather, he was using a striking slogan—which paid off handsomely, as the phrase echoed throughout the literature on postmodernism—to indicate that the reader has the power to shape the text and its meanings. This was surely always the case, but literary criticism and education routinely enshrined the author as the final authority on the texts he or she created. Readers were encouraged to search out the author's meaning. This authority long reigned as a meta-narrative of literary criticism and interpretation. Barthes recognized what has been the experience of perceivers all along but had been invalidated by scholars and critics: every person creates, *and is entitled to,* his or her own mental version of a text, based on the backlog of *his or her own* experiences. The tyranny of imposing meanings—presumably of the author—on perceivers comes from scholars and critics who try to channel and shape the ideas of a consumer of texts. In his use of the phrase "the death of the author," Barthes invoked hyperbole to point to the necessity of questioning this meta-narrative. By undermining an accepted meta-narrative, Barthes sought to take control of textual meaning away from critics and teachers operating in the name of the author and to extend that control to the reader.

Barthes's idea is powerful and has been much discussed. But we should not be seduced by the force of his slogan into rejecting all external input into our understanding of texts. I mentioned in my discussion of the music of Cage (Section 3.4) the

---

[13] Roland Barthes, "The Death of the Author," in *Image—Music—Text*, trans. Stephen Heath (New York: Noonday, 1977), pp. 146, 148. This article is discussed perceptively in Michael Newman, "Revising Modernism, Representing Postmodernism: Critical Discourses of the Visual Arts," in Lisa Appignanesi (ed.), *Postmodernism: ICA Documents* (London: Free Association Books, 1989), pp. 114–24. At the end of his essay (p. 148), written in 1968, Barthes throws down a challenge to which literary critics have responded but which music analysts are only now beginning to consider: "Classic criticism has never paid any attention to the reader; for it, the writer is the only person in literature. … To give writing its future, it is necessary to overthrow the myth: the birth of the reader must be at the cost of the death of the Author." Wolfgang Iser offers similar, though more mildly formulated, ideas: "The reader's enjoyment begins when he himself becomes productive, i.e. when the text allows him to bring his own faculties into play," *The Act of Reading: A Theory of Aesthetic Response* (Baltimore: Johns Hopkins University Press, 1978), pp. 107–8. Nicholas Cook considers the relevance of Iser's ideas to music listening in *Music, Imagination, and Culture* (Oxford: Clarendon, 1990), pp. 18–19.

necessity of people being tutored in how to listen to his indeterminate compositions. Those who seek to educate listeners in how to hear Cage often take some of their ideas from the composer: his writings, his interviews, and what he said in person to those fortunate enough to have met him. If we believe completely in "the death of the author," we should not interrogate Cage about his works. But we can (even though this particular author is now, alas, literally dead), and we should—as long as we realize that his input is but one of many sources of postmodern meaning, and that our own perceptions (whether influenced by his ideas or not) are still of foremost importance.

Although some composers may understandably balk at being declared dead, the 1960s avant garde in America in effect accepted this pronouncement when, for example, Pauline Oliveros called for the anonymity of the composer[14] and when she composed her series of *Sonic Meditations*,[15] when Cage composed pieces so open that it was impossible for even him to recognize them in performance, and when several composers made music in which performers' and even listeners' activities were as critical to the shaping of the music as were composers' choices. Cage wrote about the unique experience of an active listener: "Nowadays we would tend toward doing it ourselves (we are the listeners), that is, we would enter in[to the music]. The difference is this: everybody hears the same thing if it emerges. Everybody hears what he alone hears if he enters in."[16] (Quoting these sentences of Cage is a good example of why the author/composer is not quite dead—he still has something valuable to tell us about our understanding of his art.)

Locating experiential unity, expression, and creativity in the listener implies that, as mentioned above, there are at least as many musical texts—as many pieces—for a given compositional act or performance as there are listeners. Is this idea incompatible with the analytic project? It suggests rather that studies of compositional proce-dures, scores, performances, and perceptual mechanisms are different, perhaps even independent, enterprises.[17] Barthes's "death of the author" does not subjugate the text totally to the subjective whims of the perceiver. I continue to believe in the objective existence of music created by a composer. A composition does have some ontological status even prior to its being perceived, even prior to its being performed. Nattiez's "neutral level" does exist, even though its neutrality is not perceptually accessible. That is why poststructuralists (and perhaps some of the more extreme "new musicologists") may deny its very existence: no one can know that it is out there unless it is seen or heard, and once it is seen or heard it exists in the perceiver's mind, where it is inter-preted by each individual's perceptual and cognitive faculties. The perceived trace is

---

[14] "I think we ought to obscure the composer," *Source: Music of the Avant Garde* 2 (1967): 51

[15] Pauline Oliveros, "Sonic Meditations," *Source: Music of the Avant Garde* 10 (1971): 103–7.

[16] John Cage, *A Year from Monday* (Middletown, CT: Wesleyan University Press, 1967), p. 39.

[17] Seen in this light, set theory—about which I complained earlier—is appropriately up-to-date, since it often concerns itself with scores as autonomous entities and only peripherally with compositional procedure or with how a piece is played or heard. I find that some set-theoretic analyses describe structures that I do or can hear; other such analyses do not. Nicholas Cook's discussion (*Music, Imagination, and Culture*, pp. 233–4) suggests that I am not alone in having difficulty hearing certain structures elucidated by set-theoretical analyses. What is relevant is that set theory's *appeal* to perception, if it exists at all, is rarely primary.

no longer a trace but exists on the esthesic level (i.e. the level of the auditor). Even the most seemingly objective of analyses—e.g. Nattiez's or Ruwet's so-called semiotic studies or certain applications of Fortean set theory—necessarily proceed from the analysts' perceptions. Even if we believe in some kind of objective similarity between two musical figures, for example, this similarity is necessarily interpreted by, and indeed distorted by, the perceptual act. To go from the necessity of a perceiver to the notion that the text has no existence apart from the perceiver is too large a leap. The inaccessibility of the neutral text is no argument for its non-existence. Using quasi-objective techniques of music analysis, we can approach (but never fully reach) an understanding of the text-out-there—in the full knowledge that such understanding must be personal, subjective, and individual and that such a text becomes subjective once it is perceived as music.

Consider the pairs of musical events shown in Examples 7.1–11. [Editor's note: as explained in the Introduction, these examples are missing here and on p. 130.] Which pairs are similar, an analyst might ask. Or a music psychologist may ask, if the members of all pairs are heard, preferably within a musical context, which pairs will a listener select as similar? I am talking about degrees of similarity; I am not suggesting absolute identity: even Examples 7.1A and B are only similar, not identical. When we look at them, we find one on the left side of the page, and one on the right. When we listen, one comes first and one second. When the second is heard, the memory of the first may remain in the listener's consciousness. Thus the contexts are different, and thus the two figures are different—i.e. their similarity stops short of literal identity.

Are any of the pairs dissimilar? Traditional analysis sees similarity relationships and encourages listeners to hear them and respond to them. Thus an analyst (and presumably—but not always demonstrably—a listener) tends to feel more comfortable, to feel a greater sense of understanding, when noticing a similarity between two events. Thus, it is considered useful to notice that Example 7.2B is an arpeggiation of the chord of Example 7.2A, Examples 7.3A and B have the same harmonic root, Examples 7.4A and B have the same melodic contour, Examples 7.5A and B have the same rhythmic grouping patterns, Examples 7.6A and B have the same durational pattern, Examples 7.7A and B use the same underlying pitch-class set type, Examples 7.8A and B use complementary set types, Examples 7.9A and B use Z-related set types, Examples 7.10A and B use M5-related set types, and Examples 7.11A and B are similarly scored. Just as it is impossible to create two events so similar that they are identical (remember that even Examples 7.1A and B are similar, but not identical—because of their contexts), so it may be impossible to create two events so dissimilar that no one can discover in or reasonably impose on them some sense of similarity. Context can imply which types of similarities a listener (or analyst) may find to be salient or significant in a given work.

Noticing such similarities is a prelude to mentally constructing the unified text. Because of the large number of events in most any piece, there are too many potential relationships for anyone to consider them all. Hearing similarities is a selective act, and each listener may come up with a different set of similarity relationships and with different kinds and degrees of similarity. Furthermore, not every listener will value similarity relationships as much as music analysts would like them to, and for that reason may not privilege similarity over difference in constructing a musical text mentally.

Even if their interrelationships are available to us only through the necessarily subjective processes of perception and interpretation, it makes for good common sense to admit that Examples 7.1A and B have a greater degree of similarity than do Examples 7.11A and B. If this seemingly obvious statement is accepted, then it follows that there indeed *is* a text-out-there, a piece of music that contains events offering varying degrees of similarity and difference, which may or may not be perceived, understood, appreciated, or interpreted by analysts, performers, and listeners. It is this objective text that stimulates people to create their own internal music. The piece is not just the context for listener or performer creativity: it also provides (some of) the material with which listeners and performers operate. The musical experience is not created by each listener in a vacuum: it comes from an interaction between the piece-out-there, its performance, possibly analyses and criticisms the listener knows, and the listener's mind.

To understand music, it is therefore important not only to study (as cognitive psychology does) the perceptual mechanisms common to most people, not only to recognize (as critical theory does) the individuality of each listener and hence of her or his own mentally constructed work, not only to analyze performances, but also to understand as thoroughly as possible the structures inherent in the musical text which suggest similarities and differences (which is what analysis does). Thus I want to retain close analysis of scores and performances, even though some "new musicologists"— disillusioned with the objective and hermetic world of structural analysis—seek to overthrow it. Music analysis may rest on some dangerously unchallenged assumptions, its methods may be cumbersome, it may not hold all the answers, it may imply an objectivity that is ultimately misleading, and its overvaluing of textual unity may be anachronistic, but it remains a useful tool for anyone who wants deeply to understand music and the musical experience.

Focusing the analytic project on both the text and its perceiver/interpreter allows us not only to retain close reading but also to continue to avoid the Intentional Fallacy.[18] We turn away from studies of the cultural context of composers. Many "new musicologists" ignore the Intentional Fallacy as they seek to recontextualize music, to understand compositions in terms of the cultural values surrounding their creation. The enterprise of these musicologists is essentially different from mine. I too want to go beyond traditional analysis in order to contextualize music, but the context

---

[18] The term was coined by William K. Wimsatt and Monroe C. Beardsley to refer to the tendency of literary critics to find the meaning of a text not in the text itself but in biographical facts about the author or cultural facts about his or her era. Their article "The Intentional Fallacy" was a major document for the so-called New Critics, but it eventually fell into disfavor with the rise of poststructuralist thinking. I believe that the lessons to be learned from the Intentional Fallacy remain pertinent in today's postmodern intellectual climate: an author's intentions may be irrelevant to the meanings a perceiver constructs. The text itself is important, but—and this is where I part company from Wimsatt and Beardsley—the perceiver is even more so. Frequently reprinted, "The Intentional Fallacy" first appeared in the *Sewanee Review* 54 (Summer 1946): 468–88.

I seek is not that of composers but that of listeners *of today*. If I truly believe that meaning is created by listeners, operating under the influence of a musical text that has an objective status, then I must turn my attention away from historical studies. Of course such studies interest me, but what I look for when analyzing, say, Beethoven's Opus 135 is not an explanation of how the piece got to be the way it is (I even question whether it *is* any particular way), and not how it may reflect Beethoven's personality (an issue discussed in Section 7.4) or times, but in how and what it may mean to postmodern listeners living today.[19]

7.3. Communication and Expression

If listeners constitute their own meanings and even their own pieces, how is it possible for music to communicate? If Mozart intended to communicate in his K. 282 sonata something quite different from what most listeners today hear, does it make any sense to say that he communicates to listeners through his music? Indeed, *does* music communicate at all? Do composers communicate through music? Are a composer's ideas actually in the music, and if so do they emerge through a performance in order to reach a listener? Does the listener hear what the composer has "said"?

In attempting to answer these difficult questions, we must not lose the distinctions between music as conceived by composers (Nattiez's poietic level), as represented in the product of the composers' activities (the neutral level), and as understood by listeners (the esthesic level).[20] The composers' creative processes depend on their inspiration, personality, intentions, influences, moods, techniques, etc. Performers subsequently exercise their own creative (as well as re-creative) processes to make performances, using not only scores but also their own inspiration, personality, intentions, etc. In other words, performers receive, perceive, and reconceive scores by means of personal receptive processes, which are then turned around into creative processes.

Since he does not fully distinguish different traces of the musical work—score, performance, and recording (or broadcast)—Nattiez's ideas need further refinement. If the performance is recorded and/or broadcast (as many performances are), then an additional receptive-creative link (or, as sociologist Antoine Hennion calls it, mediator[21]) is added to the chain. Recording engineers receive, perceive, and reconceive performances, which are then turned into creative products dependent not only on the performances but also on engineers' inspiration, influences, techniques,

---

[19] Book II of this volume [Editor's note: Chapters 12–13] contains "case studies" of individual works that seek to elucidate postmodern ways of understanding them. These studies are not so much postmodern in methodology as they are postmodern in spirit. In particular, they do not assume that an analysis of a composition must simply seek to explain its textual unity. Rather, they focus on ways the music can be understood by a postmodern listener of today.

[20] Nattiez, *Music and Discourse*, pp. 10–32.

[21] Antoine Hennion, "Baroque and Rock: Music, Mediators, and Musical Taste," *Poetics: Journal of Research on Literature, the Media, and the Arts* 24 (1997): 417.

equipment, etc. When these recordings are heard, listeners' receptive processes make sense of them and personalize the music. This process can also be creative, as involved listeners construct mental images of the music which depend not only on the recorded sounds as heard but also on listeners' predilections, preferences, prior listening experiences, musical abilities, etc.

If it actually existed, the complete communication chain (with every link present) would be long and complex: from composers' initial thoughts and intentions through their creative acts to scores, which are altered somewhat by editors and/or publishers, and then through performers to performances, and then through recording engineers to recordings, and then through listeners to internalized representations of the music. While particularly strong ideas may actually be communicated through this chain all the way from composers to listeners,[22] I believe that it is rare for listeners to construe composers' messages essentially the way they were sent out. All the people in the chain interpret, read, possibly misread (in either Bloom's sense or the common meaning of the term), and add their own ideas, which may well alter or replace those of the composers. In cases where the chain is shorter—jazz improvisers playing unamplified to live audiences, for example—the communication may be more direct, but still, I maintain, it is problematic. Particularly when all mediators are present, the communication model for musical transmission is suspect. Expressiveness, yes: music is a means and a context for composers, performers, engineers, and listeners to express themselves. Emotion, yes: the expression can be quite moving. But communication? Rarely, I believe, since composers' expressions must traverse long, circuitous routes, during which what may have been intended as communication is inevitably distorted and altered.[23]

The circuitous nature of the chain is not the only reason for us to interrogate the concept of musical communication. At a more basic level, we need to consider constraints on the very nature of alleged communication through music. Language theorists of a postmodern persuasion have been questioning verbal communication lately, and music theorists would be wise to do likewise. Nowadays scholars have acknowledged that language is not fixed. According to psychoanalyst Gilbert Rose,[24] for example, "Words are flexible, meanings change, language is a living organism." People who speak and people who listen are in flux. Rose writes of "the improbability of conveying anything more than very partial truth by language. Facts, yes [I would

---

[22] An example: Justin London suggested (in a private conversation) that communication must be present for the jokes in Haydn's music to work. Even today, two centuries after the composer placed his rather specific messages into his scores, listeners "get" the jokes. The communication chain is complete, and listeners understand what Haydn wanted them to understand. So, communication *is* possible. But jokes are more specific than most musical expression, and I maintain that, on average, *most* Western art music—particularly that without verbal text—fails to communicate specific ideas from composer to listener.

[23] Just to clarify my use of two critical terms: by "expression" I refer to what artists and other people do in their utterances (whether artistic or not). By "communication" I refer to expression that reaches another person, who—on some level and to some degree—understands it.

[24] Gilbert Rose, *Between Couch and Piano: Psychoanalysis, Music, Art and Neuroscience,* "Whence the Feelings from Art?" (New York: Routledge, 2004), p. 3. This section is a revised version of the foreword I wrote for Rose's book.

have said 'maybe']; the feelings about facts, no." Objective communication—verbal as well as musical—is difficult. As Rose writes, language "leaves out more than it includes, yet it includes so much that any number of connections can be made among the elements that are encompassed."[25]

We express ourselves all the time, in all sorts of ways. And we listen to one another. Postmodern thinking teaches us that we do not simply, passively receive communications. We construct the message (and even the sender!) for ourselves, using a mix of what we have heard, what we think we have heard, what we want to have heard, what we hope we did not hear, who we are, who we think the message sender is, what our values and expectations are, what our moods and contexts are, our memories of previous interactions, etc. So, misunderstanding between two people is inevitable, no matter how clearly and painstakingly they try to communicate, no matter who they are, no matter what their relationship. This situation is unavoidable.

The same is true of reading as it is of conversation: as Rose writes, each "reader uses the given narrative as material from which to form his own fantasy."[26] And so it is with music: each listener uses the sounds presented to his or her ear, sounds which the composer may or may not have conceived in terms of some narrative structure, to create his or her own personal narrative-fantasy.

A few years ago I had an experience that showed me just how tenuous the communication model can be for music. I asked a graduate analysis seminar to study Ives's *Putnam's Camp*. Several of the seminar participants were from countries other than the United States and hence had little knowledge of American folk music and patriotic songs. Even some of the American participants did not recognize most of the quotations in Ives's score. One student recognized only "The Star-Spangled Banner" in the penultimate measure—a possibly obscure quotation, since it contains only the first four notes, which outline a generic major triad. I realized that those who did not recognize the distinction between quoted and original material, and those who did not know anything about the historical and cultural contexts of the quoted music, had a skewed understanding of the music. I was particularly intrigued by how utterly different the piece must have been for each of my students compared to how it was for me. Despite a lot of analysis about shared perceptions (of such structural aspects as rhythmic irregularities, harmony, set constructs, interplay of tonality and atonality, etc.), everyone in the seminar had different (as well as common) experiences with the music.

Such a high degree of individuality of responses should surely warm the hearts of committed postmodernists. What stronger actualization is there of the idea that art exists in the receiver, not in the creator? Yet there is also something sobering about this notion. If everyone hears different pieces while attending to the same performance, there cannot be much of a sense of community among those listeners with respect to their musical experience. Music which suggests, means, and even *is* different things for each auditor encourages the isolation of listeners. Small wonder that we sit still in our

[25] Ibid., p. 5.
[26] Ibid., p. 16.

classical/serious/art concerts, that we are annoyed by noises or actions intruding from other members of the audience! Small wonder that so many enjoy listening to music over headphones, which block out other sounds and encourage the listener to enter directly into the music, with minimal interference! And small wonder that the possibly stultifying rituals of the classical concert are perpetuated largely unchanged, despite the enormous changes in the music that is heard. Music may have changed a lot with the rise of postmodernism, but the classical concert ritual continues to isolate listeners from each other, while the music plays (although there are certainly communal rituals associated with arriving at the concert hall, preparing to listen, intermission behavior, applause, etc.). Postmodern classical music may seek to encourage the individual creativity of listeners, but in so doing it perpetuates the concert rites of modernism, which promote a view of music as pure and unrelated to stimuli outside of itself.

The situation is certainly different in the jazz and pop worlds. Audience members physically and vocally interact with each other and vicariously with the performers and the music. Their activities during concerts may seem alternatively liberating or disrespectful to the performers, but they certainly do encourage a sense of a community of listeners, even at the possible expense of their variety of responses. When everyone is swaying or shouting together at a rock concert, how likely is it that they are all hearing different pieces?

Putnam's Camp may be an extreme case of intertextuality giving rise to individual reactions, given the large number of quotations and references to other music it contains, but I believe that all music—even the most abstract modernist music—can elicit individual associations, responses, and meanings in listeners. As Rose states about a study of reading,

> Each reader interacted with the story in terms of his own personality and intrapsychic life, and in the light of this constructed something new which was most consonant with himself. ... In short, he takes from the work what is most consonant with himself, rewrites it in his own mind and becomes its co-author. ... Art does not "communicate" meanings; it *generates* them in the receptive mind.[27]

Similarly, if each listener to a piece of music constructs "something new," something which reflects the self as much or more than it reflects the music heard, then how can anyone maintain that there is direct communication from composer to listener?

I do not deny that it is tempting and comforting to believe that composers speak to listeners. Hence what I am suggesting may sound heretical: a listener who is deeply moved by a performance is not primarily responding to a message sent out by the composer. The composer has not, to any appreciable degree, communicated with this listener. I am not denying the validity or the depth of the listener's response, but only its source. The listener has a lot to do with his or her emotional experience— otherwise, how could we explain different people having different experiences while hearing the same performance?

Many in the musical community continue to accept the communication metaphor

[27] Ibid., pp. 16–17.

as literal truth. Often listeners do believe they have received a communication from the composer. Consider this not uncommon example, which appeared in a newspaper account of how Mozart's G Minor Symphony was believed to have helped a man recover from a serious operation.

> I blissfully sink back as the opening chords of his glorious 40th Symphony start easing every sore spot in my body. ... The first movement, *Molto Allegro*, is ... a cloud that picks me up, lifts me up from the pains and fear of my hospital stay. ... Today, where there was pain, the life-assuring hand of Mozart once again leads me back to joy. ... [In the second movement] Mozart will not just rescue me from despair. He will tell me of the glorious paths I have yet in front of me. ... [In the third movement] Mozart sprays me with a dozen more clear inspirations. I hear him saying, "All those delights are there for you. I know you can do them. I know your will." ... The music [of the last movement] is Mozart at his highest appreciation of life.[28]

These feelings originated in this particular listener, not in the man Mozart (who most likely did not intend to offer solace to ailing patients), and not even really in the G Minor Symphony. I do not mean to belittle the profundity of this man's experience with the symphony. I believe his account, if I take the more direct invocations of communication as metaphorical. Nor do I mean to suggest that his experience came only from within, that the actual music had nothing to do with it. That would be nonsense. This man would surely not have had a comparable experience listening to rap music! Mozart's symphony has something to do with the man's cathartic experience, even if the experience depended even more on the listener: on his needs ("I know Mozart will have something I need to hear and to hear now"[29]), his desires, his veneration of Mozart's work, his prior experiences with the symphony, and possibly the opinions others have expressed of K. 550.

Indeed, this particular work—like the second movement of Beethoven's Seventh Symphony, as Rose reports[30]—seems to have elicited a wide variety of responses throughout its two-hundred-year existence:

> Otto Jahn, for example, called it "a symphony of pain and lamentation" (1856), while C. Palmer called it "nothing but joy and animation" (1865). Alexandre Dimitrivitch Oulibicheff (1843) wrote of the finale, "I doubt whether music contains anything more profoundly incisive, more cruelly sorrowful, more violently abandoned, or more completely impassioned," while A. F. Dickinson (1927) felt that "the verve of this movement is tremendous. It is ... the best possible tonic for the low in spirits." Georges de Saint-Foix wrote in 1932 of "feverish precipitousness, intense poignancy, and concentrated energy," while Donald Francis Tovey wrote at about the same time of "the rhythms and idioms of comedy." Robert Dearling called

---

[28] Eugene E. Atlas, "The Magic of Mozart's Music Soothes a Hurting Heart," *Sarasota Herald-Tribune*, 22 January 1995, p. 5E.

[29] Ibid.

[30] Rose, *Between Couch and Piano*, p. 18.

it "a uniquely moving expression of grief," while H. Hirschbach thought it "an ordinary, mild piece of music." While Alfred Einstein found the symphony "fatalistic" and Pitts Sanborn thought it touched with "ineffable sadness," composers seem to have had happier opinions. Berlioz noted its "grace, delicacy, melodic charm, and fineness of workmanship"; Schumann found in it "Grecian lightness and grace"; Wagner thought it "exuberant with rapture."[31]

A traditional music analyst might discourage *all* such responses to the G Minor Symphony, saying that the composer never intended to convey such images (or, even if he had, that his intentions are irrelevant: only the music counts, not how or why it came to be[32]). Confronted with a student writing a comparable interpretation, such a music analyst might try to get him or her to listen more abstractly, more in terms of patterns of tension and release, rhythmic development, motivic derivation, metric structure, and harmonic drive. But we should accept that the student's hearing is perfectly appropriate—*for that particular student at that stage of development.*

It is intriguing that many of the quoted responses to the Mozart symphony are statements about the music's alleged mood, character, or atmosphere. In my arguments against musical communication from composer to listener, I have taken communication to be of ideas. But is not the communication of moods possible? I remain skeptical. As with ideas, moods exist in composers, performers, and listeners, but not necessarily the same moods at the same times. People often do not agree on what mood a passage represents, as the reactions to Mozart's G Minor Symphony show. Hence, while I would not deny the power or importance of moods, I would seriously question whether they travel in a straightforward manner from composer to listener.

Consider this direct example: a group of people are at a concert, listening to a performance of Strauss's *Till Eulenspiegel.* Most of the listeners are smiling slyly to themselves, in appreciation of the humor allegedly in the piece, or they are involved in trying to follow Strauss's detailed programmatic narrative through the piece and finding, with pleasure and satisfaction, that they can indeed do so. But one of the listeners is sitting there with tears streaming down her face. What can this mean? How can someone cry at such a sardonic piece, the rest of the listeners may wonder. Has this one person completely failed to catch Strauss's meaning? Doesn't she *understand* the music?

After the performance, they ask her why she was crying. Her answer: this piece was the favorite of her former lover, whom she misses intensely. She had her own private interaction with the music, consisting above all of grief, despite what meaning Strauss hoped he was communicating. Is her experience any less valid than those of her friends? I would say no. Is her experience any less related to the music? Again, I say no. She was hearing and responding not only to Strauss but also to her former lover and to herself, all conceived on this occasion in the context of Strauss's composition.

---

[31] Jonathan D. Kramer, *Listen to the Music* (New York: Schirmer, 1988), p. 480.
[32] Perhaps the most influential statement of this attitude is Wimsatt and Beardsley's "Intentional Fallacy." See footnote 285.

Musical amateurs (such as Eugene Atlas, the man who believed that Mozart had helped him recover after surgery) are hardly the only ones to anthropomorphize works of music into their composers, to identify the force behind the perceived music with the actual person who wrote it. This tendency is common among performers, who readily speak of, for example, "how Serkin plays Beethoven." This phrase is a telling abbreviation of "how Serkin plays the music composed by Beethoven." Such an identification of the music with its composer may be taken as a tacit equation of the music and the person who created it. To the extent that such a locution is a personification of the music, I find little trouble with it: there *is* something about music that is not badly served by the concept of a personality. But is it Beethoven's personality? Or is it a personality (or persona) created (only in part, since both Serkin and his listeners have a role in the construction of musical personae) by Beethoven, much as Shakespeare (and actors, directors, and theatergoers) created Hamlet? Because Hamlet has his own name, we do not usually conflate him with Shakespeare. We know that Hamlet's ideas came (in part) from the man Shakespeare, but we also know that a playwright is capable of creating diverse personae, none of whom need be the author's *alter ego*. The characters in a piano sonata of Beethoven do not have individual names, and indeed it is not obvious just how they inhabit the music. But the sense of personality in the music is palpable. Lacking anyone else to identify with the personalities, musicians (and listeners) happily call the personalities by the name of the composer (or, sometimes, by that of the performer: commentators have written about the personality—whether or not they use that exact word—of a Glenn Gould or a Vladimir Horowitz performance, for example). This is especially evident when performers refer, in rehearsals and other contexts, to "playing the Mozart." Less often do we hear them say they are playing the C-Major Quartet, or K. 465, or the "Dissonant" Quartet.

As I have tried to indicate, the communication chain is problematic. It is more opaque than previously believed. Nowadays music scholars are beginning to shift their focus from one end of the chain (the composer) to the other (the listener). If listeners are understood to be active in the creation of musical personae and musical meaning, then they—more than composers—are the source (not simply the destination) of what is loosely taken to be communication. Yet, many listeners—such as the essayists writing on K. 550 quoted above—still think they have received communications from composers. The composers who allegedly communicate with them are not the real flesh-and-blood people who created the scores that the performers interpreted, but rather mental constructs. Music theorist Nicholas Cook writes of denying "that the author is a free agent, the source from which meaning flows; instead the author is seen as a construction of ideological forces, and meaning is seen as being negotiated between those forces and the reader."[33]

In their minds, each of the people who wrote interpretations of the G Minor

---

[33] Nicholas J. Cook, "Music Theory and the Postmodern Muse: An Afterword," in Elizabeth West Marvin and Richard Hermann (eds.), *Concert Music, Rock, and Jazz Since 1945: Essays and Analytical Studies* (Rochester, New York: University of Rochester Press, 1995), p. 426.

Symphony created their own Mozart, who is only tangentially related to the Mozart who actually lived. These virtual Mozarts are believed to communicate to these listener-interpreters, but since all these Mozarts are different, their "communications" are different.

7.4. Postmodern Music Analysis and the New Musicology

It is hardly surprising that listeners, performers, and critics often do not clearly differentiate between the persona(e) of a work and the person who composed it.[34] This tendency is also prevalent among musicologists, even some of those who espouse the "new" musicology. Possibly in an attempt to make the Intentional Fallacy no longer a fallacy, they seek to explain the nature and meaning of a work with reference to the composer's actual personality, the ideas or even events of his or her life or times, or what the composer or those close to her or him may have said or written about the conception or genesis of the music. While I find such studies valuable, and whereas I do not deny that they may have some relevance to present-day understanding of the music, I find them finally of marginal importance to how I conceive the project of music analysis. This is why I sometimes refer to myself as an anti-musicologist. I am interested in how and what music means today, in how music that is performed and valued and enjoyed today reflects some ideas of *today's* culture. I am intrigued by how music from whatever era or culture can become important to listeners here and now. That is the reason I am excited when I find postmodern characteristics in music composed a long time ago.

When writing about music conflates or confuses the actual composer and the persona(e) of the music, or when criticism seeks to explain how the music came to be (e.g. in reference to the cultural and historical context of the composer), then I begin to become impatient. As a postmodernist, I see the past in relation to the present, and I value artistic remnants from the past for the way they find relevance in, and are (re) interpreted in, the present.

I am disappointed, for example, when I read the chapter on Ives's music, written by Lawrence Kramer, with whose projects I am usually in sympathy.[35] His observations about Ives the man, and about how the personality, values, and experiences of

---

[34] Edward T. Cone has developed an important theory of the personae of musical compositions. See *The Composer's Voice* (Berkeley, Los Angeles, London: University of California Press, 1974). Cone accepts musical communication, and he studies its origin more than its destination. Also useful is a series of papers responding to Cone's ideas. These essays—by Fred Maus, Marion Guck, Charles Fisk, James Webster, and Alicyn Warren, plus a response by Cone—appear in *College Music Symposium* 29 (1989).

[35] [Editor's note: The Lawrence Kramer work mentioned appears to be *Classical Music and Postmodern Knowledge* (Berkeley and Los Angeles: University of California Press, 1995), pp. 174–200.] It is unfair to group all so-called new musicologists together. The writings of the people usually associated with this movement are quite distinct. Some of the names most often associated with new musicology (to varying degrees) include Lawrence Kramer, Susan McClary, Rose Subotnik, Gary Tomlinson, and Richard Taruskin.

Ives informed the music, are certainly of interest,[36] but they do not tell me very much about why and how Ives's music retains its appeal to me, or about how this music is understood in the 2000s. I do not really disagree with Kramer's assertion that Ives the man was not a postmodernist, but I am interested more in exploring how and why the music of this non-postmodernist can be understood (in part) as postmodern today than in following Kramer's exploration of how Ives the man fit into the culture of late nineteenth- and early twentieth-century America.

It is partially because of my orientation toward present perceptions more than toward historical contexts that I am unwilling to forego close analysis.[37] As I have indicated, I do believe in the existence and relevance of a text out there, in the world, even though I acknowledge how differently it is perceived, interpreted, and understood from one music listener to another. By understanding the musical text only by placing it in its composer's cultural context, "new musicologists" can preclude meaningful analysis of music as understood today. All they are left with is often unverifiable assertions of what the music probably meant to the composer, or its original audiences. These notions may be perceptive, sensitive, interesting, and suggestive, but—in the absence of a structural analysis to explicate aspects of the text to which today's listeners react—they cannot be defended or argued.

If one of two listeners interprets a passage as expressive of grief and another of whimsy, both reactions may well be valid, but each listener may nonetheless want to defend his or her own response. Without structural analysis, what can either say more than: this is how I hear it? Structural analysis will not settle any interpretive arguments, but it at least helps the listeners to understand what it is in the music to which they are responding.

Two other listeners may disagree about something more objective, e.g. whether a given chord (see Example 1, Appendix, p. 320 for Example 7.12) is a dominant or not. This disagreement may seem more resolvable than one about grief vs. whimsy, but I do not think it finally is. The individuality of listeners is real and to be cherished, whether they are reacting to emotions or harmonic structures (one type of reaction hardly precludes the other). Both types of reaction are subjective. If we have no trouble invoking structural analysis to argue whether a given chord is a dominant or an agent of tonic prolongation, we should be equally willing to invoke the structures of a text in order to argue the case for grief or whimsy.

This is why I hope that postmodern analysts will not forsake structural analysis in

---

[36] A discerning reader may recall that I, too, have indulged in the habit of explaining the music in reference to the composer. See, for example, my discussion of the modernist attitudes of Stravinsky, Ives, Hindemith, and even Tchaikovsky in appropriating music from their pasts (see Section 4.3).

[37] Several new musicologists refer disdainfully to close analysis as "formalist" analysis, which they seek to replace with more subjective, more culturally relevant studies of musical texts. In an article that responds to new musicology from the perspective of music theory, Kofi Agawu points out that there are several brands of music theory that would seem to answer to the agenda of new musicology but which new musicologists generally ignore. He also points out that many of the concerns of new musicology have been addressed by ethnomusicologists. See Agawu, "Analyzing Music under the New Musicological Regime," *Music Theory Online* 2.4, http://www.mtosmt.org/issues/mto.96.2.4/mto.96.2.4.agawu.html (accessed April 24, 2016).

favor of impressionistic interpretation. Some postmodern thinkers in other disciplines feel that close reading of texts is no longer possible, now that the site of creativity and meaning has been relocated to the reader/listener. As should be clear by now, I believe that meaning comes from a subtle and varied interplay between the listener (possibly influenced by analyses) and the work. It is therefore worthwhile to understand the textual structures as thoroughly as possible, while at the same time remaining fully aware that these structures may mean different things to different listeners, and indeed may be perceived differently.

Any link in the pseudo-communication chain—composer intentions, score structures, performer interpretation, recording, listener response—may be analyzed. Most common has been to analyze the score. But the compositional process can also be analyzed, as in sketch studies or in the Darmstadt-style analyses. Performances can be analyzed, although systematic analysis has only begun to be applied to the performer's art. And recordings can be analyzed, although thus far studies of recordings seem to be mostly impressionistic reviews. And, finally, the perception of music can be analyzed, as numerous cognitive psychologists are demonstrating.

Such analyses break the pseudo-communication chain. When an analyst studies the compositional process, for example, he or she is not particularly focused on the structure of the resulting music, much less on how it is performed, recorded, or heard. When an analyst studies the score, she or he is not directly (or sometimes not at all) concerned with how that score is interpreted by performers, engineers, or listeners. Similarly, when an analyst studies a performance, he or she is usually unconcerned with how it is recorded. And, should anyone choose to study the splicing, equalization, tempo adjustments, balance changes, reverberation, etc., in a particular recording, the effect of these procedures on the listener's cognition would probably not enter very deeply into consideration.

In an important early article,[38] Edward T. Cone distinguishes between three different kinds of prose about music, which he calls prescription, analysis, and description respectively. Cone's prescription is similar to the study of the composer's poietic process. Description simply says what is in the score, without interpretation, and hence relates to Nattiez's neutral level. Analysis, which Cone favors, attempts to study the structures that are available for hearing, that ideally contribute to a listener's understanding. Analyses by Cone and those influenced by him often (whether implicitly or explicitly) ask the question, "How is it heard?" But who does this hearing? Traditional analysis of the sort Cone promotes is not really about perception, the esthesic process. It posits an ideal listener, uninfluenced by having heard the piece previously yet having the kind of perceptions and understandings that come only with repeated listening.[39]

---

[38] "Analysis Today," in Paul Henry Láng (ed.), *Problems of Modern Music* (New York: Norton, 1962), pp. 34–50.

[39] Editor's note: Kramer here referenced an article by David Temperly that he could not remember; contact with Temperly shows it was never published, but referenced ideas in Ray Jackendorff, "Musical Parsing and Musical Affect" (*Music Perception*, 1991). Temperley: "The idea is that part of our brain is 'modular' and doesn't have access to the knowledge in the rest of our brain, so it is always in some sense hearing a piece of music 'for the first time' even if we've actually heard it many times before." [Communication with editor]

This ideal listener is often the person the analyst would like to be: all-knowing (that is, knowing all that is deemed structurally significant), all-perceiving.

This ideal listener is not a mediator in the chain from composer to listener. The ideal listener, like the performer, takes the score and poietically creates a trace (the written analysis) that can be understood esthesically by the real (not ideal) reader-listener or performer. It is not surprising that Cone likens analysis to performance. However, analysis is not a substitute for performance (although some music theorists seem to treat it as such), and it is also not directly part of the chain composer-performer-engineer-listener. The kind of analyst Cone envisages—and there are many such analysts around—is more integral to the chain, however, than are the studiers of sketches, of scores, of performances, of recordings, or of mental modeling of music. Those analysts stand outside the chain and study some part of it. Cone's analyst, like Joseph Kerman's critic, seeks to improve understanding, and to enrich the esthesic process of listeners (and presumably of performers—and why not even of engineers?).

As I have said, the communication chain is long and complex. Postmodernism encourages us to focus on the listener's end (trait 16), and hence downplays the idea that a communication emanates from the composer and reaches the listener. If the listener is understood to be active in the creation of musical meaning, then he or she—more than the composer—is the one who generates what is loosely taken to be communication.

7.5. Multiple Narratives

Postmodernism recognizes and celebrates intertextuality. Some theorists of the postmodern believe that quotation is not only a decision by the artist but an unavoidable aspect of all creation, since all artworks are necessarily related to other artworks. No work is created or perceived in a vacuum. Music exhibiting a postmodern attitude is often pervasively intertextual (trait 6). It tends to include either references to other types or bodies of music, or quotations (literal or altered) of specific other pieces, or both. Since recent postmodern pieces often refer to tonality, even if they do not fully accept tonality as meta-narrative, the appearance of tonality within a larger context that also includes atonality or polytonality or distorted tonality constitutes an intertextual reference to the procedures, if not specific compositions, of the tonal period. Tonality carries historical connotations, which—particularly if brought into postmodern juxtaposition with modernist music—produce an undercurrent of association, of narrative, that counterpoints the various directed motions—whether tonal or not—within the music. Thus, in Ives's *Putnam's Camp*, for example, there are continuities created by textural/dynamic/etc. moves. There are also continuities created by the tonality itself, when it is present. And there are webs of association, wherein familiar tunes and familiar tonal gestures and progressions create narratives—which may well be different from person to person, depending on the various memories (if any) evoked by the American patriotic and folk tunes. All these temporal narratives move along in counterpoint, creating a multiplicity of musical time[40] that is more multilayered (because it is less pure) than what modernism, even at its most densely layered, ever created. Compared with the multiplicities of timelines and tempos in a dense score by Carter or Ferneyhough, those of Ives are indeed more varied. Carter's and Ferneyhough's multiplicities are very complex, but each line works by means of the same sorts of principles, whereas in a work like *Putnam's Camp*, simultaneous layers of temporality are independent because they work on different planes.

It may seem strange to label the music of Ives—the great American innovator—as postmodernist. Was it not extremely, even radically, modernist?[41] It is reasonable to call Schoenberg a forward-looking innovator, especially when we consider the musical riches the twelve-tone idea brought forth throughout the twentieth century. It is also sensible to call Webern a pioneer, when we look at what subsequent generations of composers derived from his ideas (selectively "misread," to be sure). And we can readily call Stravinsky a modernist, because of his cellular and primitivistic approaches to rhythm. But "forward-looking" (or avant garde) is a more problematic label to apply to Ives. It is certainly true that his music anticipates many later developments, and that many composers drew inspiration from his works. Yet his music is firmly rooted in its past, in a more obvious and thorough way than the early atonal compositions of Schoenberg, Webern, or Stravinsky (which do, of course, owe a lot to the past as well): Ives's music usually (not always) remains tonal, even at its most densely dissonant. And, more significantly, the music he quotes is usually not of his present but of his past: hymn tunes, marches, and patriotic songs of his youth, and classical works not of his contemporaries Strauss or Mahler but of the classical heritage, notably Beethoven. *Putnam's Camp* uses such modernist and postmodernist techniques as collage, dense dissonance, simultaneous tempos, etc., to create a work of nostalgia for remote places and times. The referential quality of the quoted folksongs gives the work a particularly evocative cast, because of both what Ives does with these materials and also what they inherently may mean to various listeners.[42]

Putnam's Camp refers to nineteenth-century America and—if we consider Ives's literary program—to the America of the Revolutionary War period. It freely intermingles sounds and procedures of Ives's (and our) past and his present, as well as

---

[40] I discuss musical time from a postmodern perspective in Chapter 8.

[41] I am not referring only to the high level of dissonance and rhythmic complexity in several of his scores, which may have been later additions—see the controversy between Maynard Solomon and Carol Baron: Maynard Solomon, "Charles Ives: Some Questions of Veracity," *Journal of the American Musicological Society* 40/3 (Fall 1987): 443–70; Carol K. Baron, "Dating Charles Ives' Music: Facts and Fictions," *Perspectives of New Music* 28/1 (Winter 1990): 20–56—but also to the indisputable forward-looking aspects of his style such as stylistic eclecticism, multilayered textures, and multiple temporalities.

[42] Although in a different context, George Lipsitz writes astutely on the power of song: "Songs build engagement among audiences at least in part through references that tap memories and hopes about particular places. Intentionally and unintentionally, musicians use lyrics, musical forms, and specific styles of performance that evoke attachment to or alienation from particular places," *Dangerous Crossroads*, p. 4.

of his future. A listener of today can hear in it echoes of patriotic tunes from eighteenth- and nineteenth-century America, and foreshadowings of experiments of the European modernists (Schoenberg et al.) and of the eclecticism of such later works as William Bolcom's Violin Concerto and Eric Stokes's *Center Harbor Holiday*. Knowing these works enriches my appreciation of the Ives piece, even though such knowledge separates my understanding of *Putnam* from that of its composer. Furthermore, knowing *Putnam* affects my listening to these later works.

This intertextuality situates *Putnam's Camp* in a directionless field rather than in a linear historical continuum. And it contributes to the temporal multiplicity of the work (trait 13, discussed in Chapter 8), which emanates from: (1) its progression through piece time, achieved by textural and tonal means; (2) the programmatic narrative Ives devised for the work and presented as a score preface; (3) the web of associations that the quoted material evokes in each listener; and (4) the relations between the piece and numerous other pieces from other historical eras.

This music does not seek to escape the past and look to the future, as an avant-garde modernist work would. If it were truly an avant-garde composition, it would deny the past in its glances toward the future. The noise music of Luigi Russolo was avant garde in this sense; perhaps the music of Satie can also be so understood; certainly a piece like Varèse's *Amériques* can. Ives may have had strong elements of modernism in his musical makeup, but it is an oversimplification to label him exclusively a vanguardist. He, like Cage (but in quite different ways; see Section 3.4), was *both* modernist and postmodernist.

Among the many tunes quoted in *Putnam's Camp*, none is as ubiquitous as "The British Grenadiers." What is this citation supposed to mean? Ives provides a clue as to *his* intended meaning in the last paragraph of his preface.

> The repertoire of national airs at that time was meagre. Most of them were of English origin. It is a curious fact that a tune very popular with the American soldiers was "The British Grenadiers." A captain in one of Putnam's regiments put it to words, which were sung for the first time in 1779 at a patriotic meeting in the Congressional Church in Redding Center; the text is both ardent and interesting.[43]

There are many ways a listener may react to the "British Grenadiers" quotations. He or she may know the tune as a patriotic American song, thus possibly having thoughts and feelings about patriotic music and its relationship to this particular context. Or he or she may know the tune as British, with somewhat different connotations. If the listener knows the words of either version (or of both), they may come back to consciousness when the tune is heard, or they may influence whatever emotional connotations the listener harbors for the melody. But the words of the two versions conjure up rather different associations.

While some listeners may know one or both sets of these words, many will not.

---

[43] Charles Ives, *Three Places in New England*, ed. James B. Sinclair (Bryn Mawr, PA: Mercury Music, 1976), p. 20.

Of those, some will nonetheless recognize the tune and perhaps have distinct and personal memories of it, perhaps from childhood. Others, like some of the students in my seminar, may not know the melody at all, and take it as an archetypal folk song or as some music Ives devised specifically for programmatic purposes.

Thus different listeners may have very different reactions to the numerous quotations of the "British Grenadiers" tune. For many listeners, their own personal associations will contribute to the creation in their minds of an unfolding narrative of the music. I do not mean to imply that every listener will hear *Putnam's Camp* as a narrative (although the intertextual references are certainly conducive to narratological interpretation), but only that those who do so hear it may experience narratives that are quite different, depending in part on each listener's prior knowledge of and associations with the material quoted.

Has Ives communicated anything by quoting "British Grenadiers"? If Ives were simply trying to communicate the existence of "British Grenadiers" and his various distortions of it and their pattern of recurrence in the piece, we could hardly argue with his success for most listeners. But that would not be much of a communication. Clearly he had more in mind, as his verbal program lays out. He was using these quotations, and several others, to tell a story, which was at least part of what he intended to communicate. But now communication becomes problematic. Listeners agreeing that "British Grenadiers" occurs at several places in *Putnam's Camp* may still have quite different ideas of what this series of citations means. The story listeners create from this pattern of quotations, distortions, and recurrences, if any, could well be very different from Ives's program, or from what other listeners concoct. So, what would seem more interesting and more worthwhile to communicate—a narrative, involving the way the quotations are arranged in the piece—is precisely what is not communicated. While certain narratives may not square with the musical facts and hence would be unlikely to occur to listeners, there are countless narratives—and countless meanings—that a listener could construct from the musical sounds and their associations. What gets communicated directly from Ives to his listeners is only the most basic, the most factual aspects of the piece. The rest is where his, and our, sense of creativity kicks in, and where we shape the stories that make this music interesting, meaningful, and pleasurable for us.

7.6. Semiosis and the Problem of Musical Communication

If intertextual references are indeed suggestive of narratological interpretation, and if intertextuality is a hallmark of postmodernism (trait 6), then it may seem strange that I am arguing against musical communication in a book on postmodernism and music. Semiotic signs (or topics) have a lot to do with musical meaning in classical-period music, as Ratner, Agawu, Hatten, Gjerdingen (discussed above), and others have argued. Surely romantic-period music is also full of signs that would seem to carry identifiable meaning. But the same cannot be said so readily about some of the music of modernism. Are we aware of references outside of the specific pieces when we listen to Babbitt's *Fourplay* or Stockhausen's *Gruppen*? Music semioticians would probably respond in the negative. Yet, as postmodern values have become more pervasive in recent music, signs with specific referents are again being heard. Indeed, one might argue that some postmodern music (of today, but also a quotation-ridden piece from the past, like *Putnam's Camp*) is little more than a series of signs, one after another, which could lead a listener to find (or construct) a narrative (or several simultaneous narratives) that meaningfully joins these signs and interprets them as they move through time.

Indeed, Susan McClary would seem to argue in such a fashion in her discussion of John Zorn's *Spillane*.[44] Finding a specific narrative in this composition, McClary claims that this is possible because postmodernism has readmitted semiosis into music. She believes that Zorn set out with a specific program in mind, and that she has heard the music his way. Surely this must add up to communication from the composer to the listener, by means of well understood signifiers. But how can this be, considering my arguments against musical communication?

Postmodern music certainly means, often in a more explicit manner than modernist music means. But that meaning does not necessarily originate in the composer. In fact, McClary chronicles a disagreement between Zorn and some of his listeners over just what his music means. While there is no denying that much intertextual postmodern music is full of signifiers, and that many of the referents are well within the range of experience of many listeners, this does not mean that the signs actually invoke the same meanings, experiences, or narratives in each listener. The familiarity and richness of signs, in fact, allows for, even necessitates, a variety of responses. Yes, a piece like *Spillane* is narrative, and, yes, it is unlikely that anyone would construct, say, a bucolic story while listening to it. But that does not by any means imply that the listener's narrative is the same as the composer's.

Is the narrative McClary constructed for herself, under the influence of what the composer said about the piece, the only possible one? Even if the musical and sonic signifiers are often too explicit to allow for much variety of interpretation, the narratives may still differ from one listener to the next. It is telling that most studies of topics in classical-period music focus on the identification of signs but do not say much about how their temporal sequence can add up to meaningful stories. Even if the stories people create (whether listening to Zorn or to Mozart) do not differ very much one from the next, that does not prove that communication has taken place from composer to listener. Listeners still construct their own narratives, ones that still have a lot to do with who they are, regardless of how explicit the musical signs of a composition are.

A lot of modernist music tries to communicate. Or, perhaps better put, many modernist composers have composed assuming that communication is possible. Their great tragedy, or so it has seemed to their supporters, is that the alleged communications failed to reach a large number of people. Listeners who experience intense

[44] Susan McClary, *Conventional Wisdom* (Berkeley, Los Angeles, and London: University of California Press, 2000), pp. 145–52.

emotions while hearing, for example, Schoenberg's String Trio or Bartók's Music for Strings, Percussion, and Celeste may be frustrated or disappointed when they encounter others unmoved by this music, listeners who feel no emotion (except, perhaps, revulsion or boredom). They feel that the communication has somehow failed, and they usually place the blame on the listeners for not "understanding." Similarly, some mid-century modernist music seems to be trying to communicate ideas. Stockhausen's *Momente* was conceived as an attempt to convey the composer's ideas about moment time; Xenakis's *Pithoprakta* was intended to communicate ideas on sonorous shapes in space. But, again, these attempts at communication fail for most people—for those who do not like this music, and even for those who do like it but who hear in it quite different things.

One might look to avant-garde compositions for instances of music that does communicate specific ideas. Was not Russolo communicating something about the bankrupt nature of Western art music in his pieces for orchestras of noisemakers? Was not Ives telling listeners something about the multiplicity of simultaneous experiences in modern life, and about the significance of American culture, in the dense collages of his Fourth Symphony? Was not Cage saying something about silence, about how listeners more than composers make or at least structure music, in *4'33"*? Was not Berio making a specific commentary on musical traditions, and about the very piece he was composing, in the third movement of *Sinfonia*?

Maybe, or maybe not.

These pieces are among the most discussed of the twentieth century. Many critics, musicologists, cultural historians, theorists, and other sorts of commentators have held forth on what these pieces mean. I would hardly deny that these works are deeply and multiply meaningful, and that many people have come up with fascinating and perceptive interpretations of them, albeit sometimes quite different one from the next. But this very richness (in both breadth and depth) of interpretation argues against the idea that Russolo, Ives, Cage, and Berio were communicating ideas through the medium of these pieces. From their writings and from what has been reported that they said, we do know something of what they were trying to achieve in these works. But we do not know everything, and in fact we may know rather little. What a composer reports after the fact, after people have begun to react to her or his works, can be colored by those reactions, just as listeners may be influenced in how they understand music by what composers (and others) write about it.

These pieces are occasions for listeners to have meaningful experiences, and they have occasioned a substantial number of commentators to write about them. But that does not mean that the sometimes fascinating ideas that commentators articulate, presumably reflecting how they have experienced these pieces, come from the composers. Even when there is some agreement between what the critics say about a work and what its creator says, there is not necessarily a direct line of communication *through the music*. The composer has an idea, or a set of ideas, that animates his or her creative activities, and a piece of music results. A listener has ideas listening to the work. These two sets of ideas—the composer's and the listener's—may be similar or quite dissimilar. Surely if they are dissimilar, we should question whether the composer has communicated through the music to the listener. But even if the ideas are similar, there is no guarantee that the listener is responding to what the composer has said, rather than coming up with comparable perceptions on his or her own—influenced by but not determined by the nature of the music.

It is ironic that postmodern music would seem to have a greater ability to communicate than modernist music does, because its intertextual references have a far better chance of being understood in a way the composer may have intended than do modernist abstractions. Yet the postmodern aesthetic, more than the modernist aesthetic ever did, questions whether music actually can communicate. So we have a plethora of signs, many with specific referents, adding up not to communication but to a multifaceted context that encourages listeners to form their own narrative paths through the thicket of quotations, references, signs, and signifiers. The overload of signs in some radically postmodern music can create such complex webs of association in listeners that the result is, paradoxically, a distancing of the signs from their referents, of the signifiers from the signifieds. And so, not surprisingly, postmodern music echoes poststructuralists' concern with the signs themselves as opposed to structuralists' concern with the signs' referents.[45] In fact, some poststructuralists seem to be calling for a non-referential semiosis, a type of meaning that does not emanate from what signs refer to but rather resides more in the signs themselves and what perceivers do with them.

Postmodern narratives are seldom straightforwardly linear. The sequence of events in a postmodern work hardly ever is simply a translation into music of a direct plot line (*Spillane* may attempt to be an exception in this sense). Some postmodern music is challenging and exhilarating precisely because the stories it suggests are not the kinds of linear tales implied in pieces like *Till Eulenspiegel*. If it was indeed Zorn's intention to create a narrative based on the gangster film genre, it is odd that he chose Mickey Spillane movies as his model. These films have linear plot lines, more or less, and are not particularly postmodern. How different it might have been had Zorn chosen to model a piece on a postmodern movie like *Pulp Fiction*, in which disagreements between story time and discourse time are acute—where, in other words, the events of the movie come in a quite different order than do the events of the plot. Zorn's basing a postmodern composition on an unpostmodern source is one further instance of a conservative strain (I already mentioned his penchant for overall unity—see Section 4.2) in the work of this quite radical composer.

---

[45] Michael Newman discusses the poststructuralist focus on the signifiers more than on the signified. "Foucault makes three points which would seem to align him with Barthes and Derrida: freed from the necessity of expression, writing is transformed 'into an interplay of signs, regulated less by the content it signifies than by the very nature of the signifier'; writing is now involved with the death or 'sacrifice' of the author into the text; and the boundaries according to which a 'work' is constituted are thrown into question." See Newman, "Revising Modernism, Representing Postmodernism," p. 116. Newman's quotation is from Michel Foucault, *Language, Counter-Memory, Practice* (Ithaca: Cornell University Press, 1977), p. 137.

7.7. Postmodernism and Communication

I have been discussing the question of musical communication at some length because of its close connection with trait 16 in my list of aspects of the postmodern musical attitude. If postmodernism truly tries to shift the locus of musical meaning to the listener, then the very possibility of communication must come under question. But we must differentiate three questions:

1. Does music of a postmodern persuasion communicate?
2. Does *any* music communicate?
3. Does any human utterance communicate?

Some extreme postmodern thinkers believe that communication is an impossibility (though they never seem to tire of writing books and articles and giving lectures communicating the impossibility of communication!). I do not take such a radical position. I am writing this book because I have certain ideas I want, and hope, to communicate—although I am fully aware that these ideas are unlikely to enter your mind without considerable influence or even distortion. Music—particularly untexted music, which, although in the minority of musics on this earth, is still an important segment of the Western "classical" tradition—can in some small way actually communicate (see, for example, footnote 23 in this chapter), but not nearly as directly or efficiently as more clearly representational arts such as photography, realist painting, narrative fiction, drama, etc. Mostly, communications sent out by composers are so distorted by the variety of mediators in the composer-to-listener chain that communication fails, or at least is less important than what listeners constitute as the music. This is true of all untexted music, I feel. Classical-period music, with its plethora of signs, and programmatic music (particularly that of the romantic era) would seem to be attempting communication in some manner. So would modernist music, though in a more abstract and less semiotic manner. Postmodernist music might seem to be trying to communicate, because its intertextual references tend to invoke extra-musical associations. But postmodern music is still music, and hence its communication suffers from the same interference as does that of any other music. However postmodern composers may be more aware of the problematic nature of musical communication than were their forebears, and thus they enter more knowingly and more skeptically into the attempt to communicate to listeners through their music.

Composers surely often intend to put specific meanings into their pieces. I question how often they actually succeed. They may control moods or affects that may correspond to what some listeners feel, but it certainly happens that intelligent, perceptive listeners experience affects and moods different from those intended by composers. When composers seek a specific meaning—as in text painting in songs or operas or oratorios—then indeed the meanings a listener constructs may be in line with the meanings a composer intends. But when the meanings are more abstract, I question to what extent those meanings really are communicated. Of course, composers (except perhaps those of a postmodernist persuasion) continue to hope, but often that hope (for direct communication) fails—and that is a good thing. It allows for, and recognizes, the creativity of listeners, responding to the physical sounds they hear.

I think we ought consider again just who these composers who are trying to communicate actually are. I believe that the person(a) about whom we informally speak as the source of musical communication is not the actual flesh-and-blood composer who really lived/lives, but rather an agent contructed in part by the listener, in part by the performer, and in part by history—all, I believe, to a greater extent than he/she was created by the actual composer. This metaphorical composer's intentions may be accessible, if at all, through the music, because he/she exists *only* through the music.

I already made an analogy to the play *Hamlet*. It contains many characters, each with a different persona. What those characters are intending to communicate is something about which theatregoers may reasonably discuss and debate. It is reasonable to try to unpack just what it is that Gertrude and Ophelia et al. are trying to communicate, intending to say. We might even go so far as to say that each of these characters is conveying ideas of Shakespeare.

But this Shakespeare is the force behind the play, not the man who lived in Stratford. The man who lived in Stratford was able to create many different personae, with different ideas to communicate, with different intentions. But those characters do not really lead us back to the man in Stratford (though his abilities surely dictated what kinds of characters he could and could not create believably). Rather, they lead us to the personae he created, which may have rather different values, ideas, thoughts, communications, etc., than did the man who lived in Stratford.

So, I think we cannot know much about what, say, Beethoven intended to communicate (in nontexted works about which he did not say much). But I think we may still go through the creative exercise of trying to unpack the intentions behind the music—what we think it is trying to communicate. Adopting the fiction that we are searching for the intentions of the man from Bonn may help us do that, but what we ultimately come up with has more to do with us than it does with the man from Bonn.

Sometimes composers write about their intentions in specific pieces. We may read these statements with interest, but I do not think they make the music any more communicative. For example, analysts reading Bartók's program note for his Music for Strings, Percussion, and Celeste have followed the composer's intention to create a highly symmetrical movement by finding innumerable symmetries in the work and by ignoring some patent asymmetries. They might go so far as to believe that the music is communicating something about symmetry. It seems to me, however, that it may be possible to come up with an even more powerful understanding of the work—and hence an even richer experience of it—by ignoring Bartók's words, or even by subverting (or deconstructing) them. I want to empower listeners and analysts to take such steps, not to be afraid to go directly against what they may believe a composer's intentions are, searching instead to find the intentions of the listeners interacting with the music Bartók created.

7.8. Intertextuality Revisited

Intertextual references meaning different things to different listeners, depending on their previous experiences with the quoted material, are not unique to postmodernist music. Leonard Meyer discusses the opening of Beethoven's *Les Adieux* Sonata, Opus 81a:

> The use of horn fifths in the first measures … is unusual in almost every way. Instead of coming at the end of a fast movement, they are the beginning of a slow introduction; instead of being accompanimental, they are the main substance; and instead of reaching emphatic closure on the tonic, they end in a deceptive cadence which is mobile and on-going.[46]

Nicholas Cook discusses Meyer's ideas about this passage in terms of listener competence:[47] a listener who does not know the "normal use" of the horn-call figure cannot understand Beethoven's distortions and commentary. Cook also mentions how Western listeners unfamiliar with the conventions of Indian music cannot fully appreciate a raga performance. The case is similar with Ives: the more you know about "The British Grenadiers"—its musical structure, its text(s), and its history, particularly with respect to the American patriotic version—the better position you are in to understand *Putnam's Camp*. But I would argue that the listener unfamiliar with "British Grenadiers" can nonetheless have a personal and meaningful experience with Ives's composition, even if that experience is less than fully informed. Similarly, you do not need to know about the horn-call tradition to enjoy and even understand (in some way, to some extent) *Les Adieux*, and you do not have to know how to keep the tala in order to listen to Indian music. Your understanding of these pieces may be somehow less authentic or less complete than that of a more knowledgeable listener, but your experience is nonetheless genuine.

The references in *Putnam's Camp* are more extensive than those in *Les Adieux*, and therein lies *Putnam's* relevance to postmodernism. In contrast to Beethoven's music, Ives's score contains a multitude of references, only some of which are identified in his preface. Not only are several American tunes broadly quoted, but also there are potential quotations of such brevity that it is difficult to decide whether or not they really are intended as citations. Some of Ives's quotations are buried so deeply within dense orchestral textures that only a most selective performance can allow them to be heard clearly. It is therefore unlikely that any one listener will even hear, let alone know, all of these references, and so the kind of competence about which Meyer and Cook write is an all but unattainable ideal for listening to Ives. With *Les Adieux*, you either know about the horn call or you do not. With the Indian raga, you either know to keep the tala or you do not. But with *Putnam's Camp*, there are so many intertextual references that it is unreasonable to expect any listener to hear and understand them

---

[46] Leonard B. Meyer, *Explaining Music: Essays and Explorations* (Chicago and London: University of Chicago Press, 1973), p. 244.
[47] Nicholas Cook, *Music, Imagination, and Culture*, pp. 143–5.

all. Each listener will have his or her own set of passages recognized, and for each recognition there may well be very different personal associations with the melodies and/or their original verbal texts.

One example is a particularly dense passage that includes several simultaneous references, including two Sousa march themes, *Liberty Bell* and *Semper Fidelis*. These marches have particular psychological resonance for me. When I was an adolescent, I spent many hours in marching bands, which often performed these and other Sousa marches in parades and at football games. Sometimes, when hearing *Putnam's Camp* I may actually recall some of these happy experiences from my youth, but more often hearing the Sousa tunes brings back pleasant and nostalgic emotions whose source may be my experiences in my high school and college bands, even though I do not conjure up specific memories or images of particular events. I usually cannot avoid these special feelings while listening to Ives's work. They form part of my own special version of his piece, part of my own narrative path through the work, a path that may not have much to do with the composer's own narrative.

I can listen to and look at the interplays of metric regularity and irregularity, thick and thin textures, consonance and dissonance, and tonality and atonality in order to create and experience a structural path through *Putnam's Camp*. Were I to make a thorough structural analysis, I would be trying to elucidate this path. When I listen in a structural manner, I am aware of and do respond to the pacing of these interplays. But my own personal narrative as I listen does not simply coincide with this structural hearing, although the two are not unrelated either. Since my narrative depends in part on my emotions and memories associated with the various tunes quoted (and also associated with other experiences I have had listening to this often-heard composition), it is uniquely my own. I am sensitive to the counterpoint among several paths: a quasi-objective structural reading, my own personal narrative based on recollections, and Ives's program. Each of these sources offers me a way through the piece, but I prefer not to choose among them but rather to savor them all—in alternation or in counterpoint. Hence the rich multiplicity of meanings people can experience in conjunction with *Putnam's Camp*, and hence my postmodernist appreciation of this work.

I hope this discussion has shown how the intertextual references in Ives's piece join hands with internal multiple structures to form a context fertile with potential for listening from multiple perspectives, and for creating diverse narratives shaped by the listener's personal associations with quoted materials, by Ives's own narrative program, by the specifics of a given performance, and by the musical structure. *Putnam's Camp* may offer particularly varied experiences (although it is not the most multilayered of Ives's creations—consider, for example, the second movement of the Fourth Symphony), but it is not unique in lending itself to a postmodernist multiple understanding. Any music which contains references outside itself, and indeed any music with any reasonable degree of complexity, can conjure different experiences in different listeners, or even in the same listener on different occasions. Thus a postmodernist understanding of any music is theoretically possible, although some pieces—like *Putnam's Camp*—have a particularly keen appeal to the postmodern sensibility.

Not everyone knows the music Ives quotes, as I have said. Those who do know several of the tunes are initiates in the special world of American folk, patriotic, and march music of the turn of the century. A work as rich in intertextual references as is *Putnam's Camp*—or several recent works I have mentioned as having a plethora of references—is hardly a work that is anti-elitist (trait 5). The tunes quoted may be vernacular, but there is still considerable experience invested in recognizing a large number of them, and not everyone has acquired that skill. Therefore some postmodernist music faces a paradox: by quoting well-known music it tries to avoid elitism, yet it does create a situation where initiates are in a better position to understand the work's multiple meanings than is someone without the requisite listening experience.

7.9. A Simple Example

Let us consider a simple example of how different listeners can understand the same music differently. Schumann's *Soldier's March* from the *Album for the Young* would seem at first to be a quite straightforward piece. [Editor's note: for the score please see John Halle's essay at the end of the book.] Not only its title but also its character suggests a march. Perhaps Schumann had in mind trying to make a little march be a small piano piece. Perhaps he was thinking about a play on the march genre. Or perhaps he was not thinking of anything in particular beyond getting the harmonies, rhythms, and tunes he liked down on paper in an orderly fashion. We can never know what, if anything, he intended to communicate, though we can reasonably guess some things he was not trying to communicate: e.g. tragedy at the death of a loved one, or gaiety at a social dance (march music is not the same as dance music). Even if he had recorded his thoughts on paper (which, as far as I know, he did not), could we fully trust them? After all, he could not have written about what he intended to communicate and also composed the actual music in the same instant; and, even if he could accomplish such a feat, we still might not fully believe him, since artists can be notoriously inaccurate reporters on their creative processes.

But I do have concrete proof that some people understand the piece differently from the way others do. For the moment, I am not talking directly about its semiotic content, or its intertextuality, or its relationship to other music. I am talking about something as basic as its metric structure. I have had performers play Examples 7.12A and 7.12B for groups of musically sophisticated listeners (upper level undergraduate music majors at Columbia University). They regularly disagree about which version of the piece they are hearing. I have also played a commercial recording of this little piece, and I have found that listeners still disagree about which version of the piece they are hearing.

The performers, whether the accomplished pianist[48] on the CD or the less experienced pianists I used in my classes, had the decided intention of playing one version or the other. These two versions would seem to communicate somewhat different

---

[48] Luba Edlina.

ideas on the march genre (more on this in a moment). But, regardless of what the performers intend to communicate (through their performance of the meter) about the nature of this march, the listeners hear what they want to hear (or what they have some predilection, for whatever reason, to hear). What happened to the performer's communication about the march-like nature of this music? Did it reach only some listeners? Or did it reach none, and was their understanding of the piano piece's relation to the march genre dependent more on their own habits and previous experiences with march music than on anything the performer or composer did?

In Example 7.12A tonic harmony begins with the first downbeat and lasts through the first measure. An apparent change of harmony coincides with the downbeat of the second measure, as is normal: harmonic changes do tend to articulate if not create metric downbeats. But it turns out that the harmony returns to tonic on the second beat of m. 2, so that in retrospect the downbeat of m. 2 is not so much a change of harmony as it is an accented neighbor chord within a still prolonged tonic. A similar thing happens at the downbeat of m. 3, where a seemingly new dominant harmony turns out to be passing within a tonic prolongation. The dominant harmony on the downbeat of m. 4, however, is more substantial, because of the skip motion in the bass. This V7 does have harmonic function, driving to the tonic cadence on m. 4's second beat.

Example 7.12B is more static harmonically. Instead of having the tension of accented dissonances needing to resolve in mm. 2 and 3, we find tonic harmony on the downbeat of every measure in the first phrase. What are accented dissonances requiring resolution in Example 7.12A, mm. 2 and 3, become in Example 7.12B more neutral, less intense, unaccented neighbor and passing chords. Even the full root-position dominant chord just before the cadence seems less active than in Example 7.12A, because it comes on the weak beat of the measure. The cadence in Example 7.12B, m. 4, is less an arrival, less a resolution, and more simply a continuation of tonic harmony than is its counterpart in m. 4 of Example 7.12A. Similar observations can be made about the tonic prolongation in mm. 11–12 (Example 7.12A, or mm. 10–12 in Example 7.12B). The non-tonic chords are incomplete neighbors or passing chords, which are more active because they fall on strong beats in Example 7.12A than they are as weak beats in Example 7.12B.

The opening rhythmic figure—dotted eighth, sixteenth, eighth—leads forward toward its final impulse. It is a quintessential upbeat figure leading to a downbeat. The meter in Example 7.12B supports this conventional understanding of this figure, and thereby makes the opening more march-like than the opening of Example 7.12A. In Example 7.12A there is a tension between the upbeat-downbeat nature of the opening figure and its metric placement as downbeat-upbeat. Similarly, the m. 4 cadence is more straightforward in Example 7.12B, where the cadence chord arrives on a strong beat, than in Example 7.12A, where the arrival chord comes on a weak beat. Similar things can be said about the arrival in m. 8.

Example 7.12B is the more straightforwardly march-like of the two. Its upbeat-downbeat figures (mm. 0–1, 4–5, 8–9, 12–13, 16–17, and 20–21) are all placed in agreement with the meter: upbeat-downbeat. The cadential arrivals (except the final one) are all on strong beats (mm. 4, 8, 12, 16, and 20). The prolonged harmonies are all extended by simple unaccented passing-neighbor chords.

By comparison, Example 7.12A is more stylized and more sophisticated. It is a commentary on the march, a deconstruction of the march, even a slight distortion of the march. It is full of dissonant chords (accented neighbor and passing) that are more prominent, more tension-laden, than we would expect in an innocent march. The opening figure, with its conventional upbeat-downbeat profile, is consistently placed against the meter, in a downbeat-upbeat position. And all the cadence points arrive on weak beats, until the very end, where finally the rhythmically accented cadential chord falls on a strong beat and thereby offers an overall resolution to the work's metric tensions.

Schumann's actual notation is shown in Example 7.12A. But that does not imply that his specific intention was to communicate a deconstruction of the march. The remarks offered on Example 7.12A are mine, not Schumann's. We do not know what Schumann wanted to communicate, and hence we cannot know whether the meanings constructed by listeners do or do not correspond to what he may have thought he was communicating.

But what do listeners hear? A performer reading from Example 7.12A presumably would want to project the metric structure in that score, and thereby possibly "communicate" a deconstructive reading such as I have outlined. A performer may want to preserve ambiguity over which version is being played, but it is unlikely that a player would read Example 7.12A and choose to try to communicate Example 7.12B (such perversity—deliberately going against the notation—is not impossible, but it is relatively rare among serious performers, who usually try to be faithful to the score's notation). Schumann probably had some intentions, possibly along the lines described here (but not necessarily), for choosing to notate the piece as in Example 7.12A rather than Example 7.12B. And a performer probably intends something specific by deciding to (or not to) bring out Example 7.12A but not Example 7.12B. But what happens to these intentions to communicate ideas about metric structure and about the work's attitude toward the march? Are they received and processed by listeners? In my experience, no! It seems not to matter whether the performer is trying to project Example 7.12A or 7.12B (unless the performer gives an unnaturally and unmusically exaggerated account of the work's accentuation). In my experience, people hearing a performer play Example 7.12A may perceive either Example 7.12A or Example 7.12B. The difference from listener to listener cannot be accounted for in the score or the performance, which are identical for all listeners. The difference must have something to do with the listeners' abilities, experiences, or attitudes—or possibly the differences are simply coincidental. Similarly, when a performer deliberately performs Example 7.12B, listeners still hear either version. Again, neither the composers' (Schumann did not compose Example 7.12B, but he did compose Example 7.12A) score nor the performers' intentions seem to be communicated to a large number of listeners.

I do not mean to imply that the only possibly communication "in" Schumann's piece lies in the area of metric structure. The potential meanings of even such a small piece are myriad, and they are related to many aspects of the music, not just the meter. But I do think it is reasonable to suggest that, particularly for a march, the metric structure is one means by which an idea would be communicated from Schumann to us if any such communication is possible. The melodic, rhythmic, and harmonic figures in this piece do suggest the archetype "march," and most listeners accustomed to the conventions of march music in European and American culture should recognize these elements as march-like. But whether the piece is a real march (Example 7.12B, at least before the end) or a deconstructed march (Example 7.12A) seems to depend more on the listener than on the score or the performance.

I also do not mean to suggest that the interpretive nuances on which performers work diligently make no difference. That would be absurd! But in this one case, where the meter is indeed ambiguous, performer nuance may be less readily accessible to listeners—even to musically trained listeners—than performers might like to believe. This example nicely demonstrates the power of listeners to create their own understanding of a heard performance, even when it flatly contradicts the way the performer thought she or he was projecting the music. Surely this does not happen all the time. Indeed, I had to search hard before finding an appropriate musical example. But this one example does suggest how strong the listener's powers of interpretation—I almost said "composition"—are. In less ambiguous pieces, what the performer does is no doubt more readily understood. In more complex pieces, performers (and composers, and listeners) find a richer layering of possible meanings, which sometimes agree and sometimes do not.

7.10. A More Complex Example: Is the Meaning in the Music or in the Perceiver?

A musicologist wanted to analyze my orchestral piece *Moments in and out of Time.* I did not wish to impose my views on her, though it *was* tempting. She came up with a reading of the piece as dialectical. I certainly do not think of it in that way. It is one of my six-note pieces: only six pitch classes appear throughout; the other six are never heard (except if/when a player makes a mistake!). You could call this particular six-note collection a harmonic minor scale on E without the fourth degree; you could also call it [013478] or 6-Z19. Perhaps these alternate labels—each of which carries quite a lot of aesthetic baggage, at least for music theorists—suggest that there *is* a dialectic aspect to my thinking, but in a far more submerged sense than my friend had in mind. The entire first section (about eight minutes) is based on a single melody and takes place over a pedal E. There is transformation but not much contrast.

So I was surprised to read about the dialectical struggles, the destruction of one kind of music by another, the conflicts of material. Was she wrong? Surely not. A European, she had been trained in a musical culture that values, perhaps even depends on, dialectical thinking. I was not so trained. Apparently she *needed* the piece to be dialectical in order to understand it. I did not. The music inevitably means something very different to her than it does to me.[49] As Katherine Hayles has written,[50] "Observational statements are always theory-laden." Furthermore, observational statements are necessarily informed by the observer's meta-narratives. Calling a piece dialectical is like calling it unified: to observe textual unity (or dialectic opposition) is to invoke (whether tacitly or explicitly) theories which rest on the assumption that music is unified (or dialectical).

As we talked, I began to enjoy her understanding of *Moments*. I had once been quite interested in European musical dialecticism, while I was studying with Boulez, Stockhausen, and Jean-Claude Eloy. When she finally asked, and I finally consented to tell her, about some of the ways I had thought about the music, she was not persuaded. My ideas did not fit her already formed notions of what the piece is. And I was telling her how I had made it, not what it was (at least for her).

Does the piece have *any* inherent characteristics that analysts of whatever persuasion would agree on? Observable facts (such as that there is a thirty-six voice canon for solo strings in the first section), yes, but no objectively verifiable qualities of expression.

But can we not say that about any piece?

7.11. *Is* Musical Communication Possible?

So, once again: is musical communication possible? Is there some objective way to test whether listeners' meanings come from, or correspond to, composers' intentions? Testing for verbal communication is possible, but does that mean that musical communication can similarly be demonstrated? A normal way to check out verbal communication is to ask the receiver to reproduce the alleged message. To make sure that the simple sounds of words (or their appearance on the page) are not being reproduced without comprehension, we might ask for a change of mode: heard speech to be reproduced in writing, or read writing to be replicated in speech.

Such tests do not work for music. If someone hears music and then reproduces it, for example, on a piano keyboard, we do not normally take what may be considered a demonstration of good musicianship as proof that the composer communicated successfully. Reproducing across modes—e.g. asking a good musician to write down in standard musical notation what she or he has heard—is a common activity: this is the basis of dictation exercises in musicianship training. But, someone with a good ear who can take down musical dictation accurately is not necessarily thought to have received and understood the composer's communication. Musical communication—especially in nontexted music—is different from verbal communication.

I am quite sensitive to this difference. As the author of this book, I am always trying to communicate (as well as to suggest, to lead you into new contexts for

---

[49] To read her take on the piece, see Dorota Maciejewicz, *Zegary nie zgadzają się z sobą* (Warsaw: Studia Instytutu Sztuki Pan, 2000), pp. 154–9, English summary p. 179.
[50] N. Katherine Hayles, *Chaos Bound*, p. 263.

thought, etc.). I realize that you may well interpret what I say in a way rather different from what I intend, but I must take that chance. I try to be as clear as I can, but I know that your meaning rests ultimately with you. If your interpretations—if the ideas you take from this book—differ considerably from what I have in mind, I may be annoyed or elated, depending on whether I like your version of my ideas or not. (Of course, your version of my ideas is not directly accessible to me. I have only your report, your transcription, to go by, and then I am necessarily interpreting, just as you necessarily did.)

I am also a composer, and I feel differently about the music I produce than I do about the prose I create. I do not try to make my compositional ideas too explicit. I prefer a certain vagueness, a certain ambiguity, a multi-meaningful situation, which encourages you to hear and understand my music in your own way. When people tell me their quite different understandings of my music, I am usually quite pleased (though some interpretations, I admit, seem so far from the mark that I question my music and/or the receiver's musical abilities). When people tell me of their diverse understandings of my expository prose, I may or may not be pleased, but I am displeased far more often than I am when a listener comes up with what seems to me to be an odd understanding of my music.

Is the difference between music and words, or is it between imaginative vs. expository creation (not a rigid distinction, to be sure)? Since I do not indulge in creative writing, I cannot offer a first-hand account of how someone feels when her or his creative prose or poetry is understood in a way quite different from what (if anything!) was consciously intended. But I suspect that novelists, poets, and playwrights feel more the way I do as a composer than the way I do as a theorist. However, everyone is different, and I should not make speculative generalizations that may not apply to everyone, or even to most of us.[51]

What does all of this have to do with postmodernism? I am certainly not trying to suggest that people today, when postmodern musical attitudes are more prevalent than in earlier eras, are likely to hear Schumann's *Soldier's March* differently than they would have 150 years ago. I do not know of anyone trying such an experiment in perception back then, but I suspect that, if someone had, the results would have been similar to what I found: that many educated listeners hear a different version from that being played. The relevance of this kind of ambiguity for postmodernism is that today, deeply influenced by postmodernist thinking, we are more likely to celebrate the fact that different listeners hear different metric structures in the same performance. We are likely to rejoice in this concrete demonstration of the individuality of listeners' responses, and to take note of how such a situation seriously calls into question the

---

[51] As I have already stated, most people involved with Western music have believed that it is a communicative art. Communication from composer to listener has been a meta-narrative of the musical process. What I have tried to do in this section is, in a quintessentially postmodern manner, interrogate the notion of musical communication, and to deconstruct it. I am trying to suggest that we should all think about it, and that in so doing we should remove it from the status of a meta-narrative. I am not trying to argue totally against musical communication, but to recontextualize it by showing in what ways it may occur and in what contexts it probably does not.

notion that a composer simply sends out a communication that listeners pick up, with the help of a sympathetic performance. Faced with diverse understandings of the metric structure of *Soldier's March* in earlier eras, before postmodern ideas were widespread, people might have concluded that some of the listeners were not as good musicians, or that the performer had failed to bring out the "true" metric structure. In some subtle (or perhaps not so subtle) way, those who heard Example 7.12B when Example 7.12A was played would be disparaged. In some sense, and to some degree, their perception would have been deemed *wrong*. Under the influence of postmodernism's respect for the individuality and creativity of listeners, we today are not comfortable with the idea that a perception can be right or wrong. And that, in a nutshell, is why postmodernist thinking is skeptical of the very idea of musical communication.

8

Postmodern Musical Time: Real or Unreal?

8.1. Multiply-Directed Time

With only a few exceptions,[1] the postmodernist critical theories of literary and visual arts with which I am familiar do little more than mention time. If any art genre exhibits a postmodern sense of time, however, it should be the quintessentially temporal art of music. Of the traits of postmodern musical thought I have mentioned, certain ones stand out as particularly relevant to the time structures of music and music perception: we should expect postmodern musical time to be created by listeners more than by composers (trait 16), to differ from one listener to another (trait 16), to be fragmented and discontinuous (trait 10), and to be nonlinear and multiple (trait 13). The notion of the multiplicity of musical time—that music can enable listeners to experience different senses of directionality, different temporal narratives, and/or different rates of motion, all *simultaneously*—is truly postmodern.

In several parts of this book I discuss music that places its temporal structure in the listener. I try to show not only how the music objectively is but also how one particular postmodern listener understands its temporality. I do not mean to imply that the music does not matter: structures that are objectively in these pieces suggest my multiple-time hearing of them. The temporalities I describe come from an inter-action between these structures and me. I describe the pieces as they are constituted in my mind. My mental representation is informed by the nature of the music, by my ideas on postmodernism, by various performances I have heard of this music, and by who and what I am.

The concept of multiple musical time began as a modernist statement, a series of avant-garde experiments. Once modernism showed listeners, performers, and analysts the richness of multiple temporal structures, it became possible to discern comparable, though not identical, forms in previous compositions. In my book *The Time of Music*, I discuss several species of multiple musical time (e.g. mobile form, gestural time, multiply-directed linear time) and also certain other temporal experiments (moment time, vertical time) that were creations of modernist composers of the early and/ or mid-twentieth century. Despite their modernist spirit, many of these temporal

---

[1] Most notably: Ursula Heise, *Chronoschisms: Time, Narrative, and Postmodernism* (Cambridge: Cambridge University Press, 1997) and Elizabeth Deeds Ermarth, *Sequel to History: Postmodernism and the Crisis of Representational Time* (Princeton: Princeton University Press, 1992).

structures also contain the seeds of postmodern thinking about musical time. Thus I wish to recapitulate (in abbreviated form) some of what I have said about modernist temporality in music, and to recast some of my descriptions in postmodernist terms.

First I want to discuss "multiply-directed time." *The Time of Music* defines a multiply-directed piece as one "in which the direction of motion is so frequently inter-rupted by discontinuities, in which the music goes so often to unexpected places, that the ... [sense of linear motion through time], though still a potent structural force, seems reordered."[2] In certain modernist works, multiply-directed time results from simultaneous motions toward different goals. Each such motion may take place in a different parameter. The pitches, for example, may be moving toward one goal while, say, the textural density is moving toward a different goal—at the same time. This hypothetical structure depends on what might be called the "parametric concept." A number of modernist composers in the mid-twentieth century thought of the various parameters of music (e.g. duration, pitch, register, timbre, loudness, etc.)[3] as separable. This idea derives from "total" or multi-parameter serialism, in which each parameter has its own construction (actually, the same serial structures often govern many parameters, so that the theoretical independence of parameters was used to make them isomorphic). Once listeners understand loudness and textural density, for example, as independent, they can ideally comprehend each of these parameters as providing its own sense of direction.

Explained in this manner, the parametric concept is essentially modernist: a struc-turalist attempt to redefine musical temporality by creating independent structures in different facets of the music. But there are undercurrents of postmodernist thinking evident as well, because what the parametric concept actually does is to deconstruct the previously holistic idea of musical structure. Thus, for example, I am able to offer (in Chapter 12) a parametric analysis of the finale of Mahler's Seventh Symphony, which tries to show how that work can be understood as temporally multiple: each of five parameters (theme, tonality, harmony, meter, and chromatic vs. diatonic pitch content) has its own quasi-independent structure. The five quasi-independent tempo-ralities, I argue, operate in counterpoint with one another, creating—at least for this listener—a richly multiple time sense.

How does time function in postmodern music? Postmodernism is profoundly temporal, but it uses, rather than submits to, time. Its music shapes time, manipulates time. Time, like tonal sounds and diatonic tunes and rhythmic regularity and textual unity, becomes no longer context but malleable material. So, many postmodern composers use tonality, often not simply referring to it but entering into it in order to utilize its temporal structures. Because they want to work with time, to create new temporalities, they use materials—i.e. those of tonality—that are inherently diachronic, whereas the materials of modernism often tend to be synchronic. The serial system, for example, is not inherently diachronic (although a particular serial

[2] Jonathan D. Kramer, *The Time of Music*, p. 46.
[3] Different composers had different concepts of the basic parameters. Some differentiated between the inherent parameters of sound and the particular parameters of a given passage or piece.

piece may indeed create directed motion contextually). Just as Edward Cone[4] demonstrates that the typical pitch-serial analysis can work just as well on the inversion of a twelve-tone piece as on the real piece, so the retrograde could be equally well analyzed: if the beginning and ending are serially indistiguishable, we might conclude, then the music—or, better stated, its underlying serial structure—must be essentially synchronic.

Of course, demonstrating that an analysis works just as well if the music is retrograded is not the same as showing the experiential synchronicity of the piece itself. Most—but not all—modernist works do differentiate their beginnings from their endings, do progress through time in one manner or another. But still their directionality, which is often created by extra-serial means, is often less acute than that of tonal works. Temporal direction is not inherent in serialism or in atonality the way it is in tonality. Posttonal works that do have a sense of directed motion through time contextually create their own means of motion.[5] If postmodernism deconstructs linear musical time, it does so by using aspects of tonality, with its inherent conventions of temporal motion, rather than by constructing a unique atonal directionality only to distort it. So, radical postmodernists' turn to tonal sounds, procedures, and materials is just that: a turn, not a *return*. Theirs is not simply a re-embracing of the metanarrative of tonal temporal linearity, but a way to deconstruct time by means of its strongest musical representation—tonality itself.

8.2. Gestural Time

Analyses in *The Time of Music* show how the first movement of Beethoven's String Quartet, Opus 135, and the third movement of Mozart's *Jupiter Symphony*, among other works, take advantage of the temporal implications of particular gestures to deconstruct the linearity of musical time.[6] In these works, piece time (the normal succession of events) is contradicted by what I call gestural time, in which temporal function is created not by the order of events but by their conventional profiles. Thus a definitive cadence is considered final in gestural time, whether or not it falls at the end of a performance in piece time. Does this mean that the temporal witticisms of Haydn (as discussed by Levy and Meyer; see footnote 6) and Mozart (which I trace briefly in

---

[4] Edward T. Cone, "Beyond Analysis," in Benjamin Boretz and Cone (eds.), *Perspectives on Contemporary Music Theory* (New York: Norton, 1972), pp. 72–90.

[5] For discussions of examples of contextually created directionality in atonal music, see *The Time of Music*, pp. 32–40, 170–83, 187–9, and 196–9.

[6] Janet M. Levy and Leonard B. Meyer have analyzed similar passages by Haydn. See Levy, "Gesture, Form, and Syntax in Haydn's Music," in Jens Peter Larsen, Howard Serwer, and James Webster (eds.), *Haydn Studies* (New York: Norton, 1981), pp. 355–62. Also see Meyer, "Toward a Theory of Style," in Berel Lang (ed.), *The Concept of Style* (Philadelphia: University of Pennsylvania Press, 1979), pp. 33–8. The Haydn passage (opening of the slow movement of the *Military Symphony*) is also discussed in Burton S. Rosner and Leonard B. Meyer, "Melodic Processes and the Perception of Music," in Diana Deutsch (ed.), *The Psychology of Music* (Orlando, FL: Academic Press, 1982), pp. 318–19. Meyer's analysis also appears in his *Style and Music*, pp. 26–30.

The Time of Music), or the intense temporal reorderings of Beethoven (as shown in *The Time of Music*) and Mahler (discussed here in Chapter 12), are postmodern? In a way they are, since they do deconstruct time, they do use musical time as material as well as context, they do create multiple time senses, and they do depend on a re-ordered linearity created not by the performer but mentally by the listener. It may take a postmodern sensibility, more likely to be understood and articulated in the late twentieth or early twenty-first century than earlier, to understand such temporal manipulations. It may well be that they can be understood and experienced as postmodern only in an "age of postmodernism." Or, more carefully put, the postmodernism of such works resides not simply in the music but in the way listeners (and critics and analysts and performers) understand them *today*.

My postmodern analysis of the first movement of Beethoven's Opus 135 begins with the observation of a prematurely strong cadence in mm. 9–10. It is possible, I argue, to understand this gesture as a *final* cadence, despite its appearance early in piece time. This gesture feels like, and has the shape of, an ending. In a certain sense, *it actually is the end*. In piece time mm. 1–10 do, obviously, constitute an opening. But, in terms of gestural time, the movement *does end* in m. 10, at least for me, because m. 10 is the place where I hear the profile of a final cadence.

In tonal music, piece time is diachronic: in it a piece unfolds note by note, gesture by gesture, phrase by phrase. Gestural time, however, is synchronic: a final cadence is recognized as such no matter where in the piece it occurs. Does it make any sense to ask which is the "real" time, piece time or gestural time? (I return to this question later in this chapter.)

The Time of Music's suggestion that there is a sense in which the ending of the first movement of Opus 135 occurs in m. 10 is a postmodernist idea. It postulates a multiple temporal continuum, with two separable orders of succession. One order depends on the succession of musical events as heard in performance (in piece time), while the other depends on conventionally defined gestures that carry connotations of temporal function (beginning, ending, climax, transition, etc.) regardless of their immediate context. Such conventions are more clearly and thoroughly defined in tonal music (and, in particular, in classical-period tonal music—they form, for example, some of the "topics" of Kofi Agawu's semiotics of classical music[7]). Hence, when recent postmodern composers began to include tonal passages in their pieces, they re-introduced (at least potentially) not only the complex directionality of tonal progression but also temporal multiplicity as defined by conventionalized gestures.

I conclude my analysis in *The Time of Music* with some observations that in essence show how disagreements between gestural time and piece time are postmodern in spirit. Since time exists within me, there are other species of temporality beyond the simple moment-to-moment succession I have been calling piece time. Gestural time is one of these species. I do not believe that I literally experience the orderings of gestural time. If I hear a gesture that sounds like a final cadence followed by a gesture that feels like an internal transition, I know in what order I have heard these events and I

---

[7]   See Agawu, *Playing with Signs*, pp. 26–50.

understand that their gestural profiles suggest a different ordering as more "logical." I *understand*, but do not really *hear*, the underlying logical ordering: internal transition before final cadence. I *understand* when a gesture seems to be misplaced in piece time, and I await the consequences of this misplacement. Eventually, I may come to understand in retrospect that the gestures of the piece imply logical progressions and virtual continuities quite different from the progressions and continuities actually heard in piece time. I call these continuities "virtual" because they do not exist objectively "out there" in the music, but rather they exist where all music I hear exists: in my mind.

8.3. Time Out of Phase

Chapter 12 uses the finale of Mahler's Seventh Symphony as an additional example of postmodern multiple temporality in tonal music. Like the first movement of Beethoven's Opus 135, it contains gestures (notably V-I cadences suggestive of sectional endings) that do not function in accord with the structural conventions they invoke. And, like the Beethoven movement (but to a greater extent), it is a piece that once proved difficult for many listeners, but today, when the postmodern impulse in music is widely recognized, begins to make a lot of sense.

Mahler called the movement "Rondo-Finale." And, indeed, it exhibits a rondo-like structure. In a more normal rondo, thematic returns would coincide with moves back to the tonic, which would usually be underlined by V-I cadential articulations. In the Mahler movement we find returns of the rondo thematic material, which may or may not begin with the first rondo motive; we find returns to the tonic, which may or may not coincide with V-I progressions; we find returns to diatonicism after chromatic passages; we find returns to metric regularity after passages in which the hypermeter[8] is uneven, and/or the heard meter conflicts with the written meter, and/or different contrapuntal voices project different meters simultaneously, and/or the meters alternate between duple and triple.

What is particularly interesting in this movement, and unsettling, and in my view postmodern, is the manner in which these various returns rarely coincide. If a progression back to the tonic has the power to create a major structural articulation, particularly when it is underlined by a V-I cadence, then why should it not coincide with a reappearance of the rondo theme? The reason is that the movement questions formal structuring by means of coinciding harmonic, tonal, and thematic recapitulation. One of the principal structures of tonal form—recapitulation, as supported in several musical parameters—is overthrown. This is not the kind of overthrowing

---

[8] The term "hypermeter," which is used by a number of theorists of meter, refers to large-scale meter. For example, the hypermetric structure of a typical four-bar phrase is a hypermeasure of four beats, respectively the downbeats of each of the four measures. The downbeat of measure 1 is the strongest, and it functions as the hypermeasure's downbeat. The downbeat of measure 3 is next strongest, functioning like the third beat of a large, slow 4/4 measure. The downbeats of measures 2 and 4 are weaker, although still stronger than any beats that are not downbeats of measures. This hypermetric structure is typical but not inviolable: there are numerous variations in actual music. For a fuller discussion of hypermeter, see *The Time of Music*, pp. 83–107.

of all of tonality that was soon to emerge in the works of Schoenberg and Webern, however. Their invention was modernist, while Mahler's was, paradoxically (since it occurred earlier), postmodernist. He did not eschew tonal, thematic, or harmonic return. He used them, but in ways that compromised, redefined, and deconstructed their traditional meanings and functions. In a postmodern manner, he used history to destroy history. He used tonality to destroy tonal form. He thereby made tonal form not the structure of the movement but its topic. He created a narrative in which the characters are tonality, harmony, and theme (*not* particular themes, but the general concept of musical theme). Tonality operates, but without the crucial component of dominant support. Harmony operates, but fundamental root movements sometimes do and sometimes do not have truly articulatory impact. And themes certainly exist. They abound, in fact. Because the rondo theme often starts at some point other than its beginning, however, thematic recapitulation is compromised. And because certain motives migrate from one thematic group to another, thematic identity is also compromised.

These out-of-phase thematic returns, tonal returns, harmonic cadences, re-emergences of metric regularity, and returns of diatonicism are not consistent throughout the movement, however. Sometimes these elements are partially in phase, i.e. some of them do occur together. When some elements cooperate, the result is not, as might be expected, a major structural downbeat, but rather just another contrast, another juncture, which happens to involve some coordination between the elements. This happens because *all* these parameters *never* work completely together. Some element always contradicts the others, always seeks to destroy whatever sectional articulation the others are creating. Thus the temporality of this movement is indeed deeply multiple.

The movement's title leads us to expect certain kinds of structures. They are not absent, but they are radically redefined, losing much of their traditional meaning and gaining new meanings in the process. Big, fully orchestrated V-I cadences, for example, rarely mark major structural junctures, whereas unexpected harmonic juxtapositions do. Thus the V-I cadential gesture becomes not so much a functional harmonic progression as a topic—a musical object rich in association, connotation, and intertextual resonance.[9] It exists prominently on the surface but not in the deep structure, where the dominant key is absent. Large-scale tonal moves by fifth or fourth

---

[9]   The V-I progression is tonality's archetypal implication-realization harmony, but it is not music's only way of moving to an expected goal. Tonal music (as Leonard Meyer and Eugene Narmour have painstakingly demonstrated), and to a lesser extent some pretonal and posttonal music, is structured by means of complex interactions of implications, resolutions, delayed resolutions, and denied resolutions. However, postmodern music, particularly today's radical variety, casts doubt on the very concepts of implications and realizations. Because the postmodern future is unpredictable, musical gestures—that might in other contexts diachronically imply their continuations—become synchronic topics. They retain their intertextual references to what they might have meant in more teleological contexts, but they are no longer loaded with implications about what should happen next. Potential realizations so seldom actually materialize that the listener (or at least this listener) comes to expect the unexpected. This may be less pervasively true of an early postmodern work like Mahler's Seventh Symphony, but even there the music goes so often to unpredictable places that it is difficult to believe in an implication.

are avoided, usually in favor of major-third modulations. Cycles of major thirds are inherently more ambiguous and more limited than cycles of fifths: in an equally tempered system, if we modulate up (or down) three major thirds, we are already back home, whereas it takes fully twelve perfect-fifth modulations to complete a cycle. We have scarcely left on the major-third tonal journey before we return. Hence tonal returns are more frequent and less articulative, and less goal-like, than in traditional tonal music.[10]

8.4. Time in Recent Modernist and Postmodernist Music

The multiple time senses in Beethoven's Opus 135 and Mahler's Seventh Symphony and, to a lesser extent, Ives's *Putnam's Camp* (discussed in Sections 7.3 and 7.6) depend on discontinuities. Some later composers have explored even more extreme discontinuities, creating what I have called "moment time,"[11] which in some ways is similar to and in other ways differs from multiply-directed time. A multiply-directed piece may have one or more beginnings (which may or may not occur at the start of the work), while a piece cast in moment time does not really begin at all but rather simply starts, as if it had already been going. A multiply-directed form can have one or several *final* cadences, not necessarily at the close of the piece, whereas a moment-time work simply ceases rather than ends. At its close we feel as if we have heard a series of minimally connected sections, or moments, that belong to a potentially eternal continuum. The moments may be *related* (through motivic similarity relationships, for example) but are not *connected* by transition. Moment forms are, therefore, inherently not organic. Moments are self-contained sections (set off by discontinuities) that are heard more for themselves than for their participation in the progression of the music. If a moment is defined by a process, that process must reach its goal and must be completed within the confines of the moment. If, on the other hand, one section leads to another section (whether adjacent to it or not), then it is neither self-contained nor in moment time. The works of Zorn I have mentioned—*Forbidden Fruit* and *Carny* in particular—are prime examples of moment forms conceived under the influence of postmodernism.

An extreme manifestation of the moment idea is mobile form, in which the order of moments not only *seems* but actually *is* arbitrary. The composer indicates that the sections of the piece may be put together in any of a number of possible orderings from one performance to the next.[12] The composition of mobile forms is considerably less common than it once was. In fact, many of the temporal experiments that I described and applauded in *The Time of Music* seem in recent years

---

[10] Another work of Mahler with several postmodern characteristics is the Third Symphony, particularly the first movement. Its postmodernism lies not so much with its temporality, however, as with its brash inclusion of all sorts of music, from the most banal march riffs to the most profound symphonic passages.

[11] See *The Time of Music*, pp. 50–5 and 201–85.

[12] For more on moment time and mobile form, see *Time of Music*, pp. 50–5 and 201–85.

to have waned along with the modernist avant garde. Since pieces cast in mobile form take some degree of formal structuring out of the hands of the composer, we might expect to find postmodernists interested in continuing the modernist experiments with variable form. But this has not happened. Modernist music's self-conscious mobility was doomed to be peripheral, I suspect, because it often rested on an artificial linearity. Instead of the subtle interplay of rates of motions toward foreseeable goals that we find in tonal music, modernist avant-gardists offered such pale substitutes as step connections without clear goals, monolithic textural moves in a direction (e.g. the move toward registral extremes in Ligeti's *San Francisco Polyphony*[13]), etc. When recent postmodernist music readmitted tonality to the *lingua franca*, however, then tonality's distortions of rates of motion, delaying or thwarting of goal achievement, etc., became once again powerful means of creating temporal progression. Other types of modernist directionality have hardly disappeared, but the re-emergence of tonality now allows a deeper multiplicity of types of motion than was possible in the purist, anti-tonal compositions of high and late modernism.

Mobile form failed also because it was not usually listener-oriented. It was a private game between composer and performer. The ideal was to create a fluid, variable time, that different listeners on different occasions (but ideally even on the same occasion) could react to, could *constitute*, themselves. But only knowledgeable listeners—often other composers of mobile music—succeeded in experiencing the mobility.[14] Hence, mobile form (as in, e.g., Stockhausen's *Momente*) was finally too elitist to become widely adopted by postmodern composers (trait 5).

Similarly, the creation of what I call "vertical" compositions seems no longer to be as seductive to composers as it once was. Compositions cast in "vertical time" (such as, e.g., Stockhausen's *Stimmung)* are temporally undifferentiated in their entirety. They lack progression, goal direction, movement, and contrast. The result is a single present stretched out into an enormous duration, a potentially infinite "now" that nonetheless feels like an elongated instant. Vertical music, such as is found in many works of Cage, tries not to impose itself on or manipulate the listener. The context of vertical music allows a listener to make contact with his or her own subjective temporality. It is music of subjectivity and individuality.[15] In *The Time of Music* I conclude that vertical music "reflects a thoroughly modernistic time sense."[16] I now realize that vertical time is also postmodernist.

---

[13] Actually, I find this work and certain others like it quite exciting, although I understand that the direct structures Ligeti and others employed are hardly capable of sustaining an entire aesthetic in the way that tonal progression has.

[14] In his composition seminars I attended in 1966–7, Stockhausen wanted us to create pieces in mobile form such that a careful listener could discern the mobility on only one hearing (in other words, without having to hear a second performance in which the order of sections was different). Several of us thought we had succeeded in making the potential mobility audible at once, but I now think we were fooling ourselves. See my article "Karlheinz in California," *Perspectives of New Music* 36/1 (1998): 247–61.

[15] For fuller discussions of vertical time, see *The Time of Music*, pp. 7–9 and 375–97.

[16] Ibid., p. 57.

Why has a temporal structure that encourages the individuality of listeners (trait 16) not thrived in an age when postmodernist thinking is widespread among composers? The reason for the diminishing popularity of vertical time structures lies not with their aesthetic purpose but with their means. The ideal of vertical time—that every listener can and should provide her or his own temporal structures—is decidedly postmodernist, but its realization is often not. Vertical music tries to offer an alternative to the elitism of high modernism. However, as I mention in my discussion of Cage (Section 3.4), to create temporal structures mentally from the undifferentiated sonic fields of most vertical pieces requires sympathy, skill, patience, practice, and education.[17] Hence there is necessarily a degree of elitism surrounding music cast in vertical time, just as there is surrounding moment-time compositions.

Postmodern music is concrete while vertical music is abstract. By this I mean that postmodern music offers more tangible materials with which listeners can form temporal structures mentally. Postmodern as well as vertical music recognizes that hearing differs from one listener to another, but in postmodern music the differences have to do with an individual's connotations with various kinds of music invoked. In their austere purity, vertical compositions offer too little material—too few clear musical shapes, too few gestures that connect with previous listening experiences—for any but the most committed listeners to structure.

Neither vertical time nor moment time is antithetical to postmodernism, although they arose from attempts to find new musical temporalities appropriate to modernism. Despite the postmodernist flavor of these species of musical time, however, they were hospitable as well to modernist music in the hands of such composers as Cage (the quintessential composer of vertical music) and Stockhausen (who invented the idea of moment form). More overtly postmodern composers have sometimes remained faithful to the ideas behind vertical and moment time, and have sometimes sought other ways to offer listeners multiple paths through the temporality of their works. Indeed, now that much music has become overtly referential, multiply-directed time is more palpable, because postmodern directionality (as opposed to vertical or moment non-directionality) can be created not only or even primarily by the syntax of succession but also by references outside the music.

Temporal multiplicity is common in postmodern music because of the re-emergence of semblances of tonality. There is a fundamental difference between tonality in traditional music and postmodern tonality, however. Traditional tonality, the musical religion into which most of us were born, creates a linear logic that moves, despite deviations, from tonic and back to tonic. We are expected to believe in this temporally linear meta-narrative, and we seek to understand each tonal piece as an instantiation of this great truth. In postmodern music we can have no such belief. Yet we are still presented with sonic icons of the "old religion." Just as vertical time and moment time

---

[17] I do not mean to suggest that someone who is an undergraduate music major receives such training, however; many musicians are notoriously poor at the skills required for deep listening to vertical music.

may exist in but probably will not totally structure a postmodern work, so postmodern music may invoke the narrative of teleology. But it is no longer a meta-narrative (trait 12): it is partial, or ironic, or incomplete, or without inevitability.

8.5. Deconstructing the Concept of Real Musical Time

Vertical time vs. linear time. Piece time vs. gestural time. Multiply-directed vs. mono-directed musical time. Linear vs. nonlinear musical time. Time out of phase vs. time in phase. What is the nature of these pairs? Is each a binary opposition? Are the members of each pair hierarchically related? Is one member of each pair understood as normal and the other as just that: an "other"?

Postmodern thinking questions the viability of such hierarchies, and of seeing one structure in terms of another, more established and more common structure. Thus it should be interesting to revisit some of these dichotomies, and to deconstruct their opposition. We will do so by asking the question: which of the two species of time in these pairs is real? We often encounter the term "real time" in discussions of music, but we rarely look at just what it means for a species of musical time to be real. Can we privilege one member of each pair as the "real" musical time, or rather should we deconstruct these oppositions as we seek to understand more deeply what musical time can mean in the context of postmodernism.

What is music's real time? At first glance, this question would seem to be trivial or else odd, but in fact it is neither. The notion of real musical time carries many interpretations and—once we examine it carefully—contradictions. First of all, what does it actually mean for any kind of time to be real? After all, we cannot touch time, see it, feel it, or hear it. Is any sort of time truly real? If time is real, surely it should be able to be perceived or experienced—although many time theorists believe that time itself is not perceptible. The title of J. J. Gibson's famous essay is telling: "Events Are Perceivable but Time Is Not."[18] If time is not in itself perceptible, it must have a strange sort of ontology. Or, perhaps we should say that time actually is not real. But then, what is it? A mental construct? But is a mental construct unreal? We live in time (and, some would say, time lives in us). Yet, how can we live in what is not real?

In the context of music, we can distinguish the time that a listener *experiences* (which is not quite the same as *perceives*) from the measurable time that a performance occupies. But which is the *real* time of music: the palpable temporality as experienced, or the measurable time filled by beats, notes, rests, etc.?

Many writers on music acknowledge, directly or indirectly, that music provides more than one kind of time experience, more than one temporality. Numerous ingenious ideas have been proposed for how to categorize the variety of temporal experiences that surround music. Some writers address implicitly, some explicitly (and

---

[18] J. J. Gibson, "Events Are Perceivable but Time Is Not," in J. T. Fraser and Nathaniel Lawrence (eds.), *The Study of Time* 2 (New York: Springer-Verlag, 1975), pp. 295–301.

some not at all), which of music's temporalities is/are "real" and which are, in some sense, virtual or illusory or transitory or imaginary.

The remainder of this chapter visits some of the ways in which musical time can be considered real. I am not trying to offer a comprehensive theory, nor even a thorough survey, of what the reality of time means in various musical contexts. But I do believe that there are some important issues to be uncovered and discussed. They surface from quite different areas of music scholarship, but they nonetheless do have some commonalities. I will take up questions of time *taken* vs. time *evoked* in a musical performance, real time as a performer's or a computer's reaction without delay to a musical stimulus, real time as objectively measurable (clock time) vs. real time as the essence of subjectively perceived music, and the relationship among the composer's, the performer's, and listener's real time.

The distinction—between musical time that is real and musical time that somehow is not—is meaningful not only on the abstract philosophical level addressed by my questions above. Even in the pared down context of a simple sequence of durations, the question of what time is real is complex. The extensive research that has been going on since the 1970s (with notable earlier precedents) into expressive deviations in the timing of musical performances offers intriguing challenges with respect to real time. We now understand that the durations implied in musical notation do not generally correspond to the "actual" durations performed, yet our *perception* of these durations corresponds more closely to the notation than to their clock-time measurement. Consider, for example, this series of durations, which has been studied by Henkjan Honing and Peter Desain.[19]

Honing and Desain have found that, in an expressive performance at a certain tempo, the duration of note A is 0.34 seconds and the duration of note B is 0.35 seconds. Note B—a sixteenth note, presumably representing a quarter of a beat—is performed slightly longer than note A—an eighth note of a triplet, presumably representing a third of a beat. Yet listeners do not perceive B as longer than A. Quite the contrary: they invariably hear A as longer than B, because of the rhythmic and metric context.

A   B

Example 8.1

[19] Honing and Desain's work is described at www.nini.kun.nl/mmm/time.html. [Editor's note: This website seems no longer to be active. Readers are directed to the authors' article "Computational Models of Beat Induction", *Journal of New Music Research* 28(1), 1999: pp. 29–42.]

So: which is the "real" time? The objectively measured time, which tells us that B is longer than A, or the musical time as interpreted by performers, which tells us that A is longer than B? The answer depends on just what we mean by "real." Is real musical time an objective time, out there in the world, or is real musical time the way listeners perceive musical events in relation to one another? Scientists may be more comfortable calling clock time "real," but performing musicians may well feel the opposite. The musical time they feel and project, and that they hope listeners sense, is for them the essential musical reality. Musicians tend to disparage or dismiss outright objective time.

The distinction between musical time as measured by the clock and musical time as experienced by listeners comes up not only in small series of notes, as in Example 8.1, but also in the larger-scale proportions of compositions or sections. There is a fairly large literature in which analysts have sought to uncover the ways in which pieces are structured temporally.[20] Many of these analyses study the proportions of the lengths of various sections of a piece, finding consistent ratios, often (but not always) related by the Fibonacci series or the golden section. Only rarely do these analyses try to determine whether such objectively measured proportions correspond to proportions as experienced. In fact, there is evidence that in most cases they do not.[21] Indeed, many analysts would agree that the nature of the music that fills these abstract durations—its denseness vs. sparseness, its shifting harmonic rhythms, its tempo, its frequency and degree of contrast, etc.—affects how long the passages feel to the listener.

So, which *is* the real time? The lengths of sections as measured by the clock, or their apparent lengths as felt by listeners?

During the last century, coinciding more or less with the rise of musical modernism, there was an ever greater concern with literal durations, understood as real time (there has also been an increasing curiosity about experienced durations). Several composers (e.g. Stockhausen) took to carefully calculating the clock-time durations of the sections in their pieces. Bartók, who sometimes produced elaborate nested golden-section proportions in his compositions, often listed in his scores the exact durations, to the second, of movements and subsections. Electronic tape music made it quite convenient to measure and hence control lengths objectively. Commercial recordings, too, have become increasingly concerned with literally measurable durations. 78 records and most 33 LPs did not list durations, but CDs regularly do. And CD players usually display exactly how long each track is, and how far (in minutes and seconds) we are from the beginning or end of the track that is playing. The apparent belief in the significance of clock time, as somehow representative of *real* musical time, has been increasing, yet there is also a move in the opposite direction, as postmodern thinking has encouraged the recognition of the uniqueness of each listener's own musical experience and hence, presumably, each listener's own sense of musical duration and proportion.

[20] See Kramer, *The Time of Music*, pp. 42–54, 296–321.
[21] This issue is discussed in *The Time of Music*, pp. 324–45.

8.6. Time Taken vs. Time Evoked

Now consider a quite different example of how strange it can be to have to decide whether real musical time is in some ways objective or in some ways subjective. Recall my discussion of gestural time vs. piece time (Section 8.2). Which of these is "real"? The moment-to-moment, measure-to-measure succession of events that I call piece time? In other words, the time that a piece takes (up) when it is performed and heard? Or the time the piece evokes, in part by its conventionally defined gestures of opening, closing, transition, climax, etc., which in some cases are and in other cases are not found in the expected places within the work's piece time?

Piece time certainly has a sense of the real about it. It essentially depends on the seemingly simple fact of succession. But is musical succession indeed simple? As a physical phenomenon, it is: sounds succeed other sounds, blending into or contrasting with one another. But within the mind of the listener, is the literal succession of events the "real" temporality of the musical experience? Surely not, because each musical event carries with it—in various ways for various listeners in various contexts—implications toward the future, realizations of or contradictions of past implications, personal resonances, etc.—all of which add up to a gradually unfolding context that is to some extent personal for each listener.

In contrast to piece time, gestural time depends not on literal succession but on the conventional meanings of musical gestures. Thus, when we hear in Beethoven's Opus 135 an apparently final gesture in the tenth bar of the piece, we may wonder what is the reality of the music's time. We know that we are in just the tenth measure and thus that the piece has barely begun: in piece time, we are still near the beginning. But we also know that we have just heard what ought to be, and hence in some sense really is, a concluding gesture: the music has already evoked its ending.

Before I attempt to discuss which of these two time senses truly represents, or corresponds to, or *is*, real musical time—if either or neither or both—I want to explore another piece which, although written long ago, offers temporal contradictions that, at least for some listeners today, can provide a decidedly postmodern listening experience that in essence asks us to deconstruct the concept of real musical time. The piece is the last movement of Haydn's Piano Sonata in E-Flat Major (1798). What I am describing as temporal contradictions and disjunctions might well have seemed to be typical witticisms to Haydn's contemporary listeners. I surely do not wish to deny the delightful wit of this music. Yet, given what we know about postmodern thinking, and what we know about the subjectivity and irrationality of temporal experiences, we can hear in this movement—especially with the aid of a sympathetic performance (the nature of which should become clear in what I am saying)—something deeper, and more unsettling, than simple witty play on temporal expectation.

Consider the first eight measures. Because of the bass pedal on E♭, the harmony is essentially unchanging. Perhaps this is simply a static opening, although the idea of beginning (at least in the classical period) suggests movement into the piece, not stasis. Perhaps, however, this phrase feels gesturally more like an extended *final* tonic, typically achieved after a movement full of progressions away from and back

Example 8.2 Haydn, Sonata in E-Flat Major, finale, opening

to the tonic. Since this "really" is the beginning, we might be predisposed to hear the first eight bars indeed as an opening. However: suppose the pianist *wants* us at least to consider these measures as final. Suppose, as might well be done at the end of a movement, a slight ritard and crescendo are taken in mm. 6–7, and suppose in addition that the *fermata* on the rest in m. 8 is held a rather long time—long enough for the listener to begin to wonder whether somehow a piece "really" *has* just ended.

Such an interpretation does not totally work, even given a sympathetic performance, because these eight measures are not quite an ending. The bars are paired, by means of the bass pedal, not as 1–2, 3–4, 5–6, 7–8, as would be regular and hence resolving, but as 2–3, 4–5, 6–7. In other words, although the eight-bar phrase length is quite normal, its subdivision is not. This irregularity is reinforced by the measures which repeat earlier measures: m. 6 repeats m. 4, and m. 7 repeats m. 5. This pattern is hardly what we would expect in a final resolution, because it makes the hypermeter 3+5 (or, on the next lower hierarchic level, 1+2+2+2+1), rather than 4+4.

Another way to consider this irregularity is to realize that the tonic harmony is fully established not at m. 1 but at m. 2. The harmonic ambiguity at m. 1 is particularly acute, with five unharmonized Gs opening the movement, since the preceding movement is in the unusually distant key of E major. Especially if the pianist does not pause too long between movements, this initial G will seem disorienting, like music from another planet—hardly what we would expect at the *final* phrase of a piece.

Furthermore, the A♭ in the V⁷ chord (over the tonic pedal) in mm. 5 and 7 does not resolve down to G at the cadence, m. 8. Haydn does not place a third in that "final" tonic. It is merely an open octave—not totally resolved (although a resolution to G is surely implied, just as it is pointedly omitted).[22]

And so we arrive at the cadence in m. 8 in a state of confusion. The simple tonic harmony suggests an ending, yet the hypermeter and the lack of total resolution suggests that the music must go on and explain those anomalies. But does the music do so? Not at all! The music simply states the whole phrase all over again, up a step. A traditional analysis might simply say that the opening I is sequenced up a step to ii. This analysis certainly has some truth, but it misses the point. The quasi-finality in m. 8, followed by a possibly longish *fermata*, can make the resumption at the upbeat to m. 9 seem like an attempt to begin (or even to end!) again, this time in F minor. No explanation, no resolution, but just a new place in time. E♭ major somehow did not work out. Let us try F minor. Since the music is exactly the same, the F minor beginning has the same problems and contradictions as the E♭ major beginning. And, again, there is no resolution, no explanation, but rather simply a cadence that in some ways seems definitive (a piece in F minor comes to an end) and in some ways does not (the hypermeter is unresolved, and the B♭ on the downbeats of mm. 13 and 15 is unresolved).

So what happens next? A third "piece" begins, and ends. This time we are back in E♭ major and hence can begin to believe in the priority of that key. Also, this time there is no bass pedal, so that the harmonies really do move. Or do they? The bass begins promisingly on B♭, the dominant, at the upbeat to m. 17. The bass line moves from this B♭ down stepwise through A♭ (end of m. 18) to G. Aha! Finally there is a resolution of an A♭ down to G, supplying what was pointedly withheld in mm. 5 and 7. Furthermore, the note G now has an explanation (which it decidedly did not have back in m. 1): it is the resolution of A♭, and hence the third of the tonic triad. So, perhaps this third attempt to get the piece off the ground (beginning with the upbeat to m. 17) is actually an explanation and a resolution of some of the questions raised by the first two attempts. But then the bass just gets caught, alternating seemingly endlessly between A♭ (mm. 20, 22, and 24) and G (mm. 19, 21, and 23). Is this a harmonic progression, or just a more subtle form of stasis? Maybe there still is something like a pedal, instead of the forward-thrusting harmonic motion we might expect of an opening. Perhaps there is also a pattern: the bass E♭ of mm. 1–8 moves up to F (mm. 10–16) and then on to G (mm. 19–23). Indeed, this stepwise upward thrust continues

---

[22] Interestingly, Beethoven plays the same game in m. 10 of Opus 135.

through A♭ (m. 24) to B♭ (mm. 25–26), acting as a normal cadential dominant, as the harmony simply goes I $^6_4$ (mm. 24–25) to V (end of m. 25) and then to I (mm. 27–28). This phrase, twelve bars long instead of the eight of the first two phrases, takes its time getting to this archetypal final cadence, which is even underlined by an overt stepwise descent from 5 to 1 (mm. 24–27). So, after two phrases that play with finality, we hear a third that does more than play: it really does end, in terms not only of harmony and gesture but also of voice-leading and hypermeter.[23]

So the piece tries to begin three times in succession, in two different keys, but each time gets sidetracked by a quasi-final cadential gesture. The third time, the sense of beginning is more palpable (because there is a modicum of harmonic motion), but the side-tracking finality is even more conventional, and hence more potent. Particularly if the performer plays mm. 25–28 as a final gesture, we will feel intriguingly lost in time by m. 28. Is this piece ever going to "really" to begin? Is there ever going to be a final cadence that comes at the end of a section, rather than near the beginning? Will the temporal gestures ever line up with the succession of events in piece time? And, which of these time senses is real: the one that tells us that the piece keeps trying, and failing, to begin and to end, or the one that tells us that the measures keep succeeding one another, without the music somehow managing to get going?

8.7. Real Time in Electroacoustic Music

So, once again, what is "real" musical time? Does it correspond to gestural time or to piece time? Is it necessarily and hierarchically superior to "unreal" musical time, whatever that might be?

The term "real time" is actually most readily associated not with gestural vs. piece time in traditional music but with computer music. For the computer musician, the ideal of "real time" is the apparently immediate response of an interactive system to some stimulus.[24] The notion of real time as so understood did not originate with music technology, however. In group improvisation, in whatever style, the real-time (i.e. almost instantaneous) response of one performer to another has always been an ideal.

It should be no surprise that computer musicians are concerned with the reality of musical time, when we recall how unreal, in a certain sense, musical time was in the infancy of computer music. In the 1960s, composers would spend days constructing what they hoped was a few seconds of coherent electronic sound. But they could not hear the results of their labors until they sent off their digital tape to a distant laboratory, which converted it to sound. When the sound tape arrived in the mail a week later, the composer finally got to hear what his/her snippet actually sounded like—with sometimes surprising results.

---

[23] Still, however, the thinness of the "final" sonority (m. 28) works against total acceptance of this gesture as a final cadence.
[24] For relevant discussion, see Jonathan Impett, "Real Times: Implementing a Temporal Phenomenology in an Interactive Music System," https://www.researchgate.net/publication/237282920_Real_times_implementing_a_temporal_phenomenology_in_an_interactive_music_system (accessed April 24, 2016).

Days of constructing the sound, more days of waiting, and then finally a few seconds of recorded music to listen to! The gap between conception and audition was massively greater than the duration of the musical excerpt. It is no wonder that composers yearned for a somehow more "real" musical time, with little or no disconnect between the construction of the sound and the hearing of it. What seemed unreal was the long wait. It was as if a pianist played a series of figures at the keyboard but did not actually hear the result of his/her finger movements until a week or two later!

Such gaps are not the sole province of computer music, even though it is within the context of musical technology that the term "real time" has gained its greatest currency. Composers of music for human performance, particularly if the music is complex or requires a large performing force, have had to wait years between conception and audition. But there is a crucial difference: an orchestral composer (take Mahler as an example) may not have heard his symphonies immediately, but he did hear them in his head, in his imagination, possibly aided by imperfect but still "real-time" renditions at the piano. But a computer-music composer, for whom composing is not only putting together known sounds but also constructing hitherto unknown sonorities, may not have a mental sonic image. Hence, computer music came of age with the advent of real-time technologies, which allow for the immediate production of sound.

The distinction between real and delayed time pertains to instrumental as well as electroacoustic and interactive music. A real-time performance of that Mahler symphony, by a flesh-and-blood orchestra, is one thing; a recorded performance is another. Traditionally, the live performance is thought of as taking place in real time, whereas the recording can be, and usually is, made up of a complex layering and inter-action of excerpts recorded and edited separately over a period of, possibly, months. Digital editing technology allows for seamless splicing together of note-perfect "performances," which—contrary to the beliefs of many performers—are not easy to distinguish from real-time recorded performances.

I had an experience which was telling and typical. There was a recording session for one of my chamber works. The musicians did several "takes"—continuous playing of a few seconds or minutes of the music. Each passage in the piece was recorded at least twice. Some of the more difficult ones were recorded up to ten times. It then became the task of the editor—in this case myself—to choose the best of these takes for each passage and to blend them together into a continuous whole, using digital techniques of splicing, cross fading, adjusting tempo (without affecting pitch or timbre), etc.

The musicians all told me that they hoped I would not have to do too much splicing, because excessive splicing can ruin the sense of continuity, of directed motion through time. I initially agreed to their request, but then had to ignore it when I got into the editing studio. Recorded music is not quite the same art form as performed music, I believe: the highest ideals of live performance are immediacy, visceral engagement, and excitement; the highest ideals of recorded music are note-perfect, rhythm-perfect, in-tune realizations of the composer's score. Since I was making a recording, I gravi-tated toward wanting a note-perfect rendition of my piece. I was willing to do almost any amount of digital manipulation to get that result.

There was one passage where the strings just could not seem to attack a series of *pizzicato* chords in unison. There was a series of nine such chords, evenly spaced in time. In order to get the desired unison of attack (without shaving the envelopes, which I could have done but preferred not to), I had to select *each chord* from a different take. I worked hard on minute timing, on equalization, and on loudness. I finally produced a good facsimile of musical continuity. I did not tell the musicians what I had done (eventually I admitted it, though). They were very pleased that I had managed to produce the edited whole with a minimum of splices. They never heard, nor suspected, that that one ten-second passage had nine splices in it!

So, where is the real time and where is the unreal time in all of this? What the musicians played in the recording studio certainly seemed like real musical time to them, but once it appeared on tape, it became subject to all sorts of electronic manipulations that made the time anything but real. I created a false, an unreal, continuity, but one which closely approached the ideal of real-time continuity that the musicians had wanted to produce but had been unable to achieve. Once the recording was finished, we all listened to it in what seemed like real time. Our temporal experience was real enough, even though it was in response to electronic manipulations that were pretty far removed from real time as it is usually understood.

When computer musicians compose and perform in real time, they too mix the real with the unreal. They often do not produce all their sounds on the spot. Some are prerecorded—sampled—to be called up and played at the appropriate moment in the performance. The technology is similar—often it is actually the same—to that which is used in digital editing. Snippets recorded in real time are disembodied by technology into an unreal time, but then brought forth in a live performance to contribute to a new real time.

8.8. Intertextuality and Real Time

The concept of real musical time is bound up with intertextuality. Real-time combinations of previously sampled music bring into confrontation two (or maybe even more) different real times—the time of the original performance, that was subsequently sampled and stored in the unreal time of a hard disk, and the real time of the new context in which these sampled bits are brought back to life and combined anew.

The intertextuality of much postmodern music brings out the complexities and contradictions in the concept of real time. I have written (in Chapter 7) about how the personal resonance each listener may have with quoted materials helps to create a unique narrative path through an intertextual work: each listener mentally creates his/her own space and time in which the music unfolds. Which time is the real one? The temporal context from which the quoted material was lifted, the new musical continuity into which it was thrust, or the mental time in which the listener understands and experiences the work? The question cannot be answered. All these times are real, each in its own way.

Having taken a Mahler symphony as an example, I am led to the third movement of Luciano Berio's *Sinfonia*, in which almost the entire third movement of Mahler's Second Symphony is played, beginning to end. Myriad quotations of other music (and literature), and commentaries (musical and verbal), are superimposed on Mahler's music. Here we are dealing with multiple temporalities: the temporality of Mahler the man, composing his movement; the temporality that he constructed within this movement; the temporality of a real-time performance of this music by a symphony orchestra; the temporality of Berio, thinking over this music and what he might do with it; the temporality of the various compositions and literary works (by Boulez, Stravinsky, Rossini, Beckett, and many others) that are sampled (although not electronically) and laid down on top of the Mahler; the temporality of a performance of Berio's newly conceived work; the temporality of the listener experiencing this fascinating melange.

Each of these temporalities has a sense of the real about it. And therefore there is no single, unique real time surrounding this work. In a thoroughly postmodern spirit, the temporality is multifaceted.

And what does this postmodern attitude toward multiple real times have to do with a work like the finale of Haydn's E♭ Piano Sonata, composed more than a century before anyone had uttered the word "postmodernism"? Actually, quite a lot. In earlier ages, before time was fully accepted as personal, subjective, multiple, or malleable, listeners may have reacted to the Haydn as a real-time sequence of measures and motives, against which Haydn played delightful games with our expectations about beginnings and endings. Implicit in such an attitude was the notion that the moment-to-moment succession that I have been calling piece time was the work's *real* time, and that Haydn's playing with listeners' expectations was somehow unreal, somehow outside of the time that a performance of the work took: a challenge, perhaps, to the orderliness of real time.

Today, however, influenced by ubiquitous postmodern values, we may not see things in such starkly opposed ways. We may well hear in the Haydn a statement of a jumbled, reordered temporality in which the *non sequiturs* on the musical surface can be ironed out in the listener's mind into a coherent temporality that may be quirky but that is no less real than the measure-by-measure unfolding of the notes in the score. It is as if we are doing the digital editing in our heads, as we listen to—or as we contemplate in retrospect after having heard—the Haydn sonata. We hear the performance at first in piece time, but as we do so we sample it (mentally), storing up Haydn's witticisms in our memories with the purpose of eventually coming to understand the temporal world of his sonata as a reordering of another temporal world which we can just barely grasp—but a world that is no less real. This, too, is real time, just as much as an on-the-spot remix of sampled source materials is in the world of contemporary technological musical performance.

8.9. Real Time and Postmodernism

To the extent that real time has to do with instantaneous responses in music, it has also to do with speed. The 1960s' delay of several days between the conception and the audition of a composed series of computer sounds has now shrunk to an instant. This is progress, or so computer musicians like to think. And yet, progress is more a modernist than a postmodernist value, since postmodernism questions the linearity of historical progress (trait 3). It is not lightly that postmodernists proclaim themselves to live in a post-historical world. For postmodernists, neither progress nor speed is to be accepted as an absolute, nor as a desirable nor even a possible, condition. This attitude stands in stark contrast to that of modernity. As Sandy Baldwin writes, "Speed is the unique experience of modernity, so it seems, and real time the terminal realization of speed."[25]

What, then, is a postmodern attitude toward real time? Technology not only recognizes the contemporary viability of real time, as in interactive musical composition, but also provides for temporal experiences which are far from the real, as in digital editing, sampling, overdubbing, remixing, etc. As an inclusive aesthetic, postmodernism questions the hierarchical relationship between real time and the various virtual times of temporal arts. Particularly under the banner of modernist experimentation, music has offered its listeners a variety of temporalities. But these musical temporalities are no longer the experiments they were for avant-gardists like Ives, Webern, Stravinsky, Varèse, Cage, or Stockhausen. Now these temporalities simply exist, to be used or not used, invoked or not invoked, by composers, performers, and listeners alike. To postmodernists, the dichotomy between linear and non-linear musical time is no longer a dialectic relationship, the way it was when modernist values held sway among contemporary composers. Perhaps the same can be said about the distinction between gestural time and piece time. The distinction remains meaningful, but neither type of musical time is necessarily the "real" one, and hence neither is relegated to the status of an "other." Each species of musical time has its own context for reality. Whereas it may once have been important to understand Haydn's temporal distortions against a backdrop of continuous piece time, to a postmodernist ear and mind they offer up a different reality. Not a distortion, but an alternative. Or, perhaps put better, just as much a distortion as is every musical temporality. For a postmodernist, all musical time is real, and all musical time is unreal. Music is both instantaneous and contemplative. Music's time is both evoked and taken. Piece time and gestural time are not the same, but they are not hierarchically related: no longer does one depend on the other, nor does one reorder the other. Each presents its own temporal ordering. Now that real, instantaneous time is readily available to interactive composers, the modernist experiments in multiple temporalities are no longer experiments. They have become the essence of the postmodern musical experience.

---

[25] Sandy Baldwin, abstract to article "Speed and Ecstasy: 'Real Time' after Virilio, or, the Rhetoric in Techno-Logistics," http://high-techne.tumblr.com/onspeedandecstasy (accessed April 24, 2016).

8.10. Real Time and Modernism

Real time is instantaneous time, a goal toward which modernism's progress has aimed.[26] Time has gotten progressively faster (increasing tempos, splashes of notes in electronic music going by so fast that a listener can barely hear them as individual tones, decreasing length of historical time during which any particular musical aesthetic is in vogue, etc.). Nothing happens faster than the instantaneous. Nothing is faster than real time. But how real is a time which allows the listener and performer no pausing for contemplation, for reflection, but rather in which responses are immediate and hence unmediated? Real time as a goal and a barrier points, in a way, to an impoverishment in modernistic thinking. If modern culture and society are forever in a race toward greater speed, then that simply shows the obsessive narrowness of the idea of historical (or artistic) progress drawn to a one-dimensional extreme. Hence the appeal of the messy multitude of times in postmodern thinking.

Instantaneous time remains a possibility, but not necessarily an ideal. Does instantaneous time therefore deserve to be thought of as the sole "real time"?

The time a composition takes—its pace—has become faster (I do not mean shorter—there are still plenty of long works being composed—but *faster*). (The time certain modernist compositions—such as several by Morton Feldman—take has also gotten slower, but that is another story, not to be addressed here.) Tempos are faster, note durations are shorter, contexts and textures change more frequently. It is certainly appropriate, therefore, to identify time taken with real time, as I did in discussing traditional pieces (by Beethoven, Haydn, Mahler, and others), in which there is a disjunction between the time a piece takes and the time it evokes. If real time is identified with the time a piece takes, then it has been getting faster, approaching the limit of instantaneous time, which in the modern world has come to be known as real time. So, the reality of time has gone in a circle, and has ended with ultra speed being called real, when in an experiential sense it is anything but real.

And what happened to the time a piece evokes, or portrays—gestural time, for example, although there are other types of temporal experience suggested by various kinds of music? Pieces still evoke or portray many kinds of temporalities—indeed, given our wide range of perspectives, probably a far greater range now than ever before. Now these times are recognized as personal and subjective: they depend not only on what the composer did, not only on what the music does, not only on what the performer does, not only on what the performance does, but also—and primarily—on what the listener does with these external musical stimuli. Hence this other time, the irrational, subjective, malleable time that was once thought of (although this term was not, to my knowledge, used) as unreal, has become all the more real, just as real time (the time music takes, which approaches the instantaneous time commonly called real) has paradoxically become unreal—fast in a way beyond the reality of experience.

---

[26] For further discussion, see David Dufresne, "Virilio—Cyberesistance Fighter: An Interview with Paul Virilio," http://www.apres-coup.org/archives/articles/virilio.html. See also David Cook, "Paul Virilio: The Politics of 'Real Time,'" http://www.ctheory.net/text_file.asp?pick=360 (accessed April 24, 2016).

Here we have an archetypal instance of how postmodern thinking deconstructs previous values, turning them inside out, or upside down. Real time in music has become unreal, and virtual time has become real.

8.11. Speed and Unrepeatability

Above I wrote: "Nothing happens faster than the instantaneous. Nothing is faster than real time." Let us explore, or deconstruct, this seemingly innocent statement. If we actually could go faster than the instantaneous, what would happen? Perhaps we would go backward in time! Now, this is not simply a science-fiction fantasy. In music, gestural time actually can provide a way to go backwards—not literally, of course, but in a palpable way nonetheless. If we hear final-like cadences in mm. 8, 16, and 28 of the Haydn sonata movement, then in a sense we have experienced (some of) the ending(s) of the piece. Then we go on to hear more of what the piece *that we just heard end* contains. This process is, in a sense, going backward: we experience the end, then we go on to experience the middle!

This kind of playing with temporal ordering is more than an intellectual game, more that a conceit, more than a peculiar way to understand Haydn's temporal disjunctions. It suggests a subjective, personal, non-linear way for a listener to understand this music upon reflection—not just as it happens in piece time but also, in a non-instantaneous manner, in contemplation after the performance has ended. This kind of jumbled temporality, this kind of subjective response to a work's temporality, is postmodern in spirit, even if the Haydn sonata existed long before the concept of postmodernism did. This kind of thinking informs certain postmodern compositions of today, in which the literal order of presentation is not the only factor by which a listener can construct a personal narrative that moves through the time the music evokes.

Real time is unrepeatable. The time of our lives—presumably real, but that notion too could well be deconstructed (though such a project is beyond the scope of this chapter)—does not repeat, despite many rituals of repetition and despite many compelling ideas of cyclical time. We repeat experiences in time, but time itself does not repeat. Listening again to a recording of a musical performance is one of these repeated experiences. We experience yet again the same temporal sequence that a composer conceived and that a performer brought to life (and, some traditionalists might say, that a recording brought to death!). In interactive music, however, the ideal of temporal unrepeatability is often a reality: not only time itself but also our experience in time is unrepeatable, because the music comes out different in each performance, each realization. (A telling word, that: *realization!*)

Steve Holtzman has written, "The digital experience is interactive, not passive. Digital worlds respond to you, pull you in, demand your participation. The unique creation is not simply a 'work' produced by an artist held high on a pedestal, but the interaction between you and the possibilities defined by the artist."[27]

---

[27] Steve Holtzman, *Digital Mosaics* (New York: Simon and Schuster, 1997), p. 128. I am indebted to Jason Freeman for pointing me to this source.

If we identify real musical time with the unrepeatable, and hence unreal musical time with the artificially repeated, then we have reversed this chapter's original identification (in the context of the Haydn sonata) of the real with the measure-to-measure succession of a performance and the unreal with the gestural-time jumbling of that literal succession into a uniquely subjective narrative which differs from one listener to another, and even from one listening to another. The measure-to-measure succession—piece time—is repeatable, on every occasion when the music is heard. But the listener's subjective path through the work, shaped (but only in part) by the work's gestural time, is unique to each listening occasion and hence not repeatable.

While such a reversal may seem confusing, this confusion is both healthy and creative. And it is postmodern in spirit. Indeed, postmodern musical thinking has contributed to a deconstruction of the concept of "real time." And that is what this chapter is about. It is about the contradictions inherent in the idea of real time—and how music and musical experience do not resolve them but rather live with them, and live through them.

8.12. Real Times in a Work by Szymański

I would like to close by looking at a work that embodies postmodern attitudes toward musical time, and that thereby offers up distinct, even contradictory, notions of real time. The music is *Quasi una sinfonietta*, by Polish composer Paweł Szymański, composed in 1990 to a commission by the London Sinfonietta.

One way to look at this piece is as a clash of temporalities, each real in its own way. It begins with some twenty seconds of a high piano trill, F to E. The regularity of this figure may suggest the inexorability of time; its unchanging nature may suggest temporal stasis or even eternity. In fact, it is virtually impossible for a pianist to play this trill utterly evenly, so the mechanical regularity implied in the score is a chimera. And so, a familiar question: which is the real time of this opening? That represented by the mechanical, clock-like regularity of the notation, or that represented by the performer's all too human, pseudo-random deviations from this regularity?

This introductory gesture gives way to other temporalities. The oboe and bassoon play a simple arpeggiation that suggests a V^9 chord of D minor (see Example 8.3), which—sure enough—progresses to a tonic-like D-minor arpeggio. The simple figuration and the clear tonality suggest a bygone historical era—quite a different sort of music from what we might expect of a piece composed in 1990. And yet, there is something disembodied about this D-minor figuration. It is played on viola, not the most likely instrument for the opening theme of a true classical-period work. Furthermore, the viola is to play without vibrato, giving a certainly unearthly quality to this music. Timbrally, it is a ghost of the past, more than a recreation. As the music continues, harmonic stasis undermines the tonality as first suggested, as do the irregular rhythmic transformations of the repeated arpeggio. Again the question arises: which is the real (historical) time (era) of this music? The era when D-minor arpeggios stood for tonal stability and served as the origin of a work's tonal motion, or

Example 8.3 Szymański, *Quasi una sinfonietta*, opening

the more recent era when they could repeat in a minimalist haze, seemingly endlessly, subject to unpredictable rhythmic permutations? The contrabass *pizzicato* rising D octaves reinforce this disjunction: they too repeat again and again, but they are not always evenly spaced in time. The eventual entrance of first and second violins (and later high cello) on A (harmonic, hence still *senza vibrato)* does nothing to break the music out of its D-minor prison.

And there is a third layer of temporal disjunction. Going against this corpse-like invocation of a classical-period D minor, the woodblock plays evenly spaced single notes—"like a metronome," the score says. These ticks appear every two and a half beats for 98 (!) successive measures. They mark time, but what time? Not the same time as the D-minor arpeggios, which are initially four beats in length, before irregularities set in. The woodblock keeps a time that, in the context of what the rest of the orchestra is doing, is no time. Yet it *is* a time of clock-like regularity.

One might also hear these woodblock strokes as an instance of intertextuality. One of the major mid-century modernist works is Iannis Xenakis's *Pithoprakta.* This work of 1955 is scored for forty-six strings, two trombones, xylophone, and woodblock.[28] The woodblock often punctuates string music (of a very different sort from what we find in Szymański's piece). So well known is this piece, with its prominent woodblock, that I find it impossible not to recall it when hearing *Quasi una sinfonietta.*

Again the familiar question: which is the work's real historical time? Does it refer to the classical period, or through the woodblock quotation to the modern period? And which of those references functions as the real time in the opening section of the work? The utterly regular woodblock strokes, whose period agrees with nothing else in the music and which stubbornly refuses to align itself with the rest of the orchestra? Or the subtly shifting variants of the D-minor arpeggio?

It would take too much space to trace all the materials and temporal issues through this entire half-hour piece. But I should explain that these various temporalities, so starkly opposed to one another at the beginning, do eventually evolve and influence each other. The D-minor sonority eventually moves tonally, giving rise to, among other things, a vigorous diatonic passage in B♭ minor. The woodblock punctuations disappear and, much later, reappear, finally agreeing with the metric cycles of the other instruments: they now recur every two beats. The ticking eventually is taken over by the entire orchestra, *ff*, punctuated by loud woodblock, piano cluster, tomtom, and bass drum strokes. Eventually all of this gives way to a slow, pulseless middle section that is oriented toward sonority more than toward pulse-like rhythm or quasi-tonal historical reference. The music of this middle section suggests mid-twentieth-century modernism.

Quasi una sinfonietta juxtaposes these various musical and historical temporalities, brings them into confrontation, and toys with their resolution but never fully achieves it. Each temporality is, in a sense, real, despite their incompatibility. Their reality is thrown down like a gauntlet at the beginning: the reality of an utterly periodic, metronome-like woodblock; the reality of tonal gestures, which concertgoers

---

[28] Woodblocks also figure prominently in other Xenakis works, such as *Metastaseis* and *Terretektorh.*

recognize readily; the reality of invocations of the modernist tradition from which the composer developed. Yes, all these temporalities are real. The real time of this work is decidedly multiple. It makes no sense to ask which of these conflicting time senses is truly the real one, against which the others are to be measured. And that is what makes this work a grand exemplar of musical postmodernism, even more than does its combinations of styles that refer to various disjunct historical periods. This work's postmodernism resides in its refusal to construct a hierarchy, its refusal to take any of its temporalities as the exotic other, as the foreign intruder into the otherwise stable world of the piece. No, none of the temporalities is stable, because *all* of them are stable. This is a blatantly concrete piece, at least until the modernistic middle section. Its intertextual and temporal meanings are right there, on the surface, palpable, and—I say it one more time—*real.*

The more I think about real musical time, the more I feel that I do not know what it is. The myriad ways in which the term is and can be used compounds the confusion. A work like *Quasi una sinfonietta* forces me to think about all these conflicting realities. But, then, so does a work like Haydn's E-Flat Sonata. Musical time is not a single thing. Perhaps it is not a thing at all. But it is indeed real, in a multitude of ways.

9

Surrealism, Neoclassicism, and Postmodernism

9.1. Did Music Have a Surrealist Period?

Before the recent publication of Daniel Albright's book *Untwisting the Serpent*,[1] there was little serious discussion of surrealism in music (although informally calling certain music surreal is certainly common enough).[2] Music has been assumed not to have gone through much of a surrealist stage. Yet, some postmodern music has characteristics in common with surrealist art, particularly in comparison with painting's unusual juxtapositions of recognizable objects.[3] Is there a musical equivalent of a recognizable object? Perhaps it is a quotation of a particular piece, or the use of an identifiable style, or the employment of a known genre such as a march or a waltz. While some neoclassic music (such as that by Schoenberg or Bartók) invokes the past by utilizing traditional forms, other neoclassic music (particularly that of Stravinsky and also Hindemith) also uses sonorities or even themes reminiscent of, or taken from, the past. How, then, does neoclassic music differ from the postmodern music I am comparing to surrealism?[4] After all, both postmodernism and neoclassicism use conventional materials in new ways. If postmodernism is truly an attitude more than a period, we cannot simply say that music's neoclassicism, trailing painting's and literature's surrealism by a decade, happened in the 1930s and 1940s while postmodernism happened in the 1980s, 1990s, and 2000s.

The two aesthetics differ in more than just chronology, although postmodernism—at least of the conservative variety—does indeed blur into neoclassicism. Neoclassicism tends to distort, postmodernism to accept;[5] neoclassicism to distance,

---

[1] Daniel Albright, *Untwisting the Serpent: Modernism in Music, Literature, and Other Arts* (Chicago and London: University of Chicago Press, 2000).

[2] Mention should be made of Nicholas Slonimsky's article "Music and Surrealism," *Artforum* (September 1966): 80–5. Subsequent to the appearance of Albright's book, Anne LeBaron published an important study called "Reflections of Surrealism in Postmodern Musics," in Judy Lochhead and Joseph Auner (eds.), *Postmodern Music/Postmodern Thought* (New York and London: Routledge, 2002), pp. 27–73.

[3] LeBaron identifies this tendency as collage, one of the two aspects of surrealism that has appeared in music. The other is automatism. She draws a parallel between the automatic writing of surrealist authors and the spontaneity of improvised music, particularly free jazz and other kinds of free improvisation.

[4] Peter Bürger discusses and criticizes the parallel Adorno draws between surrealism and Stravinsky's neoclassicism (*Theory of the Avant-Garde*, pp. 34–6).

[5] For a contrary view, see Robin Hartwell, "Postmodernism and Art Music," p. 43.

postmodernism to embrace; neoclassicism to integrate, postmodernism to revel in incongruities; neoclassicism to misread (in Bloom's sense of the term), postmodernism to read. The contrast is similar to that between cubist and surrealist painting: cubism distorts familiar objects, while surrealism juxtaposes them (I am, of course, greatly oversimplifying—there are a lot of distorted objects in surrealist art, although arguably they remain closer to their original essences than do their cubist counterparts). Like postmodern musical compositions, paintings such as Salvatore Dalí's *The Discovery of America by Christopher Columbus* and *Velazquez Painting the Infanta Margarita*, or René Magritte's *The Rights of Man* and *Personal Values*, are ironic (trait 2) and intertextual (trait 6), combine the past and the present (trait 3), offer textual discontinuities (trait 10) and disunities (trait 11), embrace contradiction (trait 8), are pluralistic (trait 7), and/or suggest multiple meanings (trait 13). And, in ways strikingly similar to certain radically postmodern music, these surrealist artworks are disordered. As Elizabeth Deeds Ermarth remarks, surrealism's "estrangement of objects from their 'normal' order calls attention *to* that order *and* to its arbitrariness."[6]

Surrealist visual artists justified their work with reference to the unconscious and to dreams. While postmodern composers—whose presentational music may be more engaged with its surfaces than with its deep interior—do not often invoke Freudian analogies when discussing their compositions, a lot of postmodern music is decidedly free-associational. In addition, postmodern music rich in quotations can have a dream-like temporal quality, in which fragments of prior listening experiences float by in strange ways.[7]

What is the point of sketching a comparison between surrealist painting of the 1920s (and beyond) and postmodern music primarily of a half century or more later? If there are stylistic and procedural similarities, that does not mean that the two genres are situated similarly with regard to their social or cultural contexts. (But, remember, this book is interested in how music relates more to its consumers of today than to its composers' contemporaries.) Furthermore, there does not seem to be much evidence of direct influence. The differences between the two aesthetics are as palpable as the similarities. If we call the recent upsurge in postmodernist ideas in music composition a long delayed surrealist period, what do we gain? Perhaps not too much, but there is one thing of value: we can adopt theories of surrealism as we try to understand, to enter into, and to listen to music that is pervasively postmodern. We have the advantage of several decades of absorption and analysis of surrealism to help us understand how to listen to the music of postmodernism.

I do not want to make too much of this parallel. I am not referring to all surrealist art, nor to all postmodernist music. Surrealist literature does not strike me as profoundly similar to postmodernist music.[8] And the art of some painters usually classified as

---

6   Ermarth, *Sequel to History*, p. 94. Ermarth offers a valuable discussion of the parallels between surrealist painting and postmodernist literature. See pp. 90–106.
7   Christopher Ballantine explores at some length the parallels between musical quotation and dreaming. See "Charles Ives and the Meaning of Quotation in Music," *Musical Quarterly* 65/2 (April 1979): 167–84.
8   I acknowledge LeBaron's parallel between automatic writing and free improvisation, but I do not

surrealists—Max Ernst, André Masson, and Juan Miró—also does not resonate directly with postmodern music. But I do find striking similarities between the paintings of artists like René Magritte, Salvador Dalí, Paul Delvaux, Yves Tanguy, and Frida Kahlo and certain recent music replete with characteristics of postmodernism.

What music? Not the mystical postmodernism of Giya Kancheli, Henryk Gorecki, Arvo Pärt, or John Tavener, but rather the polystylistic (trait 7) postmodernism of William Bolcom, Alfred Schnittke, John Zorn, and Pawel Szymański (at least in the first movement of his *quasi una sinfonia).* Thus, for example, when art critic Patrick Waldberg writes of surrealism that "the scene is unreal, but the setting, the objects, and the human figures which comprise it are painted with fidelity,"[9] it is not an enormous leap to apply his idea to pluralistic music of recent times. Recall that I am taking as the musical equivalent of realistic objects and human figures musical objects and figures that are (or could have been) taken from music of an earlier era. Thus we can indeed sense a connection in spirit and in artistic technique between surrealist painting and postmodernist composing.

Waldberg also offers this intriguing idea:

> There is among all the surrealist artists a desire to find, over and beyond appear- ances, a truer reality, a kind of synthesis of the exterior world and of the interior model. … Human figures and objects are divorced from their natural function and placed opposite one another in a relationship which is unexpected—perhaps shocking—and which therefore gives each of them a new presence.[10]

In intertextual music, quotations and other specific references correspond to the exterior world, and the way composers put these citations together into a narrative peculiar to their piece can indeed be understood as an "interior model"—whether interior to the composer or to the listener. And a useful way to understand this music is as a synthesis between the quasi-objective world of other musics as they exist in our world and the personal and idiosyncratic ways postmodernist composers put their citations together, giving these recontextualized references indeed a kind of "new presence."

Critic Yves Bonnefoy takes this idea further, offering an explication of intertextual incongruity that can give us insight into polystylistic music:

> When surrealist thought took pleasure in reuniting, after the *Songs of Maldoror,*[11] the sewing machine and the umbrella on the dissection table, those three objects

---

find the music of free improvisation necessarily postmodern in spirit. It often strikes me as hardcore modernist. I take exception to LeBaron's briefly stated parallel between automatic writing on the one hand and total serialism and random generation of musical parameters on the other, however, since surrealist writers were seeking an immediate contact with their unconscious minds, while total serialism and randomly composed music seek more to deny the composer's personality or inner self.

[9] Patrick Waldberg, *Surrealism* (New York: Thames and Hudson, 1965), p. 7.

[10] Ibid., p. 8.

[11] The reference is to a book by Lautréamont (Isidore Ducasse), written in 1868-9, and believed by André Breton to contain the first surrealist writing. The description of an umbrella and a sewing machine on a table inspired Man Ray's *The Enigma of Isidore Ducasse.*

remained specifically the instruments that we know by the integrity of their structure, which was at once abstract and rigorously defined. This structure, however, because of the obliteration of the rational perspective caused by the bizarre combination, henceforth appeared opaque, irreducible to its own meaning or to any other, and the reunited objects became mysterious, carrying us by their purposeless existence to a new form of astonishment.[12]

Consider also this similar statement by Ermarth, who writes about what happens to familiar objects when placed in the strange new contexts of surrealist art, but who just as well could have been describing the impact of encountering familiar music in an unfamiliar postmodern composition:

An object is put in crisis by radically pluralizing the context in which we must perceive it, specifically by removing it from the contexts where we conventionally perceive it and placing it in surprising ones.[13]

Another striking example of a critic writing on surrealism in a way that illuminates musical postmodernism is this paragraph that Robert Lebel wrote about painter Francis Picabia:

With that comical majesty to which he holds the secret, Picabia will espouse every style, including the worst, thereby demonstrating that everything is possible and that everything is worthwhile. Pushing desacralization to its extreme, he will be preoccupied with the unheard of and the trivial, will testify that from a certain point of view, there is no basic difference between a rather commonplace Spanish portrait and "one of the most exceptional paintings in the world"; he will rise to the loftiest poetic heights, and will counteract it by the about-face of a pun.[14]

Like surrealism, postmodernism is more than a style: it is an attitude, a context, a way of thinking about the world, a state of mind. The various surrealist painters share this attitude but do not exhibit much consistency of style among them, just as postmodernist composers have produced varied styles of music. Critic Maurice Blanchot's ideas on the ubiquity of surrealism can readily be adopted to describe the pervasiveness of the musical postmodern:

It is not so much a school, but a state of mind. Nobody belongs to this movement, but everybody is part of it. Is surrealism disappearing? No, because it is neither here nor there: it is everywhere. It is a phantom, a brilliant obsession.[15]

This quotation exemplifies why I am not happy thinking of musical postmodernism

[12] Yves Bonnefoy, *Dualité de l'art d'aujourd'hui* (Paris: Arts de France 11, 1961), translated by Waldberg, p. 29.
[13] Ermarth, *Sequel to History*, p. 93.
[14] Robert Lebel, "Picabia and Duchamp, or the Pro and Con," November, 1949, quoted in Waldberg, *Surrealism*, p. 30.
[15] Maurice Blanchot, *La Part du feu* (Paris, 1944), translated and quoted in Waldberg, p. 45. Referring to Octavio Paz, LeBaron also characterizes postmodernism as "a state of mind," "Reflections of Surrealism in Postmodern Musics," pp. 61–2.

as a historical period, nor thinking of compositions as either postmodern or not. Postmodernism today, like surrealism in the 1920s, is pervasive (though not ubiquitous in either case). All composers, even those who consciously reject it, are affected by postmodernism. All listeners (at least in the West), even those who cling to the values of modernism or antimodernism, live in a society permeated by postmodern ideas, values, and artworks, and surely they cannot avoid postmodernism's impact. The total range of music today shares no stylistic characteristics, but listening and composing today share one critical thing: they are activities carried out at a time and in a place where postmodern values are ubiquitous.

9.2. Music in the Time of Surrealism

Albright's *Untwisting the Serpent* offers a fuller account of musical surrealism than any other source I know, other than LeBaron's article. The chapter "Surrealism (Music)" begins promisingly with the question, "What is surrealist music?"[16] Although Albright never directly answers this question, he does deliver on a more modest promise: "From our vantage point at the and of the twentieth century, we can perhaps see the outlines of such a theory [of musical surrealism]."[17]

All of the music Albright discusses—by composers such as Milhaud, Stravinsky,[18] Auric, Honegger, and above all Poulenc—is linked to the theater. The majority of the surrealist qualities in these works come from their theatrical contexts more than from the music itself, although Albright does discuss what makes some of this music surreal. The composers did in certain cases (particularly Poulenc) try to create music appropriate to surrealistic theater, but—as Albright says of the five who provided music for Jean Cocteau's *Les Mariés de la Tour Eiffel*—"the composers themselves had little interest in [surrealist] incongruity for incongruity's sake."[19] To be fair, the theme of Albright's book is the interrelationship between modernist music (of various stylistic persuasions) and other art forms, so I should not expect other than a focus on music for the theater. While Albright's claim—that the loops and stasis in a work of

[16] Albright, *Untwisting the Serpent*, p. 275.
[17] Ibid., p. 275.
[18] Albright cites *Oedipus Rex* (composed in Paris in 1927, at the birth of surrealism), generally considered a neoclassic composition, as possibly understandable as surrealist. Composer Reece R. Dano similarly finds postmodernist elements in this work: "The music constantly seems to reference and juxtapose Verdian duets, Handelian choruses, popular trumpet fanfares, and can-cans, among other musical debris. But, perhaps, what is most interesting about *Oedipus* is the increasing analytical interest in it as it enters into the postmodern era and how it is increasingly viewed through a completely different hermeneutic, or perceptual/analytical filter, now that some analysts are no longer concerned with seeing the work as 'objective,' but rather highly nuanced in approach to its stylistic play," Reece R. Dano, "Stravinsky and Cocteau's *Oedipus Rex*: The Shifting Hermeneutics of Modernism and Postmodernism," http://home.earthlink.net/~rdano/stravinsky-andpomo.html (weblink no longer accessible, April 24, 2016). Also relevant is Stephen Walsh's suggestion that the fusion of styles in *Oedipus Rex* is essentially postmodern. *Stravinsky: Oedipus Rex* (Cambridge: Cambridge University Press, 1993), p. 60.
[19] Albright, *Untwisting the Serpent*, p. 279.

Milhaud render it surreal—is not completely convincing, the intertextuality he traces in Auric's and Honegger's portions of Cocteau's *Les Mariés de la Tour Eiffel* are relevant to our discussion. Where Albright is the most useful, however, is in his discussions of Poulenc's specifically musical surrealism.

> I understand Poulenc's manner of quotation—and he was a music thief of amazing flagrancy—not as a technique for making pointed semantic allusions, but as a technique for disabling the normal semantic procedures of music. ... Poulenc is a composer of surrealizing misquotations.[20]

Albright explores this idea further:

> Surrealism is a phenomenon of semantic dislocation and fissure. It is impossible to disorient unless some principle of orientation has been established in the first place. ... In other words, you can't provide music that means wrong unless you provide music that means something. ... The surrealism of Poulenc and his fellows didn't try to create a new language of music—it simply tilted the semantic places of the old language of music. Just as surrealist paintings often have a horizon line and a highly developed sense of perspective, in order that the falseness of the space and the errors of scale among the painted entities can register their various outrages to normal decorum, so surrealist music provides an intelligible context of familiar sounds in order to develop a system of meanings that can assault or discredit other systems of meanings.[21]

A significant work that Albright does not discuss is Jacques Ibert's *Divertissement*, which seems to me to embody the spirit of surrealism in music as well as any other work of its time. This unjustly neglected music was composed at the height of the surrealist movement, in 1929 in Paris, the center of surrealist activities.

Ibert sets the surrealist mood with a spirited yet brief Introduction, characterized by regular rhythms that periodically go off track as an extra half beat is added to some measures. The second of the six movements, *Cortège*, opens in mock seriousness, with violin harmonics against sustained wind sonorities. But the music then erupts into an animated passage reminiscent of the Introduction. A jaunty trumpet tune is taken over by strings and eventually by the entire orchestra. A snare-drum roll then leads to an outright incongruity and a blatant instance of intertextuality: a totally unexpected appearance of the Wedding March from Mendelssohn's *A Midsummer Night's Dream*. The quotation is brief, and it is made particularly strange by pungently dissonant harmonies.

The march rhythms, which continue even after the Wedding March disappears, are punctuated by three-note brass figures: first in the trumpet, then the horn, and then the trombone. It is obvious that a fourth statement is needed, but there are only three brass instruments in Ibert's small orchestra. Before we have much chance to wonder

---

[20] Ibid., p. 287.
[21] Ibid., pp. 289–90. Albright's remarks, intended to underline the distinction between atonal modernism and surreal modernism in music, serve as well to show how indeterminate music, such as that of Cage, differs from the music of certain strains of postmodernism.

who will play next, the most unlikely of instruments—the contrabassoon—speaks up with a "harrumpf." After this joke the music goes on as if nothing funny had happened: a brass melody and then a sweet clarinet tune.

The *Nocturne* is the only slow movement. There is little surrealism here, as a contemplative chromatic line weaves its way through the string section. The only surrealistic aspect of this movement is its utter incongruity in the suite. Specific surreality reappears in the *Valse*. After a boisterous introduction, a first waltz tune is presented by flute and clarinet. The tune's beat and that of its accompaniment do not coincide. It is as if two sections of the orchestra cannot manage to play together. This passage leads to a grand, sweeping, Viennese waltz, which is eventually joined by inappropriately banal trombone interjections.

At the opening of the next movement, *Parade*, to the accompaniment of low strings playing *col legno battuta*, a distant march tune is heard in the bassoon. As the march seems to come closer, it moves to the upper winds, while the bassoon makes irreverent comments.

The beginning of the *Finale* is the least expected music yet, and perhaps the most surreal: the piano (followed by the brass) plays extremely dissonant chords, such as might be heard in an atonal composition. Just as I am wondering what this modernist passage is doing in such a piece, the tempo brightens and the piece turns into, of all things, a can-can!

Ibert presented *Divertissement* to the concert world without a literary plot. Thus its jokes seem particularly whimsical, its juxtapositions particularly incongruous. The quotation of the Wedding March, for example, has no apparent justification other than its patent incongruity. The music's original context, however, was as incidental music for a play, in which the appearance of the Wedding March no doubt had some specific dramatic significance. Removed from the play and presented in the concert hall, however, this quotation seems particularly surreal. To make some kind of sense of this surprising juxtaposition, listeners must look within themselves, since *Divertissement* itself offers no explanations. When I hear this passage, the rationale I come up with has less to do with weddings or a Shakespearean comedy than it does with juxtapositions of unrelated musics.

Divertissement, like the works Albright discusses, originally owed its surrealistic impulses to factors outside the music. As accompaniment to Eugène Labiche's farce *An Italian Straw Hat* (first performed in 1851), the music's puns and quotations had specific references. Labiche's play is not really surrealistic, although its 1930 revival—for which Ibert composed the music—may have been. Regardless of the influence of the play, the concert suite *Divertissement* offers up (as far as I know) the most direct nontexted musical parallel to the artistic surrealism that came out of Paris in the 1920s to 1930s.

9.3. Are Musical Surrealism and Postmodernism the Same?

The reason I discuss *Divertissement* and quote at length from Albright's analyses of Poulenc's music is that this music has many postmodernist features.[22] I could just as comfortably point to its postmodernism as to its surrealism, and—tellingly—I would be pointing to essentially the same elements.[23] At least in this music, the musical connection between surrealism and postmodernism is palpable.

Divertissement and the works discussed by Albright are not the only music created well before the late twentieth century that is in some ways postmodernist. Throughout this book I have discussed several works of Ives as postmodernist, as well as to the finale of Mahler's Seventh Symphony, the first movement of his Third Symphony, the first movement of Beethoven's Opus 135, various works of Ives,[24] and Nielsen's Sixth Symphony (composed in 1925, when surrealism was first bursting forth, but in Copenhagen, which was far removed from the intellectual debates going on in Paris). And there are certainly other postmodern works that predate what I have loosely been calling the era of postmodernism. These pieces have something interesting in common: it took a long time for them to become appreciated or even understood. Although the two Mahler symphonies are today quite popular, they remained among his most hermetic works for more than half a century. Nielsen's Sixth is still his least understood, and one of his least performed, orchestral works. Opus 135 may well be the most hermetic of the late Beethoven quartets, which took several generations to gain widespread acceptance. The music of Ives was all but unknown for several decades. And Ibert's *Divertissement*, although certainly not banished from the concert hall, has yet to be taken as a serious (as well as a humorous) artwork. Ibert's work has exerted no great influence on other composers. It has appeared mostly on pop concerts, and composers have rarely paid much heed to it. Its surrealism seems rather isolated in history, particularly considering how close it is in spirit to some more recent music of a postmodernist bent.

We are well aware of the difficulty mainstream modernist music (Schoenberg, Webern, some Stravinsky, etc.) had making its way in the twentieth century. But its unpopularity never prevented this music from being at the forefront of compositional influence. The early twentieth-century postmodernist music I am discussing

---

[22]   A comparable argument is made for painting in Marc J. LaFountain, *Dalí and Postmodernism: This Is Not an Essence* (Albany: State University of New York Press, 1997).

[23]   An intriguing and challenging parallel is drawn between surrealist painting and postmodernism in the article "Panic Surrealism," in Arthur Kroker, Marilouise Kroker, and David Cook (eds.), *Panic Encyclopedia: The Definitive Guide to the Postmodern Scene* (New York: St. Martin's Press, 1989): "If the early surrealists—Magritte, Roux, Ernst, Dalí, Duchamp, and Miro—can be so popular today with their visions of the pineal eye, floating body parts, and disembodied power, it is because their artistic imaginations are brilliant anticipations of the postmodern destiny as detritus and amatory sacrifice. Indeed, if art is a semiological screen for the actual deployment and relays of political power, then remembering surrealism is also in the way of a dark meditation on the hidden logic of postmodern power. In these artistic texts, power announces itself for what it always was: cynical truth, cynical desire, and cynical sex as the postmodern aura."

[24]   LeBaron considers Ives to be the first postmodern composer, "Reflections of Surrealism in Postmodern Musics," p. 59.

seems to have been ignored not only by audiences (at least for a period) but also by composers, who—because their modernist compositional techniques led them away from works that were postmodernist/surrealist in spirit but utilized few new methods of composing—took several decades to come around to appreciating how much such music offered to them.

I hope to have made a cogent case for the music of Poulenc and others that Albright labels as surrealist also being postmodernist, in some sense consonant with the ideas developed in this book. Is there, then, any distinction between surrealist music and postmodernist music? I cannot cite as a distinction the different eras in which the two were composed, since I have been arguing against a historical time-frame for postmodernist music. If I can locate aspects of the postmodernist musical attitude in certain works of Ives and Mahler, then it is clearly no stretch to do so with some music of Poulenc and Ibert as well. Now, there are certainly many kinds of music in which I have found postmodernist strains that do not seem to have a lot in common with surrealism—music by Andriessen, Torke, Gorecki, and Bryars, for example, is quite distinct from the surrealism of Poulenc and Ibert. Yet there is postmodernist music of recent vintage that *does* share traits with Albright's version of musical surrealism— compositions by Daugherty, Schnittke, and Bolcom to name just a few composers.[25] Because of the extensiveness of their use of quotations, each of these composers has "managed to become a whole assortment of composers bundled up into one person."[26]

Albright's most direct explication of musical surrealism is quite close to my own understanding of musical postmodernism (I do not particularly care for his term "expressionistic," since it suggests expressionist art; the following quotation makes more sense to me if I substitute "communicative" for "expressionistic"):

Surrealist music is about the possibilities for lying, for self-incongruity, for calcu- lated inauthenticity of being. It isn't expressionistic [i.e. communicative], but *about* expression [i.e. communication]: it takes expressionistic [communicative] devices and arrays them into odd aesthetic constructs. It inspects the musical signs for joy, sorrow, languor, and so forth, and twists them into exotic curlicues. It cultivates a semantic vertigo, since the signs it uses both mean and do not mean what they seem to mean. Surrealist music is a far more wide-awake business than the surrealist writing of Breton; but it remains close to the surrealism of

---

[25] I should also mention the rock group Nurse with Wound (the founder and leader is Steven Stapleton), that has made quite a few CDs that Stapleton and several critics describe as surreal. The two of their releases I have heard—*A Sucked Orange* and *Live at Bar Maldoror* (Nurse's first album was *Chance Meeting on a Dissecting Table of a Sewing Machine and an Umbrella*)—strike me as excellent examples of rock music under the influence of surrealism/postmodernism. They freely juxtapose quite unrelated musics, taken from diverse social contexts. "Nurse music is Surrealist music. It's the displacement of something ordinary into an extraordinary setting. I take ordinary things—instruments, solos, what have you—and place them in unusual settings, giving a completely different angle on the way instruments and composition are looked at." Stapleton quoted at http:// www.wfmu.org/LCD/21/nurse.html.

[26] Albright, *Untwisting the Serpent*, p. 307.

Apollinaire, in that it drives wedges into our normal way of assembling sense data into a big, consistent world.[27]

I would be comfortable substituting the label "postmodernist" for "surrealist" in this quotation. In fact, I might prefer the postmodernist to the surrealist label for all this French music, since the aspects of surrealism that do not appear in postmodernist music also do not appear in Poulenc's and Ibert's efforts: an attempt to reflect the world of dreams and of the unconscious,[28] and the employment of automatic writing in an endeavor to allow for an unmediated contact between the creator's mind and that of the audience.

All music that is surrealist (according to Albright's definition) also displays several characteristics of musical postmodernism (as laid out in my list in Section 1.3).[29] But there is not a huge amount of such music. Albright mentions fewer than twenty pieces, composed by a half-dozen composers. Musical surrealism seems to have been a rather small, though nonetheless striking, movement. Eclipsed by the more hardcore modernism of atonalists such as Varèse, Schoenberg, and Webern, and by the neoclassicism of Stravinsky and Hindemith (and by surrealist painting and writing), French musical surrealism of the 1930s did not spawn a school. This eclipse is ironic, since the music of Poulenc and Milhaud has always been more popular with the general public than that of the atonalists. But the atonalists did not appear to care so much about popularity. In fact, they were suspicious of any music that gained acceptance in the arena of public opinion. Thus they discouraged their students from following the path of musical surrealism. It is hard to imagine Schoenberg, or Messiaen, or Boulez, or Stockhausen, or Babbitt telling students to look to the music of Poulenc, Ibert, and Milhaud for inspiration about feasible ways to conceive compositions. The isolation of musical modernism from the public all but guaranteed that disciples of the atonalists would not recognize musical surrealism as valuable or viable, and might not even recognize it as a musical movement at all.

In fact, as Susan McClary perspicaciously notes, tonal pieces of the twentieth century (which the surrealist compositions of Poulenc, Milhaud, and Ibert certainly are) were cast as modernism's enticing Other. McClary seems to exaggerate by implication, because surely it was not the atonalists' primary goal to suppress tonality, but rather to write beautiful and provocative music of a new sort. Nonetheless, many of the high priests of musical modernism did strive to keep surreal music out of the canon of acceptably forward-looking compositions.

Despite these modernist attempts at weeding out all traces of its Other, the paradox remains that atonal projects themselves derive their meaning from tonality. Throughout the years of its exile, tonality was kept simultaneously at bay and in its place of privilege by what Jean-François Lyotard describes as a negative theology: it

---

[27] Albright, *Untwisting the Serpent*, p. 291.
[28] As Fredric Jameson quips in reference to painting and video art, postmodernism is "surrealism without the unconscious," *Postmodernism or, the Cultural Logic of Late Capitalism*, pp. 67, 174.
[29] Victor Grauer draws interesting parallels between surrealism and postmodernism in music. See "Toward a Unified Theory of the Arts," *Semiotica* 94-3/4, 1993: 240–1.

reigned as the seductive idol against which composers and listeners were expected to practice apostasy. To be sure, some twentieth-century composers (commonly dismissed as reactionaries who failed to participate in the ongoing progressive history of musical innovation[30]) never disavowed tonality or its codes. But it could be argued that those who continued casually to employ its procedures were invested less intensely in tonality than those who based their work on circumventing it at all costs.[31]

This idea is certainly borne out by the educational values of twentieth-century composers. Most atonal composers who have taught have insisted on their students mastering tonality, even though they were not expected to use it in their compositions. Tonal composers also believe that their students need to understand traditional music, but there seems to be less of a sense of urgency, or of requirement—presumably because the relevance of tonality to composition in such cases may be assumed to be self-evident.

Atonal modernists often sought to cast their music as having a sense of purity, of remove from concerns of society or the marketplace. And they tended to disparage their contemporaries who wrote surrealist or neoclassicist tonal music as pandering to the public, as seeking an easy road to commercial success. The way postmodernists look at this situation is to believe that all music is a commodity, that it is impossible to escape the commodification of art. The music of, for example, Babbitt may have much less economic power than the music of the Beatles, but postmodernists believe that the difference in economic clout is of degree, not of kind. And so we will take a brief look in the next chapter at the economics and politics of music in an era when postmodern values are widespread.

---

[30] This would presumably include Albright's musical surrealists, although he believes that Poulenc's modernism is every bit as radical as Schoenberg's, although in vastly different ways. "Schoenberg worked to emancipate harmonic dissonance; Poulenc worked to emancipate semantic dissonance, to draw power from the inconsequentiality of musical events," Albright, *Untwisting the Serpent*, p. 305.

[31] McClary, *Conventional Wisdom*, pp. 140–1.

Part Three

Postmodern Chapters on the Concept of Music

10

Economics, Politics, Technology, and Appropriation

10.1. Postmodern Music as Commodity

One of the consequences of postmodernism's, like surrealism's, invitation of the everyday into the previously lofty realm of art is that art has become recognized as inevitably commodified. Today Boulez's rallying cry for high modernism—"there are musics ... whose very concept has nothing to do with profit"[1]—seems excessively idealistic and a trifle naïve. Because the general public was not interested in modernist music, its composers took refuge in its unmarketability as a badge of purity and even of significance. But all music has some commercial value. It may be true that Boulez did not earn very much money from composing a piece like *Le Marteau sans maître*. His composing of it was surely not directly motivated by profit. But he did copyright it, it did earn him and his publishers a bit of money, and it made his name widely known—which in turn contributed to his becoming a marketable commodity himself: a composer of some notoriety who could be hired to create music, to lecture about it, and to conduct it. *Marteau* was a small but significant part of a very profitable career, which might have developed rather differently had Boulez not composed it or had he written other kinds of music instead. These benefits may have been side issues for the composer, but they are nonetheless real. Boulez may have thought only about art for art's sake, but even a highly modernist work like *Marteau* is a commodity that was (and still is) consumed.

American institutions of higher education used to (and in a few cases still do) perpetuate such naïve modernist attitudes toward music in the marketplace. When modernist thinking was the ruling force in our universities, there was no instruction for students on how to market their musical skills: how to get jobs, how to win auditions, how to build performing careers, how to win competitions, how to get commissions, how to interest performers in playing their compositions. Art was one thing (that was nurtured in academia); promotion was something totally different (that belonged outside the campus). Postmodernism questions this separation. For postmodernists, art and its marketing are inextricably interwoven.[2] Now that postmodern thinking

---

[1] Michel Foucault and Pierre Boulez, "Contemporary Music and the Public," *Perspectives of New Music* 24/1 (1985): 8.
[2] This attitude is hardly unique to postmodernism. The careers of Mozart and Beethoven, for example, are chronicles of attempts (not always successful) to play the market. Twentieth-century

is beginning to be more prevalent in these bastions of learning, such instruction is becoming more common. Musical academics are finally coming to realize the inevitability of the commodification of the musical art, particularly in a society like that in the United States.[3] They are beginning to tell their students that the huge efforts they put into practicing, studying, composing, etc., will not find audiences if they do not also market their skills and their artistic products. Interestingly, this sort of practical education came more readily to conservatories, where modernism never had quite the stranglehold it had in universities.

There are pop as well as "classical" musicians who also seem motivated primarily by art, not business, even though many of them make a lot more money than most modernist composers. As I mentioned at the end of the preceding chapter, these are questions of degree, not of kind. In a postmodern society, with its efficient technological dissemination (i.e. sales) of all kinds of music, the art of music is also unavoidably linked with the business of music. No musician completely avoids the marketplace. To profess otherwise suggests naïveté if not outright denial.

To write and publish a book on music and postmodernism is also not immune from marketplace economics! That few musicologists, theorists, or critics get rich from their efforts is not the point. They write to communicate (while postmodernism casts severe doubts on the concept of communication between an author and a reader, it has not silenced academics!). If their meaning, as constituted by various readers, leads to more invitations to write, lecture, publish, or speak, would the authors be indifferent?

When I wrote *The Time of Music* in the mid-1980s, I was more of a modernist than I am now. Thus, although the style of the book is somewhat postmodern, my motivation was not: I thought I had something to say, I did not care about profit, I was acting out of pure scholarship. I wanted to communicate. But, in fact, the book subsequently earned me several speaking engagements, just as it helped me get a new academic position at Columbia University. The amounts of money are not comparable to what postmodernists of the pop music world garner, but that, as I have said, is not the point. Rather, the point is: with scholarship as with music, all texts are consumable commodities, and all are for sale. One difference between modernists and postmodernists is that the latter accept this fact while the former deny it, or at least are uncomfortable with it.

critics and annotators tried to recast such composers as above the mundane concerns of material success. But this decidedly modernist attitude comes more from the twentieth century than from the eighteenth. Since twentieth-century modernism has disparaged commercial values in music, and encouraged composers to ignore the commodity value of their music, postmodernism's blatant embrace of the marketplace has been seen not as a return to pre-modernist practices (since they have been obscured in most popular accounts of earlier composers' careers) but as a blurring of the distinction between high art and popular art—which is exactly what it was, given the postmodernist desire to break down the barrier between the high and the low (trait 4).
[3] I am happy to report that my travels to several countries in Eastern Europe have shown me musical cultures that still are somewhat free of the pressures of the marketplace, although in this post-Communist era such idealism is fast disappearing.

10.2. Postmodern Music as Commodity (continued)

If postmodernist composers seek to locate the nexus of musical meaning and experience in the listener (trait 16), does it not follow that they actively seek to attract audiences? Perhaps it does in some cases, particularly those of certain conservative postmodernists. I have heard many composers talk about wanting to close the mid-twentieth-century's enormous gap between composer (or, more literally, music) and audience, a gap whose blame they lay squarely with modernist composers: their technical procedures, their favored sounds, and their apparent disdain of audiences.

Other postmodernist composers, often of a more radical persuasion, retain something like the modernist disregard of listeners' preferences or predilections. They seem to want to continue the modernist trend of creating provocative music that will challenge each listener to make sense of it, albeit in her or his own individual way. Such composers may well be less absolutist than their modernist forebears in their attitude toward audiences, since they often incorporate familiar elements in their works, seeming to want to meet audiences halfway. Rather than demanding a total giving over of the self to the strong and challenging musical persona of a modernist work, they seek to draw listeners into their compositions with seductively ordinary materials. Then they may do strange things with those materials, emptying them of their original meaning and suggesting to the listeners new kinds of significance and new contexts.

Conservative postmodernists are sometimes accused of selling out, of trying to win audience approval by the most obvious of means. Radical postmodernists are sometimes accused of perpetuating the alienation of modernism, of continuing to create music for a small, elite band of initiates. What can be lost in this debate is the economic fallout from the postmodern composers' attempted rapprochement with audiences. A composer who writes a neo-tonal symphonic overture may hope—consciously or not, deliberately or not—for many performances, for publication, for recording, for broadcasts, for respect and fame, all of which will bring in money. The amount of money may not be huge, to be sure, but the allure of living off one's compositions—rather than having to teach, or give piano lessons, or play cocktail piano, or copy someone else's music, or drive a taxi—is seductive. Curiously, if predictably, a composer who earns a modest income from his or her compositions is respected and envied by colleagues who must do other things to earn their keep, whereas a composer who makes a huge amount of money (such as Philip Glass, for example) is jealously disdained.

Perhaps it is modernism's lingering contempt of the marketplace that causes composers to be ambivalent about earning money from their art.[4] It is certainly consonant with postmodern thinking (trait 15) to admit that music is unavoidably

---

[4] As Fredric Jameson remarks, "The deepest and most fundamental feature shared by all the modernists is ... their hostility to the market ... The various postmodernisms ... share a resonant affirmation, when not an outright celebration, of the market as such," *Postmodernism or, the Cultural Logic of Late Capitalism*, pp. 304–5.

a commodity; the only question worth asking is whether or not it is a successful commodity![5]

Yet, only a handful of "classical" composers are openly capitalist about their music. Many still prattle on about their lofty artistic ideals, rarely mentioning (except, presumably, to their accountants) their economic successes or failures. Yet the arts are thoroughly capitalistic, regardless of whether this fact is good or bad for art or for society. Consider the symphony orchestras, particularly in America. Economic considerations drive almost all the decisions they make. The price tag and the projected returns on monetary investments are routinely taken into consideration when the orchestra managements consider repertory, rehearsal schedules, guest soloists, guest conductors, and resident conductors, just as much as financial concerns drive decisions about ticket prices, marketing and advertising, publicity, musicians' salaries, etc.

As is well documented, symphony orchestras are in crisis, or at least believe themselves to be. Audiences are dwindling. Government support is shrinking. Recording contracts are drying up. Broadcast engagements are disappearing. People seem less and less interested in the museum-like nature of the repertory, yet they are even less interested in new music.

Could postmodern music, at least conservative postmodern music, save the day? It would be comforting to think so. Exciting new pieces that reflect today's cultural values and concerns rather than those of 200 years ago, yet that are not extraordinarily difficult for untutored audiences to appreciate, should be able to bring new, young audiences to the symphonic experience. So far, this seems not to be happening. Why?

Early in my eight-year tenure as composer-in-residence and new-music advisor for the Cincinnati Symphony Orchestra (1984–92), I tried to forge an alliance with the marketing department. I offered to find compositions of today that were vital, exciting, and user-friendly, and to try to persuade the music director to program them. The marketing people then were supposed to feature these works in their promotions and advertising, using slogans like "Today's sounds for today's audiences."

It did not work. Cincinnati's audiences are notoriously unadventurous, but I do not believe that is the main reason for the failure. It was a failure to go far enough, truly to believe in the product, that doomed these efforts and others like them at other orchestras. The failure to go far enough was everyone's fault. From among the wide variety of postmodern works I presented to him, the music director chose to program several ten-minute concert openers. By the time the audience had settled down and was ready to give its attention to the concert, the new music was (blessedly?) finished. The marketing department failed as well, because it was too cautious to feature the

---

[5] Cornel West sees the marketplace mentality as one of the main shaping forces of postmodern culture: he cites "the unprecedented impact of market forces on everyday life, including the academy and the art world." He finds this theme echoed in thinking across the spectrum from right (e.g. art critic Hilton Kramer) to left (e.g. art and social critic Fredric Jameson): "Commodification of culture and commericialization of the arts are the major factors in postmodern culture." See West's "Postmodern Culture," in his *Prophetic Reflections: Notes on Race and Power in America* (Monroe, ME: Common Courage Press, 1993), pp. 37–43. These two quotations are found on pp. 39 and 41 respectively.

new in their advertising. And, I must admit, often the composers failed as well. Seeing that they actually could get their music programmed by a major symphony orchestra, as long as it met certain criteria, they allowed those criteria—more than truly artistic values—to determine the music they wrote. It had to be simple enough to be learned in a short amount of rehearsal time. It had to be short. It had to be pleasant. It had to be colorful. It had to use the orchestral instruments in proven ways, so that the instrumentalists' well-honed skills would shine to everyone's delight. Given these strictures, it is hardly surprising that a lot of trivial ten-minute pieces have been opening orchestral programs throughout the United States (and Europe is not immune either). Often the composers were a bit foolish in feeling that incorporating some snippets of jazz or rock would lead to popularity. Listeners wanting to hear jazz or rock knew better than to seek it in a symphony concert. The world was more sophisticated by the 1990s and beyond than it had been in the 1920s (and just before and after), when such jazz-inflected symphonic works as Copland's Piano Concerto, Ravel's two piano concertos, Gershwin's *Rhapsody in Blue*, Milhaud's *La Création du monde*, and Stravinsky's *Ragtime for Eleven Instruments* captivated and excited audiences. More appropriate today is music that seeks a more potent crossover, a truer amalgamation. Such music exists, to be sure, but it seems to be too radical to gain the widespread performances, supported by extensive and sympathetic marketing, that would be needed to establish it as a cultural (and economic!) force. I am thinking of certain music by composers such as Michael Daugherty, Michael Torke, Steve Martland, Daniel Roumain, Robert Dick, and Frank Proto, to name just a few.

The symphony orchestras have continually avoided (not totally—after all, we *do* know about this music—but they have not promoted it actively enough to establish it in the public's consciousness) the longer, more challenging, more unusual pieces, such as those of these (and other) radical postmodernist composers. And so, the economic potential of new music remains modest. But that does not matter to this argument. What matters is that considerations of the marketplace have influenced the nature of the art that was (and is) produced. This situation is inevitable. Even under high modernism, the marketplace had its impact on composers, if only in a negative way: anyone who wrote music that was widely accepted was viewed with suspicion.[6] What is different in the postmodern world is that composers often no longer try to deny the economic subtext of their works. Whether the influence of the marketplace is good or bad for music is not my concern: it is no doubt both good and bad, like most other influences. Rather, my aim is to show that the economic subtext is undeniable and unavoidable.

Whereas some postmodern composers openly court audience approval and "understanding," and virtually all composers would like their works to be appreciated, few if any believe that a single composition can lead to widespread recognition and economic security. Such a situation was doubtless never possible, but surely it is

---

[6] As Koen Raes perspicaciously asks, "Was the anti-commodity posture of radical modernism not itself a final tribute to commodity-production?" See "The Ethics of Postmodern Aesthetics: Toward a Social Understanding of Cultural Trends in Postmodern Times," in Mark Delaere (ed.), *New Music, Aesthetics, and Ideology* (Wilhelmshaven, Germany: Florian Noetzel, 1995), p. 66.

not now, when there is a huge amount of music being produced and competing for performances, recordings, broadcasts, internet attention, etc. Since most music is widely available, even if it is also obscure, no piece of music is truly scarce. And, given the postmodern demise of the high value modernism placed on the uniqueness—the scarcity of each artwork—postmodern composers (at least those of a conservative bent) are by and large not struggling to create unique pieces of music (trait 6 questions the value placed on originality).

Yet uniqueness ought to lead, one would think, to a potentially high income. A particular canvas of Picasso is a highly valued commodity partly because of its scarcity: there is only one such canvas in existence. It is, furthermore, destined to be worth more than, say, a manuscript of Stravinsky, because the painting is an authentic work of art, while the manuscript is not the music but rather a representation of the music, or a graphic instruction for producing the work. The idea of a single authentic piece of music is problematic. It becomes doubly so when we consider that many conservative postmodern music works do not seek novelty nearly to the extent that modernist works do. So, whereas a unique work like *The Rite of Spring* might bring its composer a lot of money (although, in fact, it did not, since it was not covered by international copyright), that amount probably does not compare with the amount *Guernica*, for example, might sell for. *Guernica* is unique and authentic and hence commands a high price. *The Rite of Spring* is unique, but no performance of it is truly authentic. The conservatively postmodern ten-minute concert openers I have been disparaging are neither unique nor authentic (because postmodernism questions the very idea of artistic authenticity), and hence they are not going to bring their composers very much income. But, paradoxically, the postmodern composers, more than their modernist forebears, are conscious of the commodity value of their products. But it is not the single work, but rather the entire career (like that of the modernist Boulez, discussed above) that has earning power, or so composers like to believe. Seeing one's artistic career as a commodity may seem materialistic or parasitical or cynical, but such an attitude is indeed postmodern.

10.3. The Politics of Modernism and Postmodernism in New York

Reasons motivating composers to embrace postmodernism, beyond the questionable lure of economic success, concern the power structures of contemporary composition, the politics of the academies of so-called higher learning, the boards of certification who hand out grants and prizes, and the performing organizations that either do or do not encourage postmodern music (at least in the United States). These institutions are particularly strong in New York, where the issues of postmodernism vs. latter-day modernism are acutely felt, even if poorly understood. The postmodernists (the radical postmodernists more than their conservative counterparts), more often than not, are those excluded by the power structures of the musical world. Whether they became postmodernists because they were excluded, or whether they have been excluded because they are postmodernists, is a loaded question—one that seems impossible to answer.

Many young composers used to want to study at my New York university because they saw it as one of the last holdouts against the insidious inroads of postmodernism (although they did not frame their concerns in these terms), and perhaps also because they saw it as providing a credential and even an entree into the power structures that held out the promise of a certain kind of success. With the retirement of Babbitt and J. K. Randall and then Claudio Spies from Princeton, these students were seeing Columbia as the only safe haven in the New York area. We on the faculty were broader in our aesthetic inclinations than the students gave us credit for, but this is typical: students do tend to see aesthetic matters in black-and-white terms and to see aesthetic differences as calls to arms. But there is no denying that for a generation Columbia produced—with a few notable exceptions—late modernist composers who defended their aesthetic with a vengeance. The more anachronistic they seemed to the outside world, the more tightly they bonded, held together more by their mutual dislikes than by stylistic similarities in their compositions.

The following vignette is not at all unusual. When John Corigliano's postmodernist opera *The Ghosts of Versailles*[7] was premiered at the Metropolitan Opera, the young "uptown" modernist composers—most associated with Columbia in one way or another—turned out *en masse*, prepared to hate it. Eavesdropping on their conversations during the intermission was a delightful sociological exercise. Of course they disparaged it. It did not fit their meta-narrative of acceptable art music. It was too eclectic, too impure. I heard an antimodernist composer reply in defense, "What about the eclecticism of *The Magic Flute?*" "That's different," was the vague but defensive reply. The real reason the young modernists hated *Ghosts* was not its postmodernism directly, I suspect, but its success. Corigliano had a huge and lavish production at the Met! Therefore, he must have sold out. And he had even gone to Columbia (though, mercifully, only as an undergraduate)! He was a traitor! It became a matter of moral commitment to hate his opera.

I suppose this situation has been repeated countless times in history: when tonality began to replace modality, when polyphony gave way to homophony, when composers moved beyond tonality to atonality. There were always defenders of the old values, secure in their established positions, who were upset by the young turks of the new order. Some of the conservatives (such as Bach and Brahms) did, in fact, create beautiful and lasting music. And I think there are some major talents among the lingering modernists on New York's upper west side (and, of course, elsewhere). Even among the closed-minded opponents of postmodernism, worthwhile music is being written. I would not want it any other way. Since postmodernism denies the narrative of historical progress, it is inappropriate to see postmodernism as replacing

[7] For a discussion of this work as an instance of musical postmodernism, see Jane Piper Clendening, "Postmodern Architecture/Postmodern Music," in Judy Lochhead and Joseph Auner (eds.), *Postmodern Music/Postmodern Thought* (New York and London: Routledge, 2002), pp. 131–3.

modernism. Both exist today, along with antimodernism and various other "isms." I continually encourage tolerance—listening with pleasure, respect, and insight to many kinds of music—but this lesson is particularly difficult for most composition students, particularly my modernists, to learn.

Despite polemics for open-mindedness, I find that most latter-day modernists feel threatened by the popularity of some postmodern music. With a few exceptions, they are intolerant of postmodernism. Although professional jealousies run in many directions, I find that postmodernists are generally less intolerant than modernists, probably because they feel less threatened by the opposition than modernists do. It strikes me as typical that I met John Cage at Milton Babbitt's seventy-fifth birthday concert, but that I never saw Babbitt—who used to attend a great number of concerts—at a Cage performance. Since postmodernists are usually eclectics, they maintain their interest in many kinds of music, including hardcore modernism. Furthermore, it is less painful for the politically disenfranchised to extend a welcoming hand across the gulf than it is for those locked high in the established power hierarchy to do so. Those in power have little to gain but much to lose—namely, some of their credibility within their own circle, and hence some of their power. Those outside of the power structure stand only to gain.

The critical establishment has often given modernist music a hard time. That negative criticisms greeted the earliest modernist music is hardly surprising. What depresses those of us who love modernist music is that the vehemence (although not the intelligence) of negative criticism increased, rather than decreased, throughout the twentieth century. Toward the end of the century, as postmodern values led to the feeling that "classical" music could and therefore should be socially and culturally relevant, critics continued to pound the purity and abstraction of modernist music. There have certainly been critics who have defended and promoted musical modernism, but the voices of the detractors have been considerably more numerous.

This sort of criticism is found not only in newspapers and magazines but also in serious scholarly studies. Rose Rosengard Subotnik, for example, offers a typical damnation of modernist music produced by late twentieth-century academically affiliated composers:

> What social need is there for art music today? On the whole it must be admitted that whatever need manifests itself in our society for new musical artworks is an artificially created or self-perpetuating need, a situation that is scarcely surprising in a society where the need for music, among the socially elite, has given way so extensively to the need for musical artworks *as such*. Universities, for example, decide that they have a need for composers who produce autonomous works, that is, works for which there is no social need. Or composers get together and form groups that are defined as "needing" the kinds of music written by their founders. In both cases, the social foundation for such a need is neither broad nor deeply grounded in contemporary life and cannot support more than a handful of individuals.[8]

---

8   Subotnik, *Developing Variations*, p. 253.

It is evident in context that Subotnik is referring to modernist more than postmodernist music, and mainly that created in the United States by atonalitsts who hold positions in colleges, universities, and conservatories. Other critics, equally disdainful of the music these people create, inaccurately label them as "academic serialists." Numerous critics have dismissed if not outright condemned their music for its alleged impenetrability and social irrelevance.

What do people *really* mean when they refer to an academic serial establishment? They clearly do not mean whether or not the music uses twelve-tone rows. The music of Mario Davidovsky generally does not use rows, yet he is quintessentially a member of that notorious academic circle. The music of Joseph Schwantner, on the other hand, often *is* twelve-tone, yet he does not fit so comfortably into the establishment. Stravinsky—an outspoken anti-academic—embraced twelve-tone procedures in his late works, and even some earlier examples (Septet, second movement of the Sonata for Two Pianos) are serial but not twelve-tone. Yet who would ally the rhythmically motoric first movement of the twelve-tone *Requiem Canticles* with American academic serialism? Compare that music with the late works of Seymour Shifrin, whose style typifies that which seems to bother the critics of late twentieth-century modernism. Shifrin's music—although not at all serial—exemplifies what is dismissed as academic serialism, while Stravinsky's—strictly serial—seems not to belong to that category.

The condemnation of academic serialism is really a disparagement of latter-day modernism. Postmodernist ideas and musical styles are taken as threatening to this strain of lingering modernism. The conflict between late modernism and postmodernism in music is far more important to understanding twentieth-century music, including so-called academic serialism, than is the question of whether or not there is a tone row at work in a particular piece.

There certainly has been an academic establishment, at least in the United States. It has often allied itself with modernism, although the modernism of America in the latter third of the twentieth century was very different from that of central Europe in the teens. One aspect of modernism has been its elitism (trait 5), its encouragement of a specialist audience, its distrust of popularity. This is as true in today's concerts of groups (e.g. Speculum Musicae or Ensemble 21) that perform modernist music with great skill and dedication as it was in the concerts of Schoenberg's Society for Private Performance. As they have felt their musical values under ever greater threats—from dwindling audiences, fewer performance opportunities, disappearance of interested performing groups, diminishing of grant support (which tends to go to the trendy, not the staid), and fewer student disciples—many latter-day modernist composers have reacted with ever greater desperation. The academic serial establishment has indeed had power (through the ability to give out grants, commissions, prizes, prestigious performances, etc.)[9] and it has used this power for self-perpetuation. Today it is no longer as powerful as it was, but it still exists. *And*, it is important to realize, some

[9] This establishment has not been nearly as pervasive as the critics imply, however. See Joseph Straus, "The Myth of Serial 'Tyranny' in the 1950's and 1960's," *The Musical Quarterly* 83/3 (Fall 1999): 301–43.

wonderful and vital music is being created within the style that has been identified as academic serialism.

Perhaps some academic serialists seek to perpetuate their values by the way they teach, but this rarely works. Only small minds continue to imitate their teachers rather than find themselves. And only small-minded professors of composition teach by indoctrination. This is particularly true with regard to serial techniques. Virtually every undergraduate music major learns enough about serial techniques to misunderstand them totally. Yet few composition teachers require their students to be serialists. Schoenberg himself, as is well documented, refused to teach serialism to his students, particularly in his American years. Ironically, the biggest attempt to spawn imitators was that of Hindemith—hardly a serialist—and he largely failed.

To bring this discussion closer to home, I should return to Columbia University, where I have taught since 1988, when it was still known as a center of academic serialism. Writing serial music there in the 1960s and 1970s may have been actively encouraged—although I have trouble imagining Otto Luening making such demands on his students. I have found in most of the universities where I have taught (University of California at Berkeley, Oberlin, Yale, and the University of Cincinnati) that students create false ideologies rather than face creativity naked. They often pressure one another about what music is *verboten*, far more than do their teachers. Now it is certainly true that Columbia long had the reputation of being a safe haven for would-be academic serialists, even though it has been some time since there has been a serial composer teaching there. But there are no safe havens in art—only the timid like to believe so, and thus they cluster in places (like Columbia) where they feel unthreatened. But myths eventually die. Today at Columbia we have a wide variety of styles represented among our faculty composers *and* among our student composers. Our recent graduate students include experimentalists interested in new sonorities, a tonal traditionalist, a jazz composer, composers of the new complexity, and spectralists, in addition to some academic serialists—many of whom do not actually use serial techniques.

Given the vehemence of the derogation of modernist music of today, we might expect unhappy critics to embrace the music of postmodernism. This does not happen very often, however. Why? Perhaps critics feel that they have the greatest impact when they crankily take composers to task for writing the "wrong" kind of music. Perhaps they sense that articles in praise of a new aesthetic cause fewer reverberations: critics as much as artists can be influenced by the exigencies of the marketplace.

Or maybe there is another reason. Critics who denounce modernism may, despite themselves, be infected with modernist values. Are they really ready to embrace music that defies unity, or that questions musical taste, or that is fragmented and discontinuous and blatantly incongruous, or that questions the high value placed on novelty or even on originality, or that parasitically uses music of the past, or that unashamedly embraces commercialization? Or are they rather looking for the next modernist avant garde, for a new *Rite of Spring* that they can be the first to hail?

The critics often see conservative postmodernism as the only postmodernism. They often do not recognize, or do not understand, the challenges of a radical postmodernist impulse. With some exceptions, they often fail to understand and hence to explicate the uniqueness, importance, and challenges of works like Eric Salzman's *Nude Paper Sermon*, Louis Andriessen's *Writing to Vermeer*, Paul Lansky's *Idle Chatter* pieces, or John Oswald's *Plunderphonics* series.

It is understandable that critics, who take as representative of the postmodern spirit the often insipid ten-minute orchestral concert openers described above, will not find that postmodernism has any greater social relevance than late modernism has. But, in fact, in one cynical way these conservative postmodern pieces do have a relevance that latter-day modernist pieces eschew: they embrace the marketplace unashamedly. They admit, and even welcome, their status as commodity.

Is it possible for postmodern composers to accept the inevitability of the marketplace, and even to embrace commercialization, yet still produce music that is vital, that seems to reflect or, more potently, to shape contemporary cultural values? That such music is unlikely to be understood or even recognized by the majority of critics is not the point: throughout history critics have on the whole had a spotty record when it comes to understanding new music that defies known values. I am convinced that such music exists. I am disheartened but hardly surprised that critics have not rallied around works like those just mentioned, or Zygmunt Krauze's Second Piano Concerto or Steve Reich's *The Cave*.[10]

10.4. Subversive Music?

It is not coincidental that the commercialization of art music is increasing at a time when government subsidies to composers and performing organizations are dwindling. In the United States, government support of the arts was never as extensive as it has been in the wealthier countries of Europe, but even the small amount of support that peaked in the 1980s has diminished. And most European countries are following suit, as they try to find ways to shift support more and more to the private and corporate sectors of their economies.

Nowadays, composers, musicians, presenters, and performing organizations in Europe and America are forced to be ever more enterprising in finding their own funding sources. Their new-found reliance on the business world is making them into capitalists, well aware of the marketplace and beginning to think about the hitherto foreign concept of profit.

Some may decry the reliance on private and corporate funding, and on the appeal to audiences for money, since the often uninformed people who are being asked to pay for the arts may well have agendas about the kind of art they do and do not want

---

[10] These pieces have certainly received some favorable reviews, but they have not been the occasions for any critics to campaign actively for their dissemination or for many musicologists to probe their implications. I do not mean to dismiss all critics, however. Andrew Porter, for example—a critic who has largely disparaged postmodernist music in his campaign to promote the "masterworks" of late modernism, has recently become an active champion of the decidedly postmodern music of Thomas Adès.

to support. Money is rarely simply given away. Naturally, people who support the arts, whether through contributions or buying tickets and recordings, pay for what they like and avoid what they hate. So, it should not be surprising that conservative postmodernism and antimodernism are in the ascendancy: composers of such music believe that they are creating music that people will want to consume. The economy is indeed driving the stylistic and aesthetic predilections of large numbers of composers today.

But it remains to be seen whether or not the public does indeed want to support conservative postmodernism. Perhaps composers and performers who present such music will survive, or perhaps they will not. Perhaps audiences and funders will, or perhaps they will not, flock to easy listening. Perhaps the composers are not the best judges of what the consumers of music want. Perhaps they underestimate the consumers, who may come to prefer something more challenging and provocative. After all, if it is a conservative rapprochement with the past that people really want, they may well simply prefer the authentic music of the past.

Composers who complain about the diminishing of government funding are indeed right to object. It is scandalous when governments do not recognize the power and value of the arts. It is short-sighted of politicians not to recognize that the arts are a big business, as well as a national treasure. It often seems that governments appreciate art only when it is deemed subversive. Hitler and Stalin actively sought to suppress artworks they felt were threats to the kind of cultural climate they were trying to promote, or at least trying to convince the world existed in their countries. Far short of such tyrannical suppression of subversive art, we encounter all too often governments in so-called "free" societies trying to use subsidies—or, more accurately, the withholding of them—to suppress art that bothers them. Any artist who is wary of the strings attached to corporate and private donations should remember the attempts by politicians to use the National Endowment of the Arts to censor artists such as Karen Findlay, and they should remember New York Mayor Guiliani's attempt to withhold funds from the Brooklyn Art Museum because he did not like some of the art exhibited there.

Music—at least nontexted music—does not often suffer from blatant attempts to control its "content" through the awarding or denying of grants. Even our most subversive music, such as the indeterminate works of Cage, is blithely let be (though such music is rarely supported by governments). In Stalin's Russia, government officials believed that they were qualified to judge whether or not instrumental music was subversive and, if they felt it was, that they should suppress it. The stories of the indignities suffered by Shostakovich and Prokofiev, among others, are legion, as are stories about the ways they tried to subvert their persecution. Similarly, Schoenberg and Hindemith suffered in Germany, and Lutosławski suffered in Poland. The doctrine of Socialist Realism by which the Soviet government sought to control the nature of artistic products is widely damned today as a gross interference with artistic free speech. If conservative postmodernists of today choose to create music that they conceive of as for the people, it is not thought of as Socialist Realism—because this is happening in many countries, not only those with Socialist economic systems, and, more significantly, because the composers, not the governments, are making the choice. This distinction is real, even if it is not so stark as composers might like to believe: aesthetic preferences of government, private, and corporate funders can influence the nature of the art created by recipients of their donations.

The conservative postmodern embracing of what audiences and contributors are believed to want resonates more with the American populism of the 1930s and '40s than with Soviet Socialist Realism. Aaron Copland wrote the populist music for which he is best remembered with a conscious motivation to make contact with audiences. He was still modernist enough apparently not to have been primarily motivated by the commodity value of his music, but it is true that he amassed a considerable financial base from performances (often conducted by himself) of works like *Appalachian Spring, Billy the Kid, Rodeo,* and *El Salón Mexico.* He earned far less from his more overtly modernist music—such pieces as *Connotations,* Piano Variations, *Inscape,* Piano Quartet, and Nonet for Strings.

Conservative postmodern orchestral music of the past two decades does sometimes exhibit stylistic similarities to the populist music of Copland (and also to music of Roy Harris, Walter Piston, Howard Hanson, and others). That music was created in a cultural climate very different from that of today, however. American optimism was less tainted then. Many intellectuals believed in the fundamental goodness of the United States and its national and international policies and priorities. They took this populist music as a musical expression of the culture they thought they understood. They seemed to accept what today seems like a naïve equation: American populist music was saving the concert hall from the ravages of atonality, just as the American government was striving to save the world from the evils of Fascism and Communism. That Copland was briefly a member of the Communist Party, and that his populism came from a possibly naïve belief in the proletariat, did not seem to concern his audiences (these facts were not widely publicized). Today many American intellectuals are a lot more cynical than were their predecessors in the 1930s and 1940s. Also, they are more marginalized. A lot of American conservative postmodern music is aimed, furthermore, not at intellectuals but at people who are musically ignorant—thanks in no small part to the disappearance of music education from the curricula of many elementary and secondary schools in the last third of the twentieth century. So, current conservative postmodernist music may sound a bit like American populist music of several decades back, but the cultural context renders it a very different sort of commodity.

It is doubtful that American conservative postmodernism will take on a cultural niche analogous to that filled by the populist music of the 1930s and 1940s. Will there be enough people who care about concert music of any sort to sustain this new populism? Will audiences embrace the apparent naïveté of much of this music, or will they recoil from its sunny optimism? Will antimodern music enter into a fatal competition with the pre-modern music that still fills the major portion of concert programs? Will the darker and more problematic kinds of postmodern music—more radical and with more sinew—gain acceptance and generate interest as it comes to be understood as a more accurate, if less pretty, reflection of current cultural values? Or will radical postmodernism never gain a sufficient following for it to survive as a commodity in the arts marketplace, and hence will it remain on the fringe, much as modernist music has always done?

These are fascinating questions to track, but they may well turn out not to be the most relevant, since they depend on the assumed continuation of traditional performing organizations, composer training, funding strategies, and dissemination. Given the ubiquity of technology in virtually all aspects of our lives, and the attendant increase in its use in the creation and dissemination of music, these questions may become obsolete. If composers become ever more involved with technology, if concerts give way to internet transmissions, if arts funding becomes entangled with technology funding, we will indeed be living in a postmodern world in which questions of the viability of, e.g., neo-tonal orchestral music may become marginalized. Chamber music and symphonic music concerts may not disappear—and I certainly hope they do not—but they may well become even less vital to our society than they currently are.

10.5. Appropriation

There is a fundamental irony in postmodernist musicians' embracing of the commodification of art. In order for music to produce revenue, it must be owned. The forces of the marketplace revolve around ownership. Yet, exactly what is owned when someone lays claim to a piece of music? The score, the sounds, the underlying ideas, the performance, the recording? The answer is far from clear, and it is one of many of postmodernism's ironies that an age-old philosophical question—just what *is* a piece of music—has become a practical, though still unanswered, question in the late capitalistic world of commercialized music.

The question of ownership of music is being vigorously challenged by postmodern technologies. The huge flap over Napster—the internet enterprise that allowed people to download music for free, notably including music with copyrights owned by specific people (composers and/or performers and/or promoters and/or publishers and/or recording companies)—will probably turn out to be but one battle in the inevitable war between the forces of ownership and the forces of wide dissemination (trait 15). Postmodernism embraces technology (trait 14), which is making the exchange of music ever easier, regardless of who claims to own it. Yet postmodernism also embraces the commodification of music, which depends on someone owning it and thereby profiting from its use. The inevitable conflict between these two forces may delight a postmodern observer, but the problem is real and tangible and *serious* for those people invested—whether artistically or financially or, in a quintessential postmodern way, both—in making and sharing music.

Ownership has come up already in our discussions of musical values. When discussing intertextuality (see Section 4.3), I wrote about how some of today's composers tend to quote more than their predecessors, yet not put their stamp of ownership on what they cite as much as was done in the past. What I have been calling quotation, citation, and intertextual reference could just as easily be called by another name: appropriation. Some music created in our postmodern culture freely and baldly appropriates from other music (traits 3, 4, 5, and 6). Sampling technology has made such appropriation so widespread, at least in certain areas of popular music, that questions of original ownership seem so complex as to be unmanageable (at least from a legal standpoint) if not irrelevant.

One of the most blatant users of sampling technology is the Canadian John Oswald, who has for decades been appropriating not tiny snippets but whole long segments of music created (and often legally owned) by other people.[11] His original CD (preceded by a record), called *Plunderphonics*, consists of 24 electronic recompositions (Oswald calls them "revisions") of many well-known recordings from both the pop and classical fields. He offers this definition:

> A plunderphone is a recognizable sonic quote, using the actual sound of something familiar which has already been recorded. Whistling a bar of *Density 21.5* is a traditional musical quote. Taking Madonna singing "Like a Virgin" and re-recording it backwards or slower is plunderphonics, as long as you can reasonably recognize the source. But the plundering has to be blatant. There's a lot of samplepocketing, parroting, plagiarism, and tune thievery going on these days, which is not what we're doing.[12]

Oswald's use of sampling differs from that of most pop music musicians. His quotations are clear, extended, and recognizable.

The qualifier for practical appropriation most often cited by pop people, with the exception of the rappers, is that it's OK to sample as long as the sample doesn't sound too much like the original. Meaning: sampling is OK as long as you don't get caught. By this rule my policy of accrediting the sources as if I was writing a research paper is not the way to play the game.[13]

Oswald conceived the project as one of total openness. He steadfastly refused to profit from his work. Thus he painstakingly identified all of his sources, told the copyright holders what he was doing, and made sure not to make any money from his work (this seems to be a delectably postmodern reinterpretation of the art-for-art's-sake credo of high modernism!).[14] He produced only a thousand CDs, which he had begun to give away (mainly to libraries, magazines, and alternative radio stations—which often encouraged listeners to make copies from their broadcasts—but also to the press and to some of those whose music he sampled) when legal forces descended on him. The cover of the CD featured a picture of singer Michael Jackson's head attached to a nude female body. One of Jackson's songs featured prominently on the CD. After Jackson's lawyers and others came after him, Oswald had to agree to destroy

---

[11] Anne LeBaron discusses postmodern aspects of Oswald's work in "Reflections of Surrealism in Postmodern Musics," pp. 49–54.

[12] Oswald, *Plunderphonics* (Seeland 515, Fony 69/96, 1999), p. 17.

[13] Ibid., p. 25.

[14] Oswald echoes—albeit with postmodern exaggeration—modernist values in yet another ironic way. When considering his deliberately offensive juxtapositions (such as a preacher's talk about God and Jesus mixed with a decidedly secular rock band), Oswald states: "I was striving for my music to be unpopular," ibid., p. 5.

the master tape and 300 CDs he had not yet given away. He was allowed to make more *Plunderphonics* disks but not to distribute them! The fascinating question of who really owned *Plunderphonics* was lost in the flurry of legal rhetoric, as the case never went to court. Did Michael Jackson or his handlers own Oswald's work? Did Oswald own it? Did the designers of his samplers and their software own a piece of it? Did the people and institutions who had received copies of the CD own it? That no one profited from their alleged ownership of *Plunderphonics* did not matter, it seemed, though perhaps it should have: was *Plunderphonics* any less a musical commodity than Jackson's original song, or than, say, Beethoven's Seventh Symphony, the finale of which Oswald transformed into a quasi-minimalist piece?

The injunction against Oswald's further distribution hardly silenced him. In a manner reminiscent of how a religious ban on a book or movie seems to guarantee its continued notoriety and popularity, Oswald became famous and sought after. The rock group The Grateful Dead asked him to transform their song "Dark Star,"[15] and the Kronos Quartet commissioned several pieces from him. Before long, he was able to issue a tenth anniversary expansion of *Plunderphonics* (with copyright permissions apparently secured[16]), replete with a glossy booklet and high-tech packaging.[17] This two-CD set was not given away but rather offered for sale (at a notably small price). Is it possible to enter the marketplace and still profess not to be interested in making a profit? I do not know the answer, but I will be most interested in following Oswald's trajectory, which seems to typify the career of a thoroughly postmodern musical artist, one who is deeply aware of and involved in questions of technology, sampling, ownership, and intertextuality.

An equally interesting use of sampling technology to produce postmodern music is found in Bob Ostertag's ongoing composition *Say No More.*[18] Ostertag first asked three jazz musicians to improvise solo pieces and send him tapes of the improvisations. He then studied the music carefully, sampled portions of it, and composed a piece from some of the samples, altered in various ways. The three independent pieces were made to come together in a variety of ways: notes were lengthened, time intervals between downbeats were altered, etc., so that the tempos could relate. Sometimes one musician seems to follow another. The approach to tempo is complex, because the samples often play at their original tempos within beats but alter the length of beats to agree with other simultaneously sounding samples.

The samples are sometimes brief (as short as a twelfth of a second), but more often they are sufficiently long for the performing style of each musician to be heard. Ostertag's purpose was to preserve each musician's individual expression, even as he superimposed his own structural compositional ideas. Sometimes Ostertag himself

[15] Ibid., pp. 37, 39. Oswald's work, *Grayfolded*, utilizes simultaneously about a hundred different performances (1969–92) of "Dark Star."
[16] Ibid., p. 28.
[17] Significantly, this book and CD carry no copyright notices. See also Oswald and Norm Igma, "Plunderstanding Ecophonomics: Strategies for the Transformation of Existing Music," in John Zorn (ed.), *Arcana: Musicians on Music* (New York: Granary Books/Hips Road, 2000), pp. 9–17.
[18] The composer explained the details of his work in a lecture at the Center for New Music and Technology, University of California, Berkeley, November 28, 1994.

improvised with samples, so that his jazz performing style became an integral part of the piece.

That this piece creates a collaboration between musicians who work separately is fascinating, but even more intriguing is the question of authorship. Since Ostertag, like Oswald, preserves lengthy samples, the creativity and expression of the original improvisations is a part of the piece. He is not taking fragments out of context or distorting them beyond recognition. Rather, he is cherishing their context as he tries to make it part of his context as well.

It is telling that one of the musicians at first complained. Why should he put down on tape an improvised style he had worked twenty years to perfect, only to have someone else take it away and impose on it another person's style? But Ostertag sought to preserve each musician's expression as he created his electronic collaboration.

Ostertag intensified these issues in the next stage of the work. The resulting tape is a fascinating piece in itself, but Ostertag went on to transcribe it into an expanded musical notation, and then had the original musicians come together and play the notated piece. The results are quite different from the sampled tape. The performers' musical personalities reassert themselves, particularly as they confer in rehearsal about how best to render the sounds on the tape, some of which—because of the electronic manipulation—are beyond human capabilities. Who is the composer of this live piece? Its materials go back to independent improvisations, but Ostertag made the tape and from it the score. But the same musicians perform the live version. The answer is that *Say No More* is a true collaboration of four musicians, but one accomplished in a way that is possible only with sampling technology. This piece is postmodern not because it challenges unity (it does not) and not because it invokes sounds of tonality (it rarely does), but because it challenges barriers. It does not believe in the distinction between performer and composer, nor is it comfortable with the division of music into acoustic and electronic media.

When I met him in 1995, Ostertag was planning to continue the process, making a new piece from tapes of performances of the live version and then notating and asking the same musicians to perform the new version live. The process is potentially unending.

Ostertag and Oswald may take sampling to an aesthetic extreme, but they are hardly unique in taking advantage of technology to combine and recast music from many traditions. George Lipsitz offers an overview (and a sampling!) of the extent to which sampling techniques blur musical distinctions not only of style but also of national culture.

Like other forms of contemporary mass communication, popular music simultaneously undermines and reinforces our sense of place. Music that originally emerged from concrete historical experiences in places with clearly identifiable geographic boundaries now circulates as an interchangeable commodity marketed to consumers all over the globe. Recordings by indigenous Australians entertain audiences in North America. Jamaican music secures spectacular sales in Germany and Japan. Rap music from inner-city ghettos in the U.S.A. attracts the allegiance of teenagers from Amsterdam to Auckland. Juke boxes and elaborate "sound systems" in Colombia employ dance music from West Africa as the constitutive element of a dynamic local subculture, while Congolese entertainers draw upon Cuban traditions for the core vocabulary of their popular music.

These transactions transform—but do not erase—attachments to place. Through the conduits of commercial culture, music made by aggrieved inner-city populations in Canberra, Kingston, or Compton becomes part of everyday life and culture for affluent consumers in the suburbs of Cleveland, Coventry, or Cologne. At the same time, electric-techno-art music made in Germany serves as a staple for sampling within African-American hip hop; Spanish flamenco and paso doble music provide crucial subtexts for Algerian rai artists; and pedal steel guitars first developed by country and western musicians in the U.S.A. play a prominent role in Nigerian juju.[19]

10.6. Technology and Postmodernism

It may at first seem strange that my discussion of the chain from composer to listener (Section 7.3) includes recording engineers on the same level of importance as composers, performers, and listeners. I would argue strongly in favor of this equality, at least today, when technology has been effecting a revolution in how music is produced. Although one might not suspect so from observing how musicians are (still) being trained in conservatories, technology is pervasive in music production and consumption. Indeed, the distinction between composing and audio engineering is disappearing. What a composer does to create an electro-acoustic composition, and what an engineer does to create a recording, can be indistinguishable. Both work with recorded sounds. Both use some of the same software packages to combine and alter sounds and to put them together into a coherent final product, which may be a recording or a performance.

Such software is available for laptop computers. This means that composers can in their homes perform the same kinds of editing that was previously available only in huge, expensive recording/editing studios. They can carry their computers virtually anywhere, and thus can perform sophisticated sound manipulations live in concert, as integral parts of their pieces. To a composer steeped in technological possibilities— which are no longer so complex that they require years of training—composing, performing, recording, and editing all blur together as creative acts done by the same person on the same equipment for essentially the same purpose: to make music that belongs uniquely to a technological age.

10.7. Commercialization and Aesthetics

I have argued in this chapter that postmodern composers are more aware than modernist composers were or are of the inescapable forces of the marketplace and of their impact on musical life. This does not mean, however, that the postmodernists are

[19] Lipsitz, *Dangerous Crossroads*, p. 4.

necessarily content with this situation. Consider these complaints of John Zorn, who feels that the forces of the marketplace interfere with audience members' freedom to form their own individual responses to music.

> Rock. Jazz. Punk. Dada. Beat. These words and their longer cousins, the ism-family (surrealism, postmodernism, abstract expressionism, minimalism), are used to commodify and commercialize an artist's complex personal vision. This terminology is not about understanding. It never has been. It's about money. Once a group of artists, writers, or musicians has been packaged together under such a banner, it is not only easier for work to be marketed; it also becomes easier for the audience to "buy it" and for the critic to respond with prepackaged opinions. The audience is deprived of its right to the pleasure of creating its own interpretation, and the critic no longer has to think about what is really happening or go any deeper than the monochromatic surface of the label itself, thus avoiding any encounter with the real aesthetic criteria that make any individual artist's work possible.[20]

Zorn's complaint points to a postmodern contradiction. It is true that postmodern composers tend to be more aware of the inescapability of the marketplace in an age that has seen the widespread commodification of the arts (trait 15). Once music falls under the influence of marketing forces, it does become packaged in ways that are designed to appeal to the largest number of people, thereby discouraging the individuality of responses (trait 16). Thus, it is understandable when composers like Zorn complain. They may, possibly grudgingly or possibly enthusiastically, accept marketing as a prerequisite for dissemination of their work, but they may also grumble when the nature of marketing discourages listener creativity.

In earlier decades, when commercialization of music was deemed incompatible with "true" artistic values, there was a clean split between composers who sought large audiences directly and those who ignored the tastes and predilections of listeners in order to pursue their own, private, pure visions. The former were often called pop composers, whether they wrote for string quartets or for rock bands, and the latter were considered art composers, again regardless of whether they created string quartets or rock tunes. Nowadays this distinction is hard to maintain, since the forces of commodification are extensive. Although the encroaching of marketing considerations on the very nature of music produced may be troubling to many composers, like Zorn, it should not be surprising, given the deliberate attempt by many postmodern composers to break down the barrier between pop and art music (trait 4). Although this attempt has not been wholly successful in an aesthetic sense (as explained in Section 4.4), it has been much more successful in the arena of marketing. Whether they like it or not, composers and performers and their music are packaged for consumption, and those that do the packaging (at least of the more commercially successful composers and performers) make the decisions, even when those decisions come uncomfortably close to telling the composers what kind of music to write or

---

[20] John Zorn (ed.), Preface to *Arcana*, p. v.

telling the performers not only what music to play but also how to play it (in addition to how to dress, how to talk in public, how to style their hair, etc.). Zorn disparages the "attempts to simplify the work, package it for the market place, and conceal the subtle (and sometimes not so subtle) distinctions between the works of the many individual artists concerned."[21]

10.8. Marketing Musical Commodities

Marketing of "classical" music is certainly not solely a product of postmodern thinking. When Beethoven put on concerts for his own financial benefit, he was marketing his wares. Paganini and Liszt cultivated public personae of considerable magnetism, in an effort to draw attention to their product—that is, their spectacular compositions as they themselves flamboyantly played them. Were they selling out when they composed music with an eye toward the marketplace? Or is selling out a particularly modernist idea? Schoenberg refused to sell out. He did not try to market his wares. His Society for Private Performance was created to avoid all influence of commodification. At that stage in his life, he wanted his music to be heard only by those who were likely to be interested in it and sympathetic to it. He was not trying to convert outsiders to it; rather he was willing to welcome into his circle those who were ready to enjoy and appreciate his music and that by his colleagues. He decidedly did not want to use showmanship to attract large audiences. He preferred small audiences of true appreciators to huge unwashed masses. His attitude toward marketing was quintessentially modernist. Other modernist composers were less pure in their attitudes toward the commercialization of their music. Stravinsky, for example, used publicity—whether favorable or not—to promote his career, in order to bring his music to as wide a public as he could reach. But he probably did not let marketability influence the music he wrote (though he was indeed a keen businessman, and we do not really know what went on in his mind—although it is hard to imagine pieces such as *Orpheus* or *Requiem Canticles* being shaped by marketplace concerns). Mid-twentieth-century European modernists also strove to keep their music divorced from commercialization as they created it, although once it existed they did allow public relations concerns to influence how it was disseminated. I am thinking of the aggressively radical statements of the young Boulez and Stockhausen, for example, and how their contentious condemnations of various musical traditions and institutions brought them a lot of attention and thereby focused the public's eye on their controversial compositions.

So, is there a postmodern style of marketing music? Timothy Taylor suggests that it is postmodern, for example, to use semi-nude photos of performers on the covers of CDs of the music of Bach.[22] To present the performer as a sex-object, as a body

---

[21] Ibid., pp. v–vi.
[22] Taylor also gives several examples of classical-music performers who cultivate rock-star-like personae for marketing purposes. See "Music and Musical Practices in Postmodernity," in Judy Lochhead and Joseph Auner (eds.), *Postmodern Music/Postmodern Thought* (New York and London: Routledge, 2002), pp. 103–7.

evoking desire, while at the same time presenting on the disc the same performer as a serious interpreter of baroque music, is an instance of postmodern disjunction, of postmodern juxtaposition of seeming incompatibles, of postmodern combinations of disparate cultural values (trait 6). That such strategies work is undeniable. People certainly purchased this CD in far greater numbers than they purchased other recordings of Bach solo violin music. Similarly, a CRI disc devoted to music by gay male composers, which featured them stripped to the waist in a group photo on the cover, sold vastly better than did CDs of other music by the same composers. The huge success of the recording of Gorecki's Third Symphony, which went to position 6 on the *pop music* charts, owes a lot to marketing (and not a little to word-of-mouth).

Luke Howard, who has studied the phenomenon of the Gorecki symphony in considerable detail,[23] believes that the way this unlikely music was disseminated throughout the pop music world was a decidedly postmodern happening. The symphony, initially a critical failure and an object of ridicule when premiered in the context of a new-music festival, quickly became a favorite in the pop music world. Not only did literally millions buy the CD (not, incidentally, the first but the third commercial recording of the work) but also several pop musicians and soundtrack composers quoted it, referenced it, sampled it, and were influenced by it. One performing group, the English duo Lamb, went so far as to make a song entitled "Gorecki." The extraordinary success of this long, somber symphony, cast in three *adagio* movements, is certainly emblematic of postmodern crossing of boundaries between art and pop music. Howard feels that its dissemination is more postmodern than the music itself, although I do not find it particularly useful to try to decide whether or not the symphony is postmodern. It certainly has some postmodern characteristics, such as its musical style, which owes something to the distant past as well as to its present. It is typical of a spiritual movement among some recent composers which has aspects of postmodernism, but the way this piece pervaded the pop-music sensibility is indeed a postmodern phenomenon.

Similarly, the musical spirituality of John Taverner has been marketed rather successfully. People sometimes wonder how genuine it is, by which they seem to mean how much it exists in the composer's being, apart from its proven effectiveness as a marketable attitude. But no one can really know to what extent commercial values influence a composer's public spirituality. Similar is Stockhausen's mysticism, which has attracted a new-age public. Surely there is some degree of genuineness to it, as there is undoubtedly to Taverner's spirituality, but also there does seem to be a willingness to market it—or at least to allow it to be marketed.

What is perhaps postmodern in all of this is the disjunction between the product and the marketing techniques: widespread commercial advertising for deeply spiritual or mystical music, sexual suggestiveness for instrumental music of Bach, appeal to a gay sensibility for music which in most instances is not notably gay. These disjunctions

---

[23] Luke Howard, "Production vs. Reception in Postmodernism: The Gorecki Case," in Judy Lochhead and Joseph Auner (eds.), *Postmodern Music/Postmodern Thought* (New York and London: Routledge, 2002), pp. 195–206.

differ from modernist marketing, such as the high-culture appeal of Stravinsky's ballet music, or the flamboyance of Liszt's and Paganini's marketing of music that was indeed flamboyant.

To make a huge over-generalization, but one with some basis in truth: I believe that modernists may have accepted the commercialization of their music, perhaps reluctantly, because they felt that the techniques of advertising would bring their music to many people, some of whom would find it intriguing and search out more of it. Postmodernists often do more than accept marketing of their music: perhaps taking cues from stars of the pop music world, they enter actively into the marketing. They do not simply present a product for someone else to sell. They create it to sell it, and they participate in the selling. They do so for the sake of that one work, or that one CD, not necessarily with the expectation of attracting continued public interest. They realize that most fame is short lived, and they are willing to use marketing techniques to grab what they can of it.

As I have stated, using marketing to promote music is not solely a postmodern phenomenon. But the degree is different. As Taylor mentions,[24] "classical musicians are more commodified than ever before, and contemporary composers face even greater pressures to make themselves known." In today's postmodern climate, we find not only publishers and concert promoters but also composers and performers themselves spending money to promote their careers and their work. The once disdained idea of a vanity press is now pervasive: a large number of "classical" CDs are issued on labels controlled by, or at least financed by, the artists themselves. Often the composers are also the performers and/or the audio engineers. The ever-increasing dissemination of music over the internet is frequently in the hands of the composers and performers, not their agents or publishers. Some composers and performers have become quite skillful and original at marketing, which has become in some ways as creative an endeavor as making music.[25]

That musical artists have the money to pour into their own promotion, and that they are willing—indeed, eager—to do so, places them firmly in the economic middle class. The artist-as-outsider seems like a quaint remnant of another era, although I suppose a few composers of today purposefully cultivate such an image for commercial purposes. If a composer invests capital in marketing his or her compositions (or performances or recordings or broadcasts or internet dissemination of them), then he or she has truly and fundamentally bought into a capitalistic consumer culture. But what choice is there? A composer who refuses to get involved with self-marketing is doomed to obscurity, unless someone else takes up the banner for his or her works. Thus, the commodification and selling of new music is essentially unavoidable. Whether or not the music is in some sense postmodern, the process of disseminating it is all but unavoidably postmodern.[26]

A few seasons back, a New York-based new-music ensemble advertised that one of

---

[24] Taylor, "Music and Musical Practices in Postmodernity," p. 93.
[25] Ibid., p. 108.
[26] Ibid., pp. 101–2.

their concerts (of more or less modernist music) would contain nudity. A huge public showed up, including many people who had not been seen at new-music concerts in the past. The marketing worked, in that a lot of people came to the concert. But did those businessmen (they *were* mostly male) find some music they enjoyed and would return to? Probably not. No study was made of the long-term impact of this concert on attendance at new-music events, but it seems that this use of nudity to attract an audience had no impact beyond the one concert. The disjunction between the marketing ploy and the product was great—hence the postmodern spirit hovering over the event. The music had little to do with eroticism (even though there was the promised nudity at the end of the concert, when a naked female dancer appeared on stage for two minutes). The concert received attention, and then was all but forgotten. No converts to new music were made. In a world of postmodern fragmentation, this was just another event. From a modernist perspective, the concert promoters could be criticized for capitalizing on a small aspect of the concert in a sensationalist manner. From a postmodernist perspective, however, nothing much happened. You do whatever it takes to bring in an audience, you do not worry much about lasting impact, and then you go on. This particular marketing ploy was nothing special in postmodern New York, where nudity is used to sell almost anything. It was noticeable (and talked about) more in the contexts of New York's musical modernists, who may have been scandalized or at least disapproving of advertising nudity while trying to sell music.

It is not my purpose to celebrate or condemn the commodification of music in our time. There are ample reasons to do both. Rather, I want only to recognize it—something that a lot of composers and musicians are loathe to do. Never wholly absent, commercialization has become a big part of the art world. And it is likely to stay that way for some time to come, particularly as technology becomes ever more integral to the processes of creating and disseminating music of all sorts.

11

Beyond the Beyond:
Postmodernism Exemplified

11.1. Some Thoughts

An objection: earlier in this book I state that postmodernism calls for the demise of totalizing meta-narratives, but are there not meta-narratives (e.g. that of disunity) implied in my list of characteristics of postmodern music (in Section 1.3)? Actually, this list comes dangerously close to being a meta-narrative of postmodernism. Is it postmodern to invoke a meta-narrative of disunity or to try to find order in disunity? Does it inadvertently proclaim the ubiquity, omnipotence, and inevitability of meta-narratives and of order? Does postmodernism, despite its attempt to overthrow meta-narratives, end up substituting new ones for old?[1]

There is something paradoxical about discussing postmodernism in typical scholarly language. To try to capture the essence of an aesthetic that is nonlinear, disunified, and irrational by means of discourse that is linear, unified, and rational inevitably distorts. As does any discussion of anything, but perhaps here to a greater or at least a more critical degree. Like the opening movement of Haydn's *Creation*—a vision of chaos, but not the thing itself. In the earlier chapters of this book, a vision of postmodernism but not the thing itself. This problem, if indeed that is what it is (after all, there *are* certain advantages to the distancing of rational discourse), is an exaggeration of what is inherent in all description, in all analysis, in all criticism. It is also similar to a problem music analysts and particularly critics face all the time, when they use words to study a nonverbal medium. They do not usually write a piece of music to explicate other bodies of music (although they may certainly use musical notation in their analyses).

But. In this book my topic is not only postmodern music and not only postmodern listening but also postmodern discourse about music. Which has taken many fascinating turns, but may take others. If, like postmodern art, postmodern criticism freed itself from the confines of linear logic, from the need to be consistent, from the avoidance of contradiction—who knows? Perhaps some insights could be expressed, and even *communicated*, that cannot be explained linearly. A poem, not an explication of a poem. Or even a piece of music—of verbal music.

---

[1] I think I should put the Otana Bee story into this chapter. It does not have much to do with postmodernism, but it *is* a good story.

Hence the impetus behind this final chapter. But does this chapter do what its author intended, which is to exemplify what it discusses? Not totally. This chapter, like all chapters in all books, like every text, verbal or not, has a degree of autonomy. But.

Perhaps the Otana Bee story (see footnote 1) *does* have something to do with postmodernism. What, after all, is *a priori* unrelated to the postmodern? What is safe from being cannibalized? Maybe some reader will see in the story a dialectic relationship with other parts of this book. Seems unlikely, but I would have thought it equally unlikely that someone would read my orchestral work *Moments in and out of Time* as dialectical. Anyway, I am even more inclined now to include the story. But not yet.

11.2. The Otana Bee Story

I *said* "not yet." So this section is certainly not where you will find the Otana Bee story. Perhaps, if I build it up too much, it will be a disappointment. Is disappointment postmodern? After all, the concept of postmodernism *is* fundamentally dark,[2] while its manifestations may or may not be.

If this section is not about Otana Bee, what is it about? Must it be about something? I could just go on this way (rather the way Tom Johnson does in his lecture pieces or in the wonderful string bass piece *Failing*, or the way the characters in certain segments of *Seinfeld* work hard to create a TV show about nothing), and encourage readers to constitute the meaning of this section themselves. But that is just too obvious.

Postmodern composers seek to weaken the barriers between high art and pop art, between an audience of initiates (consider the typical symphony-going crowd) and an audience excluded. How ironic it is that symphony administrators despair over the shrinking sizes of their audiences but respond more in terms of programming—less modernist music, more familiar "classics," star soloists—and less in ways that would address this sociological problem sociologically! When symphony audiences are told that there are no more masterpieces, they take this pronouncement (whether it is true or not is beside the point) as an indication of the poverty of contemporary composition; when postmodern audiences hear the same message, they rejoice: "classical" music is coming to the people!

After my book *The Time of Music* was published, different people spoke to me about various parts of it. I was amazed at how their understanding differed from my own and from each other's. Had I written so badly that everyone misunderstood? As these diverse reactions continued, I began to realize that the nature of the book—"postmodern scholarship," as one reviewer called it[3]—encouraged different

---

[2] Dark? Yes. An aesthetic that upsets many accepted or even cherished meta-narratives is dark. A way of thinking that privileges surfaces over deep meanings is dark. An idea that embraces the death of authors is dark. Yes, dark.
[3] Robert Carl, *Notes*, Vol. 47, No. 4, June 1991, pp. 1109–10.

interpretations. It does not lay out a specific way of thinking or hearing, it does not offer a scientific theory that is readily verifiable or falsifiable. Rather, it tries to encourage people to think and hear in new ways, ways equally informed by their predilections and abilities and by my suggestions and formulations. So, I decided not to despair but indeed to rejoice that everyone seemed to interpret and use my ideas in different ways. Postmodern readers constitute texts, particularly postmodern texts, according to their own values, abilities, perceptions, backgrounds, and predilections. Postmodern authors ought to accept what their readers do to/with their texts.

11.3. More Quotations

"Vulgarity has its charms."[4]

"The liberating power of the arbitrary."[5]

"Not the negation of the already said, but its ironic rethinking."[6]

"True art analysis would uncover contradictions rather than pursue unities."[7]

"This is not a nostalgic return; it is a critical revisiting, an ironic dialogue with the past."[8]

"Every critic 'constructs' postmodernism in his or her own way from different perspectives, none more right or wrong than the others."[9]

"Postmodern genre is 'characterized by its appropriation of other genres, both high and popular, by its longing for a both/and situation rather than one of either/ or.'"[10]

"It's the best possible time to be alive, when almost everything you thought you knew is wrong."[11]

11.4. A Tale

While I was teaching at Yale in the late 1970s, I was invited to give some lectures at Queen's University in Canada. Unfortunately, it was the middle of winter. Still less fortunately, Queen's is located in the town of Kingston, which is halfway between Toronto and Montreal—near, in other words, no city large enough to have a real airport.

Don't worry, my travel agent assured me, you *can* fly to Kingston. "Just drive to the Hartford airport, take Eastern Airlines to Syracuse, and then change to Otana Bee.

---

[4] Hardison, Jr., *Disappearing Through the Skylight*, p. 115.

[5] Ibid., p. 168.

[6] Eco, *Postcript to The Name of the Rose*, p. 68.

[7] Monelle, *Linguistics and Semiotics in Music*, p. 320.

[8] Hutcheon, *A Poetics of Postmodernism*, p. 4.

[9] Ibid., p. 11.

[10] Marjorie Perloff, *Postmodern Genres* (Norman: University of Oklahoma Press, 1988), p. 8.

[11] The character Valentine in Tom Stoppard's play *Arcadia* (London: Faber and Faber, 1993), p. 48.

They fly to Kingston—almost every day! If—I mean, *when*—you land, it is just a short sleigh—I mean, *cab*—ride into town."

Thanks, friend, I replied. I don't appreciate a travel agent with a sense of humor. I decided to go by train. Not so easy, I soon found out. I'd have to fly to Toronto, get from the airport to the train station, and wait the better part of a day for the right train. So I told the travel agent to go ahead and book me on Otana Bee. I should have been nervous when she said it was impossible to buy an advance ticket, but I blithely agreed to fly with only a reservation.

Everything went fine as far as Syracuse. After I retrieved my luggage (it was impossible to check baggage through), I started looking around for Otana Bee. I found no sign indicating either gates or check-in counters for the airline. I searched various airport directories. Nothing. Then I started asking people behind information desks and at other airlines' counters. No one had heard of Otana Bee. Some thought I was joking.

Finally, I found a janitor sweeping the floor. He knew. "Just go to the left, down that long corridor, and keep going."

I did. No one was around. I was sure I was in the wrong place. Then I rounded the final bend, where the corridor dead-ended at a large window with a small door. There, taped to the wall, was a hand-lettered sign: "Otana Bee, Serving Kingston."

But the sign was all that was there, except for an unlabeled and unattended small table with three folding chairs. It was thirty minutes to flight time. I sat down.

After a quarter of an hour, I was near panic. Then I saw a small plane pull up outside the window. A man and a woman got out. Carrying a small box, the woman came in through the door. She put the box on the table. It was a cash box. She opened it, sat down, and announced to the waiting masses (I was alone): "Otana Bee Airlines is open for business!"

I approached the table cautiously. "Yes?" I told her I had a reservation to go to Kingston. "Doesn't matter," she replied. "We don't use reservations."

"I don't have a ticket yet," I explained. "No one does," she replied. "But you can buy one here."

Optimistically, I pulled out my MasterCard. "Sorry," she said. "Cash only." Luckily (or unluckily?), I had enough money.

"May I check my luggage," I asked naïvely. "He'll take it." She pointed to the man, who had joined us. "We don't actually check things, but he'll take care of it."

Another hopeful passenger appeared. He also purchased a ticket and gave a suitcase to the man.

"Time to go," the woman announced. We went out into the wind and cold and climbed aboard the tiny plane, so low that we couldn't stand.

Our suitcases were put on board, and then the man climbed in. He, it turned out, was the pilot, and the woman was the stewardess! She admonished the two passengers to sit on opposite sides of the plane. "For balance, you know."

We actually took off. As I looked down, I saw a wilderness of snow and ice. No sign of civilization. But the flight had a modicum of civility—we were served lukewarm coffee. The other passenger asked if there was anything to go with the coffee. "Sure," answered the stewardess. "Sugar and milk." After an hour and a half, we landed on an unpaved, frozen runway surrounded by snow drifts. There was a tiny, run-down building which served as the terminal. I called a cab. When I arrived in town, I found the university. Upon seeing me, my host asked, "Where were you?"

"What do you mean?" I replied. "We waited for you at the train station," he said. "I came by plane," I explained. "Don't be ridiculous," said this learned professor, "there is *no* airport in Kingston!"

"I think you're right," I replied, "but I came by air nonetheless."

No one at the university knew about Kingston's minuscule airport, nor had they heard of Otana Bee. Nor has anyone else whom I have told of this harrowing journey.

I returned by train to Toronto. Despite the long journey, compounded by the train getting to Kingston two and a half hours late (although I had been told that the Canadian railroad was always on time), I was happy to be on the ground, in a vehicle where I could stand up and where I could sit on either side, and in a place where they served soggy donuts with their lukewarm coffee.

11.5. Non-Musical Artworks that Exhibit Traits Found in Musical Postmodernism

Book by Robert Grudin
Barton Fink by the Coen brothers
Arcadia by Tom Stoppard
The Magus by John Fowles
Pulp Fiction by Quentin Tarantino
The Hallucinogenic Toreador by Salvatore Dalí
Arcadia by Tom Stoppard

11.6. Repetition and Other Matters

To repeat or return to the same music is to create intra-piece referentiality. Music has far more repetition than other art forms. Why? Because of its abstraction, because of the challenge to memory, because of the large amount of information? The function of the musical return is form-creating, since repetition tends to promote stability (although not if overdone, as in minimalism). Literal repetition is common in music, virtually unknown in literature, special in the visual arts. When novelist Alain Robbe-Grillet uses near-literal repetition (the differences, though, are crucial), the effect is postmodern, as when Buñuel does so in the film *The Exterminating Angel*. Why is literal repetition in, say, Schubert not postmodern? (Or maybe it is.) People have always known repetition in their lives. And folk music has, as far as we know, always been repetitive. Repetition is not necessarily oppressive. It depends on what is repeated. We tend to repeat, with some variation on a basically constant theme, rituals of life: eating, sex, bowel movements. We repeat acts and stimuli in life as in music. But we do not repeat situations or experiences. Every meal, every sex act, even every bowel movement is different. We are always somewhat different, shaped by our expanding lives as we re-experience.

O. B. Hardison, Jr., quotes fractal mathematician Benoit Mandelbrot:

Why is geometry often described as "cold" and "dry"? One reason lies in its inability to describe the shape of a cloud, a mountain, a coastline, a tree. Clouds are not spheres, mountains are not cones, coastlines are not circles, and bark is not smooth, nor does lightning travel in a straight line.[12]

This complaint echoes those of humanistic music analysts, such as Joseph Kerman, against formalist analysis. But there is a major difference: Mandelbrot's fractal geometry offers a way to describe mathematically the shapes of clouds, mountains, and coastlines, whereas music analysis has yet to come up with a way beyond the merely descriptive to deal with the infinite irregularities within the regularities that distinguish one work from another.

Earlier in this book I try to create what in essence is a meta-narrative of disunity, and maybe even a meta-narrative of postmodernism—even while applauding the demise of totalizing meta-narratives! But is that fair? Am I not proclaiming the ubiquity and omnipotence of meta-narratives despite my distrust of them? Indeed, there is something paradoxical about discussing postmodernism in ordinary language. To try to capture the essence of an aesthetic that is nonlinear, disunified, and irrational by means of discourse that is linear, unified, and rational inevitably distorts. As does any discussion of anything, I suppose, but perhaps here to a greater degree. In the earlier chapters of this book, I offered a vision of disunity but not the thing itself, a vision of postmodernism but not the thing itself. But this problem is inherent in all description, all analysis, and all criticism. It is similar to a problem music analysts and particularly critics face all the time, when they use words to study a nonverbal medium. And so, I decided to write a final chapter that to some extent not only discusses but also exemplifies postmodernism. And repetition. And also repetition.

Modernism's revolt against tradition was made possible, if not inevitable, by the rediscovery of the past. In earlier eras, when the past was less readily accessible, artists worked in and for the present, with little thought about their heritage or legacy. Renaissance composers, for example, generally knew little music even two generations old. Yet by the nineteenth century, works from the past were available and understood. Historical consciousness had entered the arts, and artists were both threatened by competition with the past and seduced by the powerful idea that their works might outlive them. The romantic artist became a genius speaking to posterity. Mahler was not the only romanticist to pin his hopes on the future: "My time will yet come." Small wonder that, once that future came to be, its artists rebelled against pronouncements from *their* past. The time rightfully belonged to them and no longer to Mahler's generation. While many twentieth-century artists continued to create for their future, most

[12] Hardison, *Disappearing through the Skylight*, p. 59.

avant-gardists (Satie and Russolo and, a generation later, Cage) rejected (ironically, not always successfully) not only their past but also the quest for immortality. They wrote of their day and for their day. The legacy of the avant garde is that it has no legacy.

11.7. Good and Bad Music

In his discussion of surreal music, Daniel Albright quips: "To some extent, what the twentieth century calls surreal is simply what earlier ages called bad."[13]

I began Chapter 5 with a reference to my activities as a composition teacher. A teacher sees a lot of bad music: pieces in which too much happens too soon, in which progressions seem illogical, in which materials are incompatible. These characterizations seem to apply equally to bad student pieces and to some radically postmodernist works that I think are "good." How is this possible? Perhaps intention has something to do with it. When a composer (and piece) aims for continuity yet produces discontinuity, when the music seeks consistency yet reaches variety, when it implies teleology yet achieves a jumble, then something is wrong. However, a work that implies discontinuity, variety, and a jumble may succeed in producing just those postmodern values. But, if postmodernism sometimes denies implications, what results when a piece implies continuity but produces discontinuity? A bad piece or a postmodern piece?

The teacher usually seems confident in criticizing the student's work for possessing the very qualities that a postmodern composer values. Perhaps it is simply a matter of technique: just as a wind instrument student must first master producing a pure tone and only then readmit into her or his repertory originally excluded sounds, now enshrined as multiphonics—so the composition student must master how to realize implications before being able to go against them in a meaningful and satisfying manner. Thus, paradoxically, disunity must be internally motivated, although it must seem as if it is not (if the motivation is evident, the intended disunity will seem rather unified).

There is more to the question of distinguishing bad music from (presumably good) postmodern music that uses similar gestures. Time is a major consideration. The pacing of discontinuities, *non sequiturs*, inconsistencies, unexpected events is critical to success. I cannot delineate what makes for successful timing, but I know it when I hear it. And I do not hear it all that often in student compositions. So, instead of telling the students to be more consistent, I may tell them to be more sensitive to the pacing of inconsistencies, to be more in control, to compose discontinuities or disunities as bold statements, not as timid responses to the dilemma of what to do next. If the music, and the composer, truly knows where it or he or she is heading, then it may be wonderfully effective to go somewhere else; if the music is meandering aimlessly, an unexpected turn may not be very striking.

Two pieces on which I have written (in Chapters 12 and 13) from a postmodernist analytic perspective are the very symphonic creations of their composers most often

[13] Albright, *Untwisting the Serpent*, p. 301.

criticized as problematic, trashy, disunified, inconsistent, etc. This was not my reason for choosing the finale of Mahler's Seventh Symphony or Nielsen's Sixth Symphony. Still, it is interesting that I chose to analyze as postmodern works that others dismissed as—in some ways and to some degree—bad.

The question of evaluation is especially critical, given the nature of postmodern music. If music is truly constituted in the minds of listeners, as I have been arguing in this book, then can we fairly criticize a composer or performer if we experience what we think is a bad work? As Justin Clemens writes, "If the spectators make the work, they have only themselves to blame for its quality."[14] Similarly, David Bennett is concerned about the evaluation of postmodern music in a culture of instantaneous art consumption, and in an artistic climate where "anything goes."[15] And Robert Morgan writes:

> When all music becomes equally acceptable, then all standards become equally irrelevant. We are left in a world where, since everything is valued, nothing has particular value. Surely no culture before ours has ever adopted a position in which any musical activity at all is considered equally worthy of acceptance.[16]

And, indeed, several other commentators are troubled by the question of how to evaluate a music that overturns traditional values and substitutes the individual subjectivity of the listener. Bennett refers to Lyotard's idea that "consensus has become an outmoded and suspect value in postmodernity."[17] If there is no consensus, can there be evaluation?

I am not troubled by postmodernism's challenge to value. I actually welcome it, provided it is not pushed to an unreasonable extreme.[18] I believe that our culture industry has been too long obsessed with evaluation: from the reviewers who make proclamations on the alleged inherent quality of compositions or performances to the pseudo-objective academics who perpetuate the canon of Western classical music from Machaut to Boulez. Recognition of the autonomy of the individual listener, who has his or her own values based on his or her own perceptions, is long overdue.

I do not believe, however, that postmodernism necessarily or totally precludes evaluation. Linda Kouvaras, for example, nicely demonstrates a meaningful

---

[14] Justin Clemens, "John Cage, Compact Discs, and the Postmodern Sublime," in Brenton Broadstock et al. (eds.), *Aflame with Music: 100 Years at the University of Melbourne* (Parkville, Australia: Centre for Studies in Australian Music, 1996), p. 395.

[15] David Bennett, "Time for Postmodernism: Subjectivity, 'Free Time', and Reception Aesthetics," in Brenton Broadstock et al. (eds.), *Aflame with Music: 100 Years at the University of Melbourne* (Parkville, Australia: Centre for Studies in Australian Music, 1996), pp. 383–9.

[16] Robert P. Morgan, "Rethinking Musical Culture," pp. 60–1. These ideas of Morgan show another reason why postmodernism is thought of as dark.

[17] Bennett, "Time for Postmodernism."

[18] The danger of postmodern pluralism, as Peter Bürger sees it, is "falling prey to an eclecticism which likes everything indiscriminately. Art thus threatens to become an insipid complement to everyday life, i.e. what it always was to the popularizations of idealist aesthetics," *The Decline of Modernism,* p. 44. In other words, eschewing value completely can turn music into Muzak. A thoroughly committed postmodernist might wish to do just that! I prefer a more moderate middleground: let us have our value judgments, and let us differentiate art from non-art, but let us remember that all perceivers have the power to decide for themselves what is valuable and what is valueless art.

postmodernist evaluation.[19] In her discussion of the opera *Sweet Death* by Andree Greenwall and Abe Pogos, she mentions the inclusion of quotations from Webern's Piano Variations. If postmodern music were exclusively listener-created, then there would be little more to say. Some listeners know the Webern piece, others do not. Those who do presumably have different associations with it. The quotations in *Sweet Death* will mean different things to different listeners. The individuality of responses does not completely preclude traditional value judgment, however. Kouvaras goes on to explain how and what the Webern quotations might mean: she says they are the diametric opposite of the slapstick they accompany, and that their subsequent treatment deconstructs the rules of twelve-tone serialism. By quoting and distorting the Webern extract, composer Greenwall seeks to break down "some of the borders that separated ideal modernist art from life." Without being familiar with *Sweet Death*, I cannot say whether or not I agree with Kouvaras's analysis or with her implicit evaluation. But I do appreciate her apparent belief that *Sweet Death* is a postmodernist work that does present specific associational and narrative structures to the listener (which the listener in turn, of course, may or may not mentally constitute into something of personal significance).

11.8. Another Tale

While I was teaching at Oberlin in the early 1970s, I offered a year-long course in music theory for nonmusicians. In the second semester I had the students compose short, two-voice tonal pieces—by successive approximation. They struggled with this difficult task, and some became discouraged. For the next topic, I had to choose something new and different.

I introduced them to avant-garde music. I asked them to listen to a lot of pieces by Cage and others, to read relevant articles, and to keep a journal about their changing impressions of this strange new music. I gave them an assignment: to compose a piece using no traditional musical instruments and no traditional music notation, yet which could be performed in a classroom such as ours.

One woman wrote a piece in five movements, each of which had a short verbal score. I don't remember the first two movements, but the third went something like this: "Performer, holding egg, comes before audience. Drops egg." The fourth movement said, "Everyone shouts 'yes' or 'no' for sixty seconds." And the fifth movement: "Nude with bell attached to ankle comes before audience. Waits thirty seconds. Leaves."

Now, you must understand that this composer was *extremely* shapely.[20] I could never do this in the politically correct climate of the 2000s, but I asked to see her after class. I told her that I thought her piece was wonderful and that we should perform

---

[19] Linda Kouvaras, "Postmodern Temporalities," in Brenton Broadstock et al. (eds.), *Aflame with Music*, pp. 405–7.
[20] I remember her name.

it at the next class meeting. She understood me only too well! She said, "Great! My boyfriend will be glad to do the last movement."

What could I say, other than, "Fine! Let's do it"?

So, at the next class, we did several other pieces before it was her turn. She did the first two movements. Then she stood solemnly before the class, holding a raw egg. She dropped it. The class gasped.

Then she explained that everyone was to shout "yes" or "no" for sixty seconds. Everyone did.

Then there was a pregnant silence. Only the composer and I knew what was about to happen. From outside the closed classroom door, we heard a faint tinkling sound. The door opened, and in came a man wearing nothing but a bell around his ankle. He too had a great body! He stood silently in front of the class, looking down, for the longest thirty seconds I have ever experienced. After about twenty of those interminable seconds, a woman in the back decided to recapitulate the fourth movement, and shouted out: "Yes!" Then the piece was over. The boyfriend left. And to this day I don't know what happened outside the classroom, which was located at the end of a long, crowded hallway, nowhere near a men's room.

11.9. Yet Another Tale

No more tales.

11.10. Thoughts from Poland and Elsewhere

I returned to Poland in 1994 to lecture again at the Summer Courses for Young Composers at Kazimierz Dolny, to listen to some of the concerts of the Warsaw Autumn Festival, and to lecture to young performers at the European Mozart Academy in Kraków. I talked and thought a lot about postmodernism. Some interesting ideas and questions surfaced.

How does a piece like Penderecki's Clarinet Quartet of 1993 fit into my pseudo-taxonomy of postmodernism? It could have been written in Western Europe in 1925 (though certainly not in 1875). Does this make it regressive? Modernist? Postmodernist? Is it less traditionalist than, say, Torke's *Bronze* because the tradition it uses is more recent? It is not really antimodern, since it uses sounds and techniques of the modernist era. It is not aggressively modernist. And it is not postmodern. It is simply beautiful. It is not making a statement on modernism vs. postmodernism vs. traditionalism. In this way it is like a lot of music written today. Pieces do not need to be aesthetic statements. And the fact that Penderecki was thinking of Schubert does not at all matter. The aesthetic confusion is not in the piece but in my cumbersome attempt to apply labels to it.

Hans Abrahamsen's Second String Quartet, also played at Warsaw Autumn, inter-mixes different styles, all of which are modernist. Does this make it postmodern? Is mixture of styles a sufficient condition for postmodernism? No matter what styles? Surely not.

Twice, students at Kazimierz Dolny said things that proved important to my thinking about postmodernism. In 1990 an Austrian complained that my *Musica Pro Musica* did not distort its references (see Section 4.3). Then in 1994 a young Greek composer complained after my exposition of postmodernism that it is superficial. I admitted the superficiality: music, especially modernist music, has been too long concerned with deep meaning and complex inner structures. In the worst cases, the depth is illusory, because it is hidden from perception. But even so, there is an attitude of pomposity about always trying, ever so hard, to be profound. So I said to this young student: yes, postmodernism is superficial. It embraces and revels in the surface. And that is its great profundity.

In Kazimierz I was accused of taking a polemic tone to promote postmodernism (actually the accusation was stronger: I allegedly used propagandistic slogans in place of logic—Eastern Europeans are still sensitive about propaganda!). I do concede a polemic tone, as I think inevitably about objections that are likely to be raised. Some parts of this book may be read as polemic justification of postmodernist ideas. But the other side to my polemics is that I, more than anyone else I know, deeply love many kinds of music. I love or hate pieces, not types. I have genuine affection for and feel deep enjoyment and emotional/intellectual satisfaction when listening to certain pieces of Ligeti, Bernstein, Cage, Rochberg, Harbison, Carter, Reich, Xenakis, Kurtág, Berio, Sessions, and Harrison, to name just a few. Often I have been on judging panels of composition contests and found myself arguing with fellow panelists, who seemed unable to separate the assessment of quality from stylistic preferences (yes, value judgments are still very much a part of the world of music). I had to defend some absolutely wonderful music modeled on that of Babbitt and some lovely sensitive tonal music and some minimalist music and some conceptual music. They were often attacked because a panelist disliked their models. Their quality of workmanship or beauty was secondary (however: was not each panelist exercising his or her right to interpret a text in a personal way? Are composition contests immune from postmodern values?). So, I am a pluralist. I would be unhappy if every composer became a postmodernist, if latter-day modernism and/or antimodernist tradition-alism were to disappear from our musical landscape. I cherish our diversity, and I enjoy concerts with many kinds of music. I may sometimes hope for higher quality (yes, I do believe in quality and I do evaluate!), but never for less diversity. It depresses me that few other composers agree, even among those who say they do. Even those who claim to like all sorts of music rarely do. So, in a way, I have the right to promote radical postmodernism polemically, since I am a radically postmodern listener as well as composer. When in 2000 I composed an orchestral suite that could comfortably find its way onto a pop concert program, and then immediately afterward wrote a dissonant exercise in modernism, I did not feel that either piece betrayed my aesthetic. Nor would I have to apologize if I next wrote a truly traditionalist piece.

I was unable to visit France or Germany while writing this book, but I did talk to a number of composers and critics and did read a few articles about postmodernism, or the lack of it, in the two countries that have long thought of themselves as central to the European art music tradition. It is ironic that postmodern music is less widespread in France—the country of such influential postmodern thinkers as Lyotard, Kristeva, Foucault, and Derrida—than elsewhere in the West. One of the few French composers interested in postmodern thinking tells me that most musicians in France do not read these critical theorists. In the 1990s, the two leading composers of the older generation—Boulez and Xenakis—remained committed to modernism, and their disdain of the postmodern created a political and aesthetic context that hardly encouraged younger composers who might want to experiment with postmodern idioms. Indeed, despite the considerable impact of French postmodern thinkers in intellectual circles, there remains a lot of suspicion. Antoine Compagnon explains that "the postmodern provokes all the more skepticism in France because the French did not invent it, yet we pass ourselves off as the inventors of modernity and the avant-garde as we do of the rights of man."[21]

11.11. Multiculturalism

If postmodernism seeks to break down barriers, then one such barrier is surely that between cultures. Yet there are dangers: not only the fragility of a culture and the importance of respecting and understanding foreign cultures, but also the cultural imperialism of using (plundering?) other cultures. An answer is to remain faithful to one's own culture (is this inevitable?), as do such composers as Lou Harrison, Jean-Claude Eloy, and Yi Manbang. Is it also a form of cultural imperialism for a Western composition teacher to expect his Eastern students to remain true to the music of their cultural heritage? How does that same teacher feel about a foreigner—Dvořák—telling American composers not to forget Black and Native American folk music?

Multiculturalism in music is hardly new. Why is it today considered postmodern to cross the borders between musical cultures? When Mahler included *chinoiseries* in *Das Lied von der Erde*, Chinese listeners may have resented his appropriation of their music or they may have disapproved of his superficial knowledge of their music (or they may have loved the results!). But these references did not really cut across cultural boundaries. Mahler was not writing Chinese music. Today, however, it is much easier to hear—and hence understand—a lot of foreign music. Thus a composer like Lou Harrison could create music that comes close to *being* (not just sounding) Korean or Indonesian. Or a Korean composer like Sukhi Kang can create music that sounds quite German. (These composers may feel, with some justification, that they are writing pan-cultural or international music.) This breakdown of barriers between musical cultures—found, for example, in music of Chen Yi, Zhou Long, Tan Dun, and Bright Sheng—is postmodernist in spirit.

Multiculturalism is possibly more pervasive in popular than in "classical" music. George Lipsitz gives many fascinating and informative examples. He mentions an

---

[21] Compagnon, *The 5 Paradoxes of Modernity*, p. 116.

accomplished performer of traditional Japanese drumming who is a Chicano who grew up in Los Angeles. Another example is an Afro-Caribbean salsa band whose members are Japanese. Lipsitz attributes the Japanese popularity of Elvis Presley songs and Jamaican reggae to similarities to Japanese music. Similarly, Koreans compare rap music to their traditional folk lyrics. He also mentions a Moroccan musician who performs rap music in Sweden, and a hit song put together by a Romanian working in Spain and using Gregorian chants. One more example from Lipsitz:

> In 1993, audiences around the world began hearing the music of an artist calling himself "Apache Indian." Because of his stage name and the title of his first album, *No Reservations*, some speculated that he might be an American Indian. But his music had the hard edge of Jamaican raggamuffin dance-hall rap, suggesting that he might be West Indian. In fact, Apache Indian turned out to be Steve Kapur, a former welder from Handsworth in England whose parents were Punjabi immigrants from the southwest Asian nation of India. Kapur grew up in the same racially-mixed neighborhood that produced the inter-racial reggae band UB40, and took his stage name in honor of his idol, the West Indian artist Wild Apache, aka Super Cat. ... Apache Indian's music mixes hip hop, reggae, and Anglo-American pop styles with the Asian-Indian dance music bhangra. ... Apache Indian's recordings enjoyed phenomenal sales among the diasporic Indian community in Toronto, largely because young Indian Canadians saw his use of bhangra as a sign of respect for Indian traditions. But when Kapur toured India he found that he had an image as a rebel. ... In England, Apache Indian's music became an important icon of unity between Afro-Caribbeans and Afro-Asians.[22]

As Lipsitz's book makes quite clear, multiculturalism in popular music is not just a matter of style but of politics. Different social groups use music for different political purposes: protest, acceptance, cultural identity, etc. When pop musicians like those Lipsitz describes use music of other cultures, they are not usually accused of cultural imperialism or of plundering, the way "classical" composers can be. Why? Perhaps because pop music is ephemeral. It has no permanence but is always changing to reflect and to promote changes in culture. The heritage of "classical" music, of whatever culture, is to remain, to be preserved, to become part of its culture's traditions. Thus for a postmodern Western composer of today to use sounds she or he finds in traditional music of Indian, Japan, or West Africa is to court danger: the danger of destroying the original. Even though many such composers approach the music of other cultures with caution and respect (though some do not), the dangers remain real. There are also dangers when a composer from outside the Western tradition is drawn to composing Western music. Many Asian composers study in Europe (usually Germany) and end up writing watered-down contemporary Western music. Many such composers eventually rediscover their roots—Takemitsu was one of the first Asians to embrace Europe before rediscovering the musical culture of Japan—but the strong lure of the Western tradition concerns me. Why is the appeal of Western music

---

[22] Lipsitz, *Dangerous Crossroads*, pp. 14–15.

so powerful? Because of the way Western culture spread to Asia after the Second World War. And because of the artistic, cultural, and scholarly forces working to preserve the Western tradition through performances, publications, recordings, and musicological research. Of course, there are strong forces trying to preserve other musical traditions as well, recognizing them as treasured cultural artifacts. It is because these forces have made music from around the globe readily available to all that postmodern composers have heard and are drawn to music of many cultures.

Just as American popular music is forcing itself on the entire world through the ubiquity of the cassette, the CD, Hollywood movies, and television, so some European and American art musics may overpower indigenous musical cultures, developed over many centuries. I applaud East-West cross-cultural fertilization in music, yet I feel that those who enter another musical culture must do so with utmost caution. I fear postmodernism's "random cannibalization" of styles even as I enjoy it. Since postmodernism revels in musical surfaces, its appropriation of distant styles can indeed be superficial. But composers should beware: they are not immune to cultural imperialism.

I am uneasy when I find composers interested only in foreign musical cultures, not their own. When I judged an international composition competition a few years ago, I was depressed to hear the entries by several young Asian composers. They had studied in Germany, and their music tried to sound like German expressionism, ranging from Alban Berg to Wolfgang Rihm. But how deeply could these people understand the cultural values that had formed these musical styles? (I realize that this music may have had Asian elements that I, unschooled in Asian traditions, failed to recognize, but to me it just sounded like poorly digested Teutonic music.) These Asian composers were apparently understanding German expressionism as a style, suscep-tible to imitation, rather than as the intensely personal and emotional expression that Europeans take it to be. As an American I feel somewhat closer to Germanic culture than these Asians probably did, yet I do not understand German expressionism well enough to write it. I am amused when I look back at some of my own early attempts to compose music of European high modernism.

I am concerned when I see Asian composers eager to come to the United States or to go to Europe to study. Now, there is nothing wrong with study. I believe I profited considerably from the tutelage of European composers (Karlheinz Stockhausen, Pierre Boulez, Jean-Claude Eloy, and Arnold Franchetti). But I hope that education is always understood in the context of the students' own cultural heritage and with a realization that even the most objective techniques of composition carry cultural implications. We cannot escape our origins and should not try.

There are signs that my worries are unnecessary. My Korean students tell me that their young countrymen and women are rediscovering their musical origins, even as they study abroad. There is a strong movement towards combining East and West in ways that understand and respect both traditions. Similarly, an ethnomusicologist explained to me a feeling among a group of young Chinese composers, known as *xinchao*—the "new wave." Their cross-cultural pieces of the early 1970s tended to be rather obvious, taking romantic Russian music as representative of the West and

Chinese folksongs of the East, but since 1976 these composers have been opposed to the social utility of music. They have embraced twelve-tone techniques, aleatoricism, microtones, etc., and they have written for ensembles containing both Chinese and European instruments. Their music seems to me, and more importantly to people who know both cultures better than I do, to be a fascinating amalgamation of equals, rather than what we find in Debussy, Mahler, or Stravinsky: the grafting of superficial aspects of one culture onto the essentially unchanged music of another.

Today not only Asian but also American and European composers travel to study. Many go to China, Korea, Japan, India, and Indonesia, perhaps not to enroll in universities or conservatories but instead to learn from masters of performance traditions. When a composer like Lou Harrison devotes a considerable portion of his life to learning other musical cultures, I am full of respect—even more so when I hear his music, which seems to be infused with his own personality, which incorporates his deep respect for and understanding of the musical cultures he quotes. His gamelan music is not Javanese or Balinese, as musicians of Indonesia readily recognize. He approached the Indonesian styles he understood deeply, but he was not trying to become Indonesian. His music remains American and, more importantly, it remains his own.

Harrison was one of many American composers who, along with counterparts in Europe, was particularly drawn to Asian musics. Why? The sounds have surely been found attractive, as have the performance contexts and rituals. But there is another value that appeals in particular to a Western postmodernist sensibility. As John Rea has written, "Paradoxically, in most of the non-Western cultures that have been subjected to examination and subsequent harvesting for artistic purposes, music itself is not condemned to the manichean distinctions so dear to us in the West, such as between old and new, or past and present. People there have learned to live in an uneasy coexistence with the surfeit of possible musics."[23]

Unless explicitly trying to deny it (as the young Asians I mentioned may have done), a composer inevitably injects his or her personality into his or her music. Is it a contradiction to claim, on the one hand, that postmodern music is presentational and quotational and, on the other hand, that every composition somehow contains its composer's unique personality? I think not. Perhaps musical personality today resides less in the materials the composer chooses than in the ways those materials interrelate: their rhythms of contrast, succession, duration, and proportion. In other words, perhaps the postmodern personality expresses itself most clearly in the temporal dimension of music, just as Debussy and Mahler showed the Asian influence on their compositions more profoundly in their occasionally static temporal structures than in their quaint pentatonic tunes and percussion sonorities. Every composer has a unique but culturally informed sense of time, a unique pacing in his or her life and in his or her music, which presumably is present even in pieces that are laden with references to and quotations of other musics.

The ideology of individual expression, however, is no longer ubiquitous. The concept of music as personal expression was born with the baroque and became

---

[23] Rea, "Postmodernisms."

increasingly more important to Western composers throughout the seventeenth, eighteenth, and nineteenth centuries, culminating in twentieth-century expressionism. While there were periodic reactions against this cult of the ego, the most sustained reaction against music as personal communication is found in the works of John Cage. It is significant that Cage based his ideas on the Zen of Suzuki, who taught the dissolution of the ego. Cage may not have been wholly successful—his opposition to personal expression took the form of personal expressions of his ideas—but he did help to bring to American, and to a lesser extent European, music a presentational as opposed to communicational aesthetic.

Although denial of the creator's ego may be a traditional idea in the East, it may seem heretical in the West. The idea that music presents but does not communicate may seem nihilistic in a society where individual expression is highly valued, but I maintain that the concept of music as personal communication is indeed culture-specific. As I indicate in Chapter 7, this attitude is being seriously questioned in the postmodern age.

11.12. Two Surprises

Back in the days when Automatic Teller Machines were in their infancy, I had reason to think they would never make it to adolescence. It was the early 1980s, and I was teaching at the University of Cincinnati. One day, I needed some cash. So, I went to the student union building, next to the College-Conservatory of Music. There was a cash machine in the lobby. I inserted my MasterCard, which did double duty as my ATM card. The door opened, and I went through the usual routine. At the end, instead of giving me the $20 I had requested, it simply shut down. The door closed, and the machine went dead. My card was inside.

I raced back to my office and called the bank's ATM security department. I told an anonymous voice what had happened. It replied, "Don't worry, sir. Your card is safely inside the machine. No one can get it. We have a man who checks every ATM in the Cincinnati area on a regular basis. When he gets to the university's machine, he will find your card and return it to the bank."

"When might that happen," I asked naïvely.

"Let me see. I have his schedule right here. Ah, yes. He will be at the university in just two weeks."

"Two weeks?! That is unacceptable. That card is my main credit card, and I cannot be without it. Who knows who might get hold of it and charge major purchases to me!"

I argued and argued, to no avail. So I hung up and called the bank's credit card department. I replayed my tale of woe. I got a response that made me somewhat hopeful.

"Security told you it would take two weeks to get your card out of the machine? No way! It will take only three days."

"But, but, … " I stammered. I launched again into my explanation of how I needed to know that the card was securely in my wallet, not floating around greater Cincinnati and not lodged in the bowels of some machine.

"Sir, please be patient. There is absolutely no way anyone can get to your card. It is perfectly safe."

I gave up. The next day, I was sitting in my office when the phone rang.

"Is this, um, Jonathan, er, Kramer?"

"Yes."

"I work at the information booth at the student center. Someone just turned in your MasterCard. It seems that as she was walking by the ATM, your card came flying out at her. Lucky for you she turned it in!"

Yes, lucky indeed. So, the bank had been wrong. I had not had to wait two weeks, or even three days, to get my card back.

I should have learned my lesson about ATMs. However, a few weeks later I received a large check in Saturday's mail. I was nervous keeping it around the house until Monday. I wanted to deposit it in the branch bank's ATM. "Don't be foolish," Norma (my wife) warned. "Something will go wrong."

"Nonsense," replied the ever naïve professor. "What could go wrong? They really have these technological gadgets perfected."

"Do you remember the machine in the student center?"

"How could something like that happen to anyone *twice*?"

So I drove to the shopping center, inserted my card in the machine, and pushed the deposit button. I entered the amount. A door opened, revealing a gaping mouth-like hole. It was waiting to swallow my check. The screen instructed me to place my deposit in an envelope taken from the dispenser above, and drop it into the slot. I reached into the dispenser. No envelopes.

I was reluctant to drop in the unprotected check and deposit slip. I waited for the transaction to abort and the mouth to close. It didn't. The machine was apparently programmed without a timing mechanism. It was willing to wait indefinitely to feel *something* slide down its throat. So I picked up a scrap of paper from the ground and threw it in. The mouth closed. It seemed to smile a bit. The screen said, "Thank you for your deposit." My card came back. I stood dumbly holding it, and my check, and the deposit slip.

I went into the grocery store next to the bank and purchased a package of envelopes. I wrote clearly on one of them: "Please disregard my previous deposit. The real deposit is in this envelope. There were no envelopes in the dispenser, so I terminated the previous transaction [let them guess how!], bought this envelope, and now enclose the true deposit in it. Thank you." I signed my name and gave my address and phone number.

Then I went through the whole routine again, this time carefully dropping the envelope containing the deposit into the smiling mouth. Or was it sneering now? Everything was fine, or so I believed.

I heard nothing from the bank and thought no more about the incident until my next monthly statement arrived. The bank had credited my account with *two* large deposits for the same amount. In order to cover the one of them for which there had been no check, the bank had taken out a loan in my name and was charging me interest! Needless to say, no one had informed me of this loan.

I thereafter swore off ATMs—for several months, anyway. I confess to using them regularly and avidly now, even though a few years ago a machine ate my card and had severe indigestion!

11.13. Postmodernism and Feminism

Some postmodern theorists have drawn parallels between postmodernism and feminism,[24] while others resist what they see as an attempt by postmodernism to co-opt and subsume feminism. I have neither the space nor the expertise to enter this debate, nor to say much about the relationship between postmodernism and feminism in the context of music. But I would like to offer a few remarks.

In some ways, hardcore modernist music—such as that by Schoenberg, Webern, Stravinsky, Hindemith, and Bartók, and that by latter-day modernists like Boulez, Babbitt, Carter, Stockhausen, Nono, and Wuorinen—can be characterized as masculine. This music can be aggressive, uncompromising, and challenging. Music which retains some form of tonality, such as the French surrealist music discussed in Chapter 9 and the latter-day music of a postmodernist bent discussed throughout this book, can be characterized in some ways as feminine. Some of the traits listed in Section 1.3 suggest a possibly feminist distrust of hierarchies, binary oppositions, totalizing ideas, and treating composers as supreme. And several of the binary oppositions in charts (quoted in Section 1.4) that contrast modernism with postmodernism imply that, just as modernism is in many ways masculine, so postmodernism is in some ways feminine.

Now, I must mention that, just as I distrust the opposition of modernism and postmodernism as mutually exclusive, so I do not think that the masculine and the feminine preclude one another. Music has masculine traits and feminine traits, sometimes within the same works and sometimes simultaneously. It should be understood that, although I am not prepared to offer definitions of the masculine and the feminine in music, I do not believe that music composed by men is necessarily masculine and that by women is necessarily feminine.[25] I am thinking about the masculine and/or feminine personae of the music itself, not of the shape of the genitalia of the actual people who wrote the music. Still, it is surely more likely for men to create predominantly masculine music and women to create mainly feminine music. Thus it may be of some significance that none of the early twentieth-century atonal modernists whose music I am familiar with was a woman (if we stretch our

---

[24] A useful discussion can be found in Amelia Jones, *Postmodernism and the En-Gendering of Marcel Duchamp* (Cambridge, UK, New York, and Melbourne: Cambridge University Press, 1994), especially the first chapter, "Introduction: Modernist Art History and the En-Gendering of (Duchampian) Postmodernism," pp. 1–28.

[25] Consider, for example, how often Schubert's music is considered feminine. See Susan McClary, "Constructions of Subjectivity in Schubert's Music," in Philip Brett, Elizabeth Wood, and Gary Thomas (eds.), *Queering the Pitch* (New York: Routledge, 1994), pp. 205–33.

dates some we can include Ruth Crawford), although there were some important female composers among those who composed tonal music at the same time: Lili Boulanger, Germaine Tailleferre, and Amy Beach, to name a few.[26]

The way hardcore modernist composers have sought (and still do seek) to marginalize current tonal music does parallel the way masculine values and attitudes have sought to subjugate feminine values and attitudes. The postmodern in music, like the feminine, is still the other—distrusted, kept from power, yet still in some ways alluring (for radical postmodernism's abiding ability to disturb audiences, or for conservative postmodernism's acceptance by audiences).

11.14. Why Tell Stories in a Book on Music?

Some postmodern pieces, as I have mentioned, move quickly from one reference or quotation to another. Others allow the music to remain for a comfortable while in one style-world, before wrenching or sliding the listeners to another. In the first kind of piece, the shock of the unexpected is crucial. Encountering the familiar in an unfamiliar context has an undeniable impact.[27] The pacing of surprises, of unexpected changes of reference, can operate somewhat like the rhythm of key changes in a traditional development section. In another kind of postmodern music, though, the shock of recognition is not enough to keep my interest going throughout a lengthy passage. I may begin, in spite of myself, to believe in the new style as context, no longer as object. I begin to hear tonality, for example, not simply as a kind of sound but as a set of hierarchic and diachronic relationships, based on degrees of stability. Tonality almost regains its historical status as a meta-narrative. And yet, I cannot forget the real context. There is inevitable tension between styles as references and styles as contexts. And this idea applies not only to tonality, but to more specific references, e.g. multi-parameter serialism, minimalism, ragtime, blues, traditional Japanese music, whatever.

This chapter tries—among other things—to show what that effect is like. There is something somewhat surprising about finding stories in a scholarly work. But, once the shock of incongruity wears off, the stories remain to be read and savored. I hope that they are engaging and that readers may enjoy following them as if they were self-contained entities, tales divorced from other contexts, like stories told around a

---

[26] Today there are certainly a lot of women composers composing music that is in some way radically postmodern (Diamanda Galas, Meredith Monk, Pauline Oliveros, Mary Jane Leach, Laurie Anderson, and many others) and music that is in some way conservatively postmodern (Joan Tower, Augusta Read Thomas, Sofia Gubaidalina, Melinda Wagner, Ellen Taafe Zwilich, et al.). And there are women who compose latter-day modernist music (Kaija Saariaho, Shulamit Ran, Marta Ptaszynska, and Betsy Jolas) and antimodernist music (Stefania de Kenessey). But I am not calling all of their music necessarily feminine.

[27] According to Kevin McNeilly, John Zorn's music does not "attempt to abandon its generic or conventional musical ties: those ties, rather, are exploited and segmented, to the point where, while retaining their ironic, parodic thrust and remaining recognizable to the t.v.-and-radio-saturated ear, they throw the accustomed listener off balance; the listeners who know their pop-culture, that is, have their expectations jolted, scattered, smashed, and re-arranged." McNeilly, *op cit.,* paragraph 13.

restaurant table on a relaxing evening (as they actually have been, many times). And yet, no one really forgets that they are actually part of a book on musical postmodernism. An underlying tension is unavoidable, no matter how engaging the stories are. Readers enter into the language conventions of story-telling easily enough, but the stories are not really the same—even if they correspond word for word—as they would be if heard in a restaurant.

When the topic of this chapter returns to postmodern music after a diverting tale, the scholarly language does not seem quite the same (indeed, it is not). The stories may be unrelated to postmodern music, but they have an impact on my discussion. And so it can be with invocations of other kinds of music within a postmodern work: no matter how incongruous, how unexpected, how unrelated to the rest of the composition, they make a difference in how it is heard and understood.

Earlier in this book I called for the demise of totalizing meta-narratives. But is it possible to get beyond totalizing ideas while hailing disunity and postmodernism? Am I perhaps inadvertently saying something about the inevitability of meta-narratives? Indeed, there is something paradoxical about discussing postmodernism in scholarly language. To try to capture the essence of an aesthetic that is nonlinear, disunified, and irrational by means of discourse that is linear, unified, and rational inevitably distorts. There is a difference between discussing postmodernism and being postmodern, between studying disunity and being disunified. The opening movement of Haydn's *Creation* is a vision of chaos, but it is not chaotic. Earlier chapters of this book offered a vision of disunity but not the thing itself. This problem, if indeed that is what it is (after all, there *are* certain advantages to the distancing of rational discourse), is an exaggeration of what is inherent in all description, in all analysis, in all criticism of music: the impossibility of invoking music with words. Analysts and critics regularly use words to study a nonverbal medium, but they do not usually write a piece of music to explicate other bodies of music. I want this book not only to discuss postmodernism but to be postmodern. One way I tried to do this was to incorporate different versions of the same paragraph in different parts of this chapter.

11.15. Almost the End

The way Section 11.14 explains the strategies of this chapter is not at all postmodern. The cadential nature of that section is also not postmodern, as it draws the chapter toward a logical conclusion. So, despite a ride on the wild side, this chapter (and hence this book) finally discusses more than exemplifies postmodernism.

Or does it?

Trait 8: embraces contradiction.

11.16. The End

The end.[28]

_____
[28] The end?

BOOK II

CASE HISTORIES

Postmodernism in the Finale of Mahler's Seventh Symphony

12.1. Overview

The last movement of Mahler's Seventh Symphony has had a curious reception history. Hailed by contemporary critics, it has been strongly criticized by more recent commentators. Complaints cite its looseness of form, its stylistic regressiveness, and its incorporation of banal if not downright trashy materials into a symphonic work.

Lack of unity, use of sonorities suggesting the past, and refusal to accept the distinction between art music and vernacular music are three characteristics of present-day postmodernist music. This essay argues that in certain ways the Mahler Seventh finale can be understood as a work exhibiting postmodern characteristics. Such an argument is possible once we recognize postmodernism not simply as a period but as an attitude. I believe that it is important to remove from the definition of postmodernism an absolute chronological component, even though so doing leads to the paradox of calling a work like the Mahler Seventh finale postmodern when it was composed prior to the modernist era in music.[1]

The postmodern musical aesthetic embraces discontinuity, discursive form, mixtures of high-art and popular-music styles, references to diverse musical traditions, playing against expectations, and lack of all-encompassing unifying structures. The Mahler finale exhibits all of these characteristics. Particularly problematic for latter-day critics has been the work's alleged disunity. Before we can discuss the

---

[1] Kathleen Higgins writes: "The term 'postmodernism' has an oxymoronic sound. How, if the word 'modern' refers to the present, can currently living people be 'postmodern'? This question arises almost as a gut reaction. The word seems a little uncanny. A 'postmodernist' sounds like one of the living dead or perhaps one of the living unborn—or maybe our sense of temporality is simply offended. We can recall Kurt Vonnegut and conceive of postmodernists as 'unstuck in time,'" "Nietzsche and Postmodern Subjectivity," p. 189.
Jean-François Lyotard suggests an even more ironic paradox: "A work can become modern only if it is first postmodern. Postmodernism thus understood is not modernism at its end but in the nascent state, and this state is constant," *The Postmodern Condition*, p. 79. Lyotard seems to mean that before a work can be understood as truly modern, it must challenge a previous modernism. Thus, in Lyotard's example, Picasso and Braque are postmodern in that their art goes beyond the modernism of Cézanne. Once their art has achieved this postmodern break with the past, it becomes modernist. Similarly, we might say that the finale of Mahler's Seventh Symphony is postmodern because it challenges some of the modernistic traits of the music of Wagner and Liszt, most notably organic unity.

meanings behind and purposes of this disunity, however, we must consider whether and how the movement is disunified. How can a work be characterized as disunified if its melodic materials rely on sophisticated motivic interrelationships and if its large-scale tonal plan revolves around the subtle hierarchic interaction of cycles of major-third related keys? One way in which these unifying constructs produce a less than thoroughly unified work is by operating out of phase with each other and with other structures. Thus, for example, tonal returns only sometimes coincide with thematic returns; harmonic contrasts rarely coincide with moves from chromaticism to diatonicism; returns to (hyper)metric regularity do not necessarily align with tonal stability or thematic articulations; motives migrate from theme to theme, ultimately compromising the identity of separate thematic groups. What results is, ironically, an episodic more than a developmental form, a nonteleological movement that is nonetheless tonal.

The movement works with the oppositions and dichotomies of metrically stable vs. unstable, diatonic vs. chromatic, in tonic vs. out of tonic, main theme vs. subsidiary theme, functional vs. nonfunctional harmonies, expectations fulfilled vs. not fulfilled, development vs. repetition of motives, sections that cadence vs. those that are interrupted, the organic vs. the episodic, teleology vs. succession. Thus this music challenges the limits and meaning of the tonal language, paradoxically within a context that is frequently diatonic and that has nothing to do with a Schoenbergian threat to tonality through increased chromaticism.

Adorno criticized the finale's diatonicism as monotonous, suggesting that it is excessive, trivial, and regressive.[2] But how regressive is it? Its purpose in this movement is to create contrasts and discontinuities, sometimes quite extreme: it is opposed to the movement's chromaticism. Hence the diatonicism challenges the tradition it purportedly serves. Because the harmonies within the diatonic passages sometimes include several distinct pitch classes (m. 517 is a good example; so are mm. 291–96, where the diatonicism allows several different motives of the rondo theme to be combined simultaneously, in an almost pandiatonic manner), the clear harmonic functionality we might expect of a diatonic passage is compromised. This is hardly a regressive use of diatonicism. Mahler may use diatonicism to invoke the past, to refer to simpler tonal styles, but he does not try to recreate classical tonality. Rather, he uses diatonicism in opposition to chromaticism. Diatonicism is not the system of the piece, but rather one extreme of a continuum stretching to high dissonance. Significantly, the opposition is never really resolved, and hence in this sense the movement is open-ended.[3] The final pages of the score (mm. 553–88) are almost purely diatonic, yet chromaticism suddenly re-emerges in the penultimate chord, an augmented triad which is followed unceremoniously—but without a sense of resolution (of the diatonic-chromatic opposition, not of the harmonic dissonance, which *is* resolved)— by the final tonic.

---

[2]   Theodor W. Adorno, *Mahler: A Musical Physiognomy*, trans. Edmund Jephcott (Chicago: University of Chicago Press: 1992, originally published in 1960), p. 137.
[3]   I am indebted for this observation to Martin Scherzinger.

Like other postmodern music, this movement is full of discontinuities of various sorts: unexpected modulations, unprepared climaxes, lack of transitions. Another reason why it is reasonable to characterize the movement as postmodern is its extraordinary range of textures, moods, references, and characters. It contains searing chromaticism and simple diatonicism, dense polyphony and stark unisons, massive orchestrations and chamber music, complexity and folk-like simplicity, intricate metric dissonance and straightforward (hyper)meter, and references to various vernacular musics: march, *Ländler*, fanfare, minuet, folktune, and popular music of Mahler's time. This melange of invocations of non-symphonic music casts its influence on more typical materials, so that V-I cadences and modulatory transitions become more references to tonal procedures of the past than functional harmonic structures. Traditional procedures become objects, not structures, forcing the movement to develop its own unique tonal framework—the major-third cycles.

Largely because of this overall tonal logic, the music does cohere. Nonetheless, its traditional unifying structures do not produce a unified listening experience. That a less than totally unified movement should upset critics writing in the mid-twentieth century is hardly surprising, since the music directly challenges the sacred cow of modernist musical thought: organic unity. In today's intellectual climate, however, we should look anew at this bizarre movement—not as an aberration or a mistake or a rejection of rationality but as a precursor (though hardly the only one) of late-twentieth-century postmodernism.

12.2. Ambiguities in the Opening

C major may be the unequivocal central key of the movement, but the way the music first gets to that key suggests ambiguity and equivocation more than tonic stability. (See Example 12.1.) The timpani Gs and Es in m. 1 may in retrospect seem like thirds and fifths of the C-major tonic, but m. 2 completes an arpeggiation of an E-minor triad (in fact, the timpani arpeggiate E minor throughout mm. 1–6). Is the movement going to be in E minor, then? The preceding movement's tonality of F major does little to either support or contradict E minor: perhaps a vestigial memory that the first movement cadenced in E minor helps support the timpani statement as tonic. Equivocation begins in m. 3, however. Over the timpani B root the triad is minor, not major. Is this chord V of E minor? When the timpani switch to G, the harmony is not E minor but G major: the dominant of C major appears just after the dominant of E minor is compromised. M. 4 begins the interpenetration of the two harmonic regions, E minor and C major, as the timpani E is not the root of an E-minor chord at all but rather a non-harmonic bass to G major, again V of C. The timpani B is still bass of B-minor chords. The lack of stepwise voice leading (in favor of nearly parallel arpeggiations) in these chord alternations focuses our attention on the chords as quasi-independent harmonic entities, rather than as part of an ongoing goal-directed progression.

The strings enter on the last beat of m. 4 with a grand anacrusis that suggests—melodically and rhythmically—V-i in E minor. But the harmony still contradicts:

the would-be V is still a B-*minor* triad, and the would-be i—despite bass support on E—has a D in it, so that the arpeggiations are of a G-major triad (V of C once again), which is embedded within what technically is but does not function as a iii⁷ chord in C major. In other words, the melody/bass line suggests V-i in E minor, while *part of* the downbeat harmony suggests V of C major. When the strings move on from E to D midway through m. 5, the functionality might seem to clarify, making the prominent E in retrospect an appoggiatura to D, a chord tone with V of C. Yet, at the moment of "resolution" the timpani (supported by fourth horn) stubbornly continue to beat out E.

In m. 6, the sixteenth-note descents in the winds include F♯, suggesting that E minor may after all be the proper tonality. From the end of m. 6 to the downbeat of m. 7, horns and trumpets echo the string anacrusis (mm. 4–5), no longer E minor's B-E but now C major's G-C. But the harmony is not C major V-I, but rather a weakened E minor (with E at first only in timpani, so that the chord on beat 3 is almost V of C) going forcefully but without harmonic functionally toward C major. The melodic 5-1 is undermined harmonically. And yet, paradoxically, this *is* the arrival at the initial tonic for the movement. The music comes to a grand, unequivocal C major at m. 7, but by a harmonically circuitous route. The C major is established not by any progression that leads to it, but subsequently by persistent and stable harmonies. Thus

Example 12.1 Mm. 1–51

[Editor's note: The example available covers only mm. 1–17]

the music sends out a mixed message about C major. The introductory gesture leads to the C-major rondo theme as if to imply that C is simply, unequivocally, and without conflict the key, while the harmonic color of E minor and the lack of a clear V of C suggest a shadowy, unstable C major.

Thus begins a movement in which C is the tonic, but in which its treatment as goal is destined to be compromised in a number of ways. C major becomes not just a key but an agent—an agent in a narrative about both the power and the weakness of tonicality, of being a tonic. C major must use non-traditional means to assert itself in this movement, because—as we shall see—traditional harmonic progression, thematic contrast, sectionalization, metric regularity, and diatonicism tell a different story about stability. It almost seems as if C major is struggling to be free of the composer, who wants to write a straightforward large-scale rondo. And so the narrative is about tonality itself, using C major in an attempt to destroy the structural functions of tonality, as supported by conventional gestures. The movement *is* tonal, but it employs tonality in idiosyncratic ways, leaving to its own unique contextual logic the real job of structuring the movement. Thus tonality in general, and C major in particular, are used ironically. Tonal returns are not necessarily articulative or section-defining; they do not necessarily mark reappearances of the rondo theme; they do not necessarily bring stability. And, they are too numerous to allow much sense of overall direction or development.

A large tonal movement, that lacks (or at least understates and underutilizes) direction and development, should not "work." And, indeed, many critics have reacted negatively to this music. And yet, there are reasons for undermining tonality while continuing to use it, for robbing progressions of their structural meaning yet not forsaking them, and for creating a new tonal structure in which the tonality-defining dominant function is largely absent, except where used ironically or parodistically on the musical surface.

12.3. The Rondo Theme

As the rondo themes unfold in mm. 7–51 (see Example 12.1), the strangeness of C as tonic and its conflict with E minor have consequences. At m. 13 the music returns to C major, this time actually preceded by its dominant (significantly, this V-I progression comes at neither the beginning nor the end of a phrase: already harmony and phrase structure are out of phase). But the V chord is immediately preceded (third beat of m. 11) by an E-minor chord, thereby reiterating the harmonic ambiguities of the intro- duction (mm. 1–6). In the subsequent measure, the tonic moves to vi and then V/vi: a new usage of an E triad, now functioning briefly (but significantly) as V of A minor. But m. 14 brings a chord that just may be V of E (although there is no D, ♯ or ♮). This pseudo-cadence in E minor (first three beats of m. 14) leads immediately to a V-I cadence in C major, at last in phase with the phrase structure. Although this move seems to be definitive (because it supports the emergence of a new rondo subtheme), it—like the pseudo V-I cadence in mm. 12–13—moves directly from an E-minor chord to V-I in C major.

Eight measures later there is another V-I cadence in C, this time even more stable (and again in phase with the phrase structure). No longer preceded by E minor, the V chord lasts a full measure. This cadence closes off the phrase that is sometimes considered to be a quotation from *Die Meistersinger.*[4] This phrase relaunches after two bars: what is heard emphasizing C in mm. 15–16 is restated (with minor variation) emphasizing A (although the key suggests D minor more than A minor). The parallelism calls our attention to the potential relationship between A and C. If I were trying to show underlying unity, I could make a (possibly convincing) case for this prominent gesture being the source of the large-scale tonal contrast between C major (with its two major-third-related keys) and A minor (with its two major-third-related keys). Actually, I am not convinced that anyone can actually *hear* that relationship. I am not sure *I* do, given that the A in m. 17 sounds like V of a temporarily tonicized D minor, which turns out to be ii in C major. Nor am I convinced that traditional analysis's ideal listener should hear this parallelism as related to the large-scale tonal contrast, since a parallelism such as this underlines similarity more than contrast. This is simply a case of the possibility of demonstrating unity in the score, a unity which I suspect is not very important to the way people (all? most? some? I alone?) hear the movement.

The real, uncompromised V-I cadence in C in mm. 22–23 has consequences. Responding to the stability of the cadential progression, the music then stays on C, as a pedal (with ornamental alternations of the dominant note) in the bass (taken from the opening timpani line). The pedal lasts all the way from m. 23 through m. 35.

So what is strange? So far, the dominant seems to be functioning in its traditional manner, as a chord that supports and leads to the tonic. Furthermore, the music establishes the stability of C major in stages. At first C is in conflict with E minor, then V-I cadences become gradually more forceful—first juxtaposed with E minor and in the middle of a phrase, then articulating a phrase but still juxtaposed with E minor, and finally articulating a phrase, divorced from suggestions of other keys, and leading to a long tonic pedal. The strangeness comes when we realize that the rondo theme is not yet done, although its harmonic process seems already to have run its course. The music does return to the tonic chord after only two measures (m. 38), but without dominant preparation. Another progression through diatonic C-major harmonies (mm. 42–44) lands the music yet again on I, with a series of arpeggiated echo fanfares in trumpets and winds. The move to tonic in m. 45 is also without dominant preparation, yet it turns out to be the final progression to I in the section: mm. 45–51 take place over another tonic pedal (interestingly, many accidentals in the running figures in mm. 47–50 suggest E minor). So, what is strange is that the most definitive and stable tonic cadence comes not at the end but in the middle of the section.

Because of the brevity and diatonicism and clear root orientation of the harmonies in mm. 36–37 and 42–44, it is reasonable to say that, in effect, the tonic pedal begins in

---

[4] John Williamson discusses some of these critical references to *Meistersinger* in writings about Mahler's Seventh. See "Deceptive Cadences in the Last Movement of Mahler's Seventh Symphony," *Soundings* 9 (1982): 87–96.

m. 24 and lasts through m. 51. Under this reading the strangeness can be explained in another way: the definitive tonic cadence, carefully prepared by more tentative earlier cadences, occurs after 16 measures of a 45-measure section. This hints at a harmonic imbalance, appropriate to the remainder of the movement but unusual for an opening tonic section of a rondo. The harmonic motion is over and done with after about one third of the section, after which the music harmonically marks time by means of an extended tonic pedal. What an odd place for tonic stasis! Just when the movement "should" be opening up and moving someplace harmonically, it stands stone still (in the harmonic domain; it is surely moving in other ways).

So, whichever way we explain the strangeness—as a prematurely forceful cadence or as an early end of harmonic motion—the harmonies of the rondo theme are quirky. They do not act the way they normally would. Yet, the music is full of chordal and arpeggiated triads. The sonic materials of tonality are present but made to act in odd ways: an apt way to begin a movement that is, in some ways, a narrative about tonality.

Mm. 38–51 furthermore juxtapose material from earlier in the opening rondo section. Yet the entire rondo theme is in C major, so the impact of this return is compromised—again setting the stage for how tonality is (or is not) treated in the movement. Thus the quasi-recapitulation in mm. 38 ff. presages thematic procedures occurring later in the movement.

The first rondo statement (mm. 7–51) offers many distinct motives, some of which are destined to retain their identity as rondo-theme material and others of which are to migrate, becoming associated with other thematic material. Each phrase introduces new material, which is a bit difficult to keep sorted out because of the prevalence of arpeggiated and stepwise melodic motion: each phrase is distinct, however, in offering its own type of complexity.

(1) In mm. 7–14 there is a complexity of phrasing. Despite the reasonably clear 4+4 phrase structure, certain repetitions suggest lengths other than 2, 4, or 8. In the trumpet, for example, the stepwise descent from C (mm. 9 and 12) recurs after three bars. Similarly, the half-note rhythm of m. 7 returns—again after three bars—in m. 10.

(2) After the largely diatonic first phrase (except for the tonicizations of A and E in mm. 13 and 14), the second phrase offers complexity of harmony. The parallel between C major (m. 15) and A major functioning as V of D minor (m. 17) has already been mentioned. Before the music actually gets to D, E♭s weaken the tonicization. When D arrives (m. 19), the triad is major, suggesting V/V. This kind of chromaticism contrasts strikingly with the first phrase's diatonicism. A move from diatonic to chromatic writing as a section unfolds is not unusual, but the music becomes quite diatonic again in mm. 23–28 (or beyond, if we accept the hint of subdominant tonicization in mm. 29–30 as essentially diatonic). This return to diatonicism reinforces the big V-I cadence in mm. 22–23.

(3) After a diatonic interlude (mm. 23–26), a third eight-bar phrase offers a new complexity: meter. Within the prevailing 4/4, there is a strong suggestion of 3-beat measures in the violins, mm. 27–29. Mm. 35–44 continue the metric complexity and raise it to the level of hypermeter, as it becomes difficult to discern unequivocal hyper-measures within the ten-bar phrase.

12.4. Second Rondo Statement

By the end of the first rondo statement (m. 51), the music has spent a lot of time in C major. Hints of other keys (F major, D minor) have been short-lived. The only other tonality with structural import is the initial E minor: not quite a key, but a definite threat to the stability of C. The big ending (without V-I cadence!) in m. 51 ends on a tonic chord in which the third and fifth are underemphasized. This almost pure C sonority is immediately reinterpreted as the third degree of A♭ major—a stark juxtaposition of keys, to be sure, with no hint of a modulatory transition. But the choice of key itself is logical (not that we realize this immediately: the stark jump to a distant key is quite unexpected after the surfeit of C major). A♭ completes a circle of major thirds with the prevailing C major and the opening hints of E minor. As the music goes to and through various other keys, often with equally sharp juxtapositions, we come to understand the pervasiveness and importance of such cycles of major-third-related keys.

A♭ brings considerable contrast. Fanfares give way to simple, folk-like music. Chamber-like orchestration replaces massive sonorities. Fluid phrase lengths displace the prevailing four- and eight-bar hypermeasures. Figures begin to cross the barline, suggesting a 4/4 two beats displaced (see the cello line in mm. 56–59 and 60–63). Thus this material is truly contrasting—a veritable second section.

Or is it? After only 26 measures, the music returns suddenly to C major and the rondo theme (see Example 12.2). Except that it is not m. 7 but rather m. 15 that is quoted in m. 79. Something is out of kilter. If this is truly a rondo return already, why does it not begin at the beginning (m. 7)? If, on the other hand, because of the brevity of the A♭ section (and because of the way that key arrives and leaves suddenly, without modulatory transition), the return in m. 79 is really a continuation after a brief interruption, why is there so much rondo music in the tonic? Indeed, C major remains for some time to come, so that this must be understood as a true return, both tonally and thematically, despite the anomalous thematic reference. But the music is out of phase with itself. C major returns unceremoniously, without preparatory dominant, in m. 79. A few bars later, in mm. 86–87, we do hear a big V-I in C. But this cadence can hardly serve to bring back C major (it is already back) nor to bring back the rondo material (which we have also been hearing). It is as if the big cadence in mm. 86–87 belongs to—should be in—mm. 78–79. What material is introduced by this out-of-place cadence? Motivically mm. 87 ff. recall mm. 23 ff. (which come after the first real V-I of the movement). The ultimate motivic source of this passage (and of many others) is mm. 5–6, although after two bars the reference switches specifically to m. 27 (echoed in m. 89).

Thus mm. 86–87 contain a cadence out of place, out of phase. In m. 86 the big ritard, the stepwise motion in eighth notes, the full orchestra, and the harmony all tell us that something of major importance is about to happen. But m. 87 is not so important, since it brings back neither tonic key nor main thematic material (although it *is* based on a main motive). This odd situation is the basis for something still stranger: the same cadential progression returns in mm. 196–97. This time we can

Example 12.2 Mm. 76–123

hardly expect a rondo return, since the cadence comes shortly after one in m. 189 (which in turn is rather surprising, since it comes in an unprepared D♭ major and interrupts a progression toward C major). But we can and do expect a tonic return. When the music actually does go V-I, after suitable delaying ritard, we may think that there has indeed been a major articulation, where a V-I cadence really does usher in a tonic return. This time, as opposed to the previous time, we *have* been away from the tonic for some time (since m. 152). So we actually do believe in the cadential return, in the tonal recapitulation, at m. 197. But our belief is short-lived. Again the force of a V-I tonic cadence is undercut. At m. 87 we cannot accept V-I as a structural downbeat because we are already in C major. At m. 197 the agent of destruction is more subtle: it comes not previously but subsequently to the cadence. The C major turns out not to be a tonic return at all, since a few measures later (m. 209) we find ourselves *still* in A minor. The thirteen measures of C major, despite the cadential articulation at their beginning, are finally a parenthesis, a tonicization of III in A minor. Again, the music is out of phase with itself.

12.5. Out-of-Phase Articulations

As a rondo structure, the movement deals with returns. But what is it that reappears? In a more normal rondo, thematic returns coincide with moves back to the tonic, which are usually underlined by V-I cadential articulations. In the Mahler movement we find returns of the rondo thematic material, which may or may not begin with the first rondo motive (first heard in m. 7); we find returns to the tonic, which may or may not coincide with V-I progressions; we find returns to diatonicism after chromatic passages; we find returns to metric regularity after passages in which the hypermeter (specifically, the phrase lengths) is uneven, and/or the heard meter conflicts with the written meter, and/or different contrapuntal voices project different meters simultaneously, and/or the meters alternate between duple and triple.

What is particularly interesting in this movement, and unsettling, and in my view postmodern, is the manner in which these various returns rarely coincide. If a progression back to the tonic has articulatory power, particularly when it coincides with a V-I cadence, then why should it not coincide with a reappearance of the rondo theme? The reason is that the movement questions formal structuring by means of coinciding harmonic, tonal, and thematic recapitulation. One of the principal structures of tonal form—recapitulation, as supported in several musical parameters—is overthrown. This is not the kind of overthrowing of all of tonality that was soon to emerge in the works of Schoenberg and Webern, however. Their invention was modernist, while Mahler's was postmodernist. He did not eschew tonal, thematic, or harmonic return. He used them, but in ways that compromised and redefined their traditional meaning and function. In a postmodern manner, he used history to destroy history. He used tonality to destroy tonal form. He thereby made tonal form not the structure of this movement but its topic. He created a narrative in which the characters are tonality, harmony, and theme (*not* particular themes, but the general concept of musical theme). Tonality operates, but without the crucial component of dominant support. Harmony operates, but fundamental root movements sometimes do and sometimes do not have truly articulatory impact. And themes certainly exist. They abound, in fact. Because the rondo theme often starts at some point other than its beginning, however, thematic recapitulation is compromised. And because certain motives migrate from one thematic group to another, thematic identity is also compromised.

Let us look at some additional instances of out-of-phase structures.

(1) The final return to C major occurs at m. 517. There is little impact at the moment of arrival, even though we have been away from C major for quite some time. There is no preparatory dominant, the harmony is a bizarre IV over a V pedal, the dynamic is soft, the material is from the third rather than the rondo theme, and the scoring is strings only: not exactly what one would expect at a major structural articulation. A few measures later, at m. 538, the rondo theme does return, with root-position tonic

Example 12.3 Mm. 506–43

support, strong brass and woodwind scoring, *fortissimo* dynamic, and clear harmony (although still no preparatory dominant). Even this close to the end, the music is still out of phase: the tonic key returns at m. 517, while the root-position tonic harmony and rondo theme return at m. 538. See Example 12.3.

(2) Consider another example: m. 268 (Example 12.4). Tonally, this is an important return to the tonic, which has been structurally absent since m. 152 (as explained above, the hint of C major in mm. 187–88 does not materialize, the harmonically prepared C major in m. 197 is short-lived, and the C-major cadence in mm. 217–18 is soon undercut by a continuation of A). The tonal return in m. 268 is subsequently understood to be stable, since it initiates a series of quick modulations (without transition) around the tonic major-third cycle (C major in mm. 268–75, E major in mm. 276–281, A♭ major in mm. 282–85, and C major in mm. 286–90). Furthermore, the return to C major in m. 268 supports a return of the rondo theme, which begins as a true recapitulation, using the initial m. 7 material. Despite the cooperation of tonality and theme, however, this recapitulation is undermined by other elements. There is no harmonic preparation: the stepwise bass ascent in mm. 262–67 (A♭—B♭—B♮—C—C♯—D—D♯) lands in m. 267 (over an E♭ bass) on V of D♭. This directional motion certainly does not point toward C major. The bass motion implies D♭, there is no dominant of C major prior to the tonic return, and the C-major sonority in m. 264 compromises the freshness of the eventual tonic return in m. 268. Furthermore, metric complexities after the tonic return hardly serve to resolve the 3/2 vs. 4/4 in mm. 262–63 or the hints of 5/4 in mm. 264–65. And, the thematic return at m. 268 is compromised, since the motivic content is fragmented, varied, and rearranged to the extent that the music seems more developmental than recapitulatory. In fact, the music at m. 291, in the key of A major, feels more recapitulatory than that at m. 268.

Example 12.4 Mm. 260–75

The thematic return at m. 291 is more believable than that at m. 268, yet m. 268 is in the tonic and m. 291 is in the "wrong" key of A major. Again, the music is out of phase with itself.

(3) In mm. 410–11, there is a big V-I progression in C major, complete with ritard. Something new is about to happen, we may be thinking in mm. 409–10. But what actually occurs in m. 411? The music does go V-I in C major, and this is a true move back to the tonic after a substantial absence. But the thematic material is not fresh: the music keeps working with the motive employed in the preceding few measures. But, ironically and cleverly, the music begins to include rondo-theme motives as it goes on (mm. 414–18, trumpets). A big tonal and harmonic articulation has little impact on the workings of the themes and motives. The expected rondo return comes a few bars later, at m. 446, where the key is no longer tonic. Thus thematic return and tonal return are out of phase. See Example 12.5.

(4) Consider the rondo return at m. 120 (Example 12.6). Thematically it would seem to be a major articulation: the rondo theme returns, with the original motives from m. 7 presented at the outset (although there are certainly changes, such as the material of mm. 11 and 13 (trumpet 1) moving at half speed in mm. 124–27 (oboes and clarinets). This return would seem to be more definitive than the previous one in

Example 12.5 Mm. 402–18

m. 79, which begins not with the initial rondo material of m. 7 but with the subsequent phrase (mm. 79 ff. correspond to mm. 15 ff.). Furthermore, at m. 79 the music moves suddenly from A♭ major to C major, while in mm. 116–20 there is a pointed progression in C: V/V/V/V/V to V/V/V/V to V/V/V to vi⁶ (a sidestep) to V/V to V to I. Also, the downbeat of m. 120 coincides with a move from chromaticism to diatonicism. All these factors would seem to point to m. 120 being a major articulation, a strong arrival. But it does not feel that way, because—despite the directional harmonic progression to I in C—the tonality has not really been away from the tonic since before m. 79. The apparent D major in m. 106 is too brief, and too clearly V/V in C major, to be heard as a tonal contrast. Tonally the big return is in m. 79, after the A♭ major passage, although it is not supported by a V-I cadence; thematically the big return is in m. 120. The two recapitulations, tonal and thematic, are therefore out of phase. As a result, the sense of formal articulation is compromised, and along with it the meaning of rondo form and of tonal structuring.

 (5) There is a big half cadence in m. 367. The music subsequently resolves this V to I in m. 368. This gesture is so blatant that it oversteps the bounds of even this all-permitting movement. It parodies, or deconstructs, tonal cadence: it *is* one, but it does not function as one. What, indeed, does this obvious V-I articulate? Not a rondo return (which occurs a few bars earlier in m. 360) and not a tonic return (the music is in B♭ major) and not even a modulation to a fresh key (the music has been in B♭ since

Example 12.6 Mm. 100–24

Example 12.7 Mm. 357–71

m. 360). The move to B♭ occurs with the rondo theme at m. 360 (without V-I cadence), while the big V-I progression occurs eight bars later, out of phase. See Example 12.7.

These out-of-phase thematic returns, tonal returns, harmonic cadences, re-emergences of metric regularity, and returns of diatonicism are not consistent throughout the movement, however. Sometimes these elements are partially in phase, i.e. some of them do occur together. When some elements cooperate, the result is not, as might be expected, a major structural downbeat, but rather just another contrast, another juncture, which happens to involve some coordination between the elements. This happens because *all* these parameters *never* work completely together. Some element always contradicts the others, always seeks to destroy whatever sectional articulation the others are creating.

A V-I cadence robbed of its structural implications provides one kind of irony. Thematic returns, tonal returns, returns to metric regularity, and returns to diatonicism also cannot be trusted to mean what they normally might. (The latter two structures have less impact, because a move back of metric regularity cannot be appreciated at a single instant, the way a harmonic or tonal return can: the music must go on for several measures to establish metric regularity. Similarly, diatonicism must last a few measures before its complete impact is felt. For this reason, I take the pacing of tonal, harmonic, and thematic returns as having greater impact than the pacing of returns of metric regularity or diatonicism.) Example 12.8 lists all places in the movement where there is an arrival in at least one domain, and tells whether or not it coincides with returns in other domains. The purpose is to see just what is and what is not in phase.

m	initiate a new section?	coincide with return of rondo theme?	coincide with tonic return?	V-I cadence?	coincide with return to diatonicism?	coincide with return to metric regularity?
7	yes	yes	yes	no	no	yes
15	no	no	no	yes	no	no
23	no	no	no	yes	yes	no
45	no	no	no	no	no	yes
67	no	no	no	no	yes	no
79	yes	yes*	yes	no	no	yes
87	yes	no	no	yes	yes	no
100	no	no	no	yes	yes	no
120	yes	yes	no	yes	yes	no
136	no	no	no	yes	yes	no
143	no	no	no	no	no	yes
166	no	no	no	yes	no	no
179	no	no	no	yes	yes	no
189	yes	yes*	no	no	no	yes
197	yes	no	yes	yes	yes	no
220	yes	no	no	no	yes	no
227	no	no	no	no	yes	yes
244	no	no	no	no	yes	no
260	yes	yes**	yes	no	yes	Yes
268	yes	yes	yes	no	yes	no
286	no	no	yes	no	no	no
291	yes	yes**	no	no	no	yes
342	no	no	no	yes	yes	no
351	no	no	no	yes	yes	no
360	yes	yes	no	no	yes	yes
368	yes	no	no	yes	no	no
377	no	no	no	no	yes	no
411	yes	no	yes	yes	no	no
430	no	no	no	yes	no	no
446	yes	yes	no	yes	yes	no
462	no	no	no	no	yes	no
486	no	no	no	no	yes	no
506	no	no	no	no	yes	no
517	yes	no	yes	no	yes	no
538	yes	yes	no	no	yes	no
554	no	no	no	yes	yes	no
573	no	no	no	no	no	yes
581	no	no	no	yes	no	no

* rondo return does not begin with initial (m. 7) material
** considerably altered
NB. If diatonicism or metric regularity continues, there is no return. If diatonicism returns two or three measures before an articulation in another parameter, it is considered to coincide (since it is impossible to sense an exact instant of return to diatonicism, and because this happens several times).

Example 12.8 Coincidence and non-coincidence of arrivals in different parameters

A few observations are in order:

(1) No two tonic returns are supported in the same way (although mm. 7 and 79 come close); notice also that the final tonic return is certainly not the most strongly supported. Similarly, no two returns of the rondo theme are similarly supported, and the final return is not the most strongly supported. In fact, no rondo theme return is fully supported harmonically, tonally, motivically, metrically, and in terms of diatonicism vs. chromaticism.

(2) There are many V-I cadential progressions in the movement, but only rarely do they coincide with returns to the tonic area (twice) or return of the rondo theme (once). In fact, only five times does a V-I cadence bring us to a new section. Hence the meaning of the V-I cadential gesture is severely challenged. What, then, are we to make of the V-I perorations in C major toward the end, mm. 553–69 and 577–85? This hypernormal ending relates intertextually to other romantic symphonies and tone poems that close by triumphantly alternating I and V, but it does not resonate with the meanings of V-I within the movement.

(3) The music drifts frequently back and forth between diatonicism and chromaticism (the chart does not model this contrast very well, since there are many degrees of chromaticism in the movement—this is not really a binary "yes/no" situation). Nonetheless, the passages of complete diatonicism are striking—not so much when they arrive (it is not possible for a return to diatonicism to create a structural arrival), but as they persist. We cannot tell whether a passage is going to be thoroughly diatonic when it begins; we can only come to know its diatonicism gradually. Thus, the shifts between diatonicism and chromaticism are not particularly articulative. When they are, the diatonicism often returns one, two, or three measures before the actual articulation: the diatonicism helps the drive toward a structural downbeat. In Example 12.8, therefore, a return to diatonicism or to metric regularity is considered in phase with another articulation if the two happen within a couple of measures of each other.

(4) Many of the same observations apply to metric regularity. There are many degrees and types of irregularity. Only thorough regularity on all hierarchic levels for several measures warrants a "yes" in the chart. Furthermore, since the re-establishment of metric regularity can be appreciated only gradually, regularity does not produce a strong sense of arrival.

(5) Tonic returns are either supported by V-I cadences or they coincide with rondo returns (or neither), but there is no single place in the entire movement where a return to the tonic coincides with a rondo return *and* is supported by a V-I cadence. The closest candidate is m. 120, which marks a rondo return, a V-I tonic cadence, and an apparent move back to the tonic, except that the previous music has not truly left the tonic. The absence of true rondo/tonal returns marked by V-I cadences is striking. Something which is normal in tonal ritornello forms, and which surely might be expected in a movement with frequent returns to the tonic and to the rondo theme, simply does not happen. If it had, that event might have become a central focus for the movement. As it is, there is no central focus: no strongest arrival back home, no biggest structural downbeat, no unequivocal recapitulation. Rather, the idea of return is multifaceted in this movement, with many types and degrees of recapitulation, all

of which are to some degree and in some way compromised. Every return is partial. Every return is also not a return.

(6) Even apart from the question of V-I support, we never experience the normal resolution of recapitulation. Every time the rondo material comes back, it is undercut either by being in a non-tonic key, or by occurring after the tonic key has already come back, or by beginning with material other than its opening motives.

The movement's title ("Rondo-Finale") leads us to expect certain kinds of structures. They are not absent, but they are radically redefined, losing much of their traditional meaning and gaining new meanings in the process. Big, fully orchestrated V-I cadences, for example, rarely mark major structural junctures, whereas unexpected harmonic juxtapositions do. Thus the V-I cadential gesture becomes not so much a functional harmonic progression as a musical object—rich in association, connotation, and intertextual resonance. It exists prominently on the surface but not in the deep structure, where the dominant key is absent. Large-scale tonal moves by fifth or fourth are avoided, usually in favor of major-third modulations. Cycles of major thirds are inherently more ambiguous and more limited than cycles of fifths: in an equally tempered system, if we modulate up (or down) three major thirds, we are already back home, whereas it takes fully twelve perfect-fifth modulations to complete a cycle. We have scarcely left on the major-third tonal journey before we return. Hence tonal returns are more frequent and less articulative, and less goal-like, than in traditional tonal music.

12.6. The Major-Third Cycles

V-I cadences are out of phase with structural articulations so often that the dominant itself becomes suspect. If we do not trust the dominant to go to the tonic, or to do so with traditional purpose, then using the dominant key area structurally to support the tonic is also suspect. Thus Mahler invents an elaborate system of major-third cycles, that pointedly avoid the dominant (and even its major-third transpositions). Third relations were not new in music, of course. Beethoven explored subsidiary keys related by major third in such works as the first movements of the *Waldstein* Sonata and the F Minor String Quartet, although in both of those works the dominant eventually establishes itself. Early romantic composers were even more interested in modulatory third relations. Therefore Mahler's tonal plan in the finale of the Seventh Symphony is not so much unique as it is an outgrowth of earlier procedures. But Mahler carries the procedure to such an extreme that the tonal directionality of the movement is threatened.

After the brief introduction (mm. 1–6) in which C major gradually emerges from E minor, the first rondo theme (mm. 7–51) is firmly in C major. At m. 51 the music slips suddenly and unexpectedly into A♭ major, thereby completing a C—E—A♭ major-third cycle. The music returns to C major when the rondo material comes back at m. 79. The music remains in the tonic major-third cycle through another C-major rondo return at m. 120.

At m. 153 the music slips into A minor, thereby initiating a new major-third cycle. There is a C-major parenthesis in mm. 168–73, but the tonality is essentially A, sometimes minor and sometimes major, through m. 186. After a deceptive hint of C major, a rondo return suggests in quick succession the other keys of the A major-third cycle: D♭ major (mm. 189–90) and F major (mm. 191–92). Having completed, however tentatively, the A—D♭—F major-third cycle, the music seems free to move on to another cycle. Hence the return to C major at m. 197. The cadential V-I suggests that we are truly back home tonally (although this is not a rondo return), but the music again slips into A minor a few measures later (m. 210), thereby rendering the C-major V-I cadence in retrospect a false tonal return. There is yet another brief hint at C major in mm. 217–19. All these hints of C within the key of A, plus the length of time spent first in C and then in A, impede the sense of forward thrust usually associated with tonal modulations.

In order to establish the A—D♭—F cycle more clearly, the music moves (suddenly) to D♭ major at m. 239. The hint of F major in m. 212 is appropriate. By m. 249 we are back in A (major), with a hint of F major at m. 260. A rare developmental passage is cut short in m. 267 by a D♭ scale over what sounds like V of D♭ major. The music returns to C major in the subsequent measure.

Now, nearly halfway through the movement, the music has explored tonalities allied with two major-third cycles: C—E—A♭ in mm. 1–152 and A—D♭—F in mm. 153–268. Other keys are rare and readily understood as supporting the major-third cycles (the D major in mm. 106–18, which functions as V/V in C) or as ironic and ambiguous hints of returns to the tonic (the C-major feints in mm. 168–73, 187–88, 197–209, and 218–19, all of which are ultimately understood as tonicizations of A minor's relative major).

The major-third cycle that begins with the return of C major in m. 268 is straight-forward and obvious, with sudden modulations to E major (m. 276), A♭ major (m. 282), and back to C major (m. 286). To help us understand this major-third cycle, not only are the modulations abrupt but also the music in each key is diatonic. After the completion of this, the second C—E—A♭ major-third cycle, the music moves deceptively and suddenly to A major (m. 291). Are we going back to the A—D♭—F cycle again? So it would seem, except to do so would be too tonally static even for this movement. This move rather suggests that the inbred nature of the two major-third cycles must somehow be broken. Thus in m. 307 the music moves—again suddenly, without preparation or modulatory transition—to a new key, G♭ major. In order to show clearly that this key is not anomalous or subsidiary, the music remains in the vicinity of G♭ a long time, through m. 359. The subsequent measure brings a rondo return, but not in C major. Rather, the key is B♭ major, suggesting that the preceding G♭ major has initiated a third major-third cycle, G♭—B♭—D. And, indeed, there is a hint of D major in mm. 323–27. The dramatic downward scale of mm. 267–68 returns in mm. 400–1; this time the scale is appropriately F♯ major over a V⁷/F♯ chord. The music moves deceptively to B♭ major in m. 404, although the deception is not great since the music remains within the G♭—B♭—D cycle, where it has been since m. 307 and where it remains through m. 410.

The long absent C major returns at m. 411, preceded by a big dominant but not coinciding with the rondo theme. Is the music returning to the tonic, and/or to the tonic major-third cycle? The length of time spent in C major might suggest so, even in the absence of a rondo statement, but the music moves—this time with a modulatory progression—to D major at m. 446. Is this the previously underemphasized third key of the G♭—B♭—D cycle? Perhaps so, for this passage moves through a rapid series of semitone descents: D major (m. 446), C♯ minor (m. 462), C minor (m. 476), B major (m. 486), and B♭ major (m. 492). These keys are rather unstable, not only because of their brevity but also because they remain much of the time over local dominant pedals. Therefore, it is of no real significance that C minor belongs to the tonic major-third cycle (the use of the minor and of extreme chromaticism further disguises the identity of mm. 476–85 as tonic), nor that C♯ minor belongs to the A—D♭—F cycle, nor that the B major in mm. 486–91 represents the *only* passage in the movement in a key of the dominant cycle G—B—D♯. But the fact that this semitonal descent begins in D major and ends in B♭ major is significant: the framing keys are both members of the G♭—B♭—D major-third cycle, in which the "space" between the D major of mm. 446–61 and the B♭ major of mm. 492 ff. is filled in by chromatic passing notes (calling the keys "passing notes" might seem odd, were it not for the harmonic stasis within each key, and the sense of motion imparted by the semitone-related dominant pedals within each successive key).

At m. 506 the music moves into D♭ major, bringing back briefly the A—D♭—F cycle, just prior to the final return of C major, mm. 517–90.

To summarize: the movement unfolds a series of keys that are related by major thirds. See Example 12.9 (the solid noteheads represent keys that are passing, fleeting, and/or not fully established; open noteheads represent more stable keys). Of the theoretical four major-third cycles, only three are used. Significantly, the omitted cycle is the one that would contain the dominant key. Dominant-tonic tonal relations are absent from the structural key scheme of the movement. Since every key is understandable as part of a major-third cycle, omitting the key of G means also omitting the keys of E♭ and B (the short passage in B in mm. 486–91, as explained above, functions in relation to the G♭—B♭—D cycle). First the tonic cycle C—E—A♭ governs the music in mm. 1–152. Then the music moves to another cycle, A—D♭—F, for mm. 153–268. The tonic cycle returns in mm. 268–90. After a brief reminiscence of the A—D♭—F cycle in mm. 291–306, the third cycle G♭—B♭—D appears in mm. 306–505 (although there is a false return of the tonic cycle in mm. 411–42). Another brief reminiscence of

Example 12.9 Major-third key cycles

the A—D♭—F cycle in mm. 506–16 prepares the final return to the tonic (C major only, not the entire cycle) in mm. 517–90. If some cycle is to be understood as substituting for the dominant cycle, it must be A—D♭—F: this is the cycle which first displaces the tonic cycle, and it is the cycle that precedes the final tonic return. If some key within that cycle is to be understood as substituting for the traditional dominant, it must be the key of A, for the same reasons: this is the key of the contrasting material that first comes in a key out of the tonic cycle, and it is the key that precedes the final C major.

Although the normal tonal hierarchy (in which the dominant is the strongest tonality supporting the tonic) is upset in this music, another hierarchy is substituted. The A—D♭—F cycle is understood as secondary to the tonic C—E—A♭ cycle, while the G♭—B♭—D cycle is more distant. Within each cycle, one key predominates as most stable (or, perhaps, as most representative of that cycle): the tonic C, the key of A (major or minor), and the key of B♭ major. Although the hierarchy of keys arranged in major-third cycles is not as rich a hierarchy as the normal tonic-dominant-subdominant hierarchy, this music does not really suggest a flattening of tonal hierarchy. In that sense—in the sense of overall tonal structure—the Seventh Symphony finale is not really postmodern, because it respects the idea of tonal hierarchy, even as it redefines it.

12.7. Themes and Theme Groups

To a certain extent it is arbitrary to label theme groups in this movement, because of the wealth of material, because of the constant transformation of motives, and because of the way many motives move from theme to theme, compromising the identity of theme groups. Nonetheless, three main themes seem to be established early in the movement, and there are places where they seem to return, even if altered. The way these themes utilize and articulate the major-third cycles is significant. The first theme, which I have been calling the rondo theme, appears several times: m. 7 (C major), m. 79 (C major), m. 120 (C major), m. 189 (beginning in D♭ major, moving to F major, and settling into C major), m. 268 (C major, but moving through E major and A♭ major), m. 291 (A major), m. 360 (B♭ major), m. 446 (D major), and m. 538 (C major). At first the rondo return idea is supported tonally, as each return to the first theme occurs in the tonic key. At m. 189 the tentative moves to D♭ major and F major suggest that the rondo theme is not completely bound up with the tonic. Indeed, after one more tonic statement (m. 268), which remains in C only a short time before moving to E major and then A♭ major, subsequent statements are in non-tonic keys. These statements not only occur in foreign keys, but also they are brief and widely spaced in time (prior to the final rondo return): the rondo theme loses some of its importance as the movement progresses. The first non-tonic key is A major (m. 291), the substitute dominant. This key carries the first appearance of the rondo theme in a key outside the tonic major-third cycle. Then, in m. 360, the rondo theme comes in a key of the remaining major-third cycle, B♭ major. And then, in m. 446, it comes (very briefly, before giving way to quotations of the first movement's main theme) in another key of that cycle, D major. At the end (m. 539), the rondo theme finally returns in the tonic key and to its full original length.

The second theme, which might be expected to present contrasting tonalities, does in fact do so. It occurs first in A♭ major (m. 53), which is a member of the tonic major-third cycle. Then it occurs in A minor (m. 153), a key of the secondary major-third cycle, a key which is a dominant substitute. Its final appearance is in a key of the third cycle, G♭ major (m. 307). The fact that the second theme never appears in the tonic suggests lack of traditional tonal resolution. The third theme, however, takes on that function. It first appears in the tonic in m. 100, after a passage already in the tonic. With no modulation, it is easy to think of this material as a continuation of the rondo material, especially since the accompaniment (second violins and cellos) was heard alone just before (mm. 87 ff.), so that its derivation from rondo material is evident: motivically m. 87 recalls m. 23, which in turn derives from mm. 5–6; the continuation, violins in m. 89, recalls the violin material in mm. 27 ff. Thus it does indeed seem rather arbitrary to call m. 100 a third theme. However, its second statement, in m. 220, helps establish its independence, in part because the tonality is A major, the dominant-substitute key. At m. 411 this material returns, now back in the tonic key, as we might expect of the second theme in a traditional two-theme-group tonal movement. The motivic similarity of this theme to the immediately preceding passage in B♭ major (mm. 402 ff.), however, compromises the impact of hearing the third theme back in the tonic. This material is heard a final time, although varied, in m. 517, where it articulates the final return to the tonic C major (preceding the final statement of the rondo theme in the home key).

Thus, the major-third cycles do articulate a quasi-traditional tonal form, in which a first theme recurs first in the tonic before migrating to other keys and finally returning to a tonic; in which another theme (the third theme) appears first as part of the C-major material, then breaks off to an independence in the dominant-like key, and finally is resolved by appearing in the tonic; and in which there is one more theme (the second, vaguely analogous to a bridge theme), which appears in various keys but avoids ever achieving tonic stability. All other keys of the major-third cycles can be thought of as developmental—keys moved through more than to.

12.8. Lack of Development

But just how developmental *is* this movement? There is no obvious development section, although there are developmental passages. What makes a passage develop-mental? It seems so if it contains some of the markers of tonal development: thematic fragmentation and recombination, tonal instability, metric dissonance, avoidance of the tonic.

Only two passages of any length feel developmental: mm. 269–90 and mm. 446–516. The former begins in the tonic with rondo-theme material, but severely fragmented and in a foreign triple meter. It modulates (we might even say it sequences) quickly through other keys (of the tonic major-third cycle), presenting the most overt statement of the major-third modulatory cycle in the movement. Thus mm. 286–91 return to C, with a V-I cadence, utilizing a mixture of first- and third-theme material. Several bars later there is a return to rondo theme (m. 291), in the wrong key and without cadence: the tonic return and the rondo return are out of phase. The A-major passage seems thematically developmental, owing to its polyphonic density, its simultaneous combination of motives from various parts of the movement. When, in m. 307, the music moves unexpectedly to G♭ major and proceeds to stay there, using second-theme material, it no longer feels developmental. Do, therefore, mm. 269–306 constitute a true development section? Not really. The passage is too short, too inconclusive, too lacking in directional thrust toward a recapitulatory goal, to be a true development.

The other candidate for a development section is more directional and more fully worked out, but it comes too late in the movement to feel truly like a development section. By the time it occurs, we have probably given up any hope of hearing a real development section. It functions, perhaps, more like the kind of extended Beethoven coda that is sometimes called a second development. The pointed downward motion by semitones of the tonalities (D major—C♯ minor—C minor—B major—B♭ major) is made particularly salient since each key is characterized by a dominant pedal, so that there is a slowly descending bass line in mm. 446–501: A—G♯—G—F♯—F. Actually, this stepwise bass descent continues to E (mm. 502–3), D (mm. 504–5), and D♭ (506–15). The variety of motives and the interplay between simple diatonicism (e.g. mm. 486–90) and dissonant chromaticism (mm. 476–85) add to the developmental flavor.

Both these passages contain vestiges of development; they are shells of development sections. As Martin Scherzinger says, "*Development* itself undergoes a transformation, therefore, from 'nature' to 'appearance,' from 'inside' to 'outside,' from 'structural' to 'topical.'"[5]

In addition to these quasi-developmental sections, there are passages that—because of their harmonic instability, intensity, and forward thrust—feel developmental. The first such passage occurs in mm. 260–68, immediately preceding the quasi-development section just discussed. The stepwise rise in the bass, the metric interplay of 4/4 vs. 3/2 and 3/2 vs. 5/4, the level of dissonance, the conflict between half- and quarter-note pulse, the quasi-sequencing—all these factors say that this music is developmental. Before it develops too much, however, it is swept aside by the descending D♭-major scale in mm. 267–68, which seems to destroy all sense of development, as it is followed by a tonic statement of rondo material. A comparably chaotic passage occurs in mm. 389–402, coming after similar material. Again the sound of a development passage is invoked, but more as a reference than as a truly functioning development. And again the music is cut short by a sweeping descending scale, this time F♯ major (mm. 400–2). The disruption by the scale is somewhat less this time,

[5]   Martin Scherzinger, "Of Grammatology in the Rondo-Finale of Gustav Mahler's Seventh Symphony," *Music Analysis*, Vol. 14, No. 1 (March 1995).

since the subsequent passage returns to the key (B♭ major) of the music before the chaotic passage (mm. 360–89).

The descending scale is heard a third time, in mm. 536–38, this time *accelerando.* The third scale (D♭ major) is less violent than the earlier ones: it is less fully orchestrated, and what it interrupts does not sound particularly developmental. Like the first scale, it leads to a tonic restatement of the rondo theme. Like the second scale, it is followed by the same key (C major) as preceded it (mm. 517–32).

Thus the movement has no long, drawn-out development section. Instead, it has a couple of brief passages that sound developmental, and a couple of sections that almost function as full-fledged developments. One of them is too inconclusive, the other too late in the movement, for us to believe in them as full-fledged developments. Does this movement in fact *need* a development section? Its length would suggest so. A movement this size is unlikely to succeed by simply continually alternating material and keys. Most large-scale rondos of the classical period contain developmental sections, for inherent structural reasons as well as by convention. The lack of a true development causes the Mahler movement to seem to go endlessly in circles. The major-third key cycles help to create this impression. The circular nature of the tonal scheme is, in fact, an apt metaphor for the whole movement. It keeps cycling through the same materials—the same third-related keys, the same motives—with variation, fragmentation and recombination, reinterpretation, but without much development and without definitive (i.e. supported in all parameters) recapitulation. What can break the endless cycling? Not a new key (except if the dominant were actually to appear), and not an old key. Not a new theme, because there already is a wealth of material, and not an old theme (we continually hear the same old themes, always in new guises). What, then? How can the music break out of these unending cycles (tonal and thematic)?

12.9. Breaking Out

There are three strategies for getting out of the endless cycling: the semitonal descent described above as a quasi-development section (mm. 446–515), the quotation of the first movement's main theme (mm. 455–514), and the perorations of a V-I progression (mm. 554–85).

(1) The semitonal descent gives tonal direction to a movement that has relied on juxtaposition of keys more than on directed motion between them. This sense of direction eventually leads back to the tonic, as one further bass semitone down is C, which arrives as a tonality in m. 517 (albeit on a curiously unstable G pedal, heard first under a IV chord), as a bass note in m. 536 (where it is bass of a dominant of D♭), and as a tonic root in m. 539.

(2) The main theme from the first movement (beginning in m. 455) is both old (since it is from an earlier part of the symphony) and new (since it has not been heard for nearly an hour). Its appearance in the finale catches us off guard, especially since its initial descending fourth sounds like the beginning of the rondo theme. It has a

critical purpose in the finale. It is more than the superficial quotation of an earlier movement's theme that we sometimes find in romantic symphonies (e.g. Tchaikovsky's Fourth). It serves to get the finale out of its rut, allowing it to push toward the end. It is a catalyst, an agent, of ending—which is paradoxical, since the main theme of an opening movement is also associated with beginning.

(3) Throughout the movement we have been led to distrust the articulative power of the V-I progression. We know what it normally means, but we also know that this meaning has not been supported in this movement. How, then, are we to take all the V-Is near the end (see Example 12.10)? Ironically? As a final, wicked *non sequitur?* As a resolution? Or perhaps as lulling us into a falsely secure belief in the comfort of V-I progressions, only to be rudely reawakened at the last possible moment by the substitution of the augmented triad (m. 589) for the cadential dominant? The V-I peroration says "this is the end!" so many times that, in spite of ourselves and despite what the movement has told us about V-I progressions, we do begin to believe. At least until that augmented triad throws us off one final time. It leads us to doubt one more time. It sarcastically and wittily tells us how foolish we had been a few measures earlier to fall prey to the easy comfort of V-I cadential reiterations.

Example 12.10 Mm. 554–90.

[Editor's note: This example is missing.]

12.10. The Augmented Triad

An analysis obsessed with unity might want to relate this penultimate chord, the augmented triad G♯—C—E, to the major-third cycles, perhaps stating that what had been a background tonal relationship becomes at the last moment a foreground harmony. But that is not the way it sounds (at least, not to me). A series of successive modulations by major third is not really the same thing as an augmented triad. Still, the penultimate chord is not unrelated. Because of the clear parallels with the opening section, this harmony recalls the juxtaposition of C major and A♭ major at m. 51 (which initiates the major-third modulatory cycles).

But how does the penultimate chord function in its immediate context? It is certainly a surprise: when we expect the continued tonic C—E—G or a dominant, we find the G raised to G♯ (so notated, but because of m. 51 it sounds more like A♭). Of course, the true tonic chord comes a measure later, reversing in a sense the order of events of m. 51. (Interestingly, in most performances I have heard, the cymbals add a richness of [additional frequencies to the][6] pitches that clouds the brief final chord's triadic consonance.) So, the G♯/A♭ must be an upper neighbor within the prevailing C major. Mahler seems to go out of his way, however, to prevent the augmented triad from sounding simply like a neighbor chord to the tonic, since no instrument

---

[6] Editor's interpolation.

descends a semitone from G♯/A♭ to G. G♯/A♭ moves down an augmented fifth to C (second horn), descends a major third to E (third trumpet), drops a minor ninth to G (third trombone), goes down an octave plus augmented fifth to C (tuba and string basses), and moves to a full chord, none of the notes of which is a semitone away (violas and cellos). Thus the voice leading encourages us to hear the augmented triad as a harmony in its own right, not just as a tonic triad with an upper neighbor temporarily replacing the fifth.

If the penultimate chord is not really an encapsulated statement of the major-third tonal relations, another passage perhaps is. In m. 130, which is toward the end of the first tonic major-third cycle, the music (which is in a chromatic C major) moves directly from an E-major chord (arrived at as V/vi) to an A♭-major chord (sounding like ♭VI). This striking harmonic juxtaposition, coming at a point where the music has been in C major but has begun in the vicinity of E minor and visited A♭ major, does indeed seem to be a surface statement of the underlying logic of key succession. The difference between m. 130 and m. 589 is that in m. 130 an actual harmonic progression reflects the order of key succession, whereas in m. 589 the major thirds become no longer a progression but a simultaneity.

12.11. Does the Movement Work?

Much of this discussion has focused on how this movement does not behave "properly," how it avoids normal tonal, harmonic, and thematic form. To many commentators, these departures from normality are fatal: the movement fails because it does not allow its materials to behave as they ought. Does this mean that the argument over the Seventh finale finally comes down to taste? If those who disapprove of the movement and those who appreciate it agree on what its elements are and how they operate, is calling the movement postmodern anything more than putting a respectable label on what otherwise could be considered deficiencies?[7]

It does not help to point to Mahler's many successes and claim that he surely had the ability to write successful music. The critic's response would be that this particular movement may have been a miscalculation, a failure to live up to his usual standards, a mistake, and if we deem it worthwhile to study this work, it is because the failures of successful composers can be fascinating. For all I know, maybe the work *was* a failure for Mahler. Perhaps it did not live up to his intentions. Perhaps he disliked it. I don't know, but what is more important, I don't care. Just as unity (of motive, of tonality, of set, etc.) does not guarantee musical comprehensibility, so lack of unity (in this case, the temporal disunity provided by the out-of-phase pacing) does not preclude comprehensibility.

The postmodernist answer to this dilemma is that success and failure are not inherent in the artwork but are a product of the interaction of the perceiver's

---

[7] Actually, in a larger context, this question is a serious challenge to all of postmodernism: is forcing traditional elements to act in non-traditional ways excitingly new or decadently perverse? Or both?

expectations and values with the work's structures and intertextual references. For me, the movement is endlessly fascinating because of the way it contextually deconstructs V-I cadences, tonal returns, and thematic recapitulations. For another listener, the willful non-coincidence of these structures dooms the movement. I am more interested in understanding than in evaluating. My postmodern reading of this work is an attempt to comprehend it, not to prove its worth (though I would hardly spend time studying a work that was not valuable to me).

12.12. Mahler as Postmodernist?

My view of the finale of Mahler's Seventh Symphony as postmodernist may seem like a postmodernist's contempt for history: I challenge historical continuity by saying that the Mahler movement exhibits an aesthetic attitude of the late twentieth century, and by positing a connection between two non-contiguous periods—that of late romanticism and that of current postmodernism. What this essay really has sought is a way of understanding this music that is meaningful to ears, minds, and sensibilities of the 1990s. But what would a committed historian feel? Is there any *historical* reason to call Mahler a postmodernist?

Perhaps there is. As Umberto Eco has written, "Postmodernism is not a trend to be chronologically defined, but, rather, an ideal category or, better still, a *Kunstwollen*, a way of operating. We could say that every period has its postmodernism."[8] Thus it is reasonable to speak of Mahler (and of some other composers as well) as postmodernists of the romantic era.

Were these composers isolated in their prescient embracing of a musical postmodernism? Maybe not. Mahler read, admired, thought about, discussed, and set texts of Nietzsche, whom some scholars consider an important source of postmodernist thinking.[9] Several critics, for example, mention the powerful discontinuities of mood, style, and narrative in *Thus Spake Zarathustra*[10] (1883-5), a work that defies the aesthetic of organic unity.[11] One writer, Kathleen Higgins, also sees a connection between Nietzsche's idea of eternal recurrence and postmodernism's denial of the linearity of time.[12] Higgins understands as postmodern Nietzsche's "predilection for

---

[8] Umberto Eco, *A Theory of Semiotics*, p. 67.
[9] I am indebted to John Covach for pointing out the Mahler-Nietzsche-postmodernism connection.
[10] See, for example, Daniel W. Conway, "Nietzsche contra Nietzsche: The Deconstruction of *Zarathustra*," in Clayton Koelb (ed.), *Nietzsche as Postmodernist: Essays Pro and Contra* (Albany: State University of New York Press, 1990), pp. 91–110. Conway mentions *Zarathustra's* "glaring discontinuities" (p. 92), "lack of a unified dramatic structure" (p. 93), and "several radical discontinuities" (p. 97). See also Koelb's "Introduction: So What's the Story?" *op. cit.*, p. 12. Koelb believes that "Nietzsche's writing is fundamentally narrative in that it constructs a process that we folow [sic] as we read, but it is never *meta-narrative* because it never promises unity, wholeness, or closure," (p. 15).
[11] Koelb, *Nietzsche as Postmodernist*, p. 8
[12] Higgins, "Nietzsche and Postmodern Subjectivity," in Koelb, *Nietzsche as Postmodernist*, pp. 208–12.

the aphoristic and the fragmentary."[13] She writes, "has not Nietzsche, like the postmodernists, insisted that we are condemned to the fragmentary?"[14]

While it is probably only coincidental that one section in the discontinuous second part of *Zarathustra* is called "The Night Song" and that Mahler's Seventh Symphony has been known as "The Song of the Night," there are striking similarities between the two works: they share discontinuous and fragmentary forms, disregard for organic unity, and stark juxtapositions of diverse materials and styles. It may not be farfetched to suggest that Nietzsche's work was an influence on Mahler. More significant, however, is to realize that some ideas we now label as postmodernist were not unknown in turn-of-the-century Europe.

[13] Ibid., p. 213.
[14] Ibid., p. 214.

13

Unity and Disunity in Nielsen's
Sinfonia Semplice

13.1. *Sinfonia Semplice* and Postmodernism

"His strangest and most private [symphony], the funniest, the grimmest, the most touching." Thus Michael Steinberg[1] describes Nielsen's Sixth Symphony, the *Sinfonia Semplice*. David Fanning[2] writes of the work's "corrupted simplicity." A list of adjectives could go on:[3] enigmatic, contradictory, eclectic, prophetic, postmodern. Postmodern? In 1925? People who debate whether Nielsen was a modernist or a latter-day romantic may be surprised to find this piece put forth as an example of an aesthetic that has received widespread recognition in music only since 1980. But, as I have emphasized numerous times in this book, postmodernism is understood better as an attitude than as a historical period: it is more than simply the music after modernism. Thus, while most postmodern pieces are recent, postmodernism has antecedents in earlier music. Some previous composers—Mahler (see Chapter 6) and Ives as well as Nielsen—embraced at least some aspects of the aesthetic. Personally, I believe the Sixth Symphony to be the most profoundly postmodern piece composed prior to the postmodern era. It freely intermixes contradictory styles and techniques, it is not overly concerned with unity, it revels in eclecticism, it delights in ambiguity, it includes aspects of both modernism and premodernism, and it does not recognize any boundaries between vernacular and art music, nor between the vulgar and the sublime. Yet at the same time the symphony incorporates such time-honored structures as tonality, motivic consistency, development, and fugue. These traditional

---

[1] Notes to the recording of Nielsen's Sixth Symphony by the San Francisco Symphony, conducted by Herbert Blomstedt, London Records 425 607-2 (1989).
[2] David Fanning, "Nielsen's Progressive Thematicism," in Mina Miller (ed.), *A Nielsen Companion* (London: Faber, 1995).
[3] Nielsen himself described the symphony various ways at different stages of the compositional process. As he began the work, he wrote of it as "idyllic" (letter of Anne Marie Telmanyi, August 12, 1924). As he approached the end of the first movement he described it as "kind/amiable" (letter to Carl Johan Michaelson, October 22, 1924). Significantly (at least with regard to the analysis offered here), he referred to the finale as "a cosmic chaos" (interview in *Politiken*, April 3, 1925). Yet, shortly after completing the work, he called the finale "jolly" while the first and third movements were "more serious" (interview in *Politiken*, December 11, 1925). I am indebted to Mina Miller for these references and translations.

elements rarely operate globally. More often they are no sooner established than—in a quintessentially postmodern manner—they are compromised.

13.2 Ambiguity at the Outset

That the first movement is tightly constructed motivically does not contradict my hearing of it as postmodern. Rather than being transformed in order to provide an impetus for motion and change, the numerous motives produce an overall consistency because of their pervasiveness. There is a more subtle and fascinating structure, however, concerned not with motivic identity but with what might be called an expressive paradigm. Often in the first movement—and elsewhere as well—a passage begins with a gesture of apparent simplicity, which is subsequently undermined. Sunny innocence—characterized normally by simple texture, straightforward rhythm, diatonic melody, clear tonality, and/or consonant harmony—gives way gradually to darker complexity—characterized by polyphonic density, involved rhythm, chromatic melody, dissonant harmony, and/or weakened tonality. The third part of the expressive paradigm is a resolution to a newly won simplicity, analogous—but usually not similar—to the initial gesture. This terminal simplicity may in turn commence a new statement of the expressive paradigm.

In this manner the first movement plays simplicity off against complexity. In accordance with the expressive paradigm, the opening offers archetypal simplicity, with its diatonicism (the first chromatic note is the B♭ in m. 5, which colors the opening G major with a tint of G minor) and rhythmic directness. But this gesture is deceptive. Is the music really so straightforward? Actually, there are hints of metric and other ambiguities right from the start. Why, for example, do the glockenspiel reiterations of D begin on the third rather than the first beat of the measure (see Example 13.4)? How are we to understand the opening as on beat 3? Do the perceived downbeats coincide with the written downbeats? Not until m. 3 does the meter clarify. One could almost make a case for a bar of 7/8 (see Example 13.1), which is reinforced by the bowing and by the placement of the longer durations.

In one sense, the violin figure does agree with the written barline: it is an extended anacrusis to the long D, which is an accented downbeat by virtue of its length and height. But there are other factors that weaken the meter. Although the figure is essentially a prolongation of G major, there is a touch of dominant. The music returns to the tonic not on a strong beat but on the fourth beat of m. 3. The tonic is then held

Example 13.1 Movement I, mm. 3–4, rebarred into 7/8

I   V   I

Example 13.2 Movement I, m. 3, rebarred into 5/8

across into m. 4 (the entrance of the clarinet on B confirms that the long violin D represents tonic, not dominant, harmony). Thus the harmonic rhythm contradicts the metric rhythm.

Just where does the G-major harmony begin? There is nothing in mm. 1–2 to suggest that the glockenspiel D is anything other than a harmonic root. If the harmony becomes G major on the second eighth of m. 3, then the string entrance has a hint of downbeat to it (as shown in Example 13.1), despite its contradiction of the beat pattern established by the glockenspiel. But if the arrival of tonic harmony produces a suggestion of downbeat, then there is also a hint of 5/8 meter embedded in m. 3 (see Example 13.2).

Neither of these alternate interpretations is strong enough to contradict the written meter definitively, but they have a sufficient degree of plausibility to provide an undercurrent of uneasiness beneath this most serene of openings. Significantly, these ambiguities are not subsequently developed. If this piece were conceived by a composer more concerned than Nielsen apparently was with exploring every impli-cation of his materials (a latter-day Beethoven, for example, or a Schoenberg), then I might look forward to a movement that works out the implications of 4/4 vs. 4/4 displaced by two beats vs. 5/8 vs. 7/8. But, in fact, these *particular* distortions have little resonance. Nielsen was satisfied to introduce the idea of metric ambiguity, without needing to explore or eventually resolve the specific ambiguities present at the opening. The initial undercurrents of irregularity serve only to introduce a movement in which meter is often compromised in one way or another (just as melody is): what often seems like a straightforward antecedent phrase trails away rather than leading to a well-formed consequent.[4]

If I look to the subsequent measures for metric clarification of the beginning, I am disappointed. The deceptively straightforward opening disintegrates into a more obvious ambiguity. The clarinet enters on beat 2 of m. 4, the one beat of the 4/4 measure that has yet to receive any accentual emphasis. Nothing happens to stress beat 3, but the bassoon enters at beat 4, reinforcing the change of harmony on beat 4 from the preceding measure (m. 3). As nothing changes at the barline of m. 5, I may begin to doubt the written measure. The winds are in mid-pattern at the barline; this pattern then repeats with an almost Stravinskian permutation in m. 5 (see Example 13.3). As the clarinet and bassoon continue to noodle, the sense of which beats are metrically

---

[4] This observation recalls David B. Greene's analyses of phrase structure in Mahler. See *Mahler, Consciousness, and Temporality* (New York: Gordon and Breach, 1984), pp. 27–8 and elsewhere.

Example 13.3 Movement I, mm. 4–5, clarinet-bassoon pattern

stronger is further weakened. The flute-oboe entrance in m. 7, followed by a textural change, serves finally to clarify the meter.

The opening, then, introduces several important issues: metric ambiguity, the important motive of m. 3, and—perhaps most significantly—the notion of disintegration, the crucial component of what I am calling the expressive paradigm. It matters that the metrically ambiguous opening does not immediately clarify but rather becomes murkier and less stable in mm. 4–6 before the resolution in m. 7.

Clarification is complete by m. 8 (see Example 13.4), where timpani and lower strings produce an unmistakable downbeat. This beat also marks the definitive return from G minor to G major (already suggested by the E♮s in m. 7, but not yet confirmed because of the persistent B♭s in the same measure).

Measure 8 begins a new cycle (see Example 13.6). Again the music seems to be in G major. Again I hear material of a beguiling simplicity but with subtle undercurrents of complexity and irregularity. The oboe-bassoon accompaniment is almost prosaic, but its spacing gives it a peculiar color that is not quite innocent: bassoons playing in close thirds two octaves below the oboes do not promote a blend so much as a timbral differentiation. The violins' repeated notes may seem at first glance (or at first hearing) as direct as possible, but there is a sense of ambiguity. Although the downbeat of m. 9 is unequivocal—because of the change of pitch from repeated Gs to repeated Ds—the last beat of m. 8 also receives emphasis. The switch from staccato to tenuto in the violins produces an unmistakable stress accent, which has the function of propelling the music away from the G on which it has been stuck. Thus the last beat of m. 8

Example 13.4 Movement I, mm. 1–8

Example 13.5 Movement I, mm. 9–11, violins' 3/4 pattern within 4/4 measures

is accented, although its accent is not metrical. Stress accent and metric accent are therefore out of phase.[5] The material of mm. 8–9 is directly related to that of mm. 3–4: both figures are played by violins in octaves, both move from a G that begins on the second eighth of the measure to a D on the downbeat of the subsequent measure, and both displace the initial G linearly to FG. And again the music threatens to disintegrate before re-establishing metric regularity. In mm. 9–11 there is a strong suggestion of 3/4 (the one meter not implied in mm. 1–4, but also the one meter that is destined to become a congenial home for the m. 3 figure—see mm. 204 ff.). The violin D in m. 9 passes through E in m. 10 before arriving on F in m. 11. The F arrives a beat late, but the meter is quickly stabilized by the downbeat of m. 12, since m. 11 omits a beat of repeated notes. The passing E, arriving logically on the downbeat m. 10, is reiterated three (!) beats later, thus producing a three-beat pattern that is literally repeated (see Example 13.5). By m. 13 metric regularity is restored once again, to remain for a while.

The high F in m. 11 is interesting not so much because it renews the G minor coloration (the F-major harmony suggests something tonally more wide-ranging) but because it sequences m. 8 down a step (the harmony also moves down a step, but not the voicing, which ascends). The idea of sequencing—particularly down a step—is important in the movement. It is immediately reinforced when the lower strings enter in m. 13 with the repeated-note figure a whole step lower than in m. 12 (see Example 13.6; this B♭, which is picked up by the second bassoon playing its lowest possible note in m. 14—thus paving the way for some important later low bassoon notes in the second and fourth movements—clarifies the harmony: the tonality suggested is no longer G minor but B♭ minor). The sequence is carried another step lower in m. 14 by the oboes, first bassoon, and third and fourth horns playing the repeated-note figure on A♭. The original sequence (high violin G in m. 8 to high violin F in m. 11) is eventually carried a whole step further: at m. 33, in an initially unclouded E♭ major, the violins relaunch the repeated-note figure from E♭. Here are the same figure, same timbre, same accompaniment, same register—but a step lower.

Why is there temporarily little metric ambiguity in mm. 13 ff.? Nielsen presents some new motives, all destined to be important subsequently. To help focus attention on these figures, to help embed them in memory, he removes any potential competition for attention from the metric/rhythmic domain. These new figures include: a largely chromatic stepwise descent (in the lower strings in mm. 15–16 and more

[5] For more on various types of accent, see Jonathan D. Kramer, *The Time of Music* (New York: Schirmer Books, 1988), pp. 86–98.

Example 13.6 Movement I, mm. 8–16

overtly in mm. 18–19), a turn motive that elaborates a single pitch (first heard in the flute and clarinet in m. 21), and a minor-third/minor-second descent (first violins and second bassoon in m. 22).

Lest this passage be too simply an exposition of new motives, Nielsen jolts us with unexpected disruptions (see Example 13.7): the flurry in the violins on the downbeat of m. 17, reiterated in flutes and clarinet in m. 23, in first violins in m. 26, and again in winds in mm. 27 and 28. As these disruptions repeat, there is a danger that they will establish a context, that they will become expected and thus no longer be disruptive. Nielsen combats this possible assimilation by making each successive disruption less integrated into the music it invades. At m. 17 the figure fits in perfectly well with the suggestion of an E♭ triad in a context potentially of G minor; furthermore, the disruption simply reiterates the main pitches of the chromatic descent in the lower strings in mm. 15–16. At m. 23 the disruption comes a beat late, and—although it does not exactly contradict the E♭ chord it invades (significantly the interruption occurs at the very moment when the harmony is clarified by the resolution of appoggiaturas F♯ and A respectively to G and B♭)—its final pitch AH has less to do with the E♭ harmony than does the final pitch F♯ (possibly an incomplete neighbor, possibly a lowered third) back at m. 17. The figure in m. 23 is uniquely diatonic, but nonetheless is disruptive because it implies an A♭ harmony while the underlying chord is E♭. At m. 26 the disruption does agree with the prevailing harmony, but it comes off the

Example 13.7 Movement I, mm. 17–32

beat. In m. 27 the disruptive figure abandons its simple descending contour, and it has a degree of harmonic independence. Strictly speaking, it does not contradict the prevailing harmony, but it changes what would otherwise be a D-minor triad into a diminished triad (acting as appoggiatura to D minor[6]). In m. 28 the disruptive figure is shorter than expected, it is anacrustic (as it was in m. 26), and it does not fit the harmony too well. Thus this figure becomes progressively more intrusive as it is reiterated.

Metric ambiguity begins to creep back into the music. There are slight hints of irregularity in two of the new motives. The ornamental figure (m. 21) hints at 3/4, since the two long B♭s arrive three beats apart. And the minor-third/second motive (m. 22) is subtly irregular because its first two descending minor thirds are metrically up-down while the last one is down-up. These suggestions of irregularity are slight indeed, but the first of the two intensifies in mm. 27–28, as the ornament migrates to a different beat and then from off the beat to on the beat.

---

[6] I am indebted for this observation to Mina Miller.

Example 13.8 Movement I, the repeated-note motive in mm. 29–32, rebeamed to show similarity to original motive

Thus is the most overt ambiguity in the piece (thus far) prepared. In m. 29 the violas bring back the repeated-note figure, but beginning a beat late and breaking off unexpectedly before the tenuto notes. In m. 30 the second violins reiterate the figure, now displaced a sixteenth-note (!) early and breaking off even earlier than in m. 29. In m. 31 the clarinets and bassoons present a syncopated version, which comes close to establishing a 3/8 meter, that is no sooner suggested than contradicted when the final repeated notes (middle of m. 32) come a half beat late and omit the final impulse (see Example 13.8).

One result of these metric manipulations is that the written meter actually changes, for the first time, to 3/4, although the various displacements do not allow the music to feel like 3/4 very long before 4/4 returns. To increase the sense of disorientation, the harmony is of nebulous tonality in this passage. Thus mm. 29–32 serve—in accordance with the expressive paradigm—as a disintegration of the relatively stable passage beginning in m. 13.

We are relieved to be back in the world of simplicity and regularity at m. 33 (see Example 13.9). The repeated-note figure returns to its proper metric position, and the harmony is a simple E♭-major chord. But the stability is short-lived, as once again the music degenerates. The first agent of destruction is the bass line in bassoons (doubled two octaves higher in clarinets) that enters in m. 34 and has little to do with the prevailing E♭ major. Then the repeated-note figure begins to meander in m. 35, as it changes notes at seemingly random points. At m. 37 the music makes a half-hearted attempt to correct itself, but the repeated-note figure's descent starts a beat early, necessitating an extra beat of repeated notes in m. 38. The meter does become regular by m. 40. Its clarity is demonstrated by the fact that the syncopations in mm. 43–48 do not threaten to move where the barline is felt. The repeated-note figure's last gasp (for now) occurs in mm. 41–42: the glockenspiel makes a futile attempt to state the figure one last time, even though the rest of the orchestra has moved on to other matters. The halting and displaced character of this statement bespeaks the impossibility of continuing this motive any longer. Its appearance in the glockenspiel, silent since m. 3, is significant, since the timbral connection back to the beginning makes explicit the connection between the repeated-note motive and the repeated Ds that open the symphony.

Example 13.9 Movement I, mm. 33–42

13.3. The Three Fugues in the First Movement

The passage from m. 41 to m. 49 is harmonically obscure but its voice leading is perfectly clear. The flute Ds in mm. 46–47 are an imaginative touch of dissonance, resolved and continued by the violin Ds in mm. 47–48. Measures 50–53 introduce one more motive, pervaded by the tritone. The tonality begins to suggest E minor, which emerges at the fugato beginning in m. 54. This E minor, particularly with its strong B (the music comes close to B minor), represents a move to the sharp side of the initial G major. Previous tonal excursions have been toward B♭ minor (minor third above G) and E♭ major (major third below G); now the music emphasizes E minor (minor third below G) and suggests B minor (major third above G), creating a tonal symmetry. (The important later tonal suggestions of F♯ major and A♭ major create another symmetry around G.)

While the fugue has certain undeniable relationships to what went before (the repeated notes, the first three-note motive as recalling the ornamental motive, and the embedded G-major triad), the overall impression is of something new and unexpected. It seems at first metrically square: the reiterated Bs strengthen the impression of a downbeat at the beginning of m. 55, the first high D to appear on the beat articulates the half measure in m. 55 (and initiates accented bowing), the return to B after repeated Ds articulates the downbeat of m. 56, the move to triplets bisects m. 56, and the return to a dotted rhythm (coinciding with the melodic low point) articulates the downbeat of m. 57. How strange, then, that subsequent statements of the fugue theme begin a beat earlier (making the beginning of the subject accord with the meter) and remain a beat displaced with respect to the written barline! This procedure results in yet another example of music which seems simple and straightforward but in fact is not.

The m. 54 fugato (see Example 13.10) is the first of three. I postpone for the moment the question of why three, but look instead at the similarities and differences between these three fugal quasi-expositions. None of the fugues is without its compromises; each distorts fugal procedures in imaginative ways. The first voice in the first fugue, for example, strangely falls silent for a beat and a half soon after the second voice enters with the theme (m. 57). This silence may help focus the ear on the new voice, but it causes the contrapuntal energy to drop off at the very place where a baroque or classical fugue would push forward, with its two voices engaged in polyphonic interplay.

The tonal pattern of fugal entries makes gestures toward tradition and also partakes of the logic of tonal symmetry prevalent in this movement. The first statement suggests E minor before moving off in the flat direction toward a final hint of the Neapolitan. The second statement is an exact transposition of the first down a fourth (actually an eleventh), suggesting the dominant key B minor (the first violins support this tonality, although in a somewhat ambiguous fashion). The third entrance balances (a fourth down balanced by a fourth up from the tonic E minor) the first by suggesting the subdominant key A minor, supported in the accompanying voices but still somewhat compromised by the insistence on the lowered seventh at the expense of the leading tone. The fourth entrance neatly returns the music to the orbit of E minor.

What might have been the anacrusis to another fugal entry (winds, end of m. 65) leads instead into a passage that destroys the fugal idea. Just as earlier passages degenerate in one way or another, so the fugato evaporates around m. 66. It is transformed into a development section, beginning canonically and with vigorous counterpoint, and continuing with various motives (from the fugato and from earlier) combined and fragmented in different ways. This soaring section itself peters out (mm. 79–80), leading (seemingly inconsequentially) to another of those deceptive passages (with an apparently new motive) that seem to be the essence of simplicity: repeated Gs interspersed with Cs a fourth above (winds, mm. 80–81), perhaps reminiscent of the very first melodic interval in the piece (the fourth in m. 3). The appearance of D♭ in m. 82 threatens the simplicity by bringing in the tritone (and switching the reference to m. 50), although the imaginative repeated notes in timpani, glockenspiel, and finally trumpets continue to remind me of the movement's initial directness.

Example 13.10 Movement I, first fugue, mm. 54–65

The second fugue (see Example 13.11) begins at the end of m. 140 (an interesting detail: the anacrusis figure is now two even notes, as hinted at the end of m. 65). The protagonists are now the four solo winds, no longer the full complement of strings. The initial key is A minor, logically prepared during the preceding passage—another instance of extremely simple writing—by E major (fifth above A). Significantly, the music comes to "rest" on a D-minor triad (mm. 138–39—fifth below A), although the E tonality is remembered because of the persistence of Es and Bs in the glocken-spiel and piccolo (the latter functioning as a reminder of repeated notes, particularly as used in mm. 81–88).

Just as the typical principle of tonal balance prepares A minor as the first key of the second fugue, so this principle generates the tonal areas of the subsequent fugue statements (as in the first fugue). This time, however, the balance is by means of semitones—not perfect fourths—on either side of the initial tonic: the clarinet suggests G♯ minor in mm. 142 ff., and the oboe suggests B♭ minor in mm. 145 ff. The fourth entrance, instead of returning to A minor, suggests C♯ minor: the process of disintegration of the fugue is already beginning.

The theme of the second fugue at first avoids repeated notes, which is appropriate after a passage full of them and before a development section that will feature (among other motives) the repeated-note figure from m. 8. Because of the absence of repeated notes from the fugue theme, its accentual shape is less clearly defined. In fact, on each successive entrance it begins on a different part of the measure. The change to triplet motion, which coincides with a change of melodic direction from up to down, does imply metric accent—which coincides with a strongly accented beat only in m. 144. The third statement (oboe, mm. 145 ff.) includes some repeated notes and is much closer to the shape of the theme in the first fugue. These repeated notes become, paradoxically, an instrument of disintegration, as the fourth statement (bassoon, mm.

Example 13.11 Movement I, second fugue, mm. 140–50

148 ff.) gets stuck on a repeated G♯ in m. 149, which serves to destroy the fugal texture. Subsequently the music moves into another soaring developmental section. This time, however, the motives include those from early in the movement: the opening figure and the repeated-note figure, both continually fragmented and distorted. As previously, the developmental music collapses into a passage of considerable simplicity: m. 171 is a dissonant and full-blooded version of m. 129.

The first fugue lasts twelve measures. The second fugue self-destructs in its ninth measure. The third fugue (beginning in m. 237) also lasts eight measures but seems shorter, because the subject—pervaded by repeated notes—has far less melodic content (see Example 13.12). The first statement is reduced to two scalewise ascents to repeated Cs (first violins, mm. 237–38). Subsequent statements consist only of the anacrusis figure followed by one ascent to repeated notes. Melodic contour is all but lost in a frantic volley of repeated notes. The headlong rush of the fugue intensifies as one entrance tumbles in soon after another—sometimes they are only three beats apart. Timpani interjections add to the confusion, particularly since they only sometimes coincide with theme entrances. Clarinets add further to the chaos by presenting non-fugal material in the form of triplets, now absent from the fugue statements. Horns, joined by flutes, complicate the already dense rhythmic polyphony with sixteenth-note figures. By m. 245 all semblance of fugal writing has been toppled, and once again the music moves into a developmental passage—more continuous than its predecessors yet still based on materials originating in different parts of the movement. As before, the development leads not to an arrival or resolution but to a dissolution to simplicity: an unaccompanied line (mm. 257 ff.), initially in A♭ minor, derived from the movement's opening motive and influenced by the turn motive.

Because the entrances in this frantic but short-lived third fugue are close together, and because they continually degenerate into repeated notes, the tonality is tenuous. Coming after a dissonant passage with a bass emphasis on C, the first statement is reasonably heard as being in F minor, even though its anacrusis does little to establish that tonality. Likewise in m. 238, the upbeat pitches do not unequivocally project a key. Perhaps this viola entry suggests D♭ minor, but the first violins hardly cooperate. The subsequent cello entry might have something to do with A minor, but again there is no supporting harmony. The same could be said for the second violin entrance in m. 239, suggesting B minor (this tonal orientation is slightly stronger than in the previous entrances, since the large descending interval is now once again an octave—F♯ to F♯—and no longer a minor ninth). The oboes, bassoons, and string basses enter in m. 242 in what might be C minor. But these keys are all fleeting, rarely lasting very long and rarely receiving much harmonic support. It is misleading to call them anything more than melodic suggestions of what might, in a more innocent context, actually establish these tonalities. The music is too troubled to be tonal in any real sense. Hence it is hardly surprising that this fugue does not utilize the principle of tonal balance to determine pitch levels of subsequent entrances—beyond the first three entrances, the "keys" of which do balance one another by means of that most ambiguous of intervals, the major third (D♭ minor is a major third below F minor, just as A minor is a major third above F minor).

Example 13.12 Movement I, third fugue, mm. 237–44

Why three fugues, each dissolving into a complex development section that in turn degenerates into a passage of disarming simplicity? Not only does each fugue and each subsequent development disintegrate, but also the fugal idea itself is progressively compromised to greater and greater degrees. While the first fugue goes through four full statements of the subject before slipping into a non-fugal developmental collage of familiar motives, the third fugue hardly begins before it falls apart. It does have five entrances, but in no real sense is any of them a complete statement of the fugue subject. The second fugue stands in the middle of this progression toward fugal instability. Its fourth statement gets trapped by repeated notes that have gradually crept into the fugue. Thus the reason for the three fugues is found in their course from relative normality to unsettling abnormality. The tonalities progress in a like manner: the first fugue is tonally balanced by means of more or less normal transpositional intervals: fourths and fifths. The second fugue is also balanced, but by means of the decidedly less normal (and less stable) interval of the semitone. The third fugue is hardly tonal at all. To the extent that it is, the transpositional levels of the first three entries do balance symmetrically, by means of a tonally ambiguous augmented triad. The remaining two entries do not participate in the logic of tonal symmetricality.

13.4. First Movement Climax

The existence of many independent motives in the first movement allows Nielsen to omit a few from developmental passages and still retain sufficient variety for contrapuntal differentiation. Thus, when the symphony's opening tune returns in the horns (mm. 110 ff., presaged two bars earlier), it has not been heard for some time. Significantly, it returns in an unabashed F♯ major. This important tonality lies a semitone below the initial tonic, creating a tonal balance with the final A♭ major. Also significant is the continuation: this material is trying to become more than a motive. It attempts to be an extended theme, but it fails as the horns are swallowed up in the dense polyphonic texture of the ongoing development section. Because this music is augmented, the initial syncopation becomes an emphasis on beat 2, which is continued in the subsequent simple passage (mm. 130, 131, 132, and 134). The beginning of the augmented version of this tune suggests 3/4, a meter that is destined to become the most comfortable home for this opening material—at once simple and subtle (as discussed above).

The music does eventually settle into 3/4 time, in a most violent and imaginative manner. The forceful passage at mm. 171 ff. can be understood in context as a simplification after the preceding dense development. Although the tonality is unsettled and the texture is not totally transparent, the straightforward rhythms (derived, of course, from the truly simple passage at mm. 80 ff.) and textural layering act as a clarification after what went before. This passage in turn initiates a new expressive paradigm, as the simplicity disintegrates into the movement's moment of greatest ambiguity, the shattering climax on the minor second B-C at mm. 187 ff. *Sinfonia Semplice* indeed! The power of this dissonance grabs my attention and demands my involvement. It is only gradually that I come to realize that the music has shifted to 3/4 time. But why? The meandering line in cellos and violas (mm. 189 ff.)—which will return in a more peaceful guise to close the movement (bassoons, mm. 263–64)—moves gradually toward a 3/4 statement of the opening motive, finally becoming unequivocal in m. 204.

How natural this material feels in 3/4! Now it can start with a long note on the beat. Now the return to tonic harmony (actually, because the tune enters over a lingering bass B♭, m. 204 feels essentially dominant and m. 205 becomes the clarification of the local tonic—E♭ minor) can coincide with a metric downbeat (beginning of m. 205). The sense of resolution is a fitting conclusion to the expressive paradigm whose disruptive middle member is the climactic minor second. But once again Nielsen compromises the apparent stability: the second violins answer a beat early, weakening the meter despite placing the high half note on a downbeat. And, although the first violins are at first unequivocal about their E♭ minor, the seconds are equally insistent on F♯ major (the identity of the third of E♭ minor and the tonic of FK major is particularly audible. The ensuing duet (texturally reminiscent of the hint of A♭ major in mm.

98 ff.) meanders both tonally and metrically, creating a pocket of instability as the music once again moves from simplicity/stability into complexity/instability. A quiet cymbal roll (imaginatively conceived to be played with metal mallets) intensifies the atmosphere but adds no tonal stability. The ubiquitous glockenspiel repeated notes offer little tonal clarification either. The resulting instability motivates a further developmental passage, of vivid counterpoint and motivic saturation (mm. 215–36), which finally gives way temporarily to the third fugue (where the music returns to 4/4 time) but finally reaches resolution only in m. 257.

13.5. Simplicity and Complexity, Unity and Disunity

The first movement is unsettled: passages of disarming simplicity and of soaring tension seem forever to disintegrate rather than resolve. Even the end, on the surface a resolution to an A♭ tonic, is tentative. The stability of A♭ is local, not global. It is impossible to accept A♭ truly as tonic. Indeed, it is a logical key, residing a half step above the opening tonic of G and thereby balancing the long passage in F♯ major.[7] This tonal symmetry is surely appropriate in a movement that features other such balances, but it does not produce an ultimate relaxation.[8] The music has not achieved A♭ through a struggle; A♭ is logical but not preordained. The music has been heading inexorably toward A♭ for only a relatively short time. Even in a movement with many developmental passages of uncertain tonality and in which truly tonal passages inhabit a wide variety of keys, the ear is not fooled into accepting A♭ as a goal. Despite the simplicity of the ending, despite its consonance, despite its stability within its own key, it is not a large-scale resolution. And so I await further movements to provide ultimate stability. And, in fact, the finale does so, for—despite its extreme variety of musical styles—it is firmly rooted in one key, B♭ major. But we are not there yet. First we must traverse the second and third movements. And the second is indeed a surprise, a bitterly sardonic *non sequitur*, a quirky little number that seems not to contribute at all to the search for stability.

The first movement's pervasive motivic consistency, which I have not traced in detail, serves to bind together its disparate parts. And disparate they are! Everything— from simple consonance to massive dissonance, from diatonic tonality to chromatic atonality, from diatonic tunes to chromatic motives, from transparently thin textures to masses of polyphony—appears in the course of the movement. Although one could perhaps make a case for the webs of motivic associations producing an overriding organic unity, I do not believe that such a characterization does justice to the

---

[7]   Robert Simpson writes—thrice, actually—about the relationship of the A♭ and F♯ major tonalities to the initial G major as "so near yet so far." See *Carl Nielsen, Symphonist* (2nd edition; New York: Taplinger, 1979), pp. 115, 116, and 124. The final reference is specifically to the relationship between the glockenspiel's initial D and final E♮ in the movement.

[8]   A♭ minor is nearer to the original home key of G major than is the balancing F♯ major (mm. 110 ff.), since there are two important notes in common (the violin timbre and register help make this relationship noticeable): G and C♭ in m. 257 correspond to G and B in m. 3.

movement.[9] The motivic identities may prevent the music from flying off into utter chaos, but they do not *generate* the form. Rather, the generative principle is what I have been calling the expressive paradigm. Again and again, in different ways and to differing degrees, the movement presents simple materials that are subsequently compromised or even destroyed by complex materials, after which there is a relaxation to a newly won simplicity.

One might react to this idea that there is nothing unusual in it, that a lot of music begins simply, becomes more complicated, and then resolves. True enough. But in this piece the means of moving through this expressive paradigm are enormously varied. Furthermore, this is no simple ABA idea, since the paradigm's final simplicity is rarely if ever identical to its initial simplicity. Because of the multitude of ways the paradigm is articulated, the music is extremely varied (despite the tight economy of motives). Thus the paradigm itself, rather than the materials that articulate it, becomes the central formal principle of the movement.

Despite its ultimate resolution, the expressive flavor of the paradigm is pessimistic. Again and again this movement presents seemingly innocent materials, which decay and disintegrate. I am saying more than that simple passages are followed by complicated passages. The process of destruction of innocence, of loss of (rather than just contrast to) simplicity, is the essence of this fundamentally dark work. That disintegration leads invariably to reintegration never seems to inspire optimism. Tensions may relax, simplicity may return, but true and total resolution is forever eluded. Thus the music must end away from its initial tonic. The final chord may be consonant, but the major triad can no longer be as sunny or innocent as it was at the outset. It is, in a word, tainted.

Another way of saying some of these same things is to suggest that Nielsen did not unquestioningly accept an aesthetic that requires a composer—or a composition—to pull every possible shred of meaning out of an opening gesture, to derive the subsequent music from the conflicts or "problems" inherent in that opening, or eventually to resolve those tensions completely and unequivocally.

I must stress that I am not accusing Nielsen of having a less than supreme command of compositional craft. Whether he consciously decided not to follow up every implication of the opening is not the issue, nor is whether or not he had the ability to probe all the implications of the opening. After all, some of the ambiguities I described in the opening result from my conception of metrical structure, which may not coincide with Nielsen's. What is significant is that the piece does not take

---

[9] Simpson's demonstration of the pervasiveness throughout the symphony of semitone figures is an excellent example of an analysis that tries to do just this. He relates these motives to the three pillar tonalities of the movement, G, F#, and Ab, *Carl Nielsen*, pp. 116–35. However elegant this analysis may be, I question its *perceptual* relevance. Listeners with absolute pitch may be aware of it, and others (with sensitive ears and powerful tonal memories) may be able to relate semitonal details to large-scale key relations, but I do not find this identity to create, elucidate, or emphasize an overriding unity that I can actually experience. Of course, I am hearing through my own values— which include a healthy respect for and enjoyment of disunity—and Simpson is hearing through his values—which presumably put a high priority on such correspondences between detail and tonal plan.

unto itself an obligation to be organic, to grow from its initial seed. Organicism is inextricable from, say, Schoenberg's aesthetic, but not from Nielsen's. The ideas of Schoenberg have resonated in the works of many composers, particularly because they have been passed on to future generations as a gospel of music education. For this reason, anyone looking at Nielsen's Sixth Symphony from the viewpoint of organicism may find the work deficient.

I am speaking of organicism, not of unity. The first movement is surely unified by the pervasive motives and the persistent expressive paradigm. But the notion of necessary growth, that everything that happens is traceable back to a fundamental idea, does not aid in understanding this symphony particularly well. It is only by bending traditional analytic perspectives out of shape that the climactic minor second (mm. 187 ff.) could be understood as an *organic* outgrowth of the opening diatonic tune.[10] It is hardly surprising that many commentators, no doubt educated in a tradition that values organicism, have had trouble with the Sixth.

But I, as a postmodern analyst, can value rather than disparage anti-organicism. I can look at the opening bars of the Nielsen Sixth and marvel at the multifaceted implications in this seemingly simple material—and yet not find all those implications dealt with subsequently. I can understand different interpretations, metric or otherwise, of the opening and not feel obligated to decide which is/are correct. And I can appreciate these diverse meanings without feeling that the piece will succeed only if they are all eventually addressed in the music.

13.6. Second Movement

The second movement turns the expressive paradigm inside out: the music begins in a disoriented, atonal manner and only after some time achieves the simplicity of diatonicism and tonality. The F♯ major tune that does eventually emerge (mm. 68 ff.) is, not unexpectedly, soon compromised—by the first of many trombone glissandos (see Example 13.13). Then the second clarinet adds a dissonant counterpoint briefly in mm. 80–83, but still the first clarinet persists with its simple scherzo, oblivious to the onslaught. The bassoon music (slightly *louder* than the clarinet line it accompanies) lends progressively less support to the clarinet's F♯ major. The B-major harmony in mm. 72–76 sends the bassoons into E major by m. 77, while the clarinet bravely continues to assert F♯. The bassoons continue to move further and further from F♯, always by falling fifths, arriving finally by means of E and A to D in m. 87. That the D turns out to be minor makes the distance from the clarinet's F♯ even greater.

When the tune is transferred grotesquely to a bassoon in m. 105, all semblance of innocent simplicity is gone. The transformation of the melody away from the diatonic

---

[10] It is instructive to compare this dissonant climax to the massive nine-pitch-class chord that forms the highpoint of the first movement of Mahler's Tenth Symphony. Whereas the Mahler climax is the result of an inexorable growth from the beginning of the movement, the Nielsen climax is less clearly integrated, less clearly motivated. It does not have the same air of inevitability. I hope it is clear that I offer this statement as an observation, not a criticism.

Example 13.13 Movement II, mm. 68–87

sphere in mm. 122–24 completes its disintegration. The movement's one element of simplicity has been progressively destroyed. What is unusual here is that simplicity does not return (the only other possible candidate, the rhythmically direct mm. 126–29, is actually rather subtle harmonically because of the chromatically descending second clarinet, which compromises the otherwise sunny F-major harmony).

The movement is full of imaginatively grotesque touches. Percussion sonorities, extreme registers, jagged atonal fragments, trombone glissandos, and wide intervals give the movement a gallows humor. The few pockets of diatonic simplicity and tonal harmonies mentioned above are foils, brief respites, before the onslaught.

Like the finale, but on a far more modest scale, this unique movement challenges the traditional concept of musical unity. There is ample evidence of motivic consistency,

Example 13.14 Movement II, mm. 109–13, compared with Prokofiev, *Peter and the Wolf*, mm. 59–62. Corresponding notes are vertically aligned

and many gestures return, yet these devices hardly serve to create a wholly unified piece. Rather, it seems forever to be stepping outside the boundaries it has established for itself: the appearance of melody in a non-melodic context, what Simpson[11] calls (apparently with precedent from the composer himself) the "yawn of contempt" (the insistent trombone glissando), the intrusion of tonality into a nontonal context, etc. The movement is wildly chaotic, with its consistencies mattering far less than its surprises.

Foremost among these surprises, at least for latter-day listeners, are the "quotations" of Nielsen's Clarinet Concerto (mm. 126–30) and Prokofiev's *Peter and the Wolf* (mm. 110–13) (see Examples 13.14 and 13.15).[12] I want to call these fragments actual (though somewhat distorted) quotations, even though Nielsen could not possibly have intended them as such: both pieces were yet to be composed in 1925. Yet, as the materials are far briefer in the *Humoreske* than in the concerto or in *Peter*, it would hardly do to call the later works quotations of the Sixth Symphony.[13] No one knowing those pieces can possibly ignore the way the *Humoreske* appears to refer to them— wittily, slyly, incongruously, even if inadvertently. There is no way to deny the impact of these "references," however inappropriate or even unfair such a hearing would have seemed to the composer.

These unintentional quotations are a demonstration—modest, to be sure—of the autonomy of an artwork. Once he composed it, Nielsen let the symphony go into the world, where it has been on its own ever since. Every listener constitutes it (and every other piece) in his/her mind in a partially unique way. For some listeners the process of possessing the piece, of understanding it in a personal way, of shaping their own mental image of it, is inevitably colored by these "quotations."

I cannot leave this necessarily brief discussion of this extraordinary movement without mentioning what Simpson[14] calls an "ugly twisted subject"—the clarinet tune in mm. 29 ff. (see Example 3.16). I might expect, given the nature of the first movement, that the first melodic statement in the *Humoreske* would clarify the

[11] Simpson, *Carl Nielsen*, p. 125.
[12] Ibid., p. 127.
[13] Apparent quotation of an as yet unwritten work is not unique to the Sixth Symphony. In his Third Symphony, for example, Mahler "quotes" the trumpet fanfare that opens his Fifth Symphony and a figure from the finale of his Fourth.
[14] Simpson, *Carl Nielsen*, p. 124.

Example 13.15 Movement II, mm. 126–30, compared with Nielsen, Clarinet Concerto, mm. 57–61

questionable tonality of the fragmented opening (mm. 1–28), but the clarinet tune is if anything less tonal, for several reasons: (1) the prevalence of whole-tone (m. 30) and semitone (m. 32) figures, (2) the frequent skips that do not suggest triad arpeggios (mm. 29 and 31), (3) the pervasive [016] trichords (three of the four descending three-note figures reduce to [016]), and (4) the large number of distinct pitch classes. From the beginning of the theme through the second note of m. 31, a string of sixteen notes traverses eleven pitch classes. Only G is missing. The duplications include three Bs, widely separated in the line (they are the fourth, ninth, and fourteenth notes), two Fs (seventh and twelfth notes), and two Ds (first and fifteenth notes). It is no coincidence that these duplicated pitches are identical to those in the diminished triad sustained in the winds in mm. 24–26: embedded in the clarinet line is the suggestion of a continuation of this prior harmony. The [016] trichords, incidentally, are significant in view of the four motivically similar presentations in the winds in mm. 23–24 (the pitches of the tritones of these arpeggios are B—D—F—G♯, thus establishing a link with the sustained diminished triad). This harmony begins with the glockenspiel A♭—D alternation in mm. 21–22. Given all the prominent statements of descending three-note arpeggios that reduce to [016], the opening of the clarinet line seems an aberration (it is the whole-tone trichord [026]). Thus, when one of the note repetitions turns out to be the initial D, prominently repeated on a downbeat (of m. 31) and as the highest note, I understand that the melody is being relaunched, but this time with a "proper" [016] beginning. The literal identity of the next three-note descents (B—F♯—C in mm. 29 and 31) confirms the relaunching of the now corrected theme.

As this brief analysis of the clarinet tune and its preceding context implies, this movement is (in part) a music of intervals, interval complexes, trichords, near-chromatic completions, etc., more than it is a music of roots, triads, or harmonic progressions. In the context of the entire symphony, this is an enormous incongruity, far more powerful (to my ear, as I keep insisting) than the gestures toward integration provided by motivic similarities.

Some readers may find it strange that I continually analyze strategies of unification (such as the trichordal discussion immediately above) and then claim a healthy measure of disunity for the piece. I find Nielsen's Sixth to be a fascinating mixture of unity and disunity. He uses some traditional and some modernist techniques—that normally serve to promote unity—yet, with delightful abandon, he juxtaposes them

Example 13.16   Movement II, mm. 20–32

with fascinating *non sequiturs*, which gain in power when understood against a context of motivic, set, rhythmic, metric, and/or tonal order. Whereas I certainly do not feel that this is the only piece to mix unity and disunity in this manner, I believe that I can best appreciate Nielsen's special aesthetic by giving equal importance to both.

One last quirk: the final long E (mm. 158–179) sounds—at least when it is well played—as if a single clarinet is producing it. The junctures where the two clarinets trade off should not be heard. As anyone knowledgeable of the instrument knows, a single player (not using circular breathing) cannot hold a note this long (at least this author, in his clarinet-playing days of long ago, was never able to come close to holding this note steady for such a long duration). The movement ends with what seems to be impossible. The idea is subtle, and Nielsen does not make a big issue of it. But the incongruity of an instrument seeming to play beyond its capacity is a fitting conclusion to a movement that has revelled in the bizarre.

13.7. Third Movement

The expressive paradigm returns to its first-movement form in the *Proposta seria*. This movement begins as a fugue (see Example 13.17), with a relatively straightforward (though not quite simple) subject. In accordance with the paradigm, the fugue soon disintegrates into a meandering passage (mm. 14 ff.) that has little to do with the fugal spirit. The catalyst for this disintegration is the disruptive high A♭ (second violins, mm. 12–13), which leads into a seemingly aimless line that wanders chromatically within a B-F tritone range. This A♭ is not wholly unprepared, however: locally it extends the first violins' fourth E♭—B♭ up a fourth to A♭, and globally it is subtly implied by the

Example 13.17 Movement III, mm. 1-15

pattern of fugal entrances (involving, as do the fugatos in the first movement, tonal balance). The first entrance (m. 1) begins on B (on the cellos' brilliant A-string); the second entrance (m. 3) begins ten beats later a fifth lower on E (first violins darkly *sul G*); the third entrance begins another ten beats later, a fifth above the opening (m. 6, violas playing as intensely and as high in their tessitura as the cellos at the beginning). The expected next entrance (ten beats later, possibly a fifth up on C♯) never materializes. But there is a prominent C♯ (violas, m. 9) that occurs two beats too late—a total of twelve beats later than the preceding entry. If the fugue had gone on another fifth higher to a statement beginning on G♯, the entry should have occurred ten or twelve beats later. And the disruptive A♭ does indeed occur twelve beats after the C♯.

The disruptive quality of the A♭ is intensified by its timbre: muted violins playing *ff.* Even as horns, bassoons, and lower strings re-enter with the head motive of the fugue subject (mm. 15-24), the second violins continue within their limited compass. Thus the music still seems aimless (not only because of the limited range but also, as Simpson points out,[15] because there are no repeated patterns in the entire long line of more than 250 notes. The music seems unable to recover the focus and assertiveness of the opening. The insistent second violins finally die away, and with them the preoccupation with the fugue's opening motive, in m. 24. A lone flute takes up the melodic fourth figure from mm. 10-12, appropriately transposed so that the top note (A♭) connects back to the disruptive A♭ in mm. 12-13. For a moment it may seem that another fugue is beginning—especially considering the precedent of the first movement's three fugato passages. But the imitation turns out to be more canonic than fugal. The pitch interval is new (clarinet in m. 25 imitating the flute a minor sixth below, and bassoon entering in m. 26 at the original pitch, although two octaves below); the time interval is inconsistent. Nonetheless, the music promises

[15] Ibid., p. 127.

some stability, some continuity, some chance to realize the thrust of imitative counterpoint, which had led nowhere in the initial fugue. The thematic reference to the first
movement's fugatos (flute in m. 27, clarinet in m. 28) helps strengthen the sense that
this passage is actually going somewhere. But it too disintegrates in m. 29, giving way
to another attempt by the original fugue.

This set of statements is destined to fail. It too promises continuation and stability
but instead evaporates. The entrance in the violins in octaves is surely dramatic and
catches my attention, but already by the end of m. 30 I know something is amiss. In
place of the melodic continuation (last beat of m. 2 to last beat of m. 3), the music
falls into an aimlessly descending, harmonically vague arpeggio, which leads to a
resumption of the meandering figure, again devoid of repeated patterns and again
restricted (once it gets going) to the tritone B-F, despite the drastically changed tonal
area. This line tries to act as countersubject, as the lower strings make a brave attempt
to keep the fugue going (again ten beats later, but at the unexpected interval of a major
sixth lower). But they inevitably fail, just as every other attempt this movement has
made to move forward has ultimately been derailed. In m. 33 the lower strings get
caught in a sequential (and almost inconsequential) repetition of the fugue theme
a fifth lower. The ensuing meandering is once again rescued—temporarily—by the
canon (mm. 36–39), now in only two voices (at the octave).

When the fugue theme tries in vain one last time to establish itself (horn, m.
39), it is unable to get beyond its initial repeated notes. The meandering line comes
along again, but even it is defeated as it leads into a series of fragmentations (violins,
mm. 39–43). As the winds and horns play around with the fugue's opening motive,
they begin to infuse it with the perfect fourth from the canon. The texture becomes
pervaded by consonant intervals, fourths in particular. The movement achieves
peacefulness as it draws to a close, but this sense of rest hardly serves to resolve earlier
tensions. The movement remains a statement of disappointed hopes. Every potentially
definitive statement or restatement of highly profiled material has petered out; never
has the movement succeeded in achieving continuity, in fulfilling the potential of its
materials. Thus this movement, like the earlier ones, is finally quite dark.

The texture is so pervaded with perfect intervals by the end that I almost believe
in the penultimate sound as stable. Again and again strongly profiled music has
crumbled, in accordance with the expressive paradigm. Finally, in the coda (see
Example 13.18), the third element of the paradigm emerges: a resolution to a new
simplicity. But the simplicity is deceptive. Essentially stacked fifths (with some octave
displacements), the penultimate sonority might be taken as stable, although the triadic
nature of the earlier materials (the fugue in particular) makes this quartal/quintal
chord a strange choice for a final cadence. As the chord dies away, I am almost ready to
accept it as pseudo-tonic, when the low D♭ finally descends to a brief C, played *pppp*.
Were all those low D♭s, then, simply an extended appoggiatura to the third of an A♭
triad? The motion from D♭ to C in second horn and first clarinet in mm. 48–52 surely
suggests this possibility, but that motion is not in the bass. The bass D♭ (mm. 50–54)
significantly descends to C only at the very end. The result is an ending that is full of
equivocation, despite the surface calm of its consonant, diatonic harmony. If the final

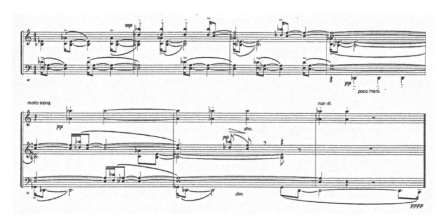

Example 13.18 Movement III, mm. 47–53

sonority is truly A♭ major, why is its overt statement so short? Why does it occur in first inversion? Why have all other notes of the chord ceased to sound by the time the appoggiatura D♭ finally resolves to C? Why is the C in such a metrically weak position? On the other hand, if D♭ is supposed to be the final root, why do the clarinet and horn keep going from D♭ to C, finally ending on C? Why do the violas and cellos descend to C at all? Why is a quartal/quintal sonority used at the end? There is, finally, a subtle ambiguity in the ending, fully appropriate to a movement that refuses to bring any of the issues it raises to definitive conclusions. The fact that the first movement ended in A♭ major seems curiously irrelevant; and the subsequent beginning of the finale in A major (or possibly in D major/minor) offers no tonal clarification.

13.8. Fourth Movement

The last movement is so disparate that it could almost be a series of independent pieces. Their timing and their order of succession give the music coherence but little consistency. The finale throws at the listener the utmost in discontinuity, disparity, surprise, variety, and juxtaposition of opposites. There are amazingly bold successions of: simplicity bordering on the simplistic, massive dissonance, modernist music, romantic music, polyrhythmic complexity, a blatant fanfare, an elegant waltz. It is only a slight exaggeration to call this movement a collage of all music. Sometimes it asks me to believe in the music it invokes, yet other times it derides its references (and perhaps its listeners as well). It is an extraordinary demonstration of a musical imagination running wild. It is amazing that a composer working in 1925 could come up with such variety. While there surely are precedents for such juxtapositions of style, it would take composers several generations before this kind of confrontation of opposites was recognized for its expressive power and no longer dismissed as naïve eclecticism.

And yet the finale *is* a set of variations. Surely the adherence to the theme grounds a potentially irrational movement, providing it with some degree of cohesion. But it is all too easy to credit the variation form and the theme in particular with unifying the finale. The sense of never letting me know what the next variation might bring, numerous unexpected little touches, the massive combinations of incompatible styles—these are not the stuff of musical unity. Whereas the persistent motives in the first movement go some way toward creating a unified, though not an organic, whole, in the finale even the presence of a constant theme ironically does not provide much unity. The sense of the unexpected is understood, to be sure, against the backdrop of comfortable thematic consistency, yet this movement—perhaps more than any other I know composed before the age of postmodernism—demonstrates the weakness of thematic consistency as a formal principle. The only earlier set of variations that occurs to me as having comparable variety is the Wedding March from Karl Goldmark's *Rustic Wedding Symphony* (composed in 1876), but there the extreme variety stops short of Nielsen's willful juxtaposition of opposing types of music.

The finale demands an unusual kind of analysis, because it demonstrates how narrow—and, in this case, futile—traditional analytic approaches can be. Surely one can trace the theme through the variations. And one can point to the centrality of B♭ major as a source of tonal unity. And one can recognize several of the theme's motives appearing in the variations. And, I imagine, a convincing set-theoretic analysis could be concocted for the movement. And perhaps some revisionist could pull off a quasi-Schenkerian analysis that would trace a unified motion. I do not deny any of these analytic possibilities. What I suggest, though, is that they would fail to elucidate in sufficient depth the disparate structure and the neurotic affect of this extraordinary movement. They would fail because their underlying premise—that music is by its nature unified and that the task of an analysis is to uncover the means of unification—is not particularly appropriate here. The last movement may well have aspects of unity, but its sense of disunity, of constant surprise, of the unexpected, and of disorder has little to do with that unity.

Alas, we theorists do not comfortably analyze disunity. We describe it, we point to it, but we do not elucidate lack of relationship in a way comparable to how we demonstrate relatedness. To explain unity is, on some level and in some way, to uncover similarity, whereas to show disunity would involve pointing to difference, and it is impossible to know positively that there are no undetected similarities still waiting to be discovered. Thus it should not be disappointing when the ensuing discussion offers specific analyses of musical consistencies but only broad descriptions of inconsistencies, despite the fact that I value the disunities *in this particular music* over its unities.

The movement begins innocently enough, with a cadenza-like introduction for winds in unisons and octaves (see Example 13.19). The first eight notes (nine, actually) are destined to be the first notes (suitably transposed into B♭ major) of the theme. The triadic contour of the first three notes of m. 2 becomes significant, as this figure leads to a series of descending arpeggiated triads (suggesting I-iv-i-V/V in the key of A). The articulation and contour support grouping into three, not four, notes, producing a syncopation of 3:4 against the beat. Since there are four descending triads of three notes each, twelve notes bring the figure back to the beat by the second beat of m. 3. The D♯ is not only the final note of the descending triads but also the first note of a sequential repetition of the opening (down a minor seventh—the A major and B major symmetrically surround the eventual tonic B♭). This pattern—the opening motive, a contrast, and the return of the opening at a new pitch level—is also important in the theme, mm. 14–19.

But there is a difference between the opening and its return in m. 3: what had been three repeated notes (the Es in mm. 1–2) becomes only two (the F♯s in m. 3). Subsequently there are only two, not four, descending triads: the pattern stops when the music returns to its original pitch level. The second triad (A-minor triad in m. 4) restores not only the initial root of A but also the third repeated note. The music then proceeds into an alternation of three-note descending figures (not always triad arpeggios) and repeated-note figures in mm. 5–8 (see Example 13.19).

The theme itself contains many of these same elements: the opening motive, repeated notes (mm. 23 and 25), descending triads (mm. 25–27) moving downward. In addition, the melodic fourths from the third movement's canon recur (mm. 16–17), motivating a repetition of the opening motive a fourth higher (mm. 18–19). The opening motive appears at pitch three times (mm. 14–15, 20–21, and 28–29), although it includes the repeated notes only the first time.

The careful integration and attention to detail in the introduction and theme hardly suggest the wildly divergent variations that follow. The first variation adheres quite closely to the theme and is sufficiently tame, but quirkiness begins to appear in the second variation, with its almost grotesque interruption by the piccolo and low horns (mm. 47–49)—an extraordinary sound.

The third variation is a parody of a fugue. The subject is absurdly long. It begins like a true fugue subject, with its first four notes paralleling those of the theme. But then it gets caught on a repeated F (mm. 62–64) and never succeeds in recapturing its melodic impulse. When its incessant up-bows finally give way to an interrupting down-bow gesture in m. 81, I have almost forgotten the fugal nature with which this unaccompanied line began. But then the second violins enter (a step lower) with what seems to be a fugal answer. As this almost literal repetition becomes stuck on repeated notes, the "counter-subject" gets caught in isolated triad arpeggiations, derived to be sure from the theme but not motivated in any organic way. The third entrance of the fugue theme (m. 103) is again almost literal. It takes the listener into the fourth variation, where the two-voice texture is more faithful to the kind of counterpoint one expects of fugues: two real lines against each other. But one is in 2/4 and the other is in 6/8, portending future complexities. Finally the fugal impulse dissipates (mm. 123 ff.), just as the fugues in the first and third movements do.

Example 13.19 Movement IV, mm. 1–6

The dissonance of Variation V, suggesting bitonality at times, is perhaps unexpected, but the urbane waltz of the subsequent variation is truly a surprise. This tonal, consonant derivative of the theme dares to go on in its simplicity (although, as both Steinberg and Simpson point out, it sometimes seems that the tonic and dominant chords are interchanged from where they should be). The most unusual the waltz gets—and this is hardly radical in context—is its combination of subdominant and dominant harmony in mm. 170–72. Even the potentially disruptive little piccolo-clarinet figure in m. 182 does not upset the engaging quality of the music. More serious disruptions emerge later on, with the metrically dissonant flute-piccolo figure in mm. 210–13. The intensification of this 4/16 vs. 3/8 in mm. 225–29 leads into the almost Ivesian complexity of Variation VII.

While the first trombone (supported by the others) blares forth with a square 4/16 version of the theme, the upper instruments blithely continue the waltz in 3/8 (mm. 230 ff.), but with winds and strings disagreeing over when their 3/8 downbeats occur. The tonal disagreement between the layers in 3/8 (B minor) and in 4/16 (B♭ major) adds to the chaos. The percussion meanwhile insists on a 2/8 pattern. When the trombones and percussion drop their metric contradictions (mm. 234–37), the piccolo returns with its 4/16 figure from the previous variation (this disruptive gesture is reiterated in mm. 247–48). The variation will not allow a single meter to sound unobstructed, until finally agreement and normality are restored toward the end.

The eighth variation begins straight-faced: an impassioned, chromatic, contra-puntal *adagio* treatment of the theme, somewhat in the mood and manner of the third movement. How can I believe in this music, after the chaos that has preceded it? In fact, disruptive gestures in those typically ornery instruments—high flute and glock-enspiel—continually remind me that the music is not what it seems. And, indeed, the variation cannot sustain this romantic mood: the texture simplifies, the harmonies become more consonant, the figuration becomes repeated notes—just before the *molto adagio* final treatment of the theme's ending.

If the eighth variation is like the third movement, the ninth recalls the second movement. Although adhering to motives from the theme (or at least their rhythmic outlines), the variation uses various grotesque sounds, some directly from the *Humoreske* and some new: bass drum, snare drum, low tuba, low bassoons, triangle, xylophone. The extraordinarily low final tuba D is an almost absurdist sonority.

Possibly the least expected thing to happen after this sardonic variation is what actually does occur next: a fanfare worthy of Hollywood. This incredible *non sequitur* (mm. 325–32) is not a variation. It is followed by another unexpected archetype: a thematically-derived cadenza for all the violins, accompanied by an insistently disruptive snare drum (suggesting the impudent snare drumming in Nielsen's Fifth Symphony and Clarinet Concerto). Brass and winds bring in fragments of the theme, and the music reaches an extraordinary level of dissonance in mm. 361 ff.

It would seem that my expectations have been thwarted so many times in this movement that I could not possibly be surprised again, but I am—by the sudden simplicity (rhythmic and harmonic) of the oom-pahs in mm. 365–71. The movement—unlike its predecessors—comes back home to the tonic key established at the beginning of the theme. There is an ultimate irony here: the most disparate movement is the most coherent tonally. And, in fact, the music stays diatonically in B♭ major, without even a single chromatic aberration, from m. 372 to the end in m. 379.

The ending is amazing. Despite the triplet eighths against triplet sixteenths against thirty-seconds in mm. 374–75, and despite the reiterations of the repeated-note figure in mm. 376–78, the close seems to be as direct as any of the purposefully simple gestures throughout the symphony. The music seems carefree, but how can that be? Because of the expressive paradigm, I have been led to distrust simplicity throughout. Can I now trust it at the end? The absurdity of the piccolo-clarinet flourish in the final bar—which is actually the end of the theme speeded up—is matched by the grotesque sound of two bassoons in unison[16] on their lowest BH♭ left hanging after everyone else has ended the symphony. This may be simple music, this may be consonant music, but it is not normal music. It deconstructs the very idea of a final cadence.

The final bars seem triumphant on the surface, but in fact this is hardly a grandiose conclusion. The good humor and tonal stability are illusory. I am reminded, possibly incongruously, of Ingmar Bergman's movie *The Magician*—a poignant and powerful drama that, almost inappropriately, ends with a hollow triumph of optimism.

And so the simple symphony is not simple. It may contain simple music, but its innocence is always compromised in one way or another. It is finally not the considerable amount of complex music that undermines this simplicity. Rather, it crumbles away whenever I expect the greatest stability or whenever it comes after a passage that seems to be heading anywhere but toward the straightforward. Because Nielsen's simplicity is not to be trusted, this music is ultimately pessimistic: not because complex, dissonant, contrapuntally dense, tonally ambiguous music wins out over direct, consonant music, but because simplicity itself becomes suspect. If I cannot believe in the stability of tonality, or in the radiance of a diatonic tune, or in the regularity of basic rhythms, then this music truly has lost its innocence, at least for me.

My characterization imputes aspects of modernism to this music. The Sixth Symphony is an accurate reflection of its times. Nielsen was by his late years not a hopeless conservative, as some critics have claimed, but thoroughly modern. His modernism in this symphony, though, is only superficially related to suspended tonality, polymeter, or pungent dissonance. More profoundly, the very nature of the work speaks of a modernist sensibility. Yet, in its extraordinary juxtapositions of opposite kinds of music, in its sardonic parodies of other styles, and above all in its use of simplicity to destroy simplicity, the symphony goes beyond modernism toward a postmodernism that few people could have foreseen in 1925. I—as one who lives in an age saturated with postmodernist ideas and artworks, where disunity, surprise, collage, and discontinuity are common in all our contemporary arts—can return to this seventy-year-old piece with renewed appreciation of its prophetic ideas.

---

[16] Theoretically, at least: it is difficult for two bassoons to play absolutely in tune on their lowest note. I suspect Nielsen may have wanted the rough sound of two bassoons *almost* but not quite in unison.

ESSAYS ON POSTMODERNISM
AND JONATHAN KRAMER

Editor's Note

As mentioned in the Introduction, from the beginning the unfinished nature of Kramer's manuscript suggested a sort of completion might occur by having a series of essay-responses, which would approach both the man and his ideas from the perspective of a decade later. This set is the result.

Appropriately, they deal with different perspectives and topics, from which emerges a portrait of Kramer's range and influence. Deborah Bradley-Kramer, as the pre-eminent interpreter of Kramer's work, discusses the challenges of his music, and how they force a performer to rethink basic premises of musical presentation. [I should also add that the musical examples come from Jonathan Kramer's own computer manuscripts and Deborah Bradley-Kramer's performer annotations; hence they are necessarily "rough" in appearance.] Brad Garton examines where the sixteen characteristics of postmodernism proposed at the beginning of the text now stand, as well as suggesting lacunae in Kramer's argument that time has made more evident (especially as regards technology). John Luther Adams would seem to be the most oppositional of the group, claiming no understanding or interest in postmodernism, yet his essay reflects key points of Kramer's argument, such as the primacy of the listener in the ultimate formation of a work, and an openness to ideas and materials that is free of any stricture. John Halle challenges Kramer's arguments from both the perspective of current politics and economics (a "commodification" far less benign than he may have imagined), and from the challenge/contribution that cognitivist theory makes to listener-centered interpretation and analysis. Duncan Neilson recalls his relationship as a student of Kramer's as a way to celebrate his unusual tolerance and curiosity about all aspects of contemporary music, and how this attitude shaped his intellectual project. And finally, Martin Bresnick remembers Kramer as a spirited colleague, and calls across the grave to him as a fellow composer to avoid categories too rigid, and to accept unconditionally the uncategorizable work of genius.

All of these reflect the breadth of Kramer's thought and curiosity. Even when they disagree with him, their imagination and intensity suggest how strong a stimulus he was to all who knew him and his work. And I think he would have been delighted with the ensuing discussion.

Two final technical matters. First, these contributors often refer to Kramer by his first name. I've kept that because of the close personal connection several had with him (and in fact I do so periodically in this volume as well), and it seems appropriate to the tone of this set. Second, whenever they have referred to the text of *Postmodern Music, Postmodern Listening*, I've converted the reference to the chapter and section (e.g. 1.3), because there were many different versions of the manuscript in circulation, and when this volume will appear in final form, the pagination will be yet again completely different.

1

Postmodern Music, Postmodern Performing

Deborah Bradley-Kramer

I first encountered Jonathan Kramer's music when I was a pianist at the European Mozart Academy in Prague, engaged primarily in playing a lot of Mozart and music of the classical canon. Midway through the summer, Lou Harrison arrived and remained with us until the end of that summer of '93. The experience of performing his music with its diverse musical languages illuminated many new worlds, and eventually led me to Jonathan Kramer's postmodern works.

His postmodern compositions were initially unfathomable—not so much from the vantage point of "postmodernism" with which I was familiar through literature, theater, and film, but through the rubric of piano performance. The level and intensity of discontinuities called into question many time-honored aspects of classical music pedagogy, which tends to foster an awareness of structure and unity within a master framework, and offers up a wealth of specific tools and techniques with which to approach these contextual constructs. Despite the obvious fragmentation, I sought this structure and unity, believing on some level that unity is "surely the indispensable thing if meaning is to exist,"[1] and aiming for a kind of organic interlacing that would make everything work.

Synchronic unity in a piece like *Serbelloni Serenade* and other postmodern works could certainly be found (Ex. 1), but didn't provide the keys needed to make every-thing work; the sonic world seemed less about these connections than about the non-sequiturs, discontinuities, jolting forays into different styles, and other aspects of disunity. When heard, the music's many related stems sometimes appeared to be roots, but they did not behave as roots, and any sense of an overarching canopy was elusive.

This perceived disconnect between score and sound reverberates through Kramer's *Postmodern Music, Postmodern Listening*. Note his discussion of the incongruous A-major tune in the finale of Bartok's *Fifth Quartet*:

> I remember first coming to know this piece while I was an undergraduate. I was struck, intrigued, overpowered by the seeming irrationality of this simple tune intruding on the last movement. More than one of my professors was quick to

---

[1] Webern's statement is discussed in Alan Street, "Superior Myths, Dogmatic Allegories: The Resistance to Musical Unity," *Music Analysis* 8 (1989): 77–8.

Example 1 *Serbelloni Serenade*, mm. 1–32

point out that what was truly admirable about this seeming *non sequitur* was how it fundamentally *did* fit in, *did* partake of and even further the tight logical consistency of the piece ... Nor was I impressed when, after I explained this point in a lecture, a theorist gleefully responded that a contour analysis reveals that the tune is "actually" a transformation of a prominent earlier melody ... The power of that passage lies in its unexpectedness and also in just when in the piece we experience the simple/familiar/tonal interrupting the complex/abstract/nontonal. An analysis—such as my friend's contour study—that shows how the tune is, in fact, textually integrated into the movement may not be false; probably it is demonstrably and objectively true. But it misses the point, if we take the point of analysis to be the explanation of how a piece is heard, how it works, and what it means.[2]

Encountering gestures like mm. 18-19 (Example 1) in postmodern compositions seemed to call for a different set of skills and a different mindset from those prescribed through traditional performance practice pedagogy. Perhaps a psychologically based approach could provide guidance, one with which I was familiar through study with certain Russian teachers, orienting the performer as an actor within a narrative. Stanislavsky considered a character's existence on the printed page there "for analysis only"; the real interpretive work was fluid, involving a search for the self as she immerses herself in the inner life of the character, working off the resonance with other actors and the vicissitudes of time and space. Some of this seemed relevant to performing Kramer's postmodern musical prisms, as they reflected so many others. Thinking not about a fixed object of practiced precision, but about fluidity and engagement in a unique sonic environment allowed risk to enter the playing field, and seemed germane to the performing experience. But some gnawing questions persisted, especially one concerning the Stanislavskian notion of a guiding super-narrative or objective—for many postmodern compositions seemed to have none.

Kramer's compositional notes for his orchestra piece *About Face* provided additional insights into postmodern performance:

While composing it, I read the well known case study by Corbett H. Thigpen and Hervey Cleckley, in which three "people"—Eve White, Eve Black, and Jane—share one body. These women are sometimes totally unaware of one another. They "come out" with changing degrees of difficulty and stay out for varying amounts of time. Sometimes they struggle with one another for dominance, but never are they present at the same time. They share some characteristics, but they nonetheless act like distinctly different people with different traits, values, and (to a limited extent) abilities. There are only occasional transitions from one personality to another, and those are brief. Often, when one personality gets herself into a difficult situation, she will "go in" and leave another to suffer the consequences.[3]

---

[2]　Jonathan Kramer, *Postmodern Music, Postmodern Listening*, Chapter 6.3.
[3]　Private correspondence between Kramer and the author.

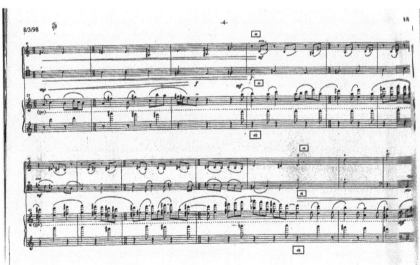

Example 2 *Surreality Check*

So, rather than seeking manifestations of unity, perhaps *disunity* should be the goal: not to seek commonalities *per se*, but the struggles with which certain common points assert themselves. In performance it now seemed that resistance of material should be demonstrated (both sonically and physically), while facile interlacings leading to cohesion should be avoided. In Kramer's Piano Trio *Surreality Check, for* example, a rhapsodic quasi-Brahmsian theme appears (Ex. 2 m. 32) and later recurs in a disfigured, disjointed state (Ex. 3 mm. 130–155) intertwined within a wild and nearly unhinged section with conflicting phrase structures among the instruments.

The goal here is not to joyously reclaim unity, but to underline fragmentation and otherness; the melody is worn like an ill-fitting glove (Example 2).

A performer might therefore think of the starkly contrasting stylistic sections (and their equally striking juxtapositions) as different manifestations of self articulated through her own *petites histoires* or units, and accompanied by their own emotional terrains which sometimes overlap uncomfortably—but which certainly lack an overarching canopy of emotional continuity. The role of emotional memory in these landscapes is critical, and—despite the fixed notation of the printed score or script—is far more fluid than the notes would suggest.

Kramer's discussion of compositional process in one of his postmodern works sheds light on fluid aspects as well when he uses phrases like "as I composed, the music insisted on becoming" and "went where it wanted to be."[4] Here, he describes the process of writing *Surreality Check*:

The way this music led me to surreality has some similarity to the "automatic writing" or surrealist authors. Instead of planning the work's overall form, I created some sounds and figures—the opening undulation, the subsequent chord, a few melodies beginning with the same interval and rhythm—and let them tell me what they wanted to do and where they wanted to go. They seemed like characters in a dream as they moved through carious situations and characters. I felt more like their observer and chronicler than like their creator.[5]

These kinds of statements, coming as they did from a composer who was also one of the country's foremost music theorists, and who spent years creating highly ordered (i.e. unified) music, led me to thoughts about the similarities between the performance of postmodern compositions and the act of improvisation.[6] While obviously differing in significant ways from true improvisation, there are nonetheless similarities to

---

[4] Private correspondence between Kramer and the author, August 2000.
[5] Program note for *Surreality Check*, inside score's cover.
[6] Kramer mentions the disorienting experience of studying with two composition teachers simultaneously, when he would go from a composition seminar with Stockhausen on Thursday, shift gears and compose music for an upcoming Monday seminar with Andrew Imbrie, after which he would again shift gears and work on his piano piece or mobile form for Stockhausen. He goes on to say: "the two composers did not have much interest in or respect for each other. This multiple personality educational ultimately planted a seed that grew into my penchant for musical pluralism. I was intrigued by the different kinds of music and values my two teachers offered, and I was comfortable trying them both out at once." Personal correspondence, July 2003.

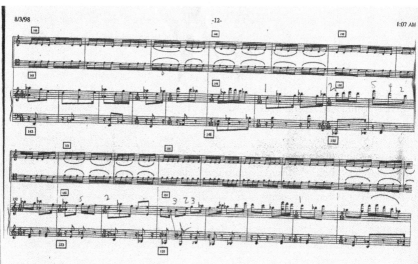

Example 3 *Surreality Check*

be found when navigating the disparate domains in pieces like *Serbelloni Serenade, Surreality Check,* and *Notta Sonata.* The shared element is: risk.

When a performer puts her main focus on reproducing something perfectly and accurately, risk avoidance is paramount. In a classical improvisation, for example, the material may sound cohesive, or it may seem fragmented, anachronistic, and even postmodern![7] But there the performer creates the music, usually drawing on clearly audible features from the concerto at hand, and always risking that the rendering will fall flat, lack vitality, miss the intended mark. Musically speaking, this could mean technical imprecision, lack of rhythmic clarity or phrase articulation, effects influenced by numerous unpredictable elements such as audience sounds, silences, and the quirks of the specific instrument. A piece like Kramer's *Surreality Check* suggests the spirit of improvisation as it whips through diverse styles (some interpenetrated by features from previous areas)—styles lacking the security of the "real," but instead reinterpreted through the moving lens of the composer's imagination.[8] Those imagined styles are ruptured at times by agonistic statements bearing no connection to previous iterations, and influencing none to come. The point is not whether it all works as part of some super-narrative, but whether one can find one's authentic voice in every far-flung statement—statements which might go against the grain, demand switching gears just when things are getting comfortable, advocate an engagement in difficult subjects or small talk, address what one reads as preposterous untruth, and go out on a limb in all kinds of ways—physically and expressively—all of which one must express and perform with utmost conviction.[9] These kinds of pieces embody many features that Kramer describes as "radically postmodern" (temporal multiplicities, intertextuality, fragmentation, disunity, to name a few) and offer rich opportunities for engagement with and interpretation of those supple "occasions of experience."[10]

The disunities and surprise in many postmodern works—whether thematically connected or utterly incongruous—are the interpretive keys that are as much about the materials as they are about the relationships between and among them. It is the sense of pacing, juxtaposition, transition, and surprise that creates the dialogue and form. Therefore, surprises should be executed in exactly that manner—as surprises[11]— within a fabric of multiplicities. When, for example, a cadence that sounds final occurs in a place far removed from the ending, something Kramer calls "gestural time," it should be played exactly as its conventional profile implies: as an ending.[12] These types of events, which occur frequently in his music, should come without preparation,

---

[7] Hear Glenn Gould's cadenza of Beethoven's Piano Concert No. 1: https://www.youtube.com/watch?v=0ObXmnpGW9M.
[8] Tellingly, the title of Kramer's last composition is *Imagined Ancestors.*
[9] Intriguing studies by Vincent Bergeron and Dominic McIver Lopes discuss risk in music from sonic and visual (somatic) standpoints. Vincent Bergeron and Dominic McIver Lopes, "Hearing and Seeing Musical Expression," *Philosophy and Phenomenological Research,* 78.1 (2009), 1–16.
[10] Alfred North Whitehead, *Process and Reality* (New York: Free Press, 1978), p. 34.
[11] Reminiscent of Magic Realism, wherein extraordinary events make their appearance in everyday events, engendering surprise, but not the kind that would label it as a foreign intruder without rights. "Surprise" as related to astonishment and wonder.
[12] See Kramer's discussion of Haydn's E-flat sonata in *Postmodern Music, Postmodern Listening;* Chapter 8.6.

without softening of edges, with a distinct sound palette, with sensitivity to the unique sonic environment of space and other site-specific peculiarities. A sense of daring and risk akin to improvisation should be in play, in contrast to the effect of a sufficiently practiced, note-perfect, cleanly ordered piece with a security system guided by shards of related material.

Music exists in time, and a major portion of Kramer's scholarly and compositional work deals provocatively with temporality. Temporal disorientation often results from disunity, and as Kramer notes, "The notion ... that music can enable listeners to experience different senses of directionality, different temporal narratives, and/or different rates of motion, all *simultaneously*—is truly postmodern."[13] Such multiply-directed time is felt in *Surreality Check*, and involves the previously noted reappearance of the quasi-Brahmsian theme which, in the new setting, coexists amid strings and piano articulating different phrase structures. Approaching this with postmodern listening strategies, we simultaneously hear the memory of the romantic tune, the fragmentation of contrasting phrase contours, the registrally displaced melody, and (if the listener knows it) a connection between this theme and one from another of Kramer's works: *Remembrance of a People: Brief Lives, Endless Memories*. The result is an amalgam of conflicting time worlds experienced at once, dreams within dreams. During a performance, the struggle is to avoid merging into one another's zones (and it may not always succeed!) along with an acute awareness of *difference*. Creating the experience of this precarious sense of danger and near chaos within order is a major challenge in such music.

One of Kramer's main points throughout *Postmodern Music, Postmodern Listening* is that what is occurring between composer, performer, and audience is far from a straightforward act of communication. Highly fragmented postmodern composi-tions offer opportunities for the performer to immerse herself in the disparate styles, treating them not as sound objects to be quoted, not as models to be imitated, but as utterances of her own voice inflected by foreign idioms. Perhaps accents can be discerned, but these just contribute to the impression of exhilaration and risk. There is no hierarchy here; within each language one presents some aspects of self that the others do not.

Meaning is generated in listeners who are open to these languages, underlining otherness and difference. A realization that the process of postmodern composition too, as in Kramer's case, also incorporates elements of spontaneity, culminating in highly fragmented music, created an opening for me, and resulted in a kind of playful dance with the material—a dance which differs from acting and improvisation, but admits some common features such as risk; a moment-by-moment, ludic engagement with distinct properties of space and time; and other qualities unique to a live perfor-mance. A vital performance incorporates a keen awareness of these elements in flux.

Kramer's exuberant advocacy of postmodernism's disunity and his celebration of stylistic variety within a given composition invited new ways of thinking about performance overall, and inspired the following questions: is there a way to reconcile

---

[13] *Postmodern Music, Postmodern Listening*; Chapter 8.1.

the postmodernist idea that meaning resides in the listener with the semiotic idea that meanings are encoded in artworks? Toward that end, could music pedagogy—even at the earliest stages—embrace modes of instruction that honor rather than try to integrate and justify fragmentation? Wouldn't this rage for unity and artificial purity enable another approach, one which fosters a turn away from the tyranny of precision-based, generic, and risk-averse performances so prevalent today?

2

Are We Postmodern Yet?

Brad Garton

Jonathan Kramer's *Postmodern Music, Postmodern Listening* was meant for publication a decade ago. It is an interesting experience to read it now, because things have changed/things have remained, and the time-lag interposes a perspective that would not be available had I been asked to write these comments "in the heat of the moment," when postmodernism was indeed the hot stuff. The very word now seems imbued with a ten-year—how fast a decade passes, now—mustiness, a historical sense that sits oddly upon a philosophy that eschewed historicity, or at least rejected a teleological unfolding of human endeavor. Much of what Kramer describes as postmodern we are now living, however. Kramer also attempts to decouple a postmodern approach from a particular point in time, stating towards the beginning of his book, "Since I take postmodernism as an attitude, I prefer not to think of it as a historical period." Why then do we no longer identify ourselves as "Postmodern," thinking instead of it as a late twentieth-century descriptor, a sociocultural moment that has come and gone?

Part of the central framework of this book is a set of sixteen "characteristics" that Kramer uses to situate his discussion of postmodernism. In true postmodern fashion, Kramer repeatedly rejects the notion that these form a constructive definition of postmodernism. Even with this cautionary constraint, it is worthwhile to consider these in understanding what has happened to postmodernist ideas.

1. Musical postmodernism is not simply a repudiation of modernism or its continuation, but has aspects of both a break and an extension
The postmodern break-and-extension perhaps worked too well. At present, it seems our musical culture is more *rootless* than anything. There isn't a sense that we are breaking or extending anything. Instead, our music feels like it simply exists. Sometimes there seems to be proximate linkages to adjacent musics, but these aren't "deep" in any meaningful sense.

2. Musical postmodernism is, on some level and in some way, ironic
This was true. I have more to say about this later.

3. Musical postmodernism does not respect boundaries between sonorities and procedures of the past and of the present, and, in fact, sometimes goes so far as to question the distinction between the past and the present
This characteristic is possibly what produced the results I describe in my comment on characteristic #1.

4. Musical postmodernism challenges barriers between "high" and "low" styles, sometimes resulting in music that can be considered of questionable taste
The postmodern "challenge" was so successful that the distinction between "high" and "low" styles no longer has any currency. I'm not even sure what "questionable taste" is today.

5. Musical postmodernism questions the mutual exclusivity of elitist and populist values
I will talk more about this later, but we are now in a period when elitist and populist values have become thoroughly entangled. An abundance of "elites" has formed around diverse musical activities, but they appear as non-hierarchical groups, each with no real claim to a "higher" or "lower" status. Musical subcultures are now better described as musical co-cultures.

6. Musical postmodernism includes quotations of or references to music of many traditions and cultures, and, in fact, is sometimes so extreme in its intertextual references that it calls into question the validity of artistic originality
This is still very much a part of the musical landscape, but not so much as a questioning of artistic originality as it is a pragmatic issue of monetary compensation. The ability to include quotations (samples) of other music is now part of an "original" artist's toolkit. Reappropriation is a creative act. This is a good example of how a vanguard aspect of postmodernism has now been subsumed into the standard operation of contemporary art-making.

7. Musical postmodernism encompasses pluralism and eclecticism
Certainly true of much music today. This ecumenicalism has surely been nurtured as a by-product of sampling technology.

8. Musical postmodernism embraces contradictions
Yes and no.

9. Musical postmodernism distrusts binary oppositions
Maybe.
Seriously, #8 and #9 were more salient when contradictions and binary oppositions were in play because there was something to contradict and oppose. That battlefield now seems vacant.

10. Musical postmodernism includes fragmentations, incongruities, discontinuities, and indeterminacy

11. Musical postmodernism shows disdain for the often unquestioned value of structural unity

Part of the success of musical postmodernism as a putative aesthetic ideology is that fragmentation, incongruity, discontinuity, and indeterminacy now form a kind of structural unity. Especially when coupled with an improvisatory approach, fragmentation, discontinuity, and so on can become powerful organizing principles.

12. Musical postmodernism avoids totalizing forms (e.g. does not want entire pieces to be tonal or serial or cast in a prescribed formal mold)

I don't think contemporary composers feel at all constrained by a specific "totalizing" style or "totalizing" aesthetic for a given piece. This may also be one of the successes of postmodernism, for composers today can choose from a range of styles and aesthetics to construct their music. There is no penalty in doing this. However, even with the rhetoric of non-totalizing narratives that supposedly distinguished postmodernism from previous philosophical systems, it seems a logical impossibility, except when the "totalizing" is carefully circumscribed like the list above (tonal, serial, formal …). Kramer himself devotes much of his book to addressing this point, asking early on, "Can there be, after all, a meta-narrative that is not totalizing?" He posits a Kuhnian-like shift from one meta-narrative to another, with the newer paradigm more fluid in terms of what it allows in multiplicity of meanings. Indeed, the latter part of the book is a delightful attempt by Kramer to realize such a postmodern text. I wish he had had access to some of the presentation tools we can now use.

13. Postmodern music presents multiple meanings and multiple temporalities

This has always been an element of music. Kramer discusses this in reference to his earlier, ground-breaking work *The Time of Music*. Postmodernism emphasized this aspect of music, but it has a prior existence, and it still functions today. This has to be a feature of a world with many co-existing musical co-cultures. Interpretations will necessarily vary.

14. Postmodern music considers technology not only as a way to preserve and transmit music but also as deeply implicated in the production and essence of music

Certainly true, but Kramer seriously underestimated the impact that technology would have on the postmodern enterprise. This is to be expected, though, given the unpredictable path that technology has taken. I don't label myself as a techno-determinist, but I do have a lot of up-close experience with music technologies. I say more about this below.

15. Postmodern music considers music not as autonomous but as a commodity responsive to cultural, social, economic, and political contexts
Again this is something that has always been a part of musical cultures, but postmodernism highlighted it by almost (perhaps truly) fetishizing it. Soon the "kick" of the fetish wears off, and it is now an accepted but more apparent part of doing music. Another postmodern success?

16. Postmodern music locates meaning and even structure in listeners more than in scores, performances, or composers
This is an ongoing discussion. Postmodernism (and post-structuralism in general) staked out anti-idealist aesthetic positions that have been passionately argued for at least the last half-century. In music, a new pole has been added to the terrain: the rise of cognitive/empirical musicology and the implications for meaning and structure it claims. Kramer discusses this in his view of postmodernism with reference to theorists such as Stephen McAdams, Fred Lerdahl, and Leonard Meyer.

Surveying my comments on Kramer's list, it seems that a lot of postmodern ideals are more or less accepted or are still actively considered as ways of being in the world. We should be in the full-throat of postmodernism. Why, then, aren't we all card-carrying members of the Postmodernist Club, worshipping ironically at the altar of radical commodification?

First of all, postmodernism has been remarkably successful at consuming itself. The demolishing of oppositions, the leveling of hierarchies, the liquidation of teleology and hegemony, these were the seeds of (and are now the fruits of) postmodernism's demise. Postmodernism has, to a large extent, become a part of our lives, and as such does not have as pronounced an existence as an independent, oppositional philosophy. Independent from *what*? *What* is opposed? Ironically(!), postmodernism's own totalizing "non-totalizing" discourse is simply the way things are.

There were other factors that led to postmodernism's association with a fixed historical period, despite Kramer's argument to unmoor its historical connection. These were things that happened after the late twentieth-century heyday of postmodernism. Because they happened in time, they retroactively determined the acme of "traditional" postmodernist thinking.

One of the biggest shifts occurred in an area close to my own work: the unexpected ways that technology has evolved. The rise of social media and the manifold uses of networking hardware and software has been one of the biggest unforeseen alterations in our lives. Social media now plays a central role in our culture. Although Kramer does mention the potential impact of technology as an ingredient of postmodernism (see his characteristic #14), the greater part of his discussion of technology is related to an older notion of commodification. He could not have predicted how Facebook or YouTube or Soundcloud would change not just the way our cultural products are disseminated in society, but would fundamentally alter how we form communities around these new social loci. To be sure, much of the erasure of the distinction between "high" and "low" art, the condition of multiple "elites" that I described above, is due to the flattening effects of peer-to-peer networks. Postmodernism in 1999 predicted that this flattening would occur, but theorists could not easily have imagined the technological mechanisms used, nor the broad scope of these mechanisms. (If Kramer had been able to anticipate all this, his heirs would be fabulously wealthy!)

Notwithstanding the increased awareness of context that accompanies postmodern critiques (characteristic #15), Kramer had his own—as do we all—contextual blind spots. I think his discounting of the potential effects of media technologies was one of those lacunae. Kramer had others, too. With the passage of time, these are now more apparent, adding to the sense that Kramer is speaking from a "postmodern era." Kramer came from a musical culture in which the concert presentation was one of the defining characteristics. That is no longer true for most of the Western world, and I have serious doubts that it was all that culturally significant ten or fifteen years ago. This led him to underestimate how strong the impact of distributive technologies would be on musical culture.

Another hidden bias in Kramer's postmodernism is the necessarily bounded scope of his musical experience. I don't mean this pejoratively, because Kramer was a voracious consumer of music and one of the most unprejudiced listeners I can name. But his knowledge had limits. He spends a fair portion of his book discussing what he deems the impossibility of a postmodern "avant garde," with particular attention paid to what he perceived as a lack of musical surrealism.

From his perspective, no active musical culture appeared as a surrealist candidate. In the late 1970s and early 1980s, the experimental post-punk music that I recall and the vibrant scene surrounding it could easily be characterized as "surreal." Kramer mentions (in a footnote) the band Nurse With Wound as a group that had been tagged by critics as an example of surrealist music. I could add many more names, bands like Pere Ubu, The Christian Lepers from India, the early Residents, and others. Even with his broad musical listening experience (I am amazed he even knew of Nurse With Wound), he simply didn't know much of this work.

There are other examples of Kramer's unavoidably finite perspective—the rise of improvisation and interactivity, the diverse uses of sampling and "appropriation" (mash-ups, etc.), the breakdown of the recording industry in the new millennium, the rise of sound art/installation presentations—but the most profound philosophical shift has been in the attitudes I see in the new generation of composers. Ironically, our current students are weary of the "been there done that" pose that characterized the cynical strain of ironism that was attached to the postmodern attitude. There seems a new seriousness of purpose, or maybe better described as a clarity of purpose, exhibited by younger creative artists. Maybe this new group is a "post-post" generation, or more likely a "pre-something" generation, but I'm not prescient enough myself to figure what that "something" will be.

I worry about that "something," and this is when I say how much I miss having Jonathan Kramer here. I fear we may be headed towards a nasty and brutish "realism," a slow anti-intellectual decline into darkness. Jonathan was always an optimist, using his keen intellect to point towards a more open, a more expansive, a *postmodern* future. Postmodernism may no longer be the name we apply to our current zeitgeist, but that's because the tenets of postmodernism have been so thoroughly integrated into our way of thinking and being. Through Kramer's writing, it is illuminating to revisit a period when the postmodern condition was being formed.

Jonathan's book is great fun to read. The last section is done as a postmodernly-written commentary on postmodernism, drawing upon the principles he describes earlier as constructive techniques. For example, his table of contents lists these chapters: 11.15, Almost the End; 11.16, The End—and the text (with an appropriate footnote) for 11.16 is delightful. Reading this book, I can hear Jonathan's voice so clearly, and I truly miss him. I will twist a postmodern trope: in this text, the author is not dead.

3

Music in the Anthropocene

John Luther Adams

Preface

I never understood what postmodernism was supposed to be. And the truth is, I never much cared. Maybe it's because I've lived much of my life in Alaska, where I imagined I was working on the fringe of contemporary culture. Maybe it's because, like Bruno Latour, I suspect that we have never really been modern. But what seems more urgent to me is what we might call "post-humanism."

Unless we humans discover our proper place, unless we create new cultures in balance with the larger community of life on this earth, our future as a species looks doubtful. This is what so many of us—in music and art, in science and in politics, in every field of human endeavor—are working on today.

I am standing alone on a beach, listening to the Pacific. As each wave rolls in—booming, roaring, growling, hissing—I listen to its voice: the unique contours of its rising and falling, its singular crescendo and diminuendo. I listen for the interval between this wave and the wave before it, and the one that comes after. I listen as the waves advance and retreat, melding and passing through one another, crashing like cymbals on the shore. I listen to the small stones clattering over one another, pulled inexorably back into the unimaginable vastness of water that stretches away toward Asia.

I do my best to listen as intently, as deeply as I can. Even so, my mind wanders.

A plastic bottle among the rocks reminds me that there are vast islands of garbage drifting far out at sea. A strong gust of wind reminds me of the increasingly capricious weather, and of the storms that lash this and other shores with growing ferocity. The burning sunlight reminds me of melting tundra and expanding deserts, of diminishing polar ice and rising seas all over the earth.

I do my best to refocus my attention, to return only to listening. Yet how can I stand here today and not think of these things?

The earth is 4,540,000,000 years old. The entire written history of the human species has unfolded in the 11,700 years since the most recent ice age, a brief moment of geologic time known as the Holocene. Throughout our history, we humans have altered the surface of the earth. But over the past century or so we have become an undeniable geologic force, making deep, troubling changes to the earth and its living systems. Today a growing number of geologists believe we have left the Holocene and entered a new period—the Anthropocene—in which the dominant geologic force is humanity itself. What does this mean for music? What does it mean for my work as a composer, or for any artist working in any medium today?

These looming threats to the biosphere compel me to write music that is more than entertainment, more than a personal narrative or a celebration of the heroic struggle of the individual. But can music be engaged with current events and at the same time detached from them? Can music resonate with the world around us, and yet still create a world of its own?

* * *

When I was younger, I was a full-time environmental activist. In the 1970s and 1980s I worked for the Wilderness Society, the Alaska Coalition, and the Northern Alaska Environmental Center. The small role that I played in the passage of the Alaska National Interest Lands Conservation Act (the largest land preservation law in history) and in helping prevent destructive dams, highways, mining, and oil drilling in Alaska remains among the most satisfying experiences of my life.

But the time came when I realized that I had to choose between a life as an activist and a life as an artist. In that moment, I decided that someone else could take my place in politics; and no one could make the music I imagined but me. So I took a leap of faith, in the belief that music and art can matter every bit as much as activism and politics. And over the years, as climate change and other global environmental threats have accelerated, and as our political systems have become increasingly dysfunctional, I've come to believe that, fundamentally, art matters *more* than politics.

As a composer, I believe that music has the power to inspire a renewal of human consciousness, culture, and politics. And yet I refuse to make political art. More often than not, political art fails as politics, and all too often it fails as art. To reach its fullest power, to be most moving and most fully useful to us, art must be itself. If my work doesn't function powerfully as music, then all the poetic program notes and extra-musical justifications in the world mean nothing. When I'm true to the music, when I let the music be whatever it wants to be, then everything else—including any social or political meaning—will follow.

From the titles of my works—*songbirdsong, In the White Silence,* or *Become Ocean*—it's clear that I draw inspiration from the world around me. But when I enter my studio, I do so with the hope of leaving the world behind, at least for a while. Yet it's impossible to sustain that state of grace for long. Inevitably, thoughts intrude. Sometimes I think about people, places, and experiences in my life. Sometimes I think about the larger state of the world, and the uncertain future of humanity. Even so, I'm not interested in sending messages or telling stories with music. And although I used to paint musical landscapes, that no longer interests me either. The truth is, I'm no longer interested in making music *about* anything.

Though a piece may begin with a particular thought or image, as the music emerges it becomes a world of its own, independent of my extra-musical associations. In the end, those initial inspirations may remain, as a title or a program note—invitations to a listener to find their way into the music. However, the last thing I want is to limit the listener's imagination. If a listener feels constrained by any words I may offer along with the music, then I encourage her to ignore them. And few things make me happier than a listener who hears something, experiences something, discovers something in the music that the composer didn't know was there. It's only through the presence, awareness, and creative engagement of the listener that the music is complete.

My desire for greater freedom for discovery—by the listener, the performing musicians, and the composer—has led me into new musical territory. For much of my life, I've made music inspired by the outdoors—but it was almost always heard indoors. Several years ago it finally occurred to me that it might be time to compose music intended from the start to be heard outdoors. Making music outdoors invites a different mode of awareness. You might call it "ecological listening." In the concert hall, we seal ourselves off from the world and concentrate our listening on a handful of carefully produced sounds. Outdoors, rather than focusing our attention inward, we are challenged to expand our awareness to encompass a multiplicity of sounds, to listen *outward*. We're invited to receive messages not only from the composer and the performers, but also from the larger world around us.

In outdoor works like *Inuksuit*, the musicians are dispersed widely throughout a large, open area. There is no conductor. Every musician is a soloist. No two musicians play exactly the same part. And each musician follows his or her own unique path through the physical and musical landscape of the piece. The same is true for the listener. There is no best seat in the house. You may choose to root yourself in one location and let the music move around you. Or you may wander freely throughout the performance, following your ears, actively shaping your own experience, creating your own "mix" of the music. For me, this relationship between the music and the listener simulates a human society in which we all feel more deeply engaged with the world, and more empowered to help change it.

Making music outdoors has also led me to a new understanding of musical polyphony, as a community of voices, an ecosystem of sounds. In a performance outdoors, it's sometimes difficult to say exactly where the piece ends and the world takes over. Rather than a single point of interest, every point around the aural horizon is a potential point of interest, a call to listen.

With characteristically radical elegance, John Cage defined music as "sounds heard." The idea that music depends on sound and listening might seem as self-evident as the idea that we human animals are an inseparable part of nature. But both these simple truths challenge us to practice ecological awareness in our individual and our collective lives.

Cage's definition of harmony was "sounds heard together." Listening to the multiplicity of sounds all around us all the time, we learn to hear the marvelous harmony they create. Hearing this harmony, we come to understand the place of our human voices within it.

* * *

An Inuit hunter scanning the tundra for game will tell you that you learn the most by watching the edges. For most of my creative life, I've lived far removed from the centers of cosmopolitan culture. In Alaska I imagined I could work on the outer edge of culture, drawing my music more directly from the earth. Over four decades I listened for that music—in the mountains and on the tundra, on the shoulders of glaciers and the shore of the Arctic Ocean, and in the northern forest, learning the songs of the birds.

And now I stand here, on this beach by the Pacific, still listening, immersed in the music of the sea. At night, as my wife and I sleep, it flows into the deepest reaches of my consciousness. There are moments when it sounds as if the waves will come crashing through the open windows, and carry us away. And then it falls to a whisper, and startles me awake. In these sudden still moments, I'm filled with an exquisite mixture of tranquility and dread. In the morning, I rise and do my best to write down the music that I heard in my dreams.

As I listen, day after day and night after night, a new sound begins to take shape— vast and amorphous, deep and inexorable. My thoughts return often to the melting of the polar ice and the rising of the seas. I remember that all life on this earth first emerged from the sea. And I wonder if we humans as a species may once again return to the sea sooner than we imagine.

Yet, if you ask me if I'm composing a piece about climate change, I will tell you, "No. Not really."

Then is this music about the sea? "Yes. Well, in a way …" But what I really hope is that this music is an ocean of its own, an inexorable sea of sound that just may carry the listener away into an oceanic state of mind.

Geologists today are engaged in a lively debate about whether the Anthropocene qualifies as a legitimate geological epoch. Regardless of the outcome of that debate, we can no longer deny the reality that human impacts on the earth are unprecedented in our history. There are some who envision a "good" Anthropocene, in which we humans manage to save ourselves and minimize our impact on the earth through new technology. But blind faith in technology is part of what got us into this predicament. And we can't simply engineer our way out of it. Others contend that the very concept of the Anthropocene leads us to the inevitable conclusion that it's already too late for us to change anything. Maybe so. But I believe that even if it is too late to avert disaster, we have both an ethical and a biological imperative to try.

My work is not activism. It is art. As an artist, my primary responsibility must be to my art as art—and yet, it's impossible for me to regard my life as a composer as separate from my life as a thinking human being and a citizen of the earth. Our survival as a species depends on a fundamental change of our way of being in the world. If my music can inspire people to listen more deeply to this miraculous world we inhabit, then I will have done what I can as a composer to help us navigate this perilous era of our own creation.

For me, it all begins with listening.

(Reprinted with the author's permission, from *Slate*, February 24, 2014.)

4

On (re-)Hearing Kramer: Five Reactions to *Postmodern Music, Postmodern Listening*

John Halle

1. Introduction

The subject of Jonathan Kramer's posthumous manuscript *Postmodern Music, Postmodern Listening* (hereafter *PMPL*) was very much in the air in the Columbia music department in the early 1990s with several of his classes devoted to the subject. These were formative on the musical and intellectual development of those who enrolled in and/or attended them, Jonathan's teaching consistently reflecting his capacity for serious and rigorous inquiry, his willingness to consider all sides of a question, and his broad awareness of trends in aesthetic theory within as well as outside the boundaries of musical scholarship.

The combination of precision and comprehensiveness characteristic of Jonathan's work is evident here and well serves his approach to the subject, which is framed around an enumeration of what Jonathan proposed as sixteen traits of music "to be understood in a postmodern manner." All of these are exhaustively, albeit not entirely systematically, considered in subsequent chapters.

The list, Jonathan stresses, should not be seen as in any way definitive. Rather it is offered as a framework both for the text that followed, and, had Jonathan been able to complete it, for discussion among those who would have regarded it as their intellectual and artistic responsibility to engage with it.

In the following I will attempt to address some of these points, picking up the threads which, with the benefit of hindsight provided by later developments in musical scholarship, allow for some resolution. But for the most part it will be apparent from my discussion that the questions Jonathan posed remain open for musicians and audiences to grapple with.

In evaluating Jonathan's contributions, it is important to recognize that his reactions are those of an observer and also a participant. Jonathan was both a distinguished composer and theorist, evincing definite sympathies with the general movement whose outlines he is attempting to sketch. The responses to *PMPL* offered here will be similarly engaged, sometimes joining in strong agreement and at others sharply dissenting with Jonathan's perspective. Most often the relationship is contrapuntal, continuing the conversations that those of us then at Columbia will recall and often recognize (in the sides we chose) as definitive of our musical identities.

2. Postmodern Analysis and Postmodern Subjectivity

A good place to begin the dialogue is with what is perhaps the tenet most philosophically central to postmodernism and most revealing of Jonathan's artistic and intellectual commitments, namely, trait 16, which suggests that postmodernism "Locates meaning and even structure in listeners, more than in scores, performances or composers."

As will be apparent, this is not just an observation about postmodern music but rather a broad claim about how we should look at music of all types and all periods, from the most contemporary and radical to the most ancient and traditional. Among the latter is Schumann's piano piece *Soldier's March* whose inherent interest, as Jonathan demonstrates (7.9), is only visible from a perspective that maintains in focus the listener and the listener's subjectivity, placing these at the core of the analytic enterprise.

Example 1

Only within this perspective is it possible for Jonathan to observe what turns out to be a paradox: Schumann's notation of the piece in 2/4 meter as well as its title unproblematically characterize it as a march. And it begins on the beat, as marches sometimes do. But is it really a march and does it really begin on the beat, as shown in A? Perhaps, on the contrary, it should be experienced, in Jonathan's words, as a "deconstructed march" heard (despite the notation) as beginning with a two-note pickup, as indicated in B, thereby reversing the associated choreography. Jonathan's analysis does not attempt to demonstrate that this is necessarily the fact of the matter. Rather, his point is that the question can have no answer as the passage is inherently ambiguous, various cues in the music arguing for either structural interpretation. Thus, for example, the harmonies on the first beat of measure 2 can be heard as either contrapuntal dissonances resulting in a tonic prolongation, or as consonances in which case a harmonic change is heard at that location. If the latter, a metrical accent is more likely to be heard; if the former, it is likely to be suppressed. One might expect that a performer would be capable of disambiguating the two potential hearings, but, as Jonathan shows, even performances attempting to project a given structural assignment fail to do so, as listeners find it easy to maintain a metrical interpretation even in the face of attempts to thwart it. Given that either can be perceptually and theoretically supported, the listener projects a structure based on any number of factors which ultimately devolve to a projection of a personal preference.

Most crucially, Jonathan argues, no knowledge of Schumann's authorial intent can help us resolve these questions. While Schumann's choice of notation seems to indicate that the piece begins on the beat, with the meter and phrase structure in phase, this notational specification could be understood as ironic, with those failing to recognize the asymmetry between what is on the page and what is heard not getting the joke. Or perhaps the passage should be understood as simultaneously in phase or out of phase. Or possibly Schumann notated the passage to efface the attribution of any metrical structure at all. These mutually exclusive options require us to conclude, as Jonathan does (7.10), that "We can never know what, if anything, (Schumann) intended to communicate." How we experience the passage is up to us.

The further conclusion emerging from Jonathan's discussion of this piece is that all links in the communicative chain from composer to listener are implicated in the construction of a musical experience. To exclusively focus on the composer's role is to impoverish our relationship to music both artistically and intellectually. The recognition of the full richness of the network of relationships implicated in a musical transaction is a fundamental requirement of any serious analytic approach to musical form and/or musical meaning.

3. Questioning Authorial Intention/Questioning Authority

Jonathan characterizes the listener's exercise of perceptual subjectivity as postmodern in a specific sense, namely, as a reaction to certain fundamental tenets of modernism. As he notes, modernism, both as a creative and analytical practice, tends to orient itself around either highly unified or organically structured compositions in which "the parts are related not only to the whole but to each other" (5.3). The sometimes oblique codes by which these are communicated are assumed to be immanent in music worthy of serious analytical scrutiny. Within this modernist paradigm is a clear division of labor: the *composer's* role is to create scores of sufficient formal complexity such that they sustain analytical engagement; the *theorist* deciphers the encoded forms in which these structures appear; while the *performer's* (significantly degraded) function is to represent the composer's intentions through faithfully realizing the increasingly detailed specifications of the score. Finally, at the end of this communicative chain, the *listener* is expected to adopt listening strategies necessary to come to terms with the encoded forms.

The postmodernist claim that structure is projected onto the musical surface by the listener fundamentally challenges this quadripartite consensus, as well as, perhaps more significantly, the underlying institutional hierarchy which it supports. Insofar as listeners perform a role in the creation of the musical experience, they are sharing in the creation of the musical experience, thereby questioning the exclusive authorial status of the composer. Secondly, musical masterpieces are seen within postmodernism through the lens of their rhetorical and/or expressive content, their meaning or meanings continually in flux with the author's intended meaning being seen as unknowable or at least problematic. Postmodern analysis itself is thereby committed to challenging the sacrosanct status traditionally accorded to the text and the role of the composer/author as creator.

Jonathan discusses the historical background of these attitudes, connecting them to Roland Barthes's highly influential "Death of the Author" thesis of the 1970s, though it should be noted that Barthes's essay was published in France in the iconic year 1968. The date is significant in that for some of its initial adherents, postmodernism was highly politicized, with Barthes's followers regarding the undermining of "the author as God" as not just an artistic preference but a political necessity. One current represented by the Situationist International promulgated in works by Guy Debord would take the form of a rejection of all forms of authority, whether the dictatorships of the Eastern bloc (then a dominant influence on the traditional European left), as well as the then slightly less institutionally rigid structures of European welfare state capitalism (McDonough 2002).

It is in this context that we should understand trait 15: that postmodernism "considers music not as autonomous but as a commodity responsive to cultural, social, economic, and political contexts." This position can be seen as a politicized response to what were perceived as exercises in modernism's "art for art's sake" self-indulgences, some of which found their justification in Boulez's claim, cited by Jonathan, that "there are musics … whose very concept has nothing to do with profit." Jonathan correctly describes these as "idealistic and a trifle naïve" (p. 309). More problematic were modernist composers who "took refuge in (modernism's) unmarketability as a badge of purity and even of significance." At an extreme, high modernist exercises would be viewed by left critics as the musical analogue of inscrutable diktats emanating from unaccountable elites.

Within this group was the Maoist Cornelius Cardew, whose manifesto "Stockhausen Serves Imperialism" (1974) would portray high modernism as defined by its failure to accept its responsibility to meaningfully contribute to the objective quality of life of the workers who provide the ultimate material foundation for artists' privileges. Rather, modernism was, according to this analysis, at base, a form of elite control, reducing the audience to passive obedience rather than functioning to liberate them from capitalist exploitation. Other postmodern works were based on different but equally radical orientations. Some would adopt the political valence and artistic intentions of radical theater projects such as the Artaud's Theater of Cruelty, the San Francisco Mime Troupe, and the Living Theater. Works inspired by this tradition include Terry Riley's *In C*, Rzewski's *Les Moutons de Panurge*, and Andriessen's *Workers Union*, all of which required performers to assume an improvisatory role, while at times breaking the fourth wall in encouraging the audience's creative participation in the artistic spectacle. Considered as a group these give a good indication of the inherent ultra-radical rejectionism of what might be called first-wave postmodernism.

***

This tendency quickly dissipated during the 1980 and 1990s, with postmodernism relatively quickly losing its counter-cultural edge. Within this increasingly depoliti-cized context, the disciplinary function of markets would play a significant role in undermining the authority not just of modernists but of all of those incapable of adapting to an increasingly Darwinian aesthetic economy. In what would become an unshakeable conventional wisdom, artists were encouraged to view their work "as a commodity," as it is referred to in trait 15. Reflecting a dominant tendency at the time, Jonathan criticizes "modernist thinking [for failing to provide] instruction for students on how to market their musical skills: how to get jobs, how to win auditions, how to build performing careers, how to win competitions, how to get commissions, how to interest performers in playing their compositions" (10.3). Furthermore, postmodernism's influence in the academy had, according to Jonathan, resulted in the widespread perception that "art and its marketing are inextricably interwoven ... Musical academics are finally coming to realize the inevitability of the commodification of the musical art, particularly in a society like that in the United States."

Jonathan was, no doubt, correct that art had become commodified and was quickly becoming more so. But his view that commodification was "inevitable" will strike many as an overly passive acceptance of Margaret Thatcher's TINA doctrine asserting that "there is no alternative" to accepting the invisible hand of markets as the organ-izing force of all aspects of society. The consequence for the musical community has been the increasing prestige of those forms of music specifically oriented towards competing effectively within the marketplace. As this has occurred, generally accepted, if not sacrosanct, barriers separating "high" from "commercial" musical culture have become regarded as unsustainable.

Within musical scholarship this tendency would find expression as the New Musicology which celebrated "a radical decentering" of the traditional canon such that work taken as central within *PMPL* would be viewed as only "one style among many and by no means the most prestigious" (Fink 1998). It is in this form that a variant of musical postmodernism has itself become as academically institutionalized as was modernism a generation prior. The difference is that its grip is arguably tighter, as its explicit endorsement of market aesthetics complements, rather than contradicts, neo-liberal capitalist economic and political orthodoxies (see Halle 2014).

This is not to suggest that Jonathan was altogether comfortable with the increasing hegemony of market fundamentalism and its influence. He protests the "diminishing of government funding" and criticizes the "scandal of governments not recognizing the power and value of the arts," accepting that "composers who complain about [this] are indeed right to object" (10.4). It is, however, disappointing that his grounds for doing so remain within market-oriented parameters, specifically referencing the "politician's short-sighted[ness]" in failing to "recognize that the arts are a big business." The view that the arts benefit from their encounters with market competition avoids the fact that the works forming the musical frame of reference assumed in *PMPL* were almost exclusively insulated from market forces, usually by some form of ecclesiastical, feudal, state, or foundation patronage. In the two decades since, the recognition of what a recent mass market book has referred to as a "Culture Crash" (Timberg 2015), induced by hegemonic dominance of markets and market ideologies, has become an increasing concern. One would like to think that Jonathan would have been on the front lines of the reaction to neoliberal austerity, though this would have required a more skeptical view of what were then dominant political and economic tendencies than is advocated in *PMPL*.

4. Cognitivism vs. Postmodernism

The postmodern view identified in trait 16 conferring determinative status to the listener in the chain of communication was surely a distinctive feature of postmodernist approaches to musical scholarship, one which can be reasonably viewed as reactive to modernism. It was, however, not unique in this respect, as those of us who were then at Columbia were well aware. At roughly the same time, in a series of articles and books, theorist and composer Fred Lerdahl along with linguist Ray Jackendoff advanced a cognitivist approach towards musical analysis which can be usefully compared with certain tenets of postmodernism as Jonathan represents them while at the same time also functioning as an independent critique of certain assumptions of modernism.

With respect to the central claim embodied in trait 16, the best known of Lerdahl and Jackendoff's works, the *Generative Theory of Tonal Music* (hereafter *GTTM*), stakes out what is a more radical position in that it uniquely privileges the structure which listeners, including the composer as listener, project onto that which they hear, taking the "intuitions of experienced listeners fluent within a musical idiom" to be the core empirical domain to be explained within theoretical analyses. Furthermore, Lerdahl goes beyond postmodernism in locating not just relevant aspects of musical structure in the psychological realm but its inherent aesthetic quality. This position is advanced in Lerdahl's essay "Cognitive Constraints on Compositional Systems" (1988), which itemizes a series of empirically supported perceptual principles. These are subsequently taken as a foundation for three fundamental aesthetic claims, including, most significantly for our purposes, the claim that the best "music utilizes the maximum range of our cognitive capacities."

Various consequences follow from this view, some consistent with postmodernism as construed by Jonathan, others sharply conflicting with it. In the former category is the conclusion deriving from the necessary recognition that, when viewed from the standpoint of cognitive science, no musical system is trivial. All of them pose cognitive challenges to listeners who, whether they are consciously aware of it, are required to devote substantial perceptual resources to even minimally organize the sounds they hear. While Western music can be shown to manifest a high degree of composed-in structural complexity (see, e.g., Bregman 1990), this turns out to be deceptive: all musical traditions—from the most prestigious to the debased—for all effective analytical purposes (see, e.g., Serafine 1988, Chapter 3) make significant "use of our cognitive capacities." It therefore follows that the cognitive perspective assumed by Lerdahl and others necessarily entails "question[ing] the mutual exclusivity of elitist and populist values" as is specified in trait 5.

Similarly, cognitivists will have no objection to music which "encompasses pluralism and eclecticism," in contrast to the narrow conception of modernists who "often sought to cast their music as having a sense of purity" (10.1), sometimes almost obsessively so, as Jonathan discusses in Chapter 10. Indeed, pluralism and eclecticism, insofar as they require a range of listening strategies to be deployed, might be viewed as more or less equivalent to multilingual discourses and thereby require a greater rather than lesser exercise of cognitive capacities which Lerdahl takes as aesthetically central.

***

A second point of commonality consists in both Lerdahl and Jonathan implicating what might be described as a neo-Empsonian (Empson 1966) position on the locus of cognitive complexity. That is, each focuses on ambiguous structures, using musical analysis to formally define the nature of the competing structures which listeners are required to perceptually resolve. Jonathan's analysis of Schumann's *Soldier's March* mentioned above is entirely consistent with *GTTM*'s approach, denoting the two potential hearings by virtue of the listener's choice to apply principles of harmonic stability, embodied in *GTTM* Metrical Preference Rule 9, or Strong Beat Early (Metrical Preference Rule 2).

Resting on the foundation of this common ground, however, is a fundamental difference in intention of the two theoretical frameworks. For Lerdahl, ambiguity can be seen as an end in itself, its role defined within what is ultimately a modernist aesthetic celebrating the non-referential purity of artistic experience. Ambiguous forms have inherent, as opposed to referential, interest, engaging our innate capacity to solve puzzles, uncover hidden structure, and our taking delight in doing so. For Jonathan, and postmodernism generally, ambiguity is a means to a broader communicative end, one taking for granted the necessity of semantic referentiality, as opposed to the autonomous syntax of musical form. How we as listeners prefer to understand and deploy this meaning of _Soldier's March_ or other works is, of course, up to us, for example poking fun at the grandiose pretentions of a highly militarized Prussian state, or maybe at General Wieck, Schumann's famously disapproving father-in-law, or we could interpret it as merely pictorial, as suggesting a dreamlike image of marching, or as toy soldiers frozen in time. Again, as Kramer insists, there are no answers to these questions, only discussions about them to be had. Structural ambiguities are a means not to provide answers but to provoke investigations into possible meanings, to encourage a deeper inquiry about particular meanings or maybe even into the nature of musical meaning itself.

***

The privileging of referentiality and encoded meanings at the expense of the austere formal complexities of modernism was, as Jonathan demonstrates, a recurrent theme of musical postmodernism and in the other arts as well, this shift in orientation nicely captured in a remark by the painter Philip Guston to his erstwhile friend composer Morton Feldman that he had become "sick and tired of all that purity! I wanted to tell stories!" (Berkson 1971). Among the "stories" which could now be told were those of "many traditions and cultures" (trait 6) as "barriers between high and low styles" were "challenged" (trait 4), resulting in the incorporation of "pluralism and eclecticism" (trait 7) in numerous postmodern works. As such, postmodernism would serve as the vehicle for multiculturalist tendencies which would become dominant in popular culture as well as in musical scholarship and across the board in academic disciplines.

Other stories told by postmodernism were inherently more problematic and challenging in comparison to what would become rather bland multiculturalist aesthetic orthodoxies. Among these is trait 2, which observes that much of what went under the banner of postmodernism was "on some level and in some way, ironic." The equation of postmodernism with ironic detachment is familiar enough by now, though its basis in an underlying cultural critique, as David Foster Wallace observes in the following (quoted in Burn 2011), is not always sufficiently recognized.

> Irony and cynicism were just what the U.S. hypocrisy of the fifties and sixties called for. That's what made the early postmodernists great artists. The great thing about irony is that it splits things apart, gets up above them so we can see the flaws and hypocrisies and duplicates. The virtuous always triumph? Ward Cleaver is the prototypical fifties father? "Sure." Sarcasm, parody, absurdism and irony are great ways to strip off stuff's mask and show the unpleasant reality behind it.

"Intertextual" works such as Michael Daugherty's *Dead Elvis*, Michael Torke's *Yellow Pages*, John Zorn's *Spillane*, and John Adams's *Grand Pianola Music* were attempts to embody in musical form the critical sensibility of postmodernism Wallace refers to. Their relevance to the discussion here resides in the perspective they provide on Lerdahl's aesthetic claims. The more a composer is focused on achieving expressive ends, in this case a cultural critique, a complex structural syntax is no longer an end in itself, as Lerdahl suggests it can be and likely is for certain composers. Indeed, it is often best achieved by the crudest and most unsophisticated statements, hence Jonathan's recognition in trait 4 that these assumptions "sometimes result in music that can be considered of questionable taste." Rather, as Jonathan notes, given that "if you take away the quotations and references, you take away the whole piece" (1.2), the impact of these works derives largely from the semantic realm—whether the juxtaposition of the pop culture and other references seems convincing, whether they convey the appropriate critical resonance with particular audiences or appear otherwise well targeted in juxtaposition or independently.

***

Similar albeit more complex issues having to do with the connection between communicative form and expressive content are provoked by trait 10, which suggests that postmodern works "include fragmentations, incongruities, discontinuities, and indeterminacy." These become the expected norm rather than the exception in postmodernism, Jonathan suggests, most notably in the works of John Zorn, which are extensively discussed in *PMPL* (e.g. 4.2). Again, within these analyses, a question is raised as to whether Jonathan is referring to the syntactic form or semantic content of Zorn's work; how we are to understand Jonathan's position depends on what turns out to be the answer.

As a discursive topic, it should be recognized that none of the characteristics Jonathan cites in Zorn's music is particularly novel or at all unique to postmodernism. To take a few examples, the depiction of incongruity is a conspicuous characteristic of Beethoven scherzos and occurs elsewhere in his works, perhaps most famously in the "horribly false" (in the words of Beethoven's friend Ferdinand Ries) horn solo concluding the exposition of the first movement of the *Eroica* symphony. The stochastic vacuum of an earth "without form" was, of course, what Haydn represents within the introduction to the *Creation*. The mad scene from Handel's *Orlando* evokes the hero's addled hallucinations conveyed by Handel's use of the then strange and unusual 5/4 meter.

That does not, of course, imply that the objective structure of the music itself embodies the characteristics of the states it is depicting. As discussed by Meyer (1956), Kivy (1990), Nattiez (1991), and others, Saussurian dictates with respect to the arbitrary relationship of sign and signifier apply to music (while not perhaps to the same degree that it does in language). Although it depicts the random chaos of a formless void, the introduction to the *Creation* is not Cage's *Winter Music* or Brown's *Available Forms*: it is a conventionally notated composition with no indeterminate or even improvisatory elements of any kind. As for the discontinuities referenced by Jonathan in relation to Zorn's music, virtually all music, not just music that is attempting to communicate the fragmentary and discontinuous nature of our experience of the world, contains them. In particular, the grouping preference rules of *GTTM* assume—and empirical research has subsequently demonstrated (Frankland and Cohen 2004)—that the parsing of the musical surface into discrete units necessarily implies discontinuities in pitch, timing, dynamics, or other musical parameters.

Rather, the aesthetic question potentially applicable to all music of all periods is whether and to what degree these discontinuities defeat the listener's capacity to assign what Lerdahl refers to in "Cognitive Constraints on Compositional Systems" as "a detailed representation". That they can do so is the basis of Lerdahl's claim with respect to the "cognitive opacity" of serialism as it is deployed in Boulez's *Le Marteau sans Maître*, the subjective experience of which Lerdahl describes as "Vast numbers of nonredundant events go[ing] by [while] the effect is of a vast sheen of pretty sounds … where a listener cannot even tell if wrong pitches or rhythms have been played." One would not describe a postmodern work like John Zorn's *Forbidden Fruit* in these terms, of course, though Jonathan's description of those listening to *Forbidden Fruit* as "never know[ing] what is coming next or when" (4.2) suggests an important family resemblance. The connection lies in our inability to predict the details of musical structure, defeated by our inability to parse the music into discrete units.

Insofar as that's the case, the absence of an audible syntax, the fragmentations, incongruities, and discontinuities, serves not to help us mentally organize what we experience but to pre-empt our capacity to do so. Deploying them in such a fashion is, it should be stressed, in no way aesthetically meaningless or expressively neutral. On the contrary, a composer doing so is engaging in a strongly communicative act. As is the case in language, disordered syntax expresses a highly specific state of mind, ranging from temporary mental stress to dementia or even psychosis. And while these are clinical diagnoses, that they are indicative of an underlying pathology has been understood by audiences going back to those of Shakespeare who recognized Ophelia's fractured utterances as "Divided from herself and her fair judgment, / Without the which we are pictures, or mere beasts." A similar emotional resonance is understood within the manic, addled, disconnectedness of *Forbidden Fruit*, reasonably seen as the musical analog to the disorientation associated with the dystopian strain of postmodernism displayed in films such as Ridley Scott's *Blade Runner*, Terry Gilliam's *Brazil*, and in the fiction of William Gibson and Mark Leyner.

That said, an aesthetic contradiction arises when an aural syntax is required to convey meanings of a fundamentally different sort than those at the core of these and other variants of postmodernism. It is here that Lerdahl's term "cognitively opaque" can legitimately be advanced as an aesthetic critique of modernism. This is not so much based on its cognitive opacity *per se*, but in its attempts to make use of an inaccessible syntax to convey states of mind and emotional valences beyond the limited range it is able to convey. The postmodern embrace of apocalypticism is arguably more consistent with the fractured, discontinuous surfaces characteristic of both modernism and variants of postmodernism. Insofar as modernist composers, most conspicuously Schoenberg and Berg, were defined to a degree by a nostalgic longing for the past, the semantic content and syntactic form are in conflict, as Boulez infamously noted in his essay "Schoenberg is Dead" (1951), though it would seem unlikely that Boulez would view postmodernism as having successfully achieved a reconciliation of form and content.

It is for these reasons, among others, that Jonathan is correct in viewing postmodernism as "not simply a repudiation of modernism or its continuation, but [as having] aspects of both: a break and an extension."

5. Cognitivist vs. (post-)Modernist Organicism

As those familiar with the work are aware, the invocation of the technical terms *syntax* and *semantics* by Lerdahl is indicative of the grounding of *GTTM* in linguistics, specifically, the X-bar variant of syntactic theory which was a major component of the Government and Binding paradigm of the 1980s. As those familiar with *GTTM* are aware, the connection is more than terminological in that it proposes applying a variant of the X-bar formalism employed by linguistics to represent the hierarchical

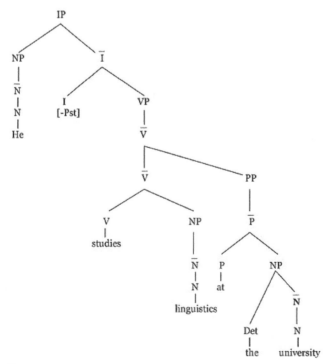

Example 2

structure of linguistic expressions to musical form. An X-bar tree applied to a simple sentence is shown below.

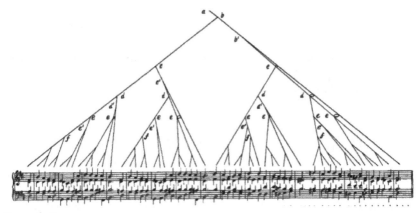

Example 3

Musical realizations of the tree proposed in *GTTM* take two forms: the time span

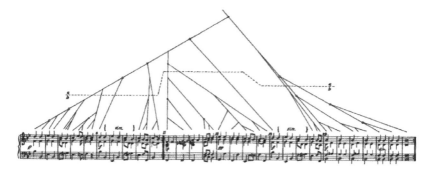

Example 4

reduction tree, here applied to the Bach chorale ...
... and the prolongational tree:
Evaluating the various forms and interpretation of tree structures which have been proposed is beyond the scope of the discussion here (see, most recently, Rohrmeier 2011). What's worth noting is that while the connection is not explicitly made in *GTTM*, the choice of the tree, an iconic if not *the* iconic organic form, places *GTTM* squarely within the organicist meta-narrative, the rejection of which Jonathan argues to be at the core of postmodernism. As for the organicist meta-narrative itself, Jonathan situates the roots of this within the German idealist tradition, and charts its trajectory through Schenker, though he omits what was the seminal inspiration for organicism, namely Goethe's studies of the morphology of living forms, most notably

his "Versuch die Metamorphose der Pflanzen zu erklären" (On the Metamorphosis of Plants) (Goethe 1790; 1991). In a series of letters to Charlotte von Stein, Goethe discusses his findings, referencing his "grow[ing] awareness of the essential form with which, as it were, Nature always plays, and from which she produces her great variety ... extend[ing] ... to all the realms of Nature—the whole realm" (Goethe 1787; 1957). The view of organic form as constituting "the whole realm" of living experience, as Jonathan notes, was at least intuitively if not consciously grasped by composers of Goethe's age, as analyses of their works by nineteenth- and twentieth-century music theorists would systematically demonstrate. This analytical work itself also had roots in Goethe's morphology, most notably that of Schenker, as John Neubeuer (2009) observes, whose "concepts of *Urlinie* and *Ursatz* [are] surely indebted to Goethe's *Urpflanze*—or rather 20th century reinterpretations of it."

It should be stressed that the *urpflanze* would turn out to be highly fruitful as a heuristic postulate for stimulating thought not only with respect to the underlying form of musical compositions but, in the works of Alexander Humboldt (see Stubb 2002), that of the deep structure of language. But given that Goethe and his successors could only speculate as to the nature of the mechanisms by which these forms would be instantiated within biological systems, it should ultimately be seen as a metaphor by which we understand reality rather than a theoretical hypothesis of the nature of biological phenomena or our brain's construction of music and language. Indeed, it would only be after the discovery of the DNA molecule and, more significantly, relatively recent advances in the field of evolutionary development that Goethe's suggestions could be formulated in precise scientific terms. In the absence of any medium through which it could be instantiated, the organicist meta-narrative as understood by Goethe and his successors is best understood as closer to a metaphysical construct rather than a biological or psychological theory.

It is in this respect that the tree structures of linguistic theory differ in their intention and function. Rather than serving as metaphors, they are, as Chomsky (2000) refers to them, "natural objects," implemented in a biological form as a cognitive faculty within our brains. The hierarchical relationships represented within them are psychologically real, just as much so as the physical properties of substances represented by familiar atomic models appealed to by chemists are taken as physically real by them. And while it is as yet unclear how the trees and the higher-level theories of computational structure which give rise to them are to be reconciled with our understanding of the neurological structures in which they are instantiated, that is no more the basis for rejecting them as it was the Newtonian theory of gravity which similarly referenced "occult" properties of action at a distance inherent in matter.

In this sense, "organic form" as it is instantiated within linguistic trees is a representation of a fundamental property of human brains just as gravitation, as represented in Newton's law, is an expression of a fundamental property of matter. According to this logic, the various attempts to "transcend" linguistic organicism simply means one is not speaking a human language, just as "transcending" gravitation means one is, quite literally, not living in the real world. It is, of course, tempting to extend this analogy to music, taking organic form as definitive of what music is, or at least should be. One must be very careful in doing so, however. As Jonathan notes, among those with inclinations along these lines are "conservative postmodernists" (3.2) on record as viewing with suspicion any attempts to "transcend" highly ordered formal and pitch relationships characteristic of common practice period organicism. And while they share very little common ground, modernist composers, as Jonathan documents in detail, were equally obsessed with organic form and followed Schoenberg in insisting on it as a characteristic of transcendent masterpieces.

But unlike language, it is by no means obvious that achieving even a weak form of organic unity is a sufficient or even necessary condition for music that is experienced as socially meaningful, emotionally fulfilling, and aesthetically engaging. Indeed, if Jonathan's analyses are correct (and those of us who were introduced to them in his classes will likely confirm that they are), widely admired works such as Nielsen's Sixth and Mahler Seventh not only lack organic unity, but directly repudiate and resist it. Furthermore, even if it were true that "music" as conventionally defined needs to embody aspects of organic form, as a strict cognitivist interpretation would require, many musicians would be perfectly happy to dispense with the definition. It was on this basis that figures such as futurist composer Luigi Rossolo, Pauline Oliveros, and the Fluxus School have self-identified as "sound artists" and not musicians. Their work, as they saw it, was problematically subsumed within traditional definitions as to what music was, is, or should be. Cognitivist analyses might offer some guidance for how some music is experienced now and has been in the more or less recent past. But it does not follow that the music of the future will engage our minds, brains, and bodies in anything like the same way, or that musical experience should be reducible to a predetermined set of psychological reactions.

6. Conclusion

All of the above should give an indication of the lines of discussion which might have developed had *PMPL* appeared a decade or so ago, as many of us were expecting. Of course, we will never know how Jonathan would engage my questions and those of others, though we can be sure that his responses would be informed, detailed, cogent, and quite possibly trenchant. It is an indication of both the breadth, rigor, and the continuing influence of his work that an uncompleted work of his from more than a decade ago not only provides many answers, but also allows us to formulate questions of a sort which point the way towards many possible musical futures. While only some of the possibilities Jonathan discussed have taken shape in the years since, it is a safe bet that Jonathan's work will continue to provoke the engagement of those passionately invested in music who will realize in musical form the answers to many of the questions he poses. To continue our discussions and arguments with him in music and in words would seem to be the most appropriate recognition of his legacy in these and many other respects.

References

Berkson, Bill, "The New Gustons," *Art News* 69/6 (1970): 44–7

Boulez, Pierre, "Schoenberg is Dead," in Piero Weiss and Richard Taruskin (eds.), *Music in the Western World: A History in Documents* (New York: Schirmer Books, 1952)

Bregman, Albert, *Auditory Scene Analysis: The Perceptual Organization of Sound* (Cambridge, MA: Bradford Books, MIT Press, 1990)

Burn, Stephen J., *Conversations with David Foster Wallace* (Jackson: University of Mississippi Press, 2012)

Cardew, Cornelius, *Stockhausen Serves Imperialism* (London: Latimer New Dimensions, 1974)

Chomsky, Noam, *New Horizons in the Study of Language and Mind* (Cambridge: Cambridge University Press, 2000)

Empson, William, *Seven Types of Ambiguity* (New York: New Directions Publishing Corporation, 1966)

Fink, Robert, "Elvis Everywhere: Musicology and Popular Music Studies at the Twilight of the Canon," *American Music* 16/2 (Summer 1998): 135–79

Frankland, Bradley and Cohen, Annalee, "Parsing of melody: Quantification and testing of the local grouping rules of Lerdahl and Jackendoff's *A Generative Theory of Tonal Music*," *Music Perception* 21 (2004): 499–543

Goethe, Johan Wolfgang von, letter to Charlotte von Stein (June 8, 1787), in M. von Herzfeld and C. Melvil Sym, *Goethe's World As Seen in Letters and Memoirs* (Edinburgh: Edinburgh University Press, 1957)

Goethe, Johan Wolfgang von, "The Metamorphosis of Plants" (1790), trans. Douglas Miller, in *Goethe: The Collected Works 12 (Scientific Studies)* (Princeton, NJ: Princeton University Press, 1991)

Halle, John, "Pop Triumphalism Redux, Neoliberal Aesthetics, and the Austerity Agenda: A Response to Robert Fink" (2014), *Musicology Now*, http://musicologynow.ams-net. org/2014/03/pop-triumphalism-redux-neoliberal.html

Hindemith, Paul, *The Craft of Musical Composition* (Melville, NY: Belwin-Mills, 1942)

Kivy, Peter, *Music Alone, Philosophical Reflections on the Purely Musical Experience* (Ithaca, NY and London: Cornell University Press, 1990)

Lerdahl, Fred and Jackendoff, Ray, *A Generative Theory of Tonal Music* (Cambridge, MA: MIT Press, 1983)

Lerdahl, Fred, "Cognitive Constraints on Compositional Systems," in J. Sloboda (ed.), *Generative Processes in Music* (Oxford: Oxford University Press, 1988)

McDonough, Tom, *Guy Debord and the Situationist International* (Cambridge, MA: MIT Press, 2002)

Meyer, Leonard, *Emotion and Meaning in Music* (Chicago: University of Chicago Press, 1956)

Nattiez, Jean-Jacques, *Music and Discourse: Towards a Semiology of Music*, trans. Carolyn Abbate (Princeton, NJ: Princeton University Press, 1991)

Neubauer, John, "Organicism and Music Theory," in Darla Crispin (ed.), *New Paths: Aspects of Music Theory and Aesthetics in the Age of Romanticism* (Leuven: Leuven University Press, 2009)

Rohrmeier, Martin, "Towards a generative syntax of tonal harmony," *Journal of Mathematics and Music* 5/1 (2011): 35–53

Serafine, Mary Louise, *Music as Cognition: The Development of Thought in Sound* (New York: Columbia University Press, 1988)

Stubb, Elsina, *Wilhelm Von Humboldt's Philosophy of Language, Its Sources and Influence* (Richardson, NY: Edwin Mellen Press, 2002)

Timberg, Scott, *Culture Crash: The Killing of the Creative Class* (New Haven, CT: Yale University Press, 2015)

5

Uncommon Kindness: Reflections on Jonathan Kramer

Duncan Neilson

To take the fragments of beauty that one knows, and arrange them in a way that one sees fit—that is the goal, it seems to me, of music exploration and composition in any era. How this plays out with each composer—Shostakovich laboring under stylistic restrictions in Stalinist Russia, Will Marion Cook battling racial prejudice in the United States, Schoenberg exploring an increasingly atonal language in a hostile Viennese concert climate, to name just a few—marks the opportunities (or lack thereof) with each respective composer in each time period. Presently we are well into an Information Age—a dazzling, unparalleled explosion of music, information, and technology that can spread this information. With simple access to a local library, a home computer or handheld phone, one has unprecedented access to a vast array of recordings, music notation, music criticism, and musical ideas—a diversity that would have astounded composers at the dawn of the twentieth century, let alone those trying to comprehend it now in 2015. How does one even begin to navigate this era of dizzying stylistic complexity? How does one police the stylistic boundaries—or is it even worth it? A person who welcomed the challenge, in my experience, was Jonathan Kramer. He navigated the stylistic riptides, undertows, and crosscurrents of the late twentieth century and early twenty-first century, as well as its graceful swells, and occasional calm seas, with refreshing courage, wit, and a quality that he exhibited time and again: uncommon kindness.

Looking back on my years of studying with Jonathan Kramer (1996 to 2003 at Columbia University), I am reminded of this trait of uncommon kindness. *Uncommon* because at the twilight of a century filled with extraordinary stylistic turf battles and squabble, Jonathan took time to genuinely explore each person's unique point of view. *Kindness* because Jonathan would routinely withhold taking sides— he refrained from value judgments about one style being more important than another, and routinely had informed opinions and kind words about other composers and their works. This struck me as refreshing (one grew used to hearing composers savage each other's works— it just seemed to go with the territory). What I learned over time was that Jonathan was engaged in a deeply thoughtful, ongoing game of perception. *He was genuinely interested in how different people perceived music.* This brought profound intellectual and emotional depth to the concepts of musical time, musical surrealism, and musical postmodernism that he explored over his career.

Chief within Jonathan's teaching ethos, in my experience, was his attitude of musical tolerance. He states in *Postmodern Music Postmodern Listening*:

> ... it is inappropriate to see postmodernism as replacing modernism. Both exist today, along with antimodernism and various other "isms." I continually encourage tolerance—listening with pleasure, respect, and insight to many kinds of music.[1]

This seemed straightforward to me, at least at first. Listening and composing, to me, was akin to being a kid in the candy store ... so many musical flavors ... and I wanted to try them all. It was exciting, with records, tapes, CDs, films, television, various piano and orchestral scores, to immerse in a huge diversity of sounds. Throughout my undergrad and Master's years, I worked at record stores. I was happy to be the guy who could freely travel between the classical, jazz, world, and rock sections—always knowing that my manager had an eye on the bottom line—but I also genuinely wanted to broaden people's horizons. For a person who didn't like modern classical: "Tried the Sibelius 5th? Copland? Prokofiev *Kije*? Steve Reich?" For a customer who couldn't stand the growing influence of electronica: "Tried Björk? Maybe Portishead?" For a customer who never listened to rock beyond King Crimson: "Tried Tortoise? Radiohead? Or Stereolab?" Or maybe something slightly more experimental: "Ligeti's Piano Concerto? Ornette Coleman?" So on and so forth ... Intriguing, too, was seeing how older works of music were being reinterpreted in the ever-growing media age—instances where Stravinsky or Holst might be quoted in a sci-fi, or Penderecki in a thriller. Or listening to the radio and hearing how Motown, funk, or Kraftwerk samples were appropriated in hip-hop music. Or seeing John Zorn's Naked City perform compositions such as *Speed Freaks*, which boasted thirty styles of music in forty seconds. It was all some beautiful game ... I loved it.

I was thoroughly impressed, though, studying with Jonathan Kramer: he had an encyclopedic mind, and he *really* practiced musical tolerance. He further opened musical areas into which I had previously delved, but had not thoroughly explored, helping me to understand Cage much more deeply, or certain twelve-tone composers, and even sounds from the natural world (a story to be relayed at end of this essay). And it is quite common among composers to *dis* each other, even a friendly *dis* ... But Jonathan just didn't do this—not in my presence anyway. I found that he really took time to look deeply into the workings of musical style, and find something positive there. Engaged in a game of perception, he did his best to view each composer and their works *on their terms*. How are *they* conceiving their work? What are the parameters that qualify as a success in *this particular work*, according to the aims of *this particular composer*? This was refreshing in my experience. It was uncommon. It was kind.

And whatever happened to musical kindness? We can read about its opposite in Slonimsky's *Lexicon of Musical Invective*. Alex Ross notes that "Slonimsky should

[1] Jonathan Kramer, *Postmodern Music, Postmodern Listening*, 10.3.

also have written a *Lexicon of Musical Condescension*, gathering high-minded essays in which now canonical masterpieces were dismissed as kitsch, with a long section reserved for Sibelius."[2] Among composers in the twentieth century it often seemed that part of the craft was to develop a hard stylistic exoskeleton, as well as various stylistic claws, barbs, and sharp appendages, and step right into the ring, swinging away. The musical styles being advanced in this way might seem dizzying in diversity, at least on the surface, but what united them was a confrontational attitude. And certainly, can't the variety of music in the Western world be explained by strong stylistic opposition, conflict, and tension, which then led to subsequent musical revolution, counter-revolution, and invention? Isn't this absolutely *essential* to the field? Maybe so ...

Jonathan identified a trend at the heart of a stylistic ethos known for strong conflict and renunciation—the modernist avant garde with notions of historical progress:

The situation for modernists was and is œdipal: they are in conflict with their antecedents, whom they reinterpret in order to possess, shape, and control their legacy. Modernists sought to displace the major figures in their past, because they were in competition with them despite their owing their very (artistic) existence to them.[3]

Jonathan also noted that the confrontational attitude seemed to relax to some degree in postmodernism:

Postmodernists, however, are more like adolescents than like children: they have passed beyond their œdipal conflicts with their modernist parents, although they may still have an uneasy relationship with them (thus, postmodernists may accept historical succession even while rejecting the idea of progress).[4]

Though Jonathan came to identify himself as a musical postmodernist, as well as a musical surrealist, what impressed me was that he was not doctrinaire about it. There was no messianic need to convert others to his system of thinking. He was already engaged in a deeply satisfying game of perception. He knew that there was a huge range of musical perception among composers, performers, students, listeners—and I saw no finger-wagging from him, or need to correct others in how they might be properly or improperly perceiving music.

Once, as Jonathan's student, to play devil's advocate I pointed out that postmodernism, specifically musical postmodernism, was not always received kindly. I had witnessed plenty of hostile reactions to postmodernism—in conversations, at concerts, in print. Even hostile reactions to Jonathan's music, which struck me as bizarre. (I find Jonathan's *Moving Music, Atlanta Licks*, and *Surreality Check* to be particularly beautiful.) When I raised questions about these hostile observations with Jonathan, he didn't take any of this personally. Instead, with a characteristic twinkle in his eye, he might discuss a certain perceptual frame to explain where a person was coming

---

[2] Alex Ross, *The Rest is Noise* (New York: Farrar, Straus and Giroux, 2007), p. 175.
[3] Kramer, *Postmodern Music, Postmodern Listening*, 1.5.
[4] Ibid.

from—and that would be why postmodernism seemed upsetting from that person's perspective. And if I mentioned that somebody might be connecting postmodernism with him personally (and by extent, perhaps wishing hostility toward him), he would smile and say, "They don't know me very well."

An example of this kind of calm reflection, or perhaps musical kindness, can be found looking back across the war-torn twentieth century, and focusing on France in 1916. In the heart of World War I, eighty French musicians signed a notice that aimed to ban all music by German and Austrian composers whose works were not already in the public domain. Advanced by the newly formed National League for the Defense of French Music, it was signed by composers such as d'Indy and Saint-Saëns, but one composer, Maurice Ravel, refused to sign. In a letter dated June 7, 1916, he replied:

> It would be dangerous for French composers to ignore systematically the productions of their foreign colleagues, and thus form themselves into a sort of national coterie: our musical art which is so rich at the present time, would soon degenerate, becoming isolated by its academic formulas.[5]

Ravel went further, and commented about Schoenberg:

> It is of little importance to me that M. Schoenberg, for example, is of Austrian nationality. This does not prevent him from being a very fine musician whose very interesting discoveries have had a beneficial influence on certain allied composers, and even our own.[6]

This is a remarkable reply, knowing the heated, polarized opinions of the time, and the devastation of the war, increasing on opposite sides of the trenches, with no end in sight. Strong opinions were common—for example, a statement made by Schoenberg in a letter to Alma Mahler from August 1914, where he denounced the music of Bizet, Stravinsky, and Ravel: "Now we will throw those mediocre kitschmongers into slavery, and teach them to venerate the German spirit and to worship the German God."[7]

Schoenberg later attributed this kind of observation to his period of "war psychosis."[8] His statement, and the sentiments of musicians who signed the notice by the National League for the Defense of French Music, were not at all uncommon. But they did stand in stark contrast to Ravel. Ravel's reply, in my opinion, was courageous. It was uncommon. On some deeply thoughtful level, it showed kindness.

Fast forward to the late twentieth century: something of this Ravelian attitude imbued Jonathan Kramer's musical thinking. He was able to stand outside of the conflict, and observe. Blazing away in New York at the time was the Uptown/ Downtown rhetoric, and though it would be naïve to ignore it, I sensed that many composers of my generation had quietly moved on. Growing up fascinated by all kinds of sounds, I felt that this was just "not my battle"—that this was something going on more among composers of Jonathan's generation. I think Jonathan was

---

[5] Arbie Orenstein, *Ravel, Man and Musician* (New York: Columbia University Press, 1968), p. 74.
[6] Ibid., p. 74.
[7] Ross, *The Rest is Noise*, p. 72.
[8] Ibid.

certainly fascinated by the Uptown/Downtown rhetoric, but once again I didn't see him spending a lot of time choosing sides. He immersed himself in a postmodern tapestry of going to concerts of all kinds. His spirit of open-ended curiosity certainly benefitted me as a student, and I felt that I could speak to him about any artistic issue. There were some differences, however, in how I was experiencing postmodernism and the way that he was experiencing it.

Jonathan openly called himself a postmodernist. But I think the idea of being put into a stylistic box is off-putting to many composers. On some level, to me, it doesn't make a lot of sense— like placing a wild bird in a cage, or trying to bottle the ocean. People change, and styles change. Music is vast, and composers, including myself, often do not feel that the stylistic labels fit. My own music, particularly *Hyperfiction*, was being called postmodern at the time and I wasn't quite comfortable with it. Reading Jonathan's *Postmodern Music, Postmodern Listening* offered a clue— an observation from N. Katherine Hayles in 1990: "The people in this country who know most about how postmodernism *feels* (as distinct from how to envision or analyze it) are all under the age of sixteen."[9]

This observation made complete sense to me. Jonathan's generation could see and analyze the patterns going on in postmodernism, but my generation distinctly *felt* it. And to have one's music labeled postmodern felt a little bit like being identified with a funny accent. I didn't have to "think" about writing postmodern. It's just that when I turned on the music faucet in my mind, and wrote down what I heard, it came out "postmodern."

Or did it? Jonathan helped identify in me several compositional tendencies that were distinctly modernist— a predilection for certain complex harmonies, a full-on embrace of dissonance, plenty of mixed meters, certain uncompromising attitudes about form, to name a few. I began working on my doctoral thesis composition with him, called *Sweet Nothing*, which displayed distinct post-minimalist tendencies. I'd also developed a sweet tooth for experimental music studying with William Albright and Michael Daugherty at the University of Michigan, and continued to explore a lot of sonic anarchy and unbridled musical experimentation in New York City, pushing the sonic boundaries as I knew them. But did I feel that some of this material might be a little too edgy to bring to composition lessons? As Jonathan points out, "Several students of one well-known modernist composer-teacher have told me how they simultaneously work on two different pieces, one that they truly believe in and one that they think that their professor will approve of."[10] This was in fact common among many of my colleagues at different schools—having compositions that you believed you could show to your professor, and then pieces that you would *never* show your professor. Happily to say, I did not have this problem with Jonathan Kramer.

That said, music can cause unexpected friction and reactions, and it turns out that in the Anything Goes concert climate of NYC (at least, as how I perceived it) one of

---

[9]   N. Katherine Hayles, *Chaos Bound: Orderly Disorder in Contemporary Literature and Science* (Ithaca, NY: Cornell University Press, 1990), p. 282.
[10]   Kramer, 1.7, footnote 37.

my compositions wound up upsetting an esteemed performer arranging a composition reading. In addition to "standard" instrumentation of flute, vibraphone, and
percussion, I had also requested "nonstandard" electric guitar, electric bass, amplified
viola, and trap set, and offered to bring in an accomplished theremin soloist. Upon
delivering the score, I received an unexpected rant from the performer that contained
a curious level of vitriol that seemed to go far beyond any immediate concerns about
instrumentation. I decided to speak to Jonathan Kramer about it.

After relaying the story to him, he smiled and said, "Oh, they're still angry about
the Beatles." I asked him to explain. He mentioned that many performers of New
Music had become performing stars in the late 1950s and early 1960s, performing
uncompromising, modernist music. They'd attracted robust, thoughtful, audiences,
and critical acclaim. They had formed their musical identities around this time.
But then came *Sgt. Pepper's Lonely Hearts Club Band* and everything changed. The
audiences went in another direction, or thinned substantially, and New Music didn't
seem to have the same unimpeachable cred. It was now one expression among many.
This left lasting wounds. "But Jonathan," I said, "I wasn't even *born* when *Sgt. Pepper's*
was released. What have I got to do with the Beatles?" He raised an eyebrow, and let
me know that I was unlikely to change this person's attitude. What I realized though,
in time, was that Jonathan was showing compassion. It was this person's *choice* to have
that attitude. New Music exists. The Beatles exist. How one feels about this reality is up
to each individual. Jonathan wasn't trying to change their opinion. And it turns out the
eventual reading went just fine, and the performers enjoyed hearing the theremin and
trying "something new." I also developed a productive relationship with the performer,
and worked with him on a number of happy occasions. I credit Jonathan's insight on
the situation, helping to broaden my understanding of the diverse performing climate
of NYC.

Speaking of diversity, Jonathan told an anecdote during a lesson one day in 2003
that I realize over time brought about a subtle yet profound shift in my musical
thinking. As the story goes, Jonathan was presenting at an electronic music seminar
at a college in the Midwest in the early 1970s. After playing various electronic music
examples, he played the composers a whale recording. The composers dove into a
discussion about how the recording must have been made—what kind of oscillator
waveform, what kind of filter slope, what kind of portamento—because they thought
that it was a purely electronic piece. Finally, Jonathan said, "Nope, its humpback
whales." They laughed and said, "No really, what is it, some kind of Buchla, or Moog
modular?" And he said, "Really, it's just whales." When Jonathan relayed the story to
me I laughed as well— I thought it was great. Then Jonathan said, "Turns out they
didn't laugh after that …" I said, "What? But isn't it wonderful that people were discovering whale sounds? Weren't they impressed that whales were making electronica-like
vocalizations long before the invention of the synthesizer? That animals other than
humans might be considered musical?" He said, "Well, they didn't think so. Not after
I told them what it was. In fact, some were offended."

Jonathan playing the whale recording in an electronic music seminar and letting
students wrestle with the implications: an innocent attempt to bring a smile? Jonathan

did have a great sense of humor. But the story led to a tipping point for me: *It's actually the oscillators that sound like the whales, not the other way around.* Until then I had experienced Messiaen's beautiful birdsong translations, had admired how indigenous cultures all over the world treated animals (and their songs) with respect, and marveled at how mockingbirds can stitch together various sonic quotations from other birds and sounds in their environment. Now, with Jonathan's story, it was as if the complexity and sweet weirdness of technologically advanced electronic music had actually "rediscovered" a language spoken by beings who had been around far longer than Western civilization, or even the human species. In this case, Jonathan helped further open a deeper understanding of music and the ecological dimension. There's a link to this in *Postmodern Music, Postmodern Listening* where Jonathan included an insight about some aspects of postmodernism:

> ... an intense concern for pluralism and a desire to cut across the different taste cultures that now fracture society... an acknowledgement of different and otherness, the keynote of the feminist movement; indeed the re-emergence of the feminine into all discourse; the re-enchantment of nature, which stems from new developments in science and A. N. Whitehead's philosophy of organicism; the commitment to an ecological and ecumenical world view ...[11]

So, over time, I realize that Jonathan's story took root and flowered into a broadening of my own compositional work and philosophy: exploring more *ecological* questions. I'd say a good deal of this shift in thinking occurred from studying with Jonathan, and from anecdotes such as his inclusion of humpback whale vocalizations in an electronic music seminar. And though Jonathan encouraged listening with musical tolerance, I think he was also interested in genuinely opening doors to greater experiences of *beauty*.

Regarding beauty, if one unburdens, or expands, the notion of beauty from a mooring in the realm of *pretty*, then one may enter a mode of exploration—encountering the vast complexity of how others might be perceiving. There is beauty in paradox. There is beauty in exploration. There is beauty in danger. There is beauty in exposing truths. There is beauty in *ugly* things. There is beauty in boredom. There is beauty in the unknown. Well over a hundred years ago, Emerson evoked the myriad implications of beauty in a poem called "Music":

Let me go where'er I will
I hear a sky-born music still:
It sounds from all things old,
It sounds from all things young,
From all that's fair, from all that's foul,
Peals out a cheerful song.

It is not only in the rose,
It is not only in the bird,

---

[11] Charles Jencks, "Post-Modernism—The Third Force," in Charles Jencks (ed.), *The Post-Modern Reader* (New York, St. Martin's, 1992), p. 7.

Not only where the rainbow glows,
Nor in the song of woman heard,
But in the darkest, meanest things
There always, always something sings.

'Tis not in the high stars alone,
Nor in the cup of budding flowers,
Nor in the redbreast's mellow tone,
Nor in the bow that smiles in showers,
But in the mud and scum of things
There alway, alway something sings.

The *mud and scum of things* is akin to language one hears with regard to musical dislikes. And how does one listen "with pleasure, respect, and insight to many kinds of music"—as Jonathan Kramer encouraged—to the remarkable diversity of sound that one has in the present day? As open-minded as I think I might be, I fully admit to moments of information overload. How does one keep listening—keep ears open, and listen with tolerance?

Jonathan passed away suddenly in 2004. And over the course of writing this essay about him, I realize that I have been referring to him both in the past *and* present tense. (I realize that there are only two composers that I do this with: John Cage and Jonathan Kramer.) In Jonathan's case it's not only that there was so much music left to be composed, and ideas to be explored, but that there was (and is) also something *timeless* about Jonathan's approach to music and perception. Right in the opening of *Postmodern Music, Postmodern Music* he raises the question, "Postmodernism ... Does the term refer to a period or an aesthetic, a listening attitude or a compositional practice?"[12] These are questions I still wrestle with, but I'd say in a mostly playful manner. Perhaps something of Jonathan's playfully inquisitive approach to these questions rubbed off. And with regard to *timelessness*, Jonathan also notes about postmodernists, "Theirs is an inclusive and pluralistic art, trying to bring as much as possible into the here and now."[13]

In retrospect, I received great encouragement from Jonathan, and he broadened my horizons significantly. The notion that composers could be given full reign to explore their creative vision is something that I could only hope for composers in any time period, and certainly wish for in the present millennium. And this connects with Jonathan Kramer's aesthetic and how I still experience it. Opening doors. Allowing a plurality of voices. Listening. Allowing composers to speak in their own voices. Jonathan approached this through the kaleidoscopic lens of musical postmodernism. He knew that the music that he would write would differ naturally from others, and he found this welcome, and truly fascinating. He approached the diversity of the musical world with deeply informed, open-minded listening, and practiced this with uncommon kindness.

[12] Kramer, 1.1.
[13] Ibid., 3.2.

6

Kramer Post Kramer

Martin Bresnick

This past autumn (2014), in my class at Yale, "Analysis from the Composer's Perspective," we were discussing George Rochberg's extraordinary and disturbing String Quartet #3. I mentioned that my old friend and colleague Jonathan Kramer had had a very interesting exchange with Rochberg about modernism in the journal *Critical Inquiry* (11/2, December 1984). Rochberg's opening article was entitled "Can the Arts Survive Modernism?" to which Jonathan, in an answering essay, had replied "Can Modernism Survive George Rochberg?" Rochberg concluded the exchange with a final article entitled "Kramer versus Kramer."

It was quickly apparent that very few of my students had ever even heard of *Kramer versus Kramer* (the Academy Award winning 1979 movie starring Dustin Hoffman and Meryl Streep). The humor of Rochberg's riposte was completely lost on them. Moreover they gave me the impression they thought the significance of the debate between modernism and postmodernism had vanished, like so many other ideological disputes, into the dustbin of musical history.

My name appears in Jonathan's *Critical Inquiry* article among those thanked for "careful critical readings ... and several helpful suggestions." I cannot recall what particular suggestions I made then that induced Jonathan to extend his generous acknowledgment. It is true that in those years at Yale (1976-8) we were constantly talking together about music and ideas about music. He and I also taught joint seminars in Composition and, because we were so stimulated by each other's ideas (at least I was by his), we even gave an informal course in musical analysis (gratis) during the summers to a group of interested students.

Once in an animated conversation I asked Jonathan if he thought it might be possible to create a method of composition that would approach the kind of hierarchical layering of responsive, pluralistic musical materials previously available in tonal practice. He seemed interested (or amused) by what I proposed but very doubtful it could be done. His rueful, skeptical observations were useful, cautionary, and very often humorous (Jonathan could be a very funny guy). In any case I did not, of course, succeed in my utopian ideas and I never went on, as he did, to pursue stylistic or theoretical matters in a written, scholarly way.

I always admired Jonathan's ability to grow intellectually and musically—to refine, transform, and elaborate new insights forthrightly while, at the same time, candidly reassessing positions he previously held. For myself, I feel everything I have ever written about music (including this article) seems to be badly in need of revision and improvement whenever I re-read it. Regarding my musical compositions, on the other hand, because they are not "true" in any semantic or conventional sense of the word, so (I hope) they cannot then be "false." My compositions seem to me to be simply exemplary of what they were when they were written.

In the early 1980s, as a composer (rather than as a theorist or scholar) I believe Jonathan considered himself to be a radical modernist with prominent avant-garde tendencies. However, it seems he was slowly changing his intellectual views, gradually moving toward a re-evaluation of the new phenomenon of postmodernism, with a special focus on the aspects of non-linear, "timelessness" in music and listening. A discussion of such non-linearity comprises a significant part of his book *The Time of Music* (1988).

At that same time I considered musical postmodernism to be interesting but peripheral (though not necessarily inimical) to my own compositional trajectory. Jonathan, however, despite the subterranean changes roiling in his views, took up the cudgels on behalf of modernism. In his *Critical Inquiry* piece he argued that Rochberg's article (but not his music) had failed to make a significant case against the expressive limitations of modernism and its historical lacunae. Defending his own version of modernism, Jonathan attacked Rochberg's postmodernism from a number of positions. For example, contra Rochberg, he claimed:

> Modernism has been profoundly reflective of late nineteenth and twentieth century values. Is that not enough? It is not that modernism has forgotten the past—an art that rebels against its past must understand its adversary—but rather that it asks us not to forget the present.

He considered there were distinctions to be made between European modernism and American modernism:

> If it [modernism] is understood as rebellion then it did indeed emanate from Europe … but … if modernism is about discovery more than revolution, then its inception can be found in a culture [American] where tradition was not felt to be an enormous weight on an artist's spirit.

With regard to unity he wrote, "While single unifying ideas have characterized Western thought for centuries, modernism has challenged us to regard unity as a choice rather than a universal."

By the time of his last book, it appears that Jonathan had taken over, on behalf of postmodernism, many of the features he had previously admired and defended in modernism. What was left of modernism could almost be described as a desiccated, austere, humorless, academic hulk. From Jonathan's newly achieved standpoint, composers such as Satie, Berg, Kagel, Partch, Harrison, Ives, Nancarrow, and Grainger (among others), whom he might have previously considered as modernists, could now be better identified as postmodernists and moved over to that conceptual side. Consider these perceptive, polemical observations from the new book:

Postmodernist music is not conservative ... it simultaneously embraces and repudiates history. Postmodernists are not threatened by the past. Postmodernism takes from history, but it often does not interpret, analyze, or revise. (4.3)

Unlike the modernists, among whom he could never be fully counted, "Berg was not content simply quoting."

Regarding musical unity now as problematic, Jonathan declared it was modernism that promulgated "the totalizing metaphor of musical unity (i.e. all good pieces are 'unified'), an unspoken assumption that theorists and analysts have accepted, often uncritically. It prejudices music analysis and it can prevent critics (and listeners who read and believe their criticism) from finding other values in music." (4.1)

On the other hand, postmodernist music has shown that, "Musical unity is not an objective fact but rather a value projected onto music."

It is postmodernism that "rejects the meta-narrative of structural unity ... it demotes unity from the status of a totalizing meta-narrative to one of many smaller narratives." (4.1)

At about the same time that Jonathan wrote his response to Rochberg, Gyorgy Ligeti was searching for a way out of the dilemma represented by the formulation—modernism or postmodernism. Struggling with the new postmodern inclinations of his students in the Hamburg seminar, he said that he wanted his music to be neither modern nor postmodern. Ligeti wished to escape from the prison of both conceptual formulations, to leap, as it were, out of history itself. Considering history, whether it is the history of the world, the "idea" of history, or more poignantly his, Ligeti's history, who could blame him?

In James Joyce's *Ulysses*, a book that is at once modernist, postmodernist, and surely so much more, Joyce famously wrote, "History is a nightmare from which I am trying to awake ..." But for me there is, finally, no possible leap out of history, no possible awakening that can fully banish the nightmare or avoid the morning sobriety that must be endured in order to face the new day.

In 1976 I had a brief but memorable conversation with the scholar and archaeologist Frank E. Brown while standing on the steps of the American Academy in Rome. At the time, Brown was engaged in the excavation and preservation of the port of the ancient Roman town of Cosa, about eighty miles to the northwest. As we stood looking at the complex spectacle of Rome below us, I asked Brown what he thought of the tumultuous circumstances then roiling the streets and piazzas of the city—the collapse and absence of the government for months, the endless strikes and street demonstrations on behalf of the "Compromesso Storico" or historic compromise that would have brought the Italian Communist party into the government with the Christian Democrats, the odd connivance of the US with the Socialist party in order to undermine the "Compromesso Storico" since the Socialists supported a plan to make abortion and divorce legally available, programs opposed by both the Communists and the Christian Democrats. At night, gunshots could be heard nearby at the Spanish

Embassy as Franco lay dying in Fascist Spain, and the voices of lost Chilean refugees of the Pinochet coup, among them *Inti ilimani*, could be found playing their wonderful neo-Andean folk music in the streets of Rome.

Brown gestured at the vista before us and spoke of the persistence of the city despite so many events, both wonderful and catastrophic, that had taken place in the ancient capitol over the last 3,000 years. And yet, there it was—still Rome, still the eternal city.

How I envied Professor Brown's Olympian wisdom, his calm, dispassionate demeanor, and comforting observations! Of course, he was right, or, at the very least, more right in the long run than any of my on-the-spot concerns or judgments about Rome or art or music could be. Some time later I began to study the "Annales" group of French scholars who had attempted to understand human history, somewhat in the manner of Frank Brown, in longer arcs of time. Such viewpoints would position concepts such as modernism and postmodernism in the context of extended ongoing trends and long-term developments, or, as Fernand Braudel would have put it, the "longue durée." I understood how the projection of great temporal distances could help sort things out, to clarify obscurities and separate present surface noises from extended historical signals.

Despite my best efforts, however, I must concede that I still often fail to rise above my distressed, spontaneous responses to the world as I find it.

At the same time I feel constantly, even morally, obliged to adjust my current ideas and feelings in the light of some "meta-narrative" of the historical past, the past we simply call history. That is one of the reasons I have come to believe all topical theories about art are almost invariably wrong—while works of art are variably, but necessarily, right.

In this book, Jonathan Kramer acknowledged very candidly, in the light of contemporary developments (in which he, like all of us, was irretrievable enmeshed), that his views on modernism and postmodernism had altered. He considered his new responses and subsequent changes of opinion (correctly, I think) to be an occupational hazard, a matter of course for intelligent scholars.

Still, I remain puzzled, perhaps even distressed, that Jonathan Kramer took pains to parse at such length the myriad, but to my mind inevitably ill-formed, definitions of modernism and postmodernism that circulated in the late twentieth and early twenty-first centuries, to write a vast book about this subject rather than create more of the music he clearly wanted to see and hear in the world. It must have been that his capacious mind was intrigued and challenged by the provocative proliferation of fuzzy ideologies that swirled around the debates. But I knew his musical compositions also to be capacious, generous, and stimulating!

Abruptly, surprisingly, while reading Jonathan's book for this article, my grief at my friend's death was painfully revived. For there in the middle of Chapter 3.2, Jonathan veered away from a detailed attempt to define and elaborate the term avant garde, to distinguish the idea of the avant garde from the "original," in order to give us this extraordinary digression:

> Some uses of the term "avant garde" ought to be dismissed outright. Avant-gardism is not the same as utter originality, for example. To my ears, two of the

most original works of the twentieth century were composed by men not regularly thought of as vanguardists: Sibelius's *Tapiola* and Janáček's *Sinfonietta* (discussed briefly in section 4.7). I am awe-struck at the visionary quality of this music. In admiration I wonder how these composers managed to find such striking and stunning ideas. These pieces are not unprecedented, however. It is possible to hear their special sound-worlds presaged in earlier pieces by the same composers. Yet these works are unquestionably original—in part for the techniques employed in their making but more substantially because of their amazingly fresh ways of thinking of musical impulse, gesture, form, continuity, and expression.

Why are these not avant-garde works? Is the reason simply that they were created toward the ends of their respective composers' careers, whereas avant-gardism is a youthful phenomenon? While there surely is more to the avant garde than the age of an artist, I do not completely discount this factor. Most avant-garde music is the product of brash young artists out to show the world something revolutionary, to state starkly what is wrong with mainstream music, to redefine what music can or ought to be, and to challenge listeners by shaking the foundations of their understanding of the musical art. The Sibelius and Janáček works are not pathbreaking in any of these ways, but they are special for more subtle, interior, and personal reasons. Instead of breaking with tradition, as youthful vanguard art relishes doing, they build on lifetimes of music-making within a known tradition. They represent an ultimate refinement of their composers' art and heritage, not a breaking away from the past. These qualities contrast considerably with those of music normally considered avant garde. Such music focuses on its surface and on its technical means of production, while works like those by Sibelius and Janáček are deep, with their technical means operating in the service of expressive ideas, and with their intriguing surfaces serving as gateways to their inner depth.

Yes, I say! Yes! Jonathan has hit on something elementally profound here, expressed beautifully and with amazement—an observation that is perhaps peripheral to the aims of *Postmodern Music, Postmodern Listening*. For Jonathan Kramer, Sibelius and Janacek revealed originalities indispensable to creators and listeners alike, especially in the face of all attempts to define those masters in terms of a school or ideology today or even in their own time. To me this is the passionate insight of Jonathan Kramer the composer breaking into the world of Jonathan Kramer the scholar with all his rigorous, painstaking, diligent parsing. These are ideas about the art of composition that underscore the continuing human need for expressive, creative ingenuity in the acknowledged flux of history, however understood—the remarkable persistence of great music to wordlessly move us even after vast oceans of time—durations that go on long after the span of any single human life.

On reading the passage, I desperately wanted to call Jonathan to talk as we did years ago, to ask him for more of his thoughts on this vital subject that mattered so deeply to us both.

Dear Jonathan.

Jonathan?

Biographies

Author

Jonathan Kramer (1942–2004) was one of the most visionary musical thinkers of the second half of the twentieth century. In his *The Time of Music* he approached the idea of the many different ways that time itself is articulated musically. This book has become influential among composers, theorists, and aestheticians. He was program annotator for both the San Francisco and Cincinnati orchestras, and his notes for the latter were collected in the book *Listen to the Music*. His undergraduate and graduate studies were at Harvard and the University of California Berkeley respectively; he then taught both composition and theory at Oberlin, Yale, the University of Cincinnati, and Columbia. He also traveled worldwide as a lecturer and presenter at countless conferences and educational institutions. A recognized and widely performed composer, he worked in a range of genres from solo piano to orchestra.

Editor

Robert Carl studied with Kramer as an undergraduate composer at Yale, and currently chairs the composition department of the Hartt School, University of Hartford. For further information, consult his website, http://uhaweb.hartford.edu/CARL/ (accessed April 24, 2016). He is the author of Terry Riley's *In C*.

Contributors

John Luther Adams received the Pulitzer Prize for Music in 2014 for his orchestral work *Become Ocean*. He has received the William Schuman and Heinz Awards, and the Nemmers Prize, all for the totality of his work. He has built his creative practice on close observation of and listening to the environment, in Alaska and now Mexico.

Deborah Bradley-Kramer, PhD, is Lecturer in Music at Columbia University, and was Director of Music Performance at Columbia from 1999 to 2013, where she created many new initiatives for performers and composers. She is founder and pianist of the Moebius Ensemble and SPEAKmusic, and has given numerous US and international premieres by pre-eminent American and Russian composers. She is a dedicated pedagogue, teaching and presenting master classes throughout the USA, Europe, the

Middle East, and Asia. Her CD of Jonathan Kramer's chamber works was released by Leonarda Records in 2016.

Martin Bresnick is a prominent composer and professor of composition at the Yale School of Music. More information may be found on his website, martinbresnick.com (accessed April 24, 2016).

Brad Garton received his PhD from Princeton University in music composition. He was fortunate to have been a colleague of Jonathan Kramer's, serving on the Columbia University music faculty for the past several decades. He is currently Professor of Composition and Director of the Computer Music Center at Columbia. For further information, see http://music.columbia.edu/~brad (accessed April 24, 2016).

John Halle teaches music theory at the Bard College Conservatory. His articles on music, culture, and politics appear regularly in *Jacobin*, *Counterpunch*, and *New Politics*. A CD of his politically themed compositions, *Outrages and Interludes*, was recently released on the Innova label.

Composer, pianist, and educator *Duncan Neilson* resides in Portland, Oregon, where he is composer in residence for the Portland Chamber Orchestra. He has taught on the music faculties of Columbia University, the College of William and Mary, and Lewis and Clark College. His recent work addresses environmental themes through the inclusion and exploration of electronica, acoustic instruments, and sounds from the natural world.

Musicologist, pianist, and documentary filmmaker *Jann Pasler* has published widely on contemporary American and French music, modernism and postmodernism, interdisciplinarity, intercultural transfer, and especially cultural life in France and the French colonies in the nineteenth and twentieth centuries. Her writings include numerous articles and the books *Writing through Music: Essays on Music, Culture, and Politics* (Oxford University Press, 2008) and *Composing the Citizen: Music as Public Utility in Third Republic France* (University of California Press, 2009). Her video documentaries have been shown at the Smithsonian, as well as national meetings of the Association for Asian Studies and American Anthropological Society, and she is the editor of AMS Studies in Music (Oxford University Press).

Bibliography

[*Editor's Note: There was no bibliography following the manuscript used for this edition. The Editor has gone through all the footnotes to the text and assembled what follows. In addition, a couple of documents were later recovered by Jann Pasler, which came respectively from an early version of the text from 1992 and a seminar on Postmodernism Kramer taught at Columbia in 1997. The additional references from these texts are marked * and ** respectively. In total this list provides a survey of the literature on musical postmodernism that is hoped to be a comprehensive resource for future scholarship.*]

Adorno, Theodor, "On the Fetish Character in Music and the Regression of Listening," in Andrew Arato and Eike Gebhardt (eds.), *The Essential Frankfurt School Reader* (Oxford: Basil Blackwell, 1978)

Adorno, Theodor, *Aesthetic Theory*, trans. C. Lenhardt (London: Routledge, 1984)

Adorno, Theodor, *Mahler: A Musical Physiognomy*, trans. Edmund Jephcott (Chicago: University of Chicago Press: 1992, originally published in 1960)

Agawu, V. Kofi, *Playing with Signs: A Semiotic Interpretation of Classic Music* (Princeton, NJ: Princeton University Press, 1991)

**Agawu, Kofi, "Does Music Theory Need Musicology?," *Current Musicology* LIII (1993): 89–98

Agawu, V. Kofi, "Analyzing Music under the New Musicological Regime," *Music Theory Online* 2.4. Available online: http://boethius.music.ucsb.edu/mto/issues/mto.96.2.4/ mto.96.2.4. agawu.html#FN23REF

Albright, Daniel, *Untwisting the Serpent: Modernism in Music, Literature, and Other Arts* (Chicago and London: University of Chicago Press, 2000)

*Anderson, Walt, *Reality Isn't What It Used To Be* (San Francisco: Harper and Row, 1990)

Antokoletz, Elliott, *The Music of Béla Bartók: A Study of Tonality and Progression in Twentieth-Century Music* (Berkeley: University of California Press, 1984)

*Appignanesi, Lisa (ed.), *Postmodernism: ICAM Documents* (London: Free Association, 1989)

Atlas, Eugene E., "The Magic of Mozart's Music Soothes a Hurting Heart," *Sarasota Herald-Tribune*, 22 January 1995: p. 5E

Bailey, Kathryn, "Webern's Opus 21: Creativity in Tradition," *Journal of Musicology* 2 (1983): 195

Baldwin, Sandy, "Speed and Ecstasy: 'Real Time' after Virilio, or, the Rhetoric in Techno-Logistics." Available online: http://www.lcc.gatech.edu/events/wips/1999-2000.html

Ballantine, Christopher, "Charles Ives and the Meaning of Quotation in Music," *Musical Quarterly* 65/2 (April 1979): 167–84

** Barkin, Elaine, "A Dedication, Five ADmusements, & A Digression", *Perspectives of New Music* 18 (1979–80): 407–21

** Barkin, Elaine, "WORDSWORTH (sic) Semi-Serial Postludes un amusement sur L'aaM," *Perspectives of New Music* 22 (1983–84): 247–52

Baron, Carol K., "Dating Charles Ives' Music: Facts and Fictions," *Perspectives of New Music* 28/1 (Winter 1990): 20–56

Barth, John, "The Literature of Replenishment: Postmodernist Fiction," *The Atlantic Monthly* 254/1 (January 1980)

Barthes, Roland, "The Death of the Author," in *Image—Music—Text*, trans. Stephen Heath (New York: Noonday, 1977)

Bennett, David, "Time for Postmodernism: Subjectivity, 'Free Time', and Reception Aesthetics," in Brenton Broadstock, Naomi Cumming, Denise Grocke, Catherine Falk, Ros McMillan, Kerry Murphy, Suzanne Robinson, and John Stinson (eds.), *Aflame with Music: 100 Years at the University of Melbourne* (Parkville, Australia: Centre for Studies in Australian Music, 1996), pp. 383–9

Best, Steven and Kellner, Douglas, *Postmodern Theory: Critical Interrogations* (New York: Guilford Press, 1991)

**Beverly, John, "The Ideology of Postmodern Music and Left Politics", *Critical Inquiry* 31 (1989): 40–56

Bicket, Dougie (K.I.S.S.—Keep It Simple Stupid—of the Panopticon), "Modernism and Postmodernism: Some Symptoms and Useful Distinctions." Available online: http://carmen.artsci.washington.edu/panop/modpomo.htm (weblink no longer active, April 24, 2016)

Blanchot, Maurice, *La Part du feu* (Paris: n.p., 1944)

Bloom, Harold, *The Anxiety of Influence* (New York: Oxford University Press, 1973)

**Blum, Stephen, "IN Defense of Close Reading and Close Listening," *Current Musicology* LIII (1993): 55–65

Bonnefoy, Yves, *Dualité de l'art d'aujourd'hui* (Paris: Arts de France 11, 1961)

**Boretz, Benjamin, "Interface Part I: Commentary: The Barrytown Orchestra on Hunger Day November 15, 1984," *Perspectives of New Music* 23/2 (Spring–Summer 1985): 90–4

Born, Georgina, *Rationalizing Culture: IRCAM, Boulez, and the Institutionalization of the Musical Avant-Garde* (Berkeley: University of California Press, 1995)

Boulez, Pierre, "Le système et l'idée," *InHarmoniques* 1 (1986): 97

Boulez, Pierre and Foucault, Michel, "Contemporary Music and the Public," *Perspectives of New Music* 24/1 (1985): 6–13

Brackett, David, "'Where It's At?': Postmodern Theory and the Contemporary Musical Field," in Judy Lochhead and Joseph Auner (eds.), *Postmodern Music/Postmodern Thought* (New York and London: Routledge, 2002)

**Bürger, Peter, *Theory of the Avant-Garde* (Manchester: Manchester University Press, 1984)

Bürger, Peter, *The Decline of Modernism*, trans. Nicholas Walker (University Park: Pennsylvania State University Press, 1992)

*Burgin, Victor, *The End of Art Theory: Criticism and Post-Modernity* (Atlantic Highlands, NJ: Humanities Free Press International, 1986)

**Burnham, Scott, *Beethoven Hero* (Princeton, NJ: Princeton University Press, 1995)

*Butler, Christopher, *After the Wake: An Essay on the Contemporary Avant Garde* (Oxford: Clarendon 1980)

Cage, John, *A Year from Monday* (Middletown, CT: Wesleyan University Press, 1967)

Carpenter, Patricia, "*Grundgestalt* as Tonal Function," *Music Theory Spectrum* 5 (1983): 15–38

Caygill, Howard, "Architectural Postmodernism: The Retreat of an Avant Garde?," in Roy Boyne and Ali Rattansi (eds.), *Postmodernism and Society* (New York: St. Martin's, 1990)

*Citron, Marcia, "Gender and the Field of Musicology", *Current Musicology* LIII (1993): 66–75

Clemens, Justin, "John Cage, Compact Discs, and the Postmodern Sublime," in Brenton Broadstock et al. (eds.), *Aflame with Music: 100 Years at the University of Melbourne* (Parkville, Australia: Centre for Studies in Australian Music, 1996)

Clendening, Jane Piper, "Postmodern Architecture/Postmodern Music," in Judy Lochhead and Joseph Auner (eds.), *Postmodern Music/Postmodern Thought* (New York and London: Routledge, 2002)

Clifton, Thomas, *Music as Heard* (New Haven, CT: Yale University Press, 1983)

*Cogan, Robert, "Composition: Diversity/Unity," *Interface* 20 (1991): 137–41

**Cogan, Robert, "The Art-Science of Music After Two Millenia," in Elizabeth West Marvin and Richard Herman (eds.), *Concert Music, Rock, and Jazz Since 1945* (Rochester, NY: University of Rochester Press, 1995), pp. 34–52

Cohn, Richard, "The Autonomy of Motives in Schenkerian Accounts of Tonal Music," *Music Theory Spectrum* 14 (1992): 150–70

Cohn, Richard, "Schenker's Theory, Schenkerian Theory: Pure Unity or Constructive Conflict?," *Indiana Theory Review* 13/1 (1992): 1–19

**Cohn, Richard and Dempster, Douglas, "Hierarchical Unity, Plural Unity: Towards a Reconciliation," in Katherine Bergeron and Philip V. Bohlman (eds.), *Disciplining Music: Musicology and Its Canons* (Chicago: University of Chicago Press, 1992), pp. 156–81

*Collins, Jim, *Uncommon Cultures: Popular Cultures and Postmodernism* (New York: Routledge, 1989)

Compagnon, Antoine, *The 5 Paradoxes of Modernity*, trans. Philip Franklin (New York: Columbia University Press, 1994)

Cone, Edward T., "Analysis Today," in Paul Henry Láng (ed.), *Problems of Modern Music* (New York: Norton, 1962), pp. 34–50

Cone, Edward T., "Beyond Analysis," in Benjamin Boretz and Edward T. Cone (eds.), *Perspectives on Contemporary Music Theory* (New York: Norton, 1972), pp. 72–90

Cone, Edward T., *The Composer's Voice* (Berkeley, Los Angeles, London: University of California Press, 1974)

*Connor, Steven, *Postmodernist Culture: An Introduction to Theories of Contemporaneity* (New York: Basil Blackwell, 1989)

Conway, Daniel, "Nietzsche contra Nietzsche: The Deconstruction of *Zarathustra*," in Clayton Koelb (ed.), *Nietzsche as Postmodernist: Essays Pro and Contra* (Albany: State University of New York Press, 1990), pp. 91–110

Cook, David, "Paul Virilio: The Politics of 'Real Time.'" Available online: http://www.ctheory.net/text_file.asp?pick=360 (accessed April 24, 2016)

Cook, Nicholas, "The Future of Theory," *Indiana Theory Review* 10 (1989): 71–2

Cook, Nicholas, *Music, Imagination, and Culture* (Oxford: Clarendon, 1990)

Cook, Nicholas, "Music Theory and the Postmodern Muse: An Afterword," in Elizabeth West Marvin and Richard Hermann (eds.), *Concert Music, Rock, and Jazz Since 1945: Essays and Analytical Studies* (Rochester, NY: University of Rochester Press, 1995)

*Cooke, Philip, *Back to the Future* (Boston: Unwin Hyman, 1990)

**Dahlhaus, Carl, "Some Models of Unity in Musical Form," trans Charlotte Carroll Prather, *Journal of Music Theory* 27 (1983): 2–30

Dahlhaus, Carl, *Schoenberg and the New Music*, trans. Derrick Puffett and Alfred Clayton (Cambridge: Cambridge University Press, 1987)

Dano, Reece R., "Stravinsky and Cocteau's *Oedipus Rex*: The Shifting Hermeneutics of Modernism and Postmodernism." Available online: http://home.earthlink.net/~rdano/ stravinskyandpomo.html (weblink no longer active, April 24, 2016)

Davies, Stephen, "Attributing Significance to Unobvious Musical Relationships," *Journal of Music Theory* 27 (1983): 203–13

Deak, Edit, "The Critic Sees through the Cabbage Patch," *Artforum* (April 1984): 56

Desain, Peter and Honing, Henkjan, http://www.academia.edu/3356873/Peter_Desain_ and_Henkjan_Honing_Music_Mind_and_Machine_Studies_in_Computer_Music_ Music_Cognition_and_Artificial_Intelligence (accessed April 24, 2016)

Deutsch, Diana (ed.), *The Psychology of Music* (Orlando, FL: Academic Press, 1982)

*Docherty, Thomas, *After Theory: Postmodernism/Postmarxism* (New York: Routledge, 1990)

Dubiel, Joseph, "Senses of Sensemaking," *Perspectives of New Music* 30/1 (1992): 210–21

Dubiel, Joseph, "Hearing, Remembering, Cold Storage, Purism, Evidence, and Attitude Adjustment," *Current Musicology* 60-1 (1996): 26–50

Dufresne, David, "Virilio—Cyberesistance Fighter: An Interview with Paul Virilio." Available online: http://www.apres-coup.org/archives/articles/virilio.html (accessed April 24, 2016)

Eco, Umberto, *A Theory of Semiotics* (Bloomington: Indiana University Press, 1976)

Eco, Umberto, *Postscript to the Name of Rose* (New York and London: Harcourt Brace Jovanovich, 1984)

Edwards, George, "Music and Postmodernism," *Partisan Review* 58 (1991): 693–705

Epstein, David, *Beyond Orpheus* (Cambridge, MA: MIT Press, 1979)

Ermarth, Elizabeth Deeds, *Sequel to History: Postmodernism and the Crisis of Representational Time* (Princeton, NJ: Princeton University Press, 1992)

Fanning, David, "Nielsen's Progressive Thematicism," in Mina Miller (ed.), *A Nielsen Companion* (London: Faber, 1995)

*Fekete, John (ed.), *Life After Mostmodernism: Essays on Value and Culture* (New York: St. Martin's, 1987)

Foster, Hal (ed.), *The Anti-Aesthetic: Essays on Postmodern Culture* (Port Townsend, WA: Bay Press, 1983)

Foster, Hal, "(Post)modern Polemics," in *Recodings: Art, Spectacle, Cultural Politics* (Seattle: Bay Press, 1985)

**Foucault, Michel and Boulez, Pierre, "Contemporary Music and the Public," *Perspectives of New Music* 24/1 (Fall/Winter 1985): 6–13

Fraser, J. T., "From Chaos to Conflict," in J. T. Fraser, Marlene P. Soulsby, and Alexander J. Argyros (eds.), *Time, Order and Chaos: The Study of Time* IX (Madison, CT: International Universities Press, 1998)

Frisch, Walter, *Brahms and the Principle of Developing Variation* (Berkeley and Los Angeles: University of California Press, 1984)

*Gablick, Suzy, *Has Modernism Failed?* (New York: Thames and Hudson, 1984)

Gaggi, Silvio, *Modern/Postmodern: A Study in Twentieth-Century Arts and Ideas* (Philadelphia: University of Pennsylvania Press, 1989)

Gann, Kyle, "Boundary Busters: How to Tell New Music from Music that Happens To Be New," *Village Voice* (September 3, 1991): 85–7

**Gans, Eric, "Art and Entertainment", *Perspectives of New Music* 24/1 (Fall/Winter 1985): 24–37

Gergen, Kenneth J., *The Saturated Self: Dilemmas of Identity in Contemporary Life* (New York: Basic Books, 1991)

Gibson, J. J., "Events Are Perceivable but Time Is Not," in J. T. Fraser and Nathaniel Lawrence (eds.), *The Study of Time* 2 (New York: Springer-Verlag, 1975), pp. 295–301

Gjerdingen, Robert O., "Courtly Behaviors," *Music Perception* 13 (1996): 365–82

Gleick, James, *Chaos: Making a New Science* (New York: Viking, 1987)

*Goodman, Nelson, "When is Art?," in *The Arts and Cognition* (Baltimore: Johns Hopkins University Press, 1977)

Grauer, Victor, "Toward a Unified Theory of the Arts," *Semiotica* 94/3–4 (1993)

Greene, David B., *Mahler, Consciousness, and Temporality* (New York: Gordon and Breach, 1984)

*Grossberg, Lawrence, Fry, Tony, Curthoys, Ann, and Patton, Paul, *It's a Sin: Essays on Postmodernism, Politics, and Culture* (Sydney: Power, 1988)

Guck, Marion, A., "Two Types of Metaphoric Transference," in Jamie C. Kassler and Margaret Kartomi (eds.), *Metaphor: A Musical Dimension* (Paddington, Australia: Currency Press, 1991)

*Habermas, Jurgen, "Modernity versus Postmodernity," *New German Critique* 22 (1981)

Hardison Jr., O. B., *Disappearing Through the Skylight: Culture and Technology in the Twentieth Century* (New York: Viking, 1989)

Hartwell, Robin, "Postmodernism and Art Music," in Simon Miller (ed.), *The Last Post: Music after Modernism* (Manchester, UK and New York: Manchester University Press, 1993)

Harvey, David, *The Condition of Postmodernity* (Oxford: Blackwell, 1990)

Hassan, Ihab, "The Culture of Postmodernism," *Theory, Culture, and Society* 2 (1985)

Hassan, Ihab, *The Postmodern Turn: Essays in Postmodern Theory and Culture* (Columbus: Ohio State University Press, 1987)

Hawkes, Terence, *Structuralism and Semiotics* (London: Methuen, 1977)

Hayles, N. Katherine, *Chaos Bound: Orderly Disorder in Contemporary Literature and Science* (Ithaca, NY: Cornell University Press, 1990)

Heile, Bjorn, "Collage vs. Compositional Control: The Interdependency of Modernist and Postmodernist Approaches in the Work of Mauricio Kagel," in Judy Lochhead and Joseph Auner (eds.), *Postmodern Music/Postmodern Thought* (New York and London: Routledge, 2002)

Heise, Ursula, *Chronoschisms: Time, Narrative, and Postmodernism* (Cambridge: Cambridge University Press, 1997)

Hennion, Antoine, "Baroque and Rock: Music, Mediators, and Musical Taste," *Poetics: Journal of Research on Literature, the Media, and the Arts* 24 (1997): 417

Higgins, Kathleen, "Nietzsche and Postmodern Subjectivity," in Clayton Koelb (ed.), *Nietzsche as Postmodernist: Essays Pro and Contra* (Albany: State University of New York Press, 1990)

Höller, York, "Composition of the Gestalt, or the Making of the Organism," *Contemporary Music Review* 1 (1984)

Holtzman, Steve, *Digital Mosaics* (New York: Simon and Schuster, 1997)

Honig, Henkjan and Desain, Peter, "Computational Models of Beat Induction," *Journal of New Music Research* 28/1 (1999): 29–42

Howard, Luke, "Production vs. Reception in Postmodernism: The Gorecki Case," in Judy Lochhead and Joseph Auner (eds.), *Postmodern Music/Postmodern Thought* (New York and London: Routledge, 2002)

Hubbs, Nadine, "Schoenberg's Organicism," *Theory and Practice* 16 (1991): 143–62

Hutcheon, Linda, *A Poetics of Postmodernism: History, Theory, Fiction* (New York and London: Routledge, 1988)

Huyssen, Andreas, *After the Great Divide: Modernism, Mass Culture, Postmodernism* (Bloomington: Indiana University Press, 1986)

Hyer, Brian, *Figuring Music* (Cambridge: Cambridge University Press, 2002)

Impett, Jonathan, "Real Times: Implementing a Temporal Phenomenology in an Interactive Music System." Available online: https://www.researchgate.net/publication/237282920_Real_times_implementing_a_temporal_phenomenology_in_an_interactive_music_system (accessed April 24, 2016)

Ingarden, Roman, *The Work of Music and the Problem of Its Identity*, trans. Adam Czerniawski (Berkeley and Los Angeles: University of California Press, 1986)

Irvine, Martin, "The Postmodern, Postmodernism, Postmodernity: Approaches to Po-Mo." Available online: http://faculty.georgetown.edu/irvinem/theory/pomo.html (accessed April 24, 2016)

Iser, Wolfgang, *The Act of Reading: A Theory of Aesthetic Response* (Baltimore, MD: Johns Hopkins University Press, 1978)

Ives, Charles, *Three Places in New England*, ed. James B. Sinclair (Bryn Mawr, PA: Mercury Music, 1976)

*Jameson, Fredric (ed.), *Aesthetics and Politics* (London: New Left Books, 1977)

Jameson, Fredric, *Postmodernism, or, the Cultural Logic of Late Capitalism* (Durham, NC: Duke University Press, 1991)

*Jencks, Charles, *The Language of Post-Modern Architecture* (5th edn; New York: Rizzoli, 1987)

*Jencks, Charles, *Post-Modernism: The New Classicism in Art and Architecture* (New York: Rizzoli, 1987)

Jencks, Charles, "The Post-Modern Agenda," in Charles Jencks (ed.), *The Post-Modern Reader* (New York: St. Martin's, 1992)

Jencks, Charles, "Post-Modernism—The Third Force," in Charles Jencks (ed.), *The Post-Modern Reader* (New York: St. Martin's, 1992)

**Jencks, Charles, *What Is Post-Modernism?* (2nd edn; New York: St. Martin's, 1992)

Jones, Amelia, *Postmodernism and the En-Gendering of Marcel Duchamp* (Cambridge, UK, New York, and Melbourne: Cambridge University Press, 1994)

Kaplan, D. Ann, *Postmodernism and its Discontents* (London: Verso, 1988)

*Kariel, Harvey, *The Desperate Politics of Postmodernism* (Amherst: University of Massachusetts Press, 1989)

*Kellner, Douglas (ed.), *Postmodernism/Jameson/Critique* (Washington, DC: Maisonneuve, 1989)

Kerman, Joseph, "How We Got into Analysis, and How to Get Out," *Critical Inquiry* 7 (1980): 317

**Kingman, Daniel, "Every New Wave Must Break on Some Shore," *Perspectives of New Music* 27 (Winter 1989): 124–7

*Kolb, David, *Postmodern Sophistication: Philosophy, Architecture, and Tradition* (Chicago: University of Chicago Press, 1990)

**Kompridis, Nikolas, "Learning from Architecture: Music in the Aftermath to Postmodernism," *Perspectives of New Music* 31/2 (1993): 6–23

Korsyn, Kevin, "Towards a New Poetics of Musical Influence," *Music Analysis* 10 (1991): 3–72

Kouvaras, Linda, "Postmodern Temporalities," in Brenton Broadstock, Naomi Cumming, Denise Grocke, Catherine Falk, Ros McMillan, Kerry Murphy, Suzanne Robinson, and John Stinson (eds.), *Aflame with Music: 100 Years of Music at the University of Melbourne* (Melbourne: Centre for Studies in Australian Music, 1996)

Kramer, Jonathan D., "Can Modernism Survive George Rochberg?," *Critical Inquiry* 11/2 (1984): 341–54

Kramer, Jonathan D., *Listen to the Music* (New York: Schirmer, 1988)

Kramer, Jonathan D., *The Time of Music* (New York: Schirmer, 1988)

Kramer, Jonathan D., "Beyond Unity: Postmodernism in Music and Music Theory," in Elizabeth West Marvin and Richard Hermann (eds.), *Concert Music, Rock, and Jazz Since 1945: Essays and Analytical Studies* (Rochester, NY: University of Rochester Press, 1995)

**Kramer, Jonathan D., "Postmodern Concepts of Musical Time," *Indiana Theory Review* 17/2 (1997)

Kramer, Jonathan D., "Karlheinz in California," *Perspectives of New Music* 36/1 (1998): 247–61

**Kramer, Lawrence, "The Musicology of the Future," *Repercussions* I/I (Spring 1992): 5–18

**Kramer, Lawrence, "Music Criticism and the Postmodernist Turn: In Contrary Motion with Gary Tomlinson," *Current Musicology* LIII (1993): 25–35

**Kramer, Lawrence, *Classical Music and Postmodern Knowledge* (Berkeley: University of California Press, 1995)

*Kroker, Arthur, *The Postmodern Scene: Excremental Culture and Hyper-Aesthetics* (New York: St. Martin's, 1986)

Kroker, Arthur, Kroker, Marilouise, and Cook, David (eds.), *Panic Encyclopedia: The Definitive Guide to the Postmodern Scene* (New York: St. Martin's, 1989)

Kuhn, Thomas, *The Structure of Scientific Revolutions*, vol. 2, no. 2 of *International Encyclopedia of Unified Science* (Chicago: University of Chicago Press, 1970)

LaFountain, Marc J., *Dalí and Postmodernism: This Is Not an Essence* (Albany: State University of New York Press, 1997)

LeBaron, Anne, "Reflections of Surrealism in Postmodern Musics," in Judy Lochhead and Joseph Auner (eds.), *Postmodern Music/Postmodern Thought* (New York and London: Routledge, 2002), pp. 27–73

Lebel, Robert, "Picabia and Duchamp, or the Pro and Con," November 1949, in Patrick Waldberg, *Surrealism* (New York: Thames and Hudson, 1965), p. 30

Lerdahl, Fred, "Cognitive Constraints on Compositional Procedures," in John Sloboda (ed.), *Generative Processes in Music: The Psychology of Performance, Improvisation, and Composition* (New York: Clarendon, 1988)

Lerdahl, Fred, *Tonal Pitch Space* (New York: Oxford University Press, 2002)

Levine, Lawrence W., *Highbrow/Lowbrow: The Emergence of Cultural Hierarchy in America* (Cambridge, MA: Harvard University Press, 1988)

Levy, Janet, "Gesture, Form, and Syntax in Haydn's Music," in Jens Peter Larsen, Howard Serwer, and James Webster (eds.), *Haydn Studies* (New York: Norton, 1981), pp. 355–62

Lewin, David, "Music Theory, Phenomenology, and Modes of Perception," *Music Perception* 3 (1986): 327–92

Lipsitz, George, *Dangerous Crossroads: Popular Music, Postmodernism, and the Poetics of Place* (London and New York: Verso, 1994)

*Lovejoy, Margot, *Postmodern Currents: Art and Artists in the Age of Electronic Media* (Ann Arbor, MI: UMI, 1989)

Lyotard, Jean-François, *The Postmodern Condition: A Report on Knowledge*, trans.

Geoff Bennington and Brian Massumi (Minneapolis: University of Minnesota Press, 1984)

Maciejewicz, Dorota, *Zegary nie zgadzają się z sobą* (Warsaw: Studia Instytutu Sztuki Pan, 2000), pp. 154–9, English summary p. 179

*Madison, G. B., *The Hermeneutics of Postmodernity: Figures and Themes* (Bloomington: Indiana University Press, 1990)

Mann, Paul, *The Theory-Death of the Avant Garde* (Bloomington: Indiana University Press, 1991)

**Mark, Christopher, "'Rigorous Contemplation of Essentials': Material and Structure in the Concerto for Piano and Orchestra," in *The Music of Roger Smalley* (Perth: Evos, 1994), pp. 45–58

Marzorati, Gerald, "Kenny Scharf's Fun-House Big Bang," *Art News* (September 1985): 81

** Maus, Fred Everett, "Recent Ideas and Activities of James K. Randall and Benjamin Boretz: A New Social Role for Music," *Perspectives of New Music* 26/2 (Summer 1988): 214–22

Maus, Fred Everett, "Concepts of Musical Unity," in Nicholas Cook and Mark Everist (eds.), *Rethinking Music* (Oxford and New York: Oxford University Press, 1999), pp. 171–92

McAdams, Stephen, "The Auditory Image: A Metaphor for Musical and Psychological Research on Auditory Organization," in W. R. Crozier and A. J. Chapman (eds.), *Cognitive Processes in the Perception of Art* (Amsterdam and New York: Elsevier Science Publishers, 1984)

** McClary, Susan, *Feminine Endings* (Minneapolis: University of Minnesota Press, 1991)

** McClary, Susan, "Narrative Agendas in 'Absolute' Music: Identity and Difference in Brahms's Third Symphony," in Ruth Solie (ed.), *Musicology and Difference: Gender and Sexuality in Music Scholarship* (Berkeley and Los Angeles: University of California Press, 1993), pp. 326–44

** McClary, Susan, "Constructions of Subjectivity in Schubert's Music," in Philip Brett, Elizabeth Wood, and Gary Thomas (eds.), *Queering the Pitch: The New Gay and Lesbian Musicology* (New York: Routledge, 1994), pp. 205–34

McClary, Susan, *Conventional Wisdom: The Content of Musical Form* (Berkeley, Los Angeles, London: University of California Press, 2000)

McNeilly, Kevin, "Ugly Beauty: John Zorn and the Politics of Postmodern Music," *Postmodern Culture* 5 (1995)

Meyer, Felix and Shreffler, Anne C., "Webern's Revisions: Some Analytical Implications," *Music Analysis* 12/3 (October 1993): 355–79

Meyer, Leonard, *Music, the Arts, and Ideas* (Chicago and London: University of Chicago Press, 1967)

Meyer, Leonard, *Explaining Music: Essays and Explorations* (Chicago and London: University of Chicago Press, 1973)

Meyer, Leonard, "Toward a Theory of Style," in Berel Lang (ed.), *The Concept of Style* (Philadelphia: University of Pennsylvania Press, 1979), pp. 33–8

Meyer, Leonard, "A Pride of Prejudices; or, Delight in Diversity," *Music Theory Spectrum* 13 (1991)

Meyer, Leonard, *Style and Music* (Chicago and London: University of Chicago Press, 1997)

Meyer, Leonard and Burton, Rosner, "Melodic Processes and the Perception of Music," in Diana Deutsch (ed.), *The Psychology of Music* (Orlando, FL: Academic Press, 1982)

Monelle, Raymond, *Linguistics and Semiotics in Music* (Chur, Switzerland: Harwood, 1992)

Monelle, Raymond, "The Postmodern Project in Music Theory," in Eero Tarasti (ed.), *Music Semiotics in Growth* (Bloomington, IN and Imatra: Indiana University Press, 1996)

Morgan, Robert P., "Rethinking Musical Culture: Canonic Reformulations in a Post-Tonal Age," in Katherine Bergeron and Philip V. Bohlman (eds.), *Disciplining Music: Musicology and Its Canons* (Chicago: University of Chicago, 1992), pp. 44–63

**Myers, Julian, "PMC Reader's Report on Kevin McNeilly, 'Ugly Beauty: John Zorn and the Politics of Postmodern Music," *Postmodern Culture* 6/1 (1995)

Narmour, Eugene, *The Analysis and Cognition of Basic Musical Structures: The Implication-Realization Model* (Chicago: University of Chicago Press, 1990)

Nattiez, Jeans-Jacques, *Music and Discourse: Toward a Semiology of Music*, trans. Carolyn Abbate (Princeton, NJ: Princeton University Press, 1990)

Neff, Severine, "Schoenberg and Goethe: Organicism and Analysis," in David Bernstein and Christopher Hatch (eds.), *Music Theory and Its Exploration of the Past* (Chicago: University of Chicago Press, 1992), pp. 501–22

Neumeyer, David, "Reply to Larson," *In Theory Only* 10/4 (1987): 34

Newman, Michael, "Revising Modernism, Representing Postmodernism: Critical Discourses of the Visual Arts," in Lisa Appignanesi (ed.), *Postmodernism: ICA Documents* (London: Free Association Books, 1989), pp. 114–24

**Norris, Charles, "Utopian Deconstruction: Ernst Bloch, Paul de Man, and the Politics of Music," *Paragraph* 11 (1988): 24–57

Nowotny, Helga, "The Times of Complexity: Does Temporality Evolve?," in J. T. Fraser, Marlene P. Soulsby, and Alexander Argyros (eds.), *Time, Order and Chaos: The Study of Time* IX (Madison, CT: International Universities Press, 1998), pp. 91–146

Nyman, Michael, *Experimental Music: Cage and Beyond* (New York: Schirmer Books, 1974)

Oliveros, Pauline, "Sonic Meditations," *Source: Music of the Avant Garde* 3 (1968); 10 (1971)

*Osmond-Smith, Gerald, *Playing on Words: A Guide to Luciano Berio's Sinfonia* (London: Royal Musical Association, 1985)

Oswald, John, *Plunderphonics* (Seeland 515, Fony 69/96, 1999)

Oswald, John and Igma, Norm, "Plunderstanding Ecophonomics: Strategies for the Transformation of Existing Music," in John Zorn (ed.), *Arcana: Musicians on Music* (New York: Granary Books/Hips Road, 2000)

Pasler, Jann, "Musique et Institution aux Etats-Unis," *Inharmoniques* (May 1987)

*Pasler, Jann, "Narrative and Narrativity in Music," in J. T. Fraser (ed.), *Time and Mind: The Study of Time* 6 (Madison, CT: International Universities Press, 1989)

Pasler, Jann, "Postmodernism, Narrativity, and the Art of Memory," in Jonathan D. Kramer (ed.), *Time in Contemporary Musical Thought*, *Contemporary Music Review* 7/1 (1993)

Pastille, William A., "Heinrich Schenker, Anti-Organicist," *Nineteenth-Century Music* 8 (1984): 32

Patterson, David W., "Appraising the Catchwords, c. 1942–1959: John Cage's Asian-Derived Rhetoric and the Historical Reference of Black Mountain College," diss., Columbia University, 1996

*Peckham, Morse, *Man's Rage for Chaos* (Philadelphia: Chilton, 1865)

Peckham, Morse, *Man's Rage for Chaos* (New York: Schocken, 1967)

**Perloff, Marjorie, "Music for Words Perhaps: Reading/Hearing/Seeing John Cage's *Roaratorio*," in Marjorie Perloff (ed.), *Postmodern Genres* (Norman: University of Oklahoma Press, 1988), pp. 193–228

Perloff, Marjorie, *Postmodern Genres* (Norman: University of Oklahoma Press, 1988)

Perloff, Marjorie, "Postmodernism/Fin de siècle: The Prospects for Openness in a Decade of Closure," *Criticism* 35/2 (March 1993)

*Porphyrios, Dmitri, "Architecture and the Postmodern Condition," in Lisa Appignanesi (ed.), *Postmodernism: ICAM Documents* (London: Free Association, 1989)

*Poster, Mark, *The Mode of Information: Poststructuralism and Social Context* (Chicago: University of Chicago Press, 1990)

Potter, Keith, "James Dillon: Currents of Development," *Musical Times* 131 (1990): 253–60

Raes, Koen, "The Ethics of Postmodern Aesthetics: Toward a Social Understanding of Cultural Trends in Postmodern Times," in Mark Delaere (ed.), *New Music, Aesthetics, and Ideology* (Wilhelmshaven, Germany: Florian Noetzel, 1995)

Rahn, John, "Aspects of Musical Explanation," *Perspectives of New Music* 17/2 (1979)

**Randall, James K., "Are You Serious?" *Perspectives of New Music* 23/2 (Spring–Summer 1985): 72–88

Rea, John, "Postmodernisms," in Jean-Jacques Nattiez (ed.), *Einaudi Enciclopedia* vol. 2. English translation www.andante.com/reference/einaudi/EinaudiRea.cfm [Editor: this link is no longer active, but *Einaudi Enciclopedia* is still in print]

Réti, Rudolph, *The Thematic Process in Music* (London: Macmillan, 1961)

Riemann, Hugo, *Lexikon* (Mainz: Schott, 1967)

*Risatti, Howard (ed.), *Postmodern Perspectives: Issues in Contemporary Art* (Englewood Cliffs, NJ: Prentice Hall, 1990)

Rochberg, George, "Can the Arts Survive Modernism?," *Critical Inquiry* 11 (1984): 317–40

Rochberg, George, "Kramer vs. Kramer," *Critical Inquiry* 11/3 (1984): 509–17

Rose, Margaret A., *The Post-Modern and the Post-Industrial* (Cambridge: Cambridge University Press, 1991)

Rosen, Charles, *Arnold Schoenberg* (New York: Viking, 1975)

Salzman, Eric, "Charles Ives, American," *Commentary* (August 1968): 39

Sarup, Madan, *An Introductory Guide to Poststructuralism and Postmodernism* (Athens, GA: University of Georgia Press, 1989)

Schenker, Heinrich, *Das Meisterwerk in der Musik* 1 (n.p.p.: n.p., 1925)

Schenker, Heinrich *Das Meisterwerk in der Musik* 2 (n.p.p.: n.p., 1926)

Schenker, Heinrich, *Das Meisterwerk in der Musik* 3 (n.p.p.: n.p., 1930)

Schenker, Heinrich, *Free Composition*, trans. Oswald Jonas (New York: Longman, 1979)

Scherzinger, Martin, "Of Grammatology in the Rondo-Finale of Gustav Mahler's Seventh Symphony," *Music Analysis* 14/1 (March 1995)

Schiff, David, "Ah, for the Days When New Music Stirred the Blood," *New York Times*, October 4, 1998: 34

Schoenberg, Arnold, *Style and Idea*, ed. Leonard Stein (Berkeley and Los Angeles: University of California Press, 1984)

Schoenberg, Arnold, *Zusammenhang, Kontrapunkt, Instrumentation, Formenlehre*, trans. Severine Neff and Charlotte M. Cross, ed. Severine Neff (Lincoln: University of Nebraska Press, 1994)

Schoenberg, Arnold, *The Musical Idea and the Logic, Technique, and Art of Its*

Presentation, ed., trans., and commentary by Patricia Carpenter and Severine Neff (New York: Columbia University Press, 1995)

Schulte-Sasse, Jochen, "Foreword: Theory of Modernism versus Theory of the Avant-Garde," in Peter Bürger, *Theory of the Avant-Garde*, trans. Michael Shaw (Minneapolis: University of Minnesota Press, 1984)

*Shapiro, Gary (ed.), *After the Future: Postmodern Times and Places* (Albany, NY: SUNY Press, 1990)

*Silverman, Hugh J., *Postmodernism: Philosophy and the Arts* (New York: Routledge, 1990)

Simpson, Robert, *Carl Nielsen, Symphonist* (2nd edn; New York: Taplinger, 1979)

Slonimsky, Nicholas, "Music and Surrealism," *Artforum* (September 1966): 80–5

Solie, Ruth A., "The Living Work: Organicism and Musical Analysis," *Nineteenth-Century Music* 4 (1980): 147–56

**Solie, Ruth, "Changing the Subject," *Current Musicology* LIII (1993): 55–65

Solomon, Larry, "What is Postmodernism?" Available online: http://solomonsmusic.net/postmod.htm

Solomon, Maynard, *Beethoven* (New York: Schirmer, 1977)

Solomon, Maynard, "Charles Ives: Some Questions of Veracity," *Journal of the American Musicological Society* 40/3 (Fall 1987): 443–70

Stewart, Ian, *Does God Play Dice?* (Cambridge, MA: Basil Blackwell, 1989)

Stoppard, Tom, *Arcadia* (London: Faber and Faber, 1993)

Straus, Joseph, *Remaking the Past: Musical Modernism and the Influence of the Tonal Tradition* (Cambridge, MA: Harvard University Press, 1990)

Straus, Joseph, "The Myth of Serial 'Tyranny' in the 1950's and 1960's," *Musical Quarterly* 83/3 (Fall 1999): 301–04

Street, Alan, "Superior Myths, Dogmatic Allegories: The Resistance to Musical Unity," *Music Analysis* 8 (1989): 77–8

Strickland, Edward, *American Composers: Dialogues on Contemporary Music* (Bloomington: Indiana University Press, 1991)

Subotnick, Rose Roseengard, *Developing Variations: Style and Ideology in Western Music* (Minneapolis: University of Minnesota Press, 1991)

**Subotnick, Rose Roseengard, *Deconstructive Variations* (Minneapolis: University of Minnesota Press, 1996)

Taylor, Timothy, "Music and Musical Practices in Postmodernity," in Judy Lochhead and Joseph Auner (eds.), *Postmodern Music/Postmodern Thought* (New York and London: Routledge, 2002)

Thorn, Benjamin, "Why Postmodern Music is Impossible," *Sounds Australian* 33 (Autumn 1992): 39–42

**Tomlinson, Gary, "Musical Pasts and Postmodern Musicologists: A Response to Lawrence Kramer," *Current Musicology* LIII (1993): 18–24

**Tomlinson, Gary, "Tomlinson Responds," *Current Musicology* LIII (1993): 36–40

*Trachtenberg, Sidney (ed.), *The Postmodern Moment: A Handbook for Contemporary Innovation in the Arts* (Westport, CT: Greenwood, 1985)

Treitler, Leo, *Music and the Historical Imagination* (Cambridge, MA: Harvard University Press, 1989)

*Turner, Bryan S. (ed.), *Theories of Modernity and Postmodernity* (London: Sage, 1990)

Ulmer, Gregory L., "The Object of Post-Criticism," in Hal Foster (ed.), *The Anti-Aesthetic, Essays on Postmodern Culture* (Port Townsend, WA: Bay Press, 1983)

**Uusitalo, Jyrki, "The Recurring Postmodern: Notes on the Constitution of Music

Bibliography

Artworks," in Veikko Ranala, Lewis Rowell, and Eero Tarasi (eds.), *Essays on the Philosophy of Music* (Helsinki: Acta Philosophica Fennica vol. 43, 1988), pp. 257–77
Vaggione, Horacio, "Determinism and the False Collective: About Models of Time in Early Computer-Aided Composition," in Jonathan D. Kramer (ed.), *Time in Contemporary Musical Thought, Contemporary Music Review* 7/1 (1993)
**Van den Toorn, Pieter C., *Music, Politics, and the Academy* (Berkeley: University of California Press, 1995)
*Vattimo, Gianni, *The End of Modernity: Nihilism and Hermeneutics in Post-Modern Culture*, trans. John R. Snyder (Cambridge: Polity, 1988)
Venturi, Robert, *Complexity and Contradiction in Architecture* (London: Architectural Press, 1966)
Venturi, Robert, Scott Brown, Denise, and Izenour, Steven, *Learning from Las Vegas* (Cambridge, MA: MIT Press, 1972)
*Wakefield, Neville, *Postmodernism: The Twilight of the Real* (Winchester, MA: Pluto, 1990)
Waldberg, Patrick, *Surrealism* (New York: Thames and Hudson, 1965)
*Wallis, Brian (ed.), *Art After Modernism: Rethinking Representation* (Boston: Godine, 1984)
**Walsh, Christopher, "Musical Analysis: Hearing is Believing?," *Music Perception* 2/2 (1984): 237–44
Walsh, Stephen, *Stravinsky: Oedipus Rex* (Cambridge: Cambridge University Press, 1993)
Ward, Glenn, *Teach Yourself Postmodernism* (New York: McGraw-Hill, 2003)
**Watkins, Glenn, *Pyramids at the Louvre: Music, Culture and Collage from Stravinsky to the Postmodernists* (Cambridge, MA: Belknap, 1995)
Webern, Anton, *The Path to the New Music*, trans. Leo Black (Bryn Mawr, PA: Theodore Presser, 1963)
West, Cornell, "Postmodern Culture," in *Prophetic Reflections: Notes on Race and Power in America* (Monroe, ME: Common Courage Press, 1993)
Whittall, Arnold, "The Theorist's Sense of History: Concepts of Contemporaneity in Composition and Analysis," *Journal of the Royal Musical Association* 112/1 (1986-7): 1–20
Whittall, Arnold, "Complexity, Capitulationism, and the Language of Criticism," *Contact* 33 (1988): 20–3
Williamson, John, "Deceptive Cadences in the Last Movement of Mahler's Seventh Symphony," *Soundings* 9 (1982): 87–96
Wilson, Edwin, "Authors' Rights in the Superhighway Era," *Wall Street Journal*, January 25, 1995: A14
Wimsatt, William K. and Beardsley, Monroe C., "The Intentional Fallacy," *Sewanee Review* 54 (Summer 1946): 468–88
Wolff, Janet, *Feminine Sentences: Essays on Women and Culture* (Berkeley and Los Angeles: University of California Press, 1990)
Zavarzadeh, Mas'ud and Morton, Donald, *Theory, (Post)Modernity, Opposition: An "Other" Introduction to Literary and Cultural Theory* (Washington, DC: Maisonneuve, 1991)
Zorn, John (ed.), *Arcana: Musicians on Music* (New York: Granary Books/Hips Road, 2000)

Index